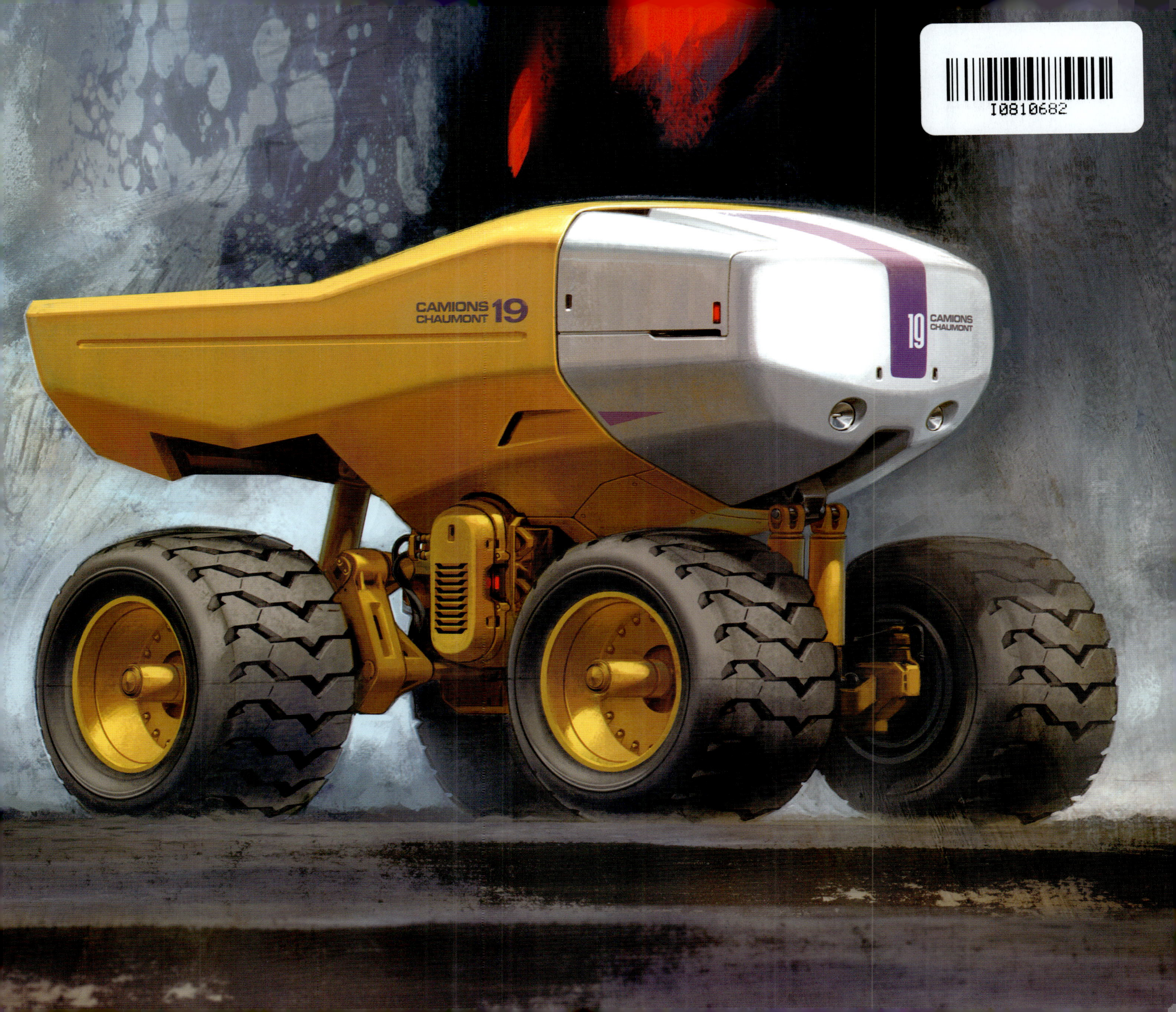
CAMIONS
CHAUMONT 19
19
CAMIONS
CHAUMONT

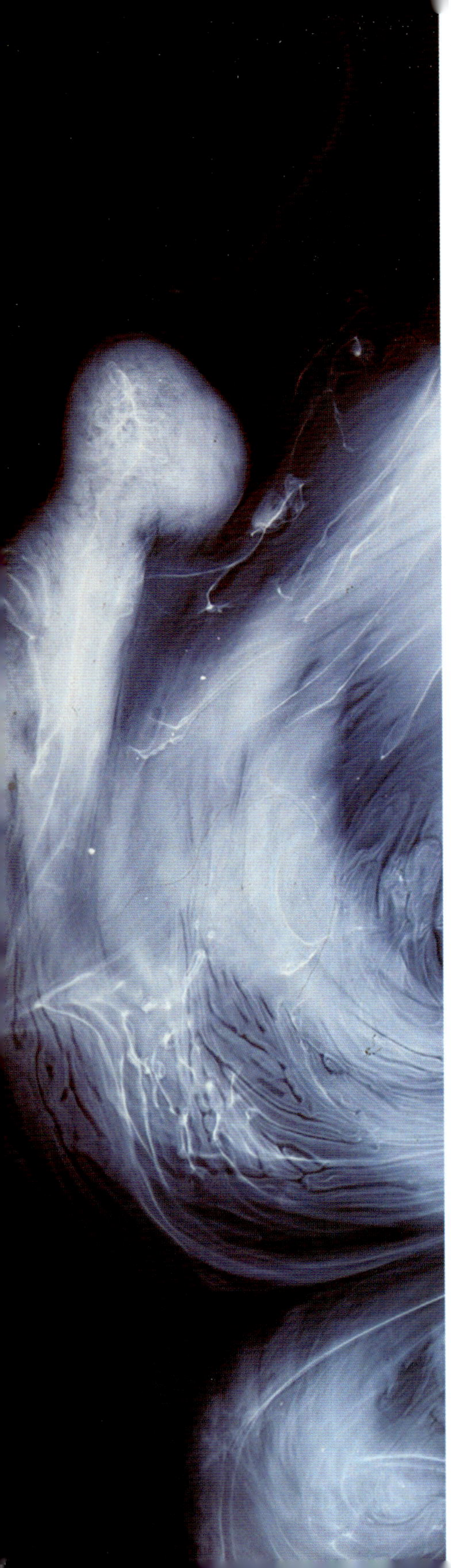

fryewerk 2.0

CONCEPT VEHICLE ILLUSTRATIONS BY JOHN A. FRYE

Hardcover ISBN: 978-1-62-465075-8 | Softcover ISBN: 978-1-62465-084-0

Library of Congress Control Number: 2023952145

First edition printed in China, 2024

10 9 8 7 6 5 4 3 2 1

Cover and Book Design by Spun Sugar Creative, LLC

www.fryewerk.com

FSC www.fsc.org MIX Paper | Supporting responsible forestry FSC® C104723

fryewerk 2.0

CONCEPT VEHICLE ILLUSTRATIONS BY **JOHN A. FRYE**

designstudio | PRESS

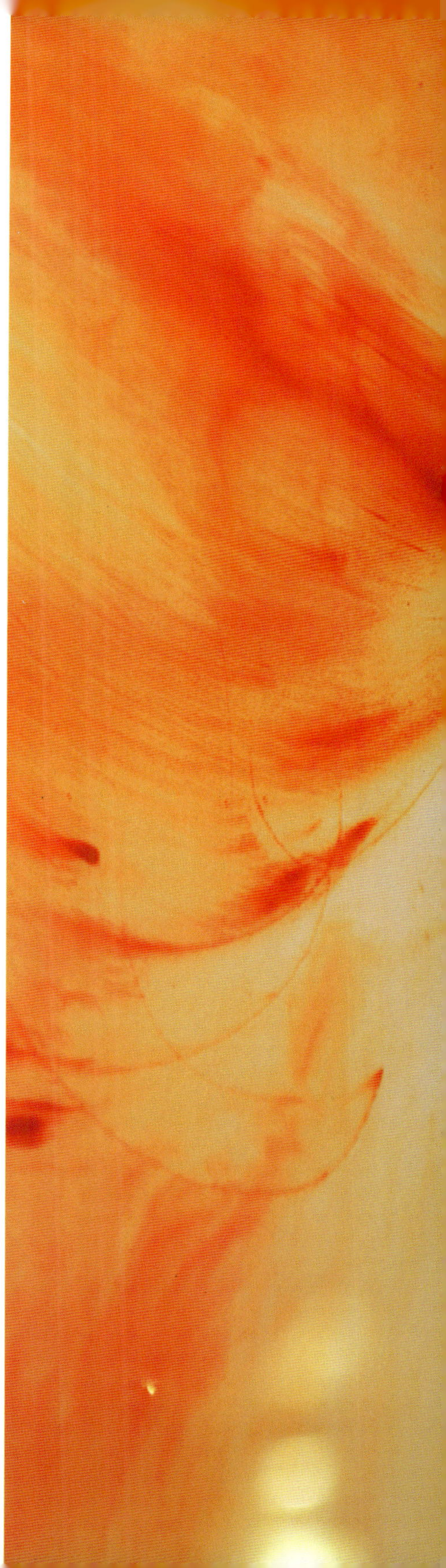

TABLE OF CONTENTS

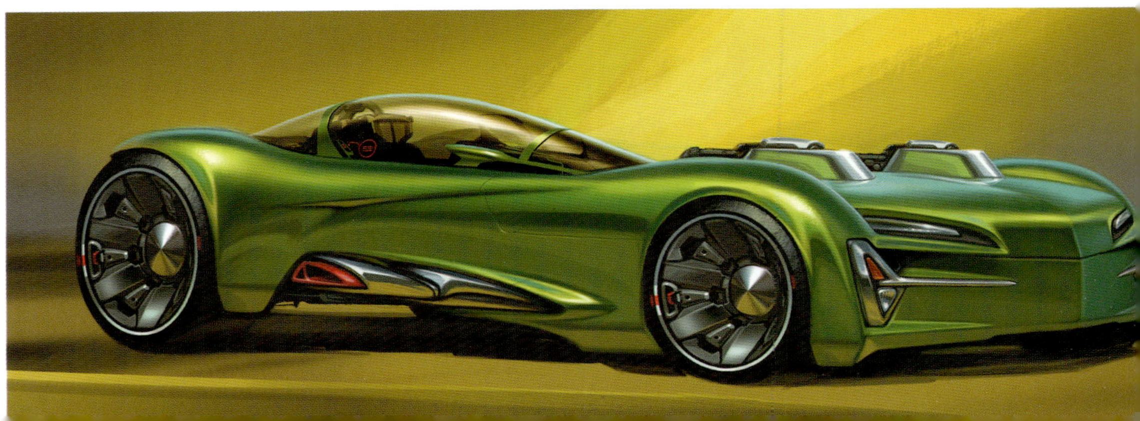

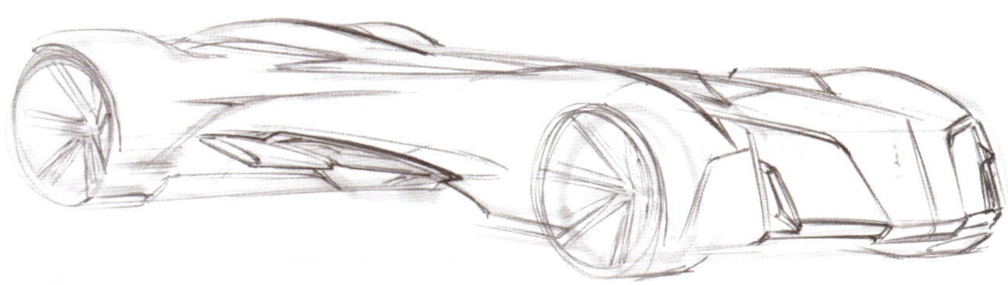

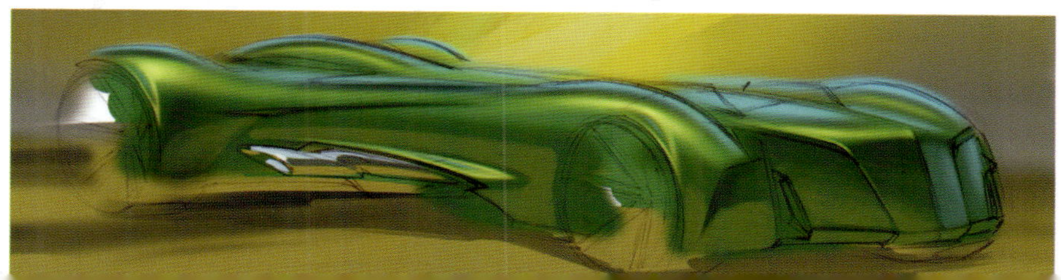

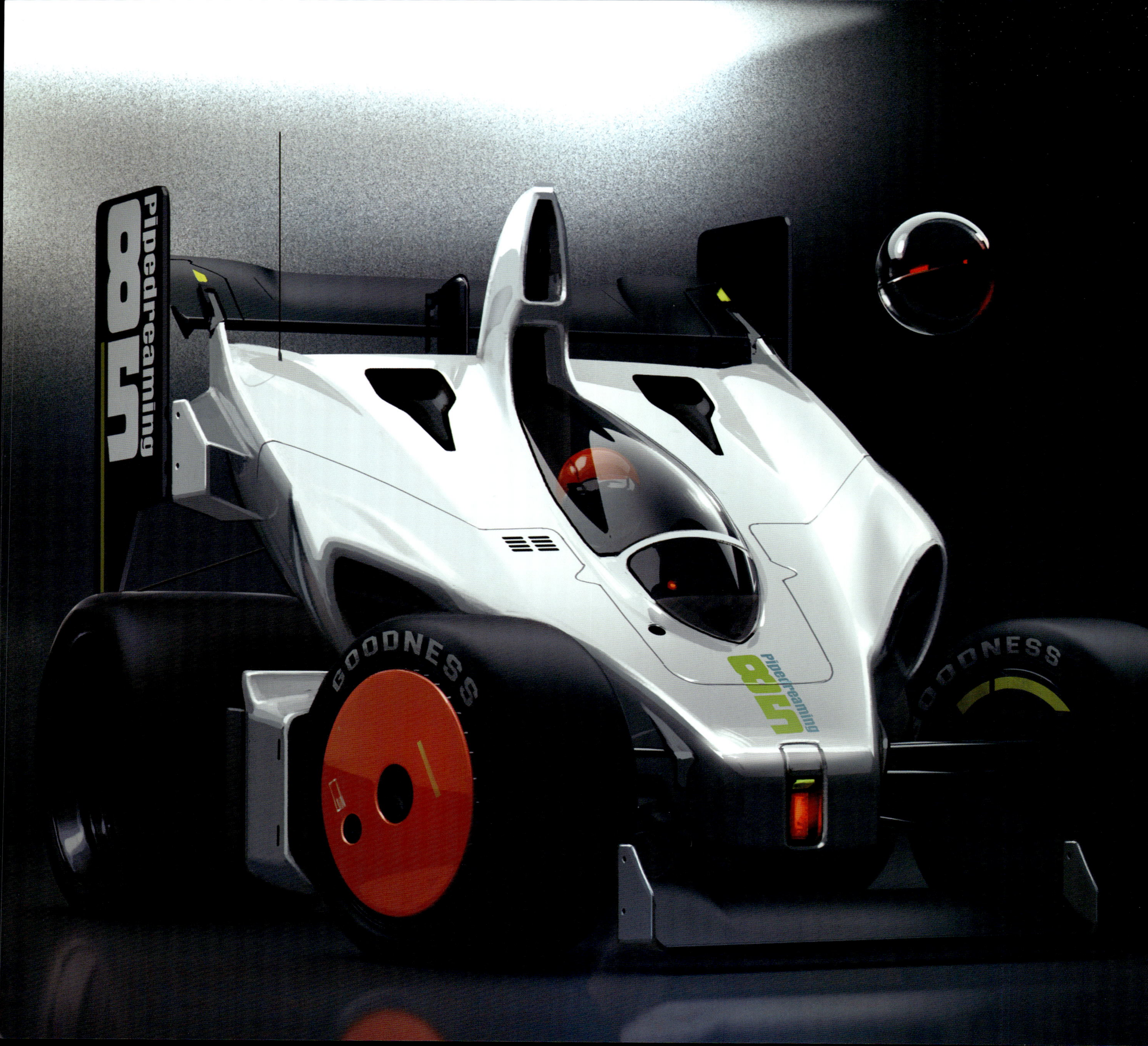

Pipedreaming
85
GOODNESS
Pipedreaming
85
GOODNESS

I first met John in school at the ArtCenter College of Design. In fact, for a year we were roommates. It was an incredible time to study art and design. We were lucky enough to be surrounded by like-minded, young, talented designers who all had the same ambition to learn and succeed. Working late nights, seven days a week, using inexpensive Home Depot bedroom doors for work desks, we were constantly inspired by our classmates and roommates alike. Decades later I find continued inspiration from John's work.

Unlike myself, John stuck with transportation design, specifically automotive design, though we both share a love for not only cars but also vehicles of all sorts. From sci-fi spaceships to high-speed airplanes, NASA rocket ships to F1 cars and futuristic utility vehicles, there's a shared interest in things that move.

Who knows where the curiosity of machines on land and air comes from? Maybe it's the love of engineering something new and evolved? Or simply the need to dream up beautiful-looking objects that have purpose and functionality?

Technically speaking, John's work has a precision to detail that is unmatched. His use of form language to build shapes and surfaces with new and interesting intersections is so fun to look at and explore. Today we take for granted knowing how to render and draw by hand—for example, knowing how to render a surface that is metallic versus matte with marker and pen. Using 3D tools, we just drag and drop with ease. In this book you'll find techniques for rendering surface materials, perspective, and design methodology—tools that will help you better express your ideas and visions.

From a design standpoint, John has always had a "personal look" to his work, something that is hard to come by today. In a world where so much art and design has a homogenized style and feel, John's work sets itself apart. I always know it's his hand when I see his work. I feel like it's perhaps a reflection of his personality, or to go even further, a reflection of his inner thoughts and dreams.

You'll find not only cool-looking vehicles of all sorts on these pages. You'll also discover the inner workings of a designer's brain, transcribed from thoughts and dreams. Ultimately, you'll have a better understanding of how it's all done.

James Clyne
VFX Art Director / Production Designer

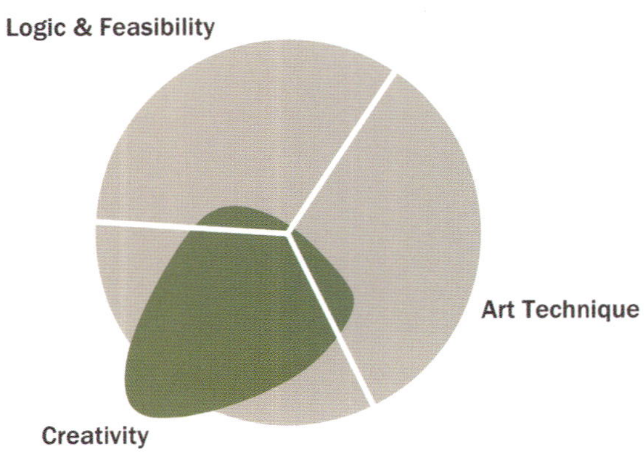

CHILDHOOD RECREATION DRAWING

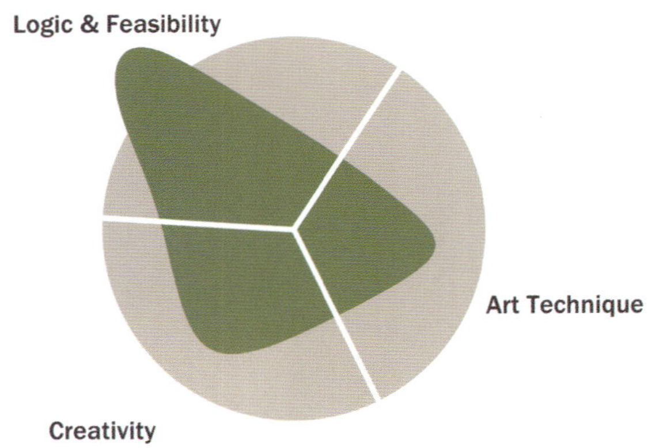

PROFESSIONAL DESIGN DEVELOPMENT DRAWING

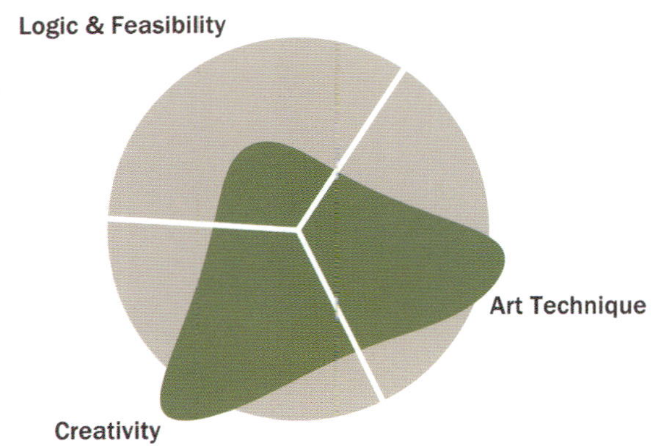

DRAWING FOR MYSELF

I was an insatiable image sponge in my formative years: race-car books, vintage aircraft magazines, Star Wars concept-design sketchbooks, Belgian ligne claire–style comics, vintage *MAD Magazine*, Wally Wood, Escher, how-to-draw art books, history photo books, die-cast cars, World War II movies, plastic-model kits. Something drove me to want to mash deep furrows into my brain with mechanical imagery and art techniques, a desire to try to understand how it was done, what it all was, how stuff worked. I took that mental hodgepodge of bolts and panels and wires and wheels and wings and produced piles of drawings with cheap markers and scrap paper and built vehicles out of Lego bricks. And looking toward my future, I incrementally began to realize that this could become sort of a career—that drawing for a living wasn't just a fine artist pushing oil in a sad apartment or an architect buried in the drudgery of math and building codes.

Throughout elementary school, I was drawing spacecraft or cars, and I got better and better at it, looking at magazines with car-development sketches and trying to guess what media they used, how they were able to draw a car, and all the right reflections before it existed. Design school found me in a bizarre way, when in high-school art class, I got curious about a stylish, gloss-black, thick book that was being used to level out a table in the center of the classroom. That book was an overview of ArtCenter College of Design. In that catalog I saw the car sketches, I saw the scale models, I saw pictures of the class studio with all of the drawing supplies laid out on tables and spectacular sketches of vehicles covering the walls. I must have stared at the ArtCenter studio photo hundreds of times, looking at every detail and dreaming of attending. After a couple more years of high school, then two at Central Oregon Community College (where I took mostly jazz trumpet and orchestra classes), I went home and drew cars, refining my portfolio. That hard work got me into ArtCenter, which was a blur and one of the best experiences of my life. And, of course, it got me my dream job in the car-design business.

Years of being in this business and taking on different essential roles, I've come to conclude that a fully realized professional designer is essentially a problem-solver with three distinct attributes. The first one is a wild creativity and unbridled drive to create something new. We generally are blessed with plenty of this essential quality at a young age. This is the foundation of design inspiration and the source of joy as a creative individual. It's an aspect of our human character that inherently drives us to seek to improve upon the world around us.

Second, art technique or 2D/3D visualization skills take the ethereal and ill-defined ideas from the mind and express them concisely in a medium that can be presented to others. The higher the level of this visual communication skill, the easier it is for a designer to sell the idea and convince others of the vision. In design school, we so rapidly learn the magical skills to produce the illusion of reality with hard skills that, if not unchecked, we may even neglect everything else in pursuit of the perfect image.

The last attribute is logic: a realistic voice that can understand all the realities that frame the constraints of the breadth of the original vision. Safety, economy, manufacturability, marketability—all are elements that provide challenges to be solved or roadblocks to be dodged in a good design. The customers are always at the forefront: What do they need? What do they want? Feasibility is essential in successful real-world design. Pretty-looking designs that do not satisfy the needs of the customer have no longevity as viable products.

We can look at any design activity with those three attributes and consider redistributing the weighting of each. There is a distinct difference in the balance between creativity, technique, and logic when I move from an activity where I am designing a real-world product for real customers to a personal illustration project where I am illustrating an idea that exists only as a single, thought-provoking image.

When one considers artistic technique, real-world design-studio technique is optimized for efficiency in the design workflow. Creating rapid visualization sketches that are clear in concept and attractive, but fast to produce, are of much more value than tight, tediously detailed illustrations—as enjoyable as those may be to create. Visual-communication skills are the shorthand 2D communication techniques that help teams arrive at design decisions without being slowed down by artistic process. We are already seeing changes within the design industry to reduce the amount of 2D work in the process and jump quickly into 3D form development. The beautiful 2D illustration has its place in selling the idea, but realistically, it takes too much time to have much value in the design-development process. By shifting the emphasis to unencumbered creativity, away from logic, I exercise those attributes to an extent that I am unable to when having to work within the critical and essential confines of real-world feasibility. Unfortunately, this last attribute of logic will all too frequently grow over the course of a design career into a heavyweight that can snuff out that youthful foundation of freethinking and make the attributes of creativity and artistic skill irrelevant.

Later in my life I understood that unique ideas and thinking could come from removing the burden of deeply logical thinking: to shrug off the shackles of critical realism. Constraint-free sketching at a professional skill level with a childlike creative energy, free of negativity and cynicism, has become the pastime that has brought me the same sort of joy as creative play did as a child. It's something that all designers should set out to do—to let their creativity loose on a regular basis and think like a kid with the horsepower of professional artistic skill. I believe we have the ability to train ourselves to more easily tap into that intense creative fuel source for more productive and passionate real-world project work. This is personal concept design; this is an illustration of a fleeting idea for the pure enjoyment of process and idea creation.

My suggestion is, as you read through this book, don't start to price out manufacturing in your mind. Don't stumble into considering the ergonomics of the entry hatch, the forward visibility, the drag, lift, center of gravity, or the compromised sales of a low-slung vehicle in states with icy-road conditions. Those hinge points don't line up; that windshield is impossible; there's not enough thrust in those engines to get out of Neptune's orbit? Forget about it! Relax!

Why don't we get out some old, multicolored scrap paper and a cigar box full of scented markers and odd, old stationery pens? Let's have a go at drawing some cool-looking spaceships at the dining table all afternoon, fueled by gingersnaps and glasses of cold milk, and imagine new and wild vehicular things.

Maybe by pushing beyond what we logically think is possible, we will break through to discover that which we never thought could ever be—and more likely and greater than we could have ever dreamed.

John A. Frye
South Pasadena, California
January 2023

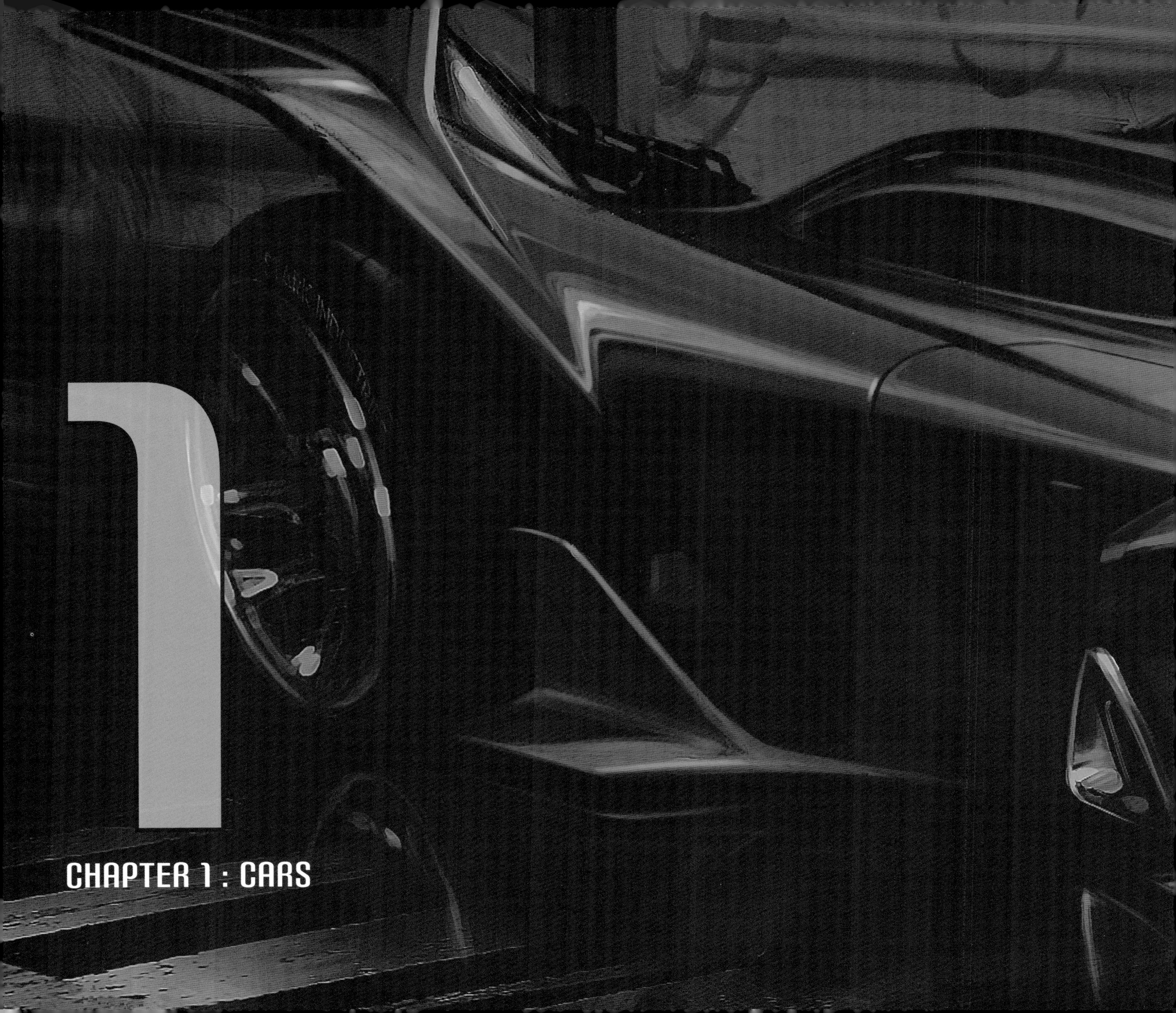

1

CHAPTER 1 : CARS

When you put pen to paper or stylus to screen, your brain is really looking out for you, trying to make your life easier. It will try to automate the process of drawing for you so that you can devote more mental processing resources to other things: listening to music or worrying about the burrito you ate from the vending machine a few hours ago. When you're a car designer, your hand and drawing instrument will tend to go through a familiar process, if you let it. You'll start with the same part of the vehicle that you've done hundreds of times before, draw the same comfortable perspective on the same size on the paper, and start to sketch out similar line gestures to describe form. Seasoned designers can draw some very ordinary and benign vehicles with their eyes closed, and some designers spend their careers drawing essentially the same car over and over again with little tweaks.

For veterans in the field, it's especially hard to push oneself to create something really new. Parts of the brain may need to shake off some dust. It takes a conscious effort to break away from the muscle memory of 10,000 cars of the past. This may come by drawing with a completely different medium, hand, or grip on a pen, for instance. You can also try drawing your subject from a completely awkward and uncomfortable perspective, or tackling a radically different scale, such as producing actual thumbnail-size sketches or filling giant sheets of paper with gestures of the arm and torso. Tiny sketches can be created with the wrist and fingers, but if you activate the elbow and shoulder, for instance, you get a different feeling in the gesture, form, and appearance of the strokes on the paper. I have tried all of these approaches. I also bounce between eras and consider new designs that could have existed, blow up ideas of current or past manufacturing limitations, and shrug off logic that constrains shape.

To spark creativity during my personal work, I'll often pull the rug out from under myself and suddenly switch from spaceships to cars, planes to trucks, from past to future. I'll try anything to keep my idea flow from stagnating and prevent my brain from going into autopilot mode.

With the car designs that follow, I wished to go well beyond what is expected and familiar. Instead, I maximized visual motifs of sleekness and volume and completely reimagined vehicles from decades past to dream up cars yet to exist to our world.

You will see how I jump through different themes to keep things fresh. I push the types of cars and eras that I can sketch from my mind in different directions, with convincing detail to match the style and time frame. I take ingredients from one decade and transport it into another, working them into an alternate reality for concept design but not inconceivably anachronistic.

But it's still important for a designer at any stage of their career, particularly in the concept-design field, to familiarize oneself with the history of things through sketching, reading, and observing. How has technology developed in terms of safety, manufacturing capabilities, packaging, and **powertrain**? Technology as well as fashion drives aesthetic evolution. Being able to understand the cars of the past in depth helps you design logically and insightfully for the future.

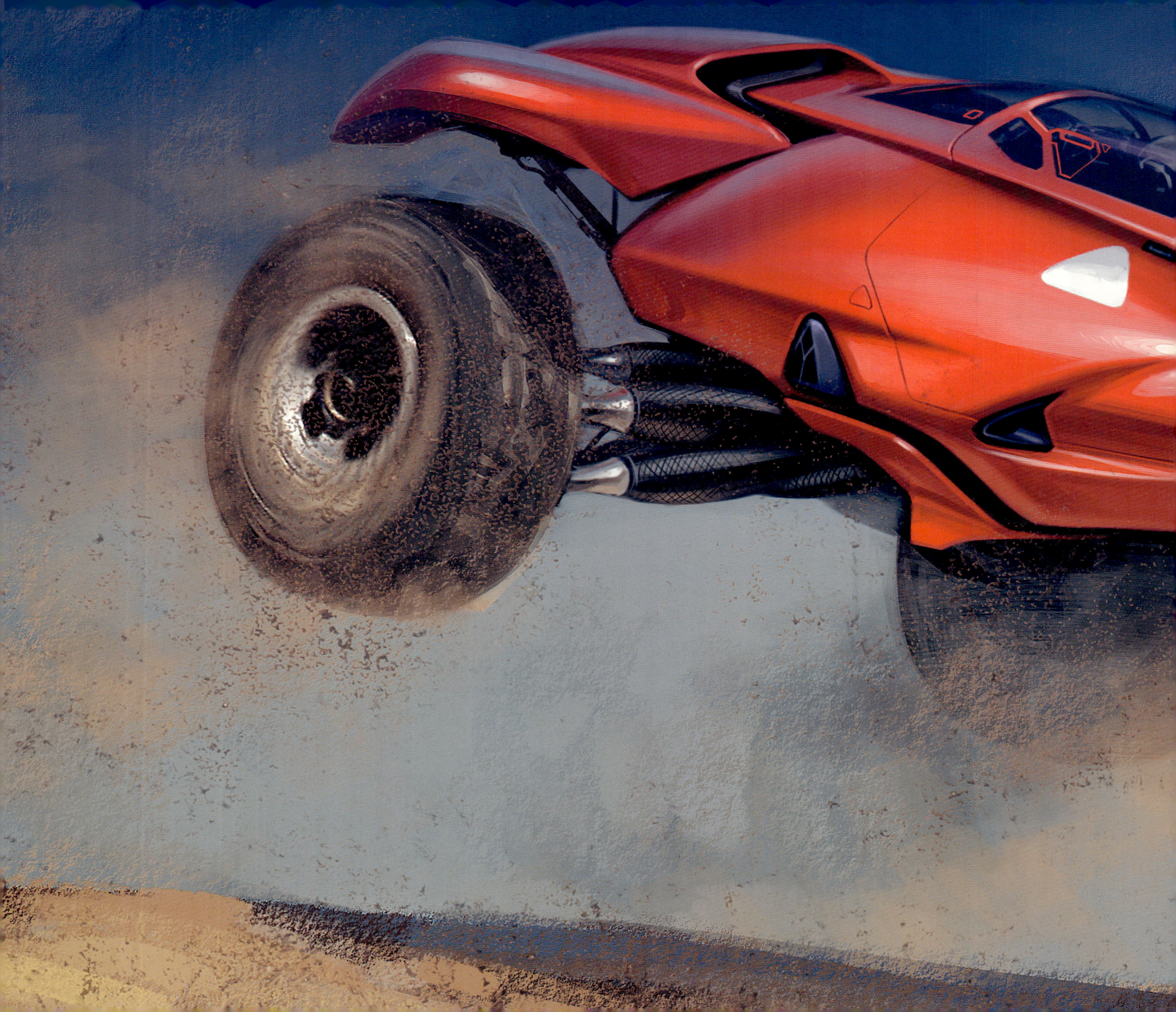

AERIT

A vehicle featuring a jet-aircraft canopy, floating fenders, and ruby-glistening carapace takes flight in the Dakar desert. I loved illustrating this scene with kicks of dust that go into sun and shadow for a little dramatic action. The car's unusual suspension is made from bundles of electrically charged, fiber-wrapped tendons that can absorb impacts, stiffen for lateral support, or even push out of fast corners like a running dog at full tilt.

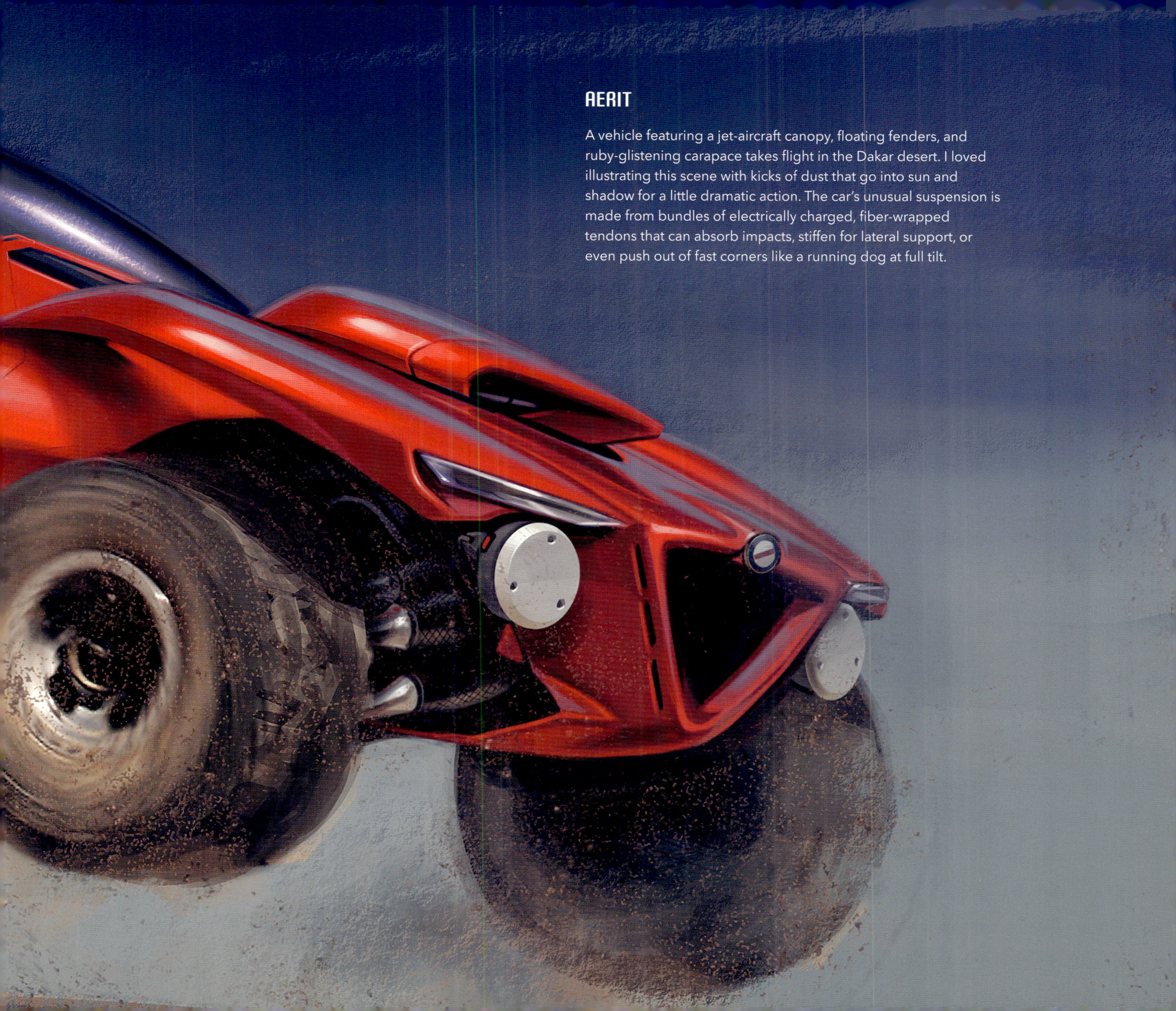

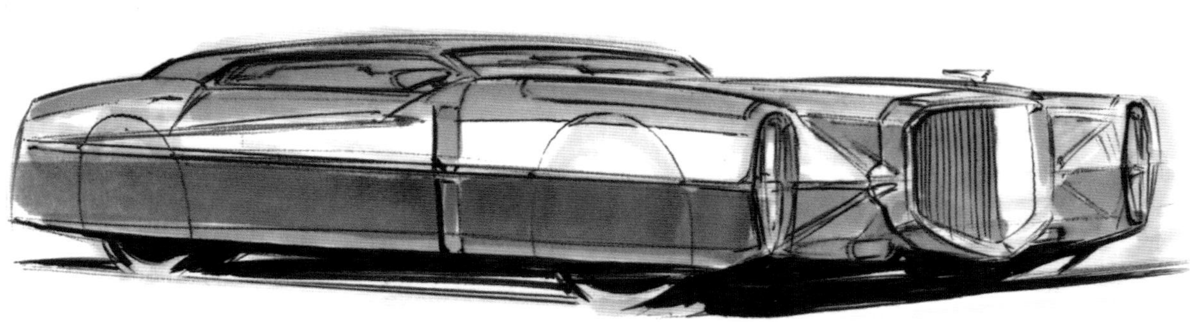

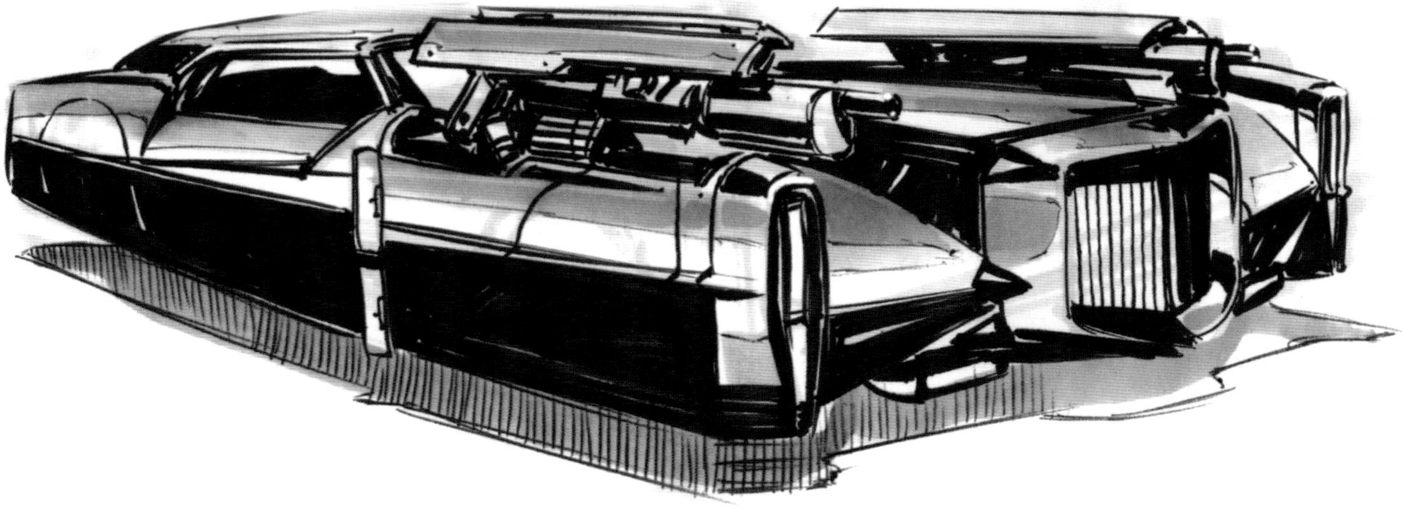

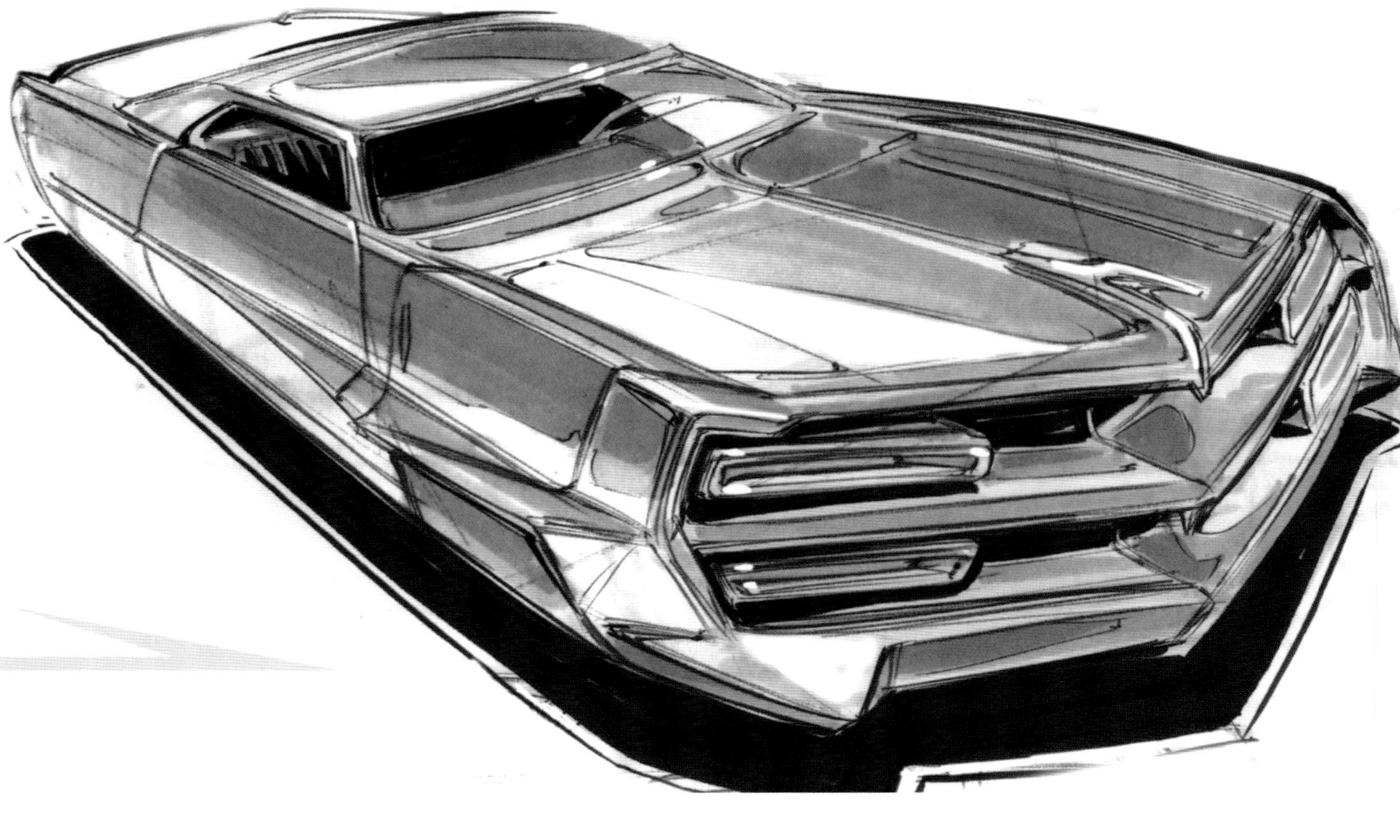

Inefficient, slabby behemoths were the cars of my childhood. The 1970s marked the last hurrah of Detroit styling excess. While their engines withered in power under the choking new fuel-efficiency requirements, their exterior styling still heralded the postwar American Dream of a surplus of money, material, and space. The low-eye-level shots of architectural grids of mesh grille, rectangular stacked headlights, and all sorts of trim bits and garnishes for fine detail distinguished the largest and grandest of each of the Big Three's top-tier brands. In retrospect, as the next generation of fuel-efficient, tighter-packaged cars became commonplace, experiencing one of these relics was less like being in a car than in a luxury yacht, in terms of its velour-wrapped ambience and floaty ride.

Sketched with marker and ballpoint pen, these designs were created for a world with a very dangerous urban landscape, so dealer-installed weapons were as common as other more luxurious options, such as velour seats and an eight-channel stereo. I only vaguely suggested wheels, as they were treated as a minor element of this 1970s equation.

Many years ago, when I started working for the car design studio, I noticed that there was always a demand for custom illustrations as gifts. If a manager was going back to Japan after a few years' stint working in California, or someone was retiring, it was the job of one of the talented senior designers to create a beautiful illustration with some special meaning to the recipient. Maybe it would depict their dream car, a project they were proud to have been a part of, or a project car of their own that they planned to finish building when they had the time. The illustration would be done in gouache or markers and chalk on high-quality vellum, often 20 x 40 inches in size. It would then be matted, usually with black board, and the studio would pass it around for everyone to sign their well wishes in a silver or gold fine-tipped paint pen. In a frame and under glass, it was always such a fantastic and unique personalized gift, and to be the one asked to be the artist was a great honor.

Over the years, I was lucky to fill that role many times. I've long since retired from the technique of drawing on 20 x 40-inch vellum and producing grand ideas in marker and chalk, and instead create such illustrations using digital drawing implements. This particular image is a mash-up car-design concept that was done for my boss of two decades. It combines a couple of real-world cars (Porsche 917 and 914/6) to produce something that doesn't exist but certainly could if someone wanted it to. The sky blue and orange race livery is one I love, yet one that I tend to avoid, because it's been done to death. But in this special instance, it was absolutely right for this particular car and my boss, and I was very happy to finally do those colors once.

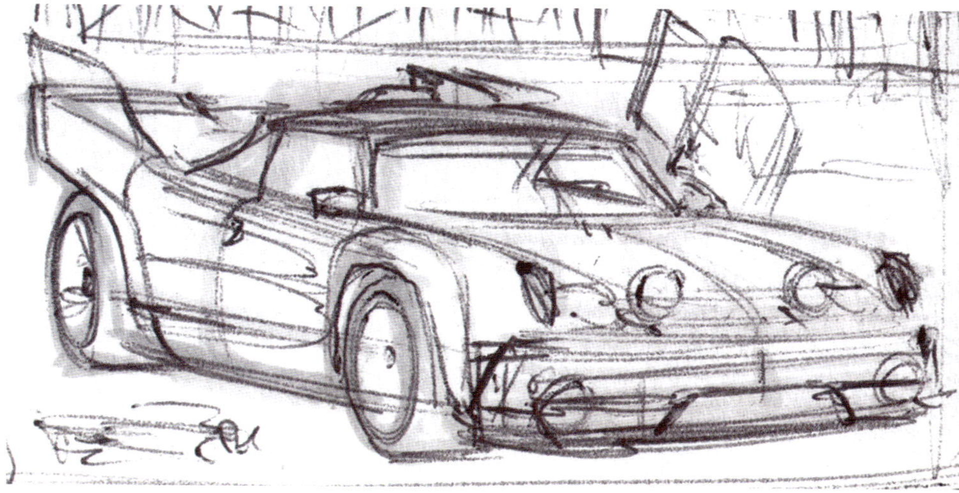

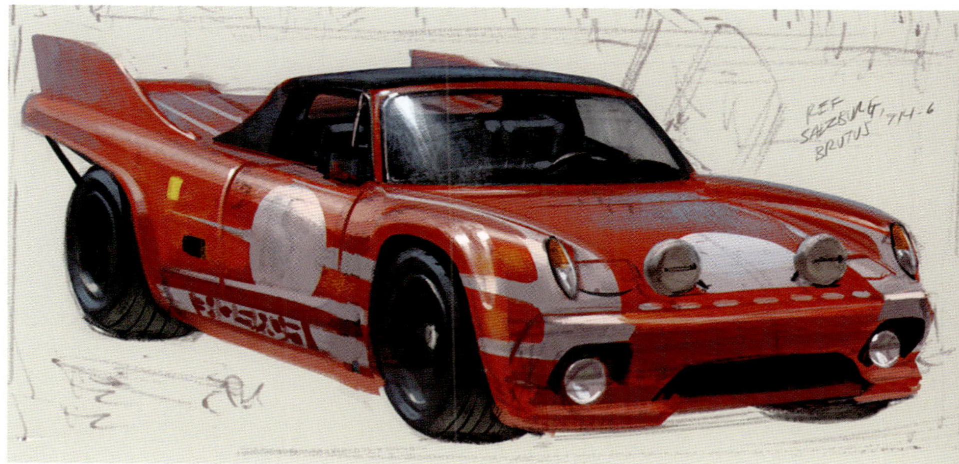

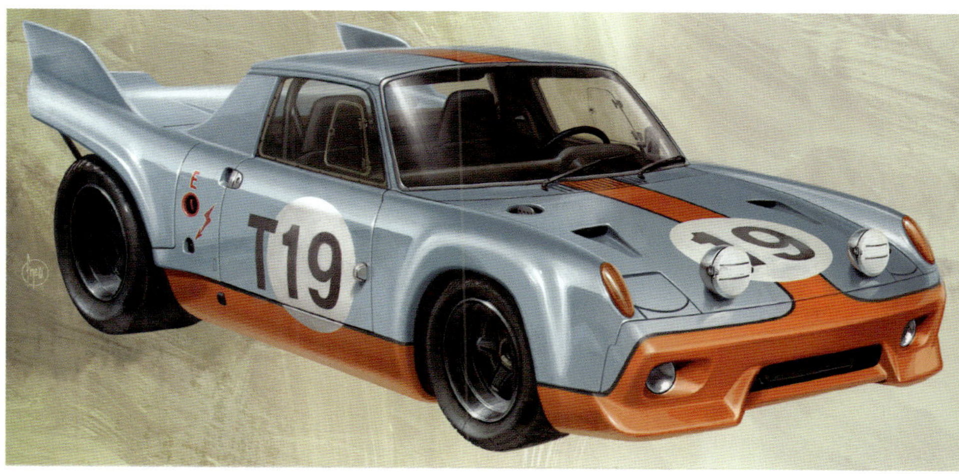

BERLINE

This classic concept design is at or near the top of many auto stylists' lists of favorite car designs. Apart from the wheels and rims, which date it quickly, the surface forms and spare, flowing, hard edges come together to embody iconic and timeless expressions of directional, automotive-streamlined beauty.

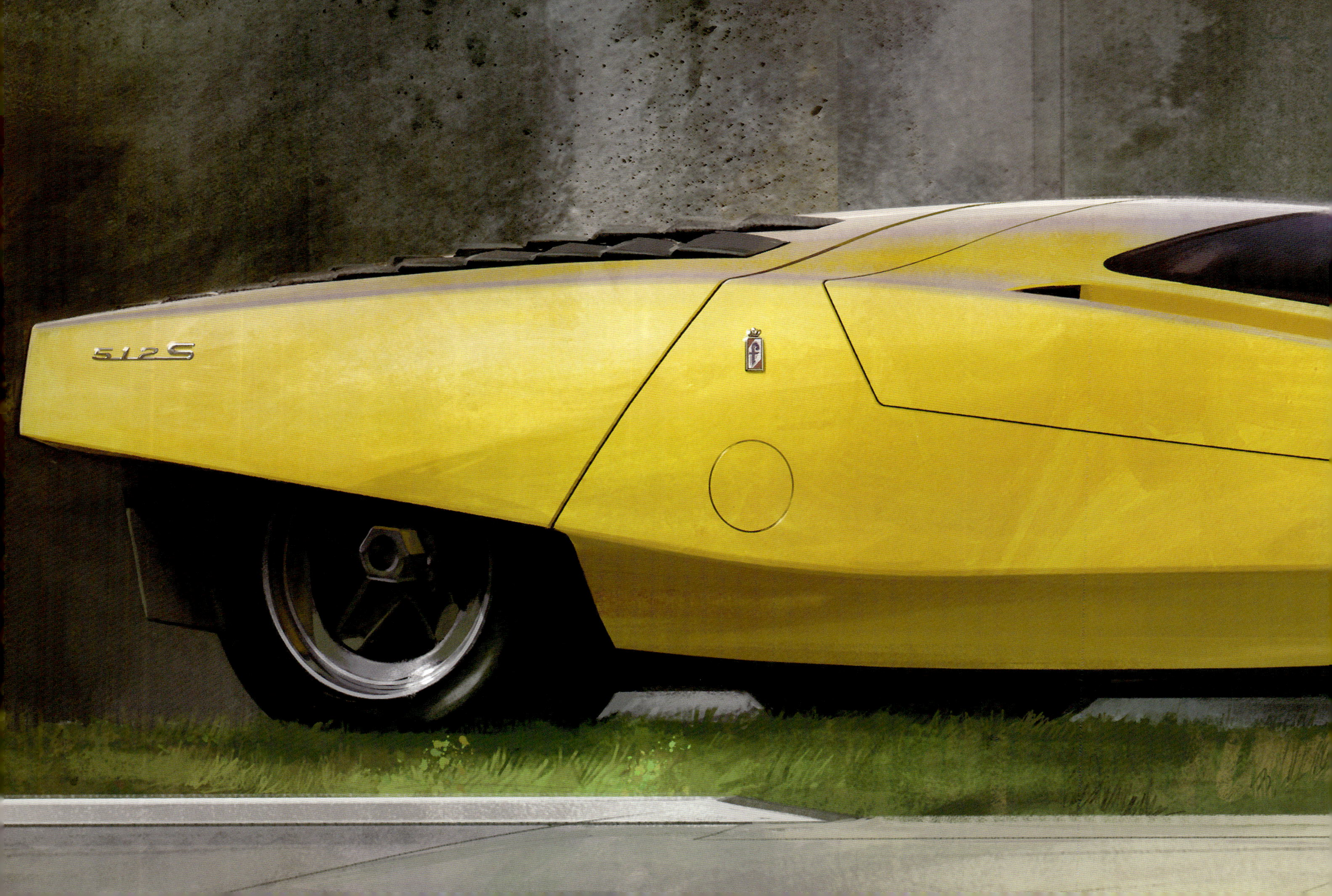

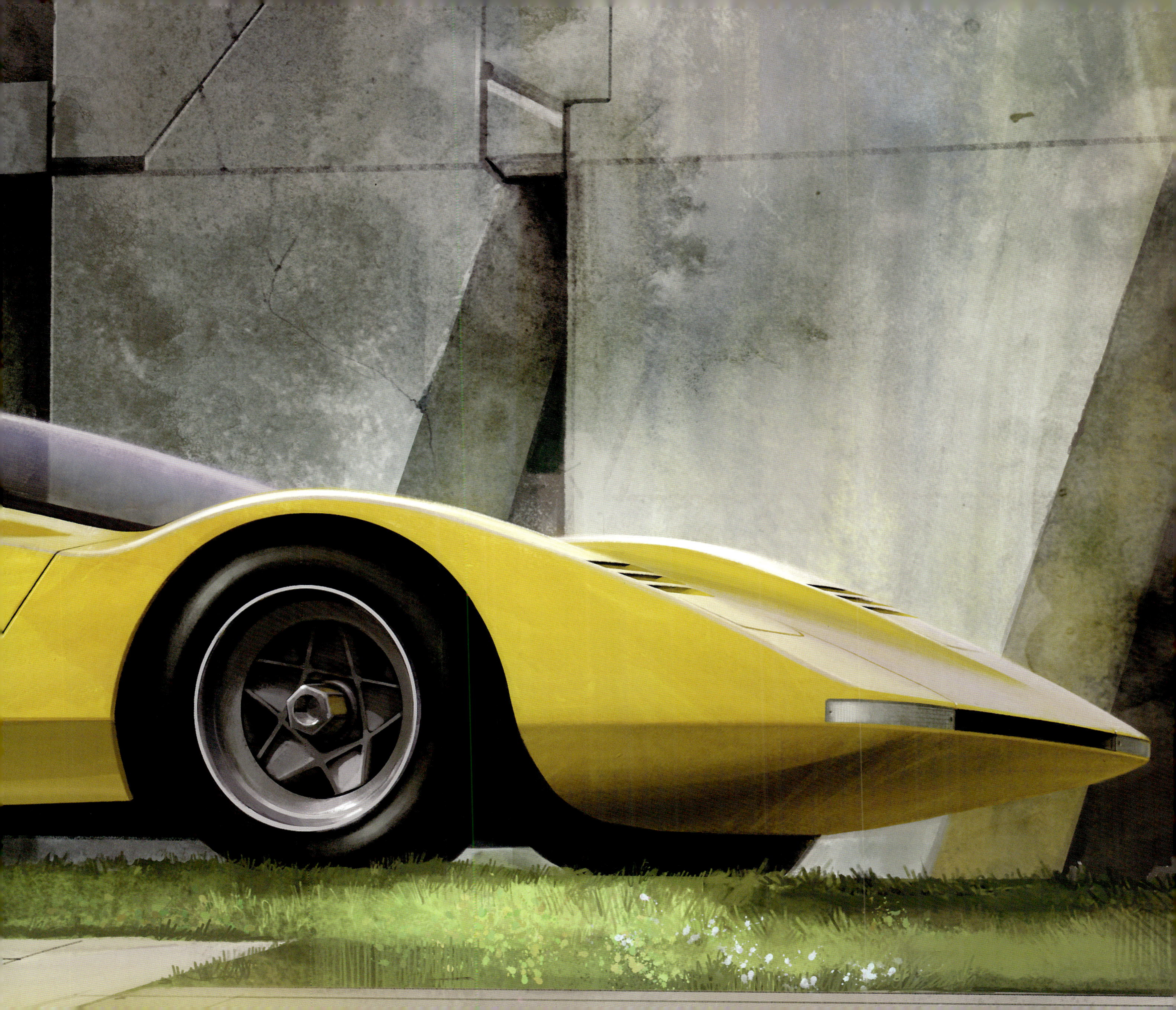

TUTORIAL: BIVENS "THERMONUCLEAR PANCAKE"

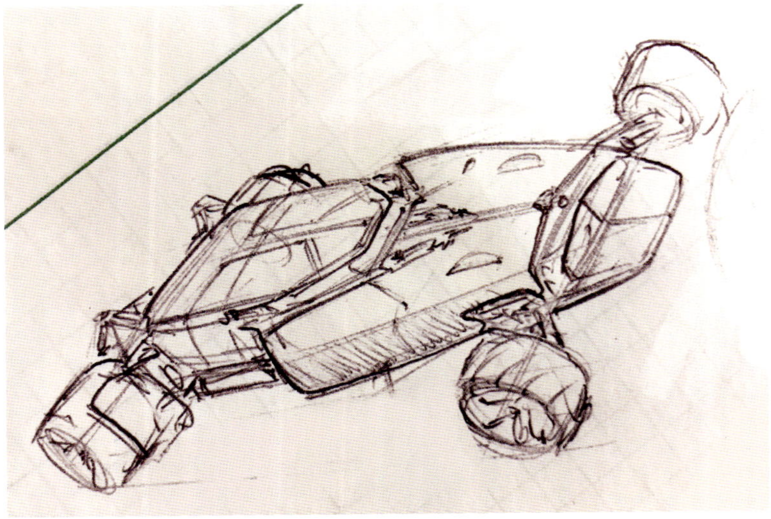

A rapid-fire ballpoint-pen sketch to digital illustration sequence takes advantage of the digital process. Seeing scores of earthy green and gritty, bolted-together vintage Bentleys at Laguna Seca racetrack in Monterey, California, one year, I was inspired to do a take on the 1929 "Blower" Bentley race car. This took form in all sorts of dead-end thumbnail sketches—most of which were spacecraft—but the theme of a tall fuselage pulling back off of a vertically proportioned, polished-chrome grille was consistent throughout until I intentionally tossed it. (The vertical proportion was too predictable and too literal to the original car from which I was trying to derive some inspiration.) Instead, I went the opposite direction, with a very flat car, a sort of hot-rod spin on a classic prewar British sports car that triggered **Ed Newton**-style brain firings. The sketch dictated the design and the likely best viewpoint. All sketches that I did from a lower eye level did not show enough of a car that flat—just wheels and a thin sandwich of metallic green and tonneau black leather and glass.

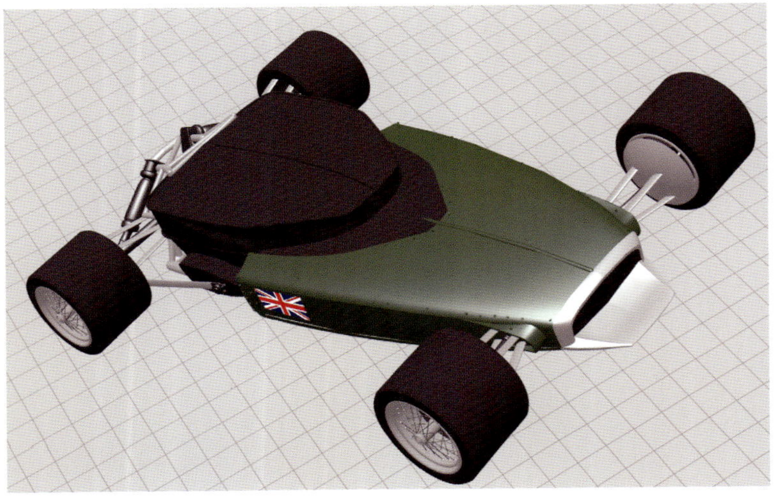

I took a photo of the sketch and dropped it into Gravity Sketch, a VR modeling application. Pulling surfaces out of the air in mime-like gestures (to the outside observer), I established the proportions and simple layout and blocked in a basic suspension to get the car and its wheels working together visually.

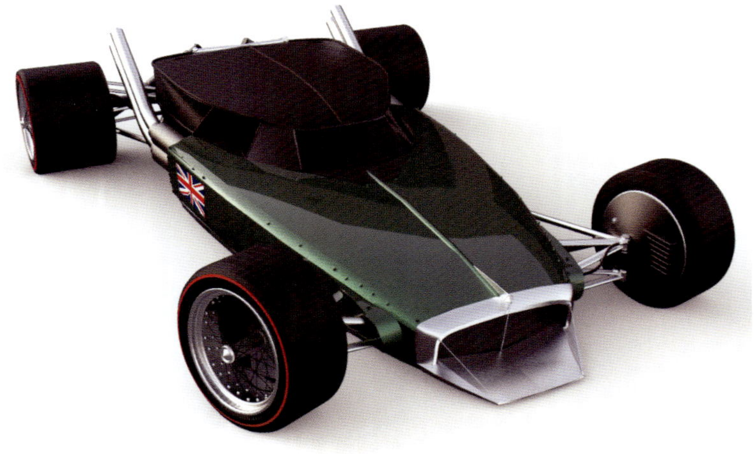

After dropping the model into the rendering application Luxion Keyshot, environment reflections, lighting angle, metallic-paint hue, and flake intensity were all tuned to use as an underlay, which did a very generous amount of the heavy lifting for the final illustration.

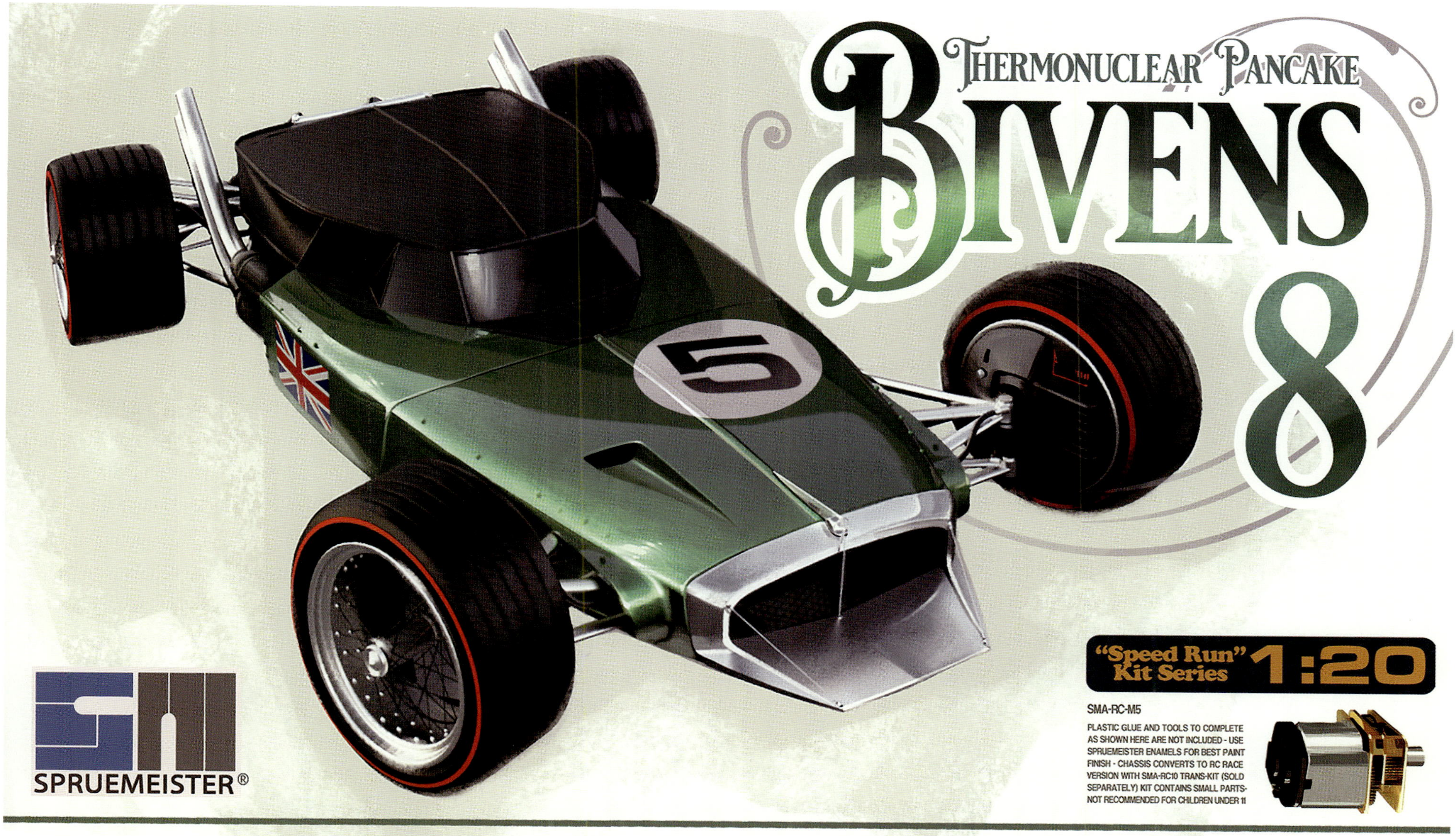

In the final illustration, the **shutlines**, the chrome-edge finishes, wheel and tire detail, and the overall finessing of surfaces are worked out. The strong asymmetry of the graphics and hood duct add interest. The long chrome pipes, which trail well beyond the body into the wake of the car, bring street-rod visual cred and reference the exhaust setup on Jack Calori's '29 Ford roadster that raced at El Mirage in the 1940s. I grew up with model-kit box art, which often was a fantastic, energetic painting that was much more detailed and realistic than the actual plastic kit inside. I have a lot of nostalgia for that style of illustration and also the graphic design of the box top itself, including the branding and details about the kit.

DESECRATION 1

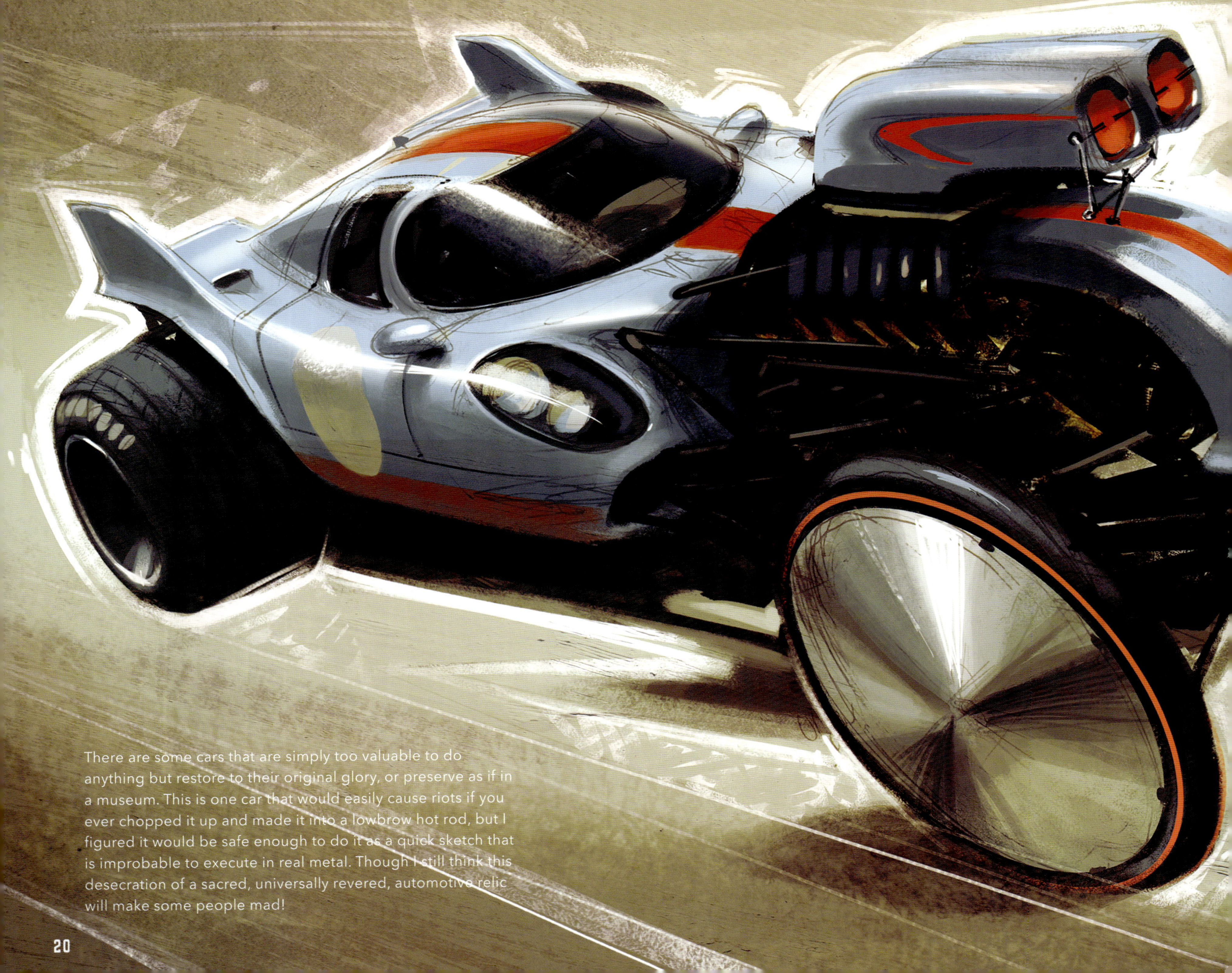

There are some cars that are simply too valuable to do anything but restore to their original glory, or preserve as if in a museum. This is one car that would easily cause riots if you ever chopped it up and made it into a lowbrow hot rod, but I figured it would be safe enough to do it as a quick sketch that is improbable to execute in real metal. Though I still think this desecration of a sacred, universally revered, automotive relic will make some people mad!

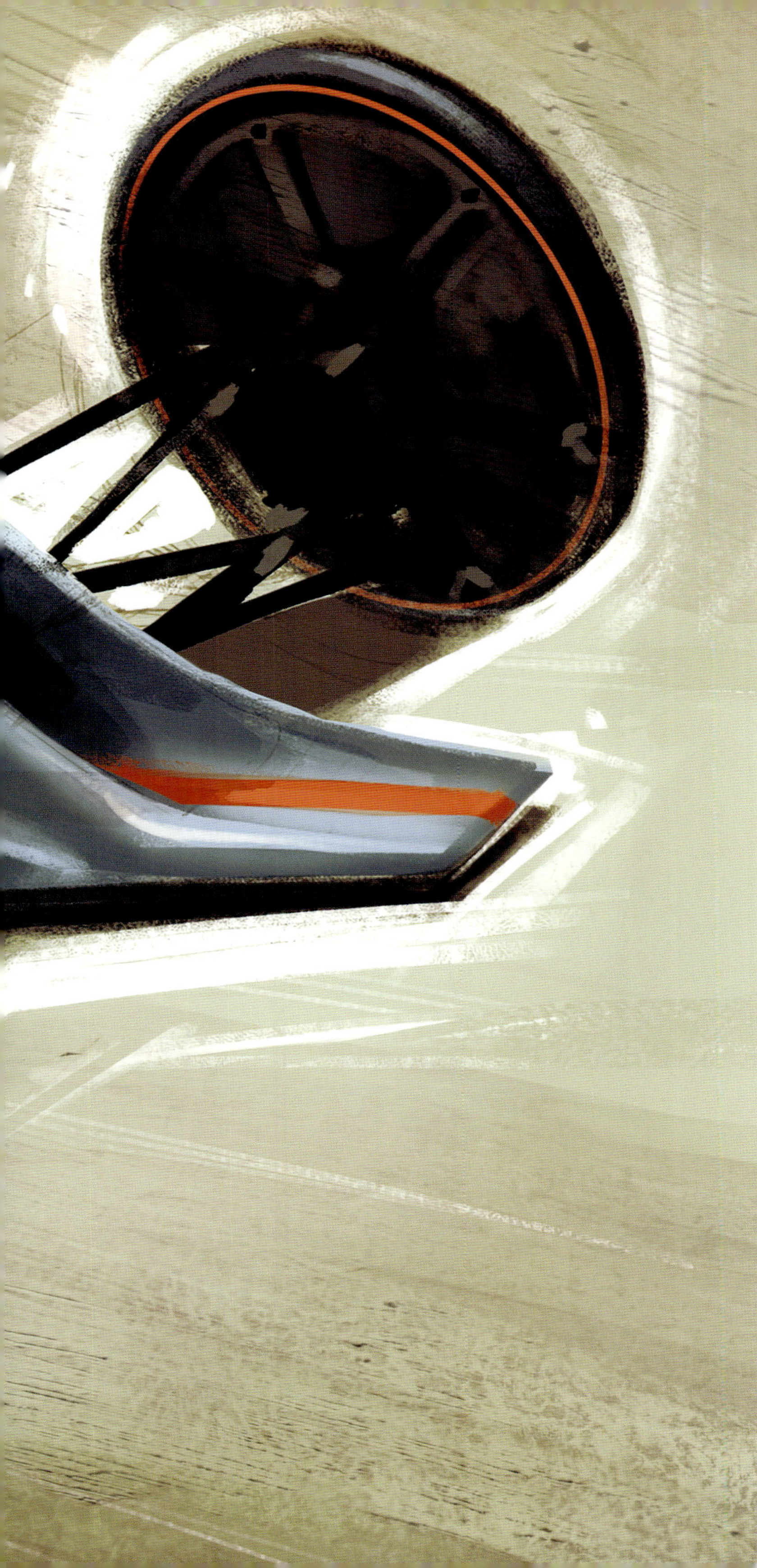

TIP: WHEEL POSITIONING

Many of my cars and trucks are illustrated with wheels in a steered position. This is done to add a bit of life and character to the vehicle, since illustrating it with all wheels pointed in line is more static. As for the direction of the steer, this can be done with some logic and purpose. Visually, a vehicle's proportional appearance is a combination of height, length, and the body's scale relative to the wheels.

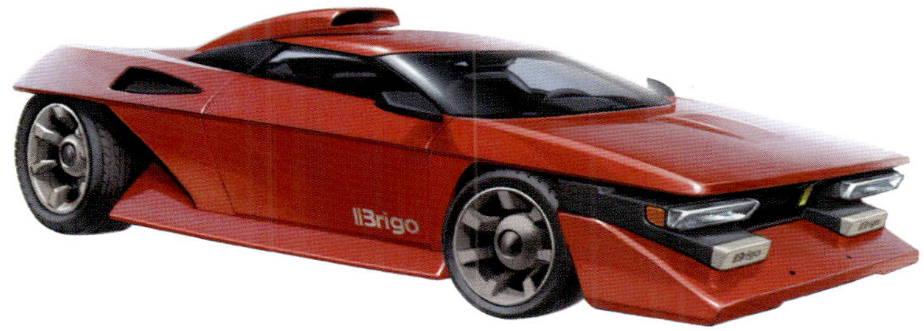

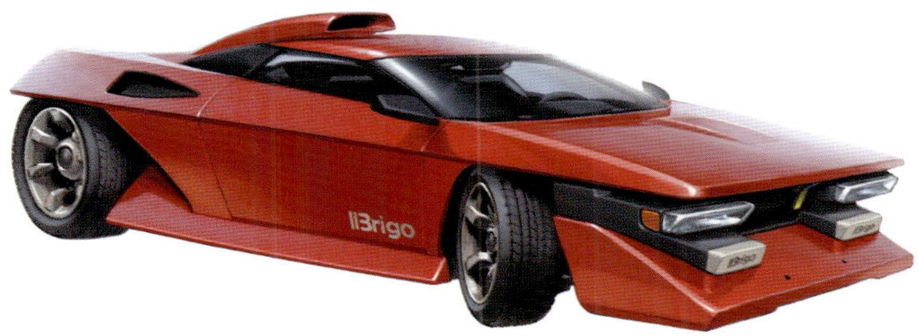

In design school, most instructors suggest turning the wheel face toward the viewer (upper image), saying, "You are designing the car and its wheels, not the tires. No one is interested in the tire tread." In itself, this is sound advice, but we have to think about what the wheels do for the overall appearance of the car.

In a front 3/4 view, the distance between the wheels is increased optically when the tire is steered toward the viewing plane (lower image). You visually lengthen the car by narrowing the wheel slightly. While the optical effect is subtle, in many cases, I find the overall impression of the design to be more attractive. In addition, as design schools typically instruct students to turn the wheel face toward the viewer, the de rigeuer practice to me is somewhat overdone and feels too posed in place. I feel turning it in the other direction feels more natural and gives the appearance of a candid image of the car in motion.

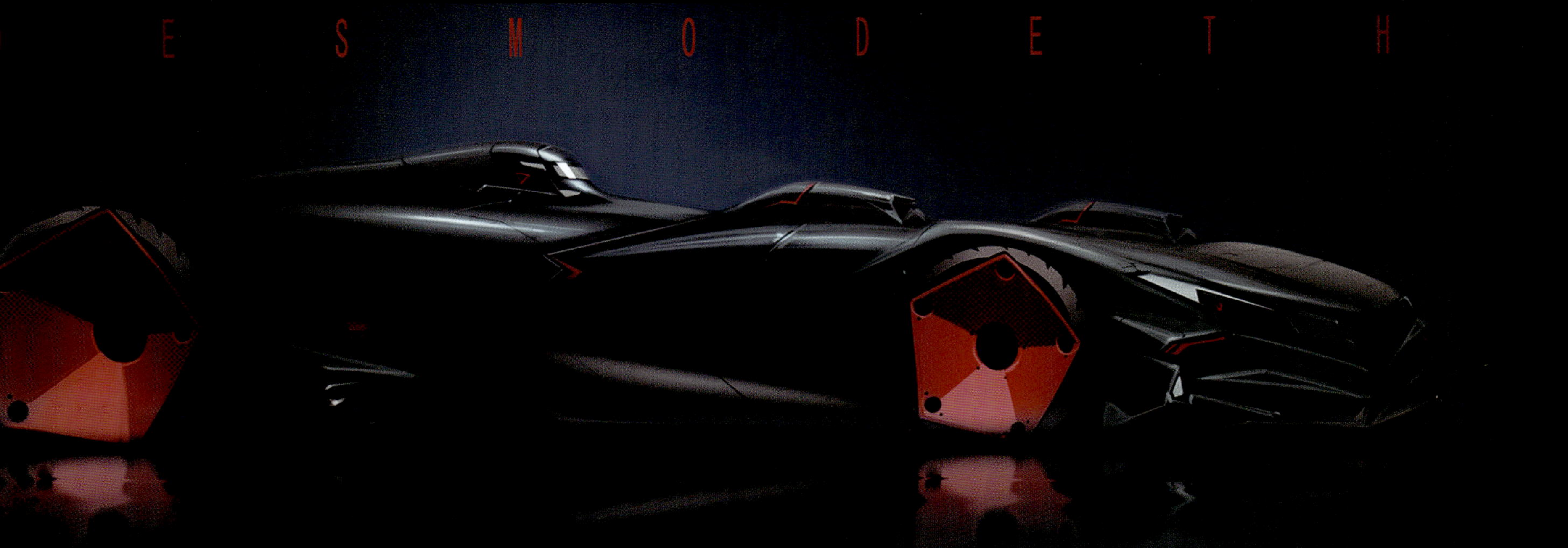

This series of expressive vehicles are geared toward those who may consider themselves midnight-shift superheroes of sorts. Hypnotize your enemies into a submissive trance with the pentagonal wheels on this svelte and angular little number. There's enough mystery in this black-on-black sketch that no one knows exactly what this thing looks like from any other angle.

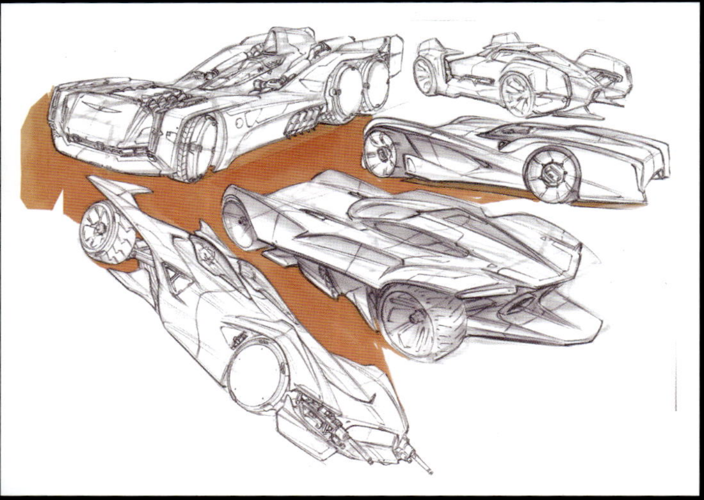

Marker, ballpoint pen, and a blaze of orange make it all pop. In the development phase of an idea, I try to stick with a theme but at the same time push in different directions from the theme's center point to sufficiently explore aesthetic turf.

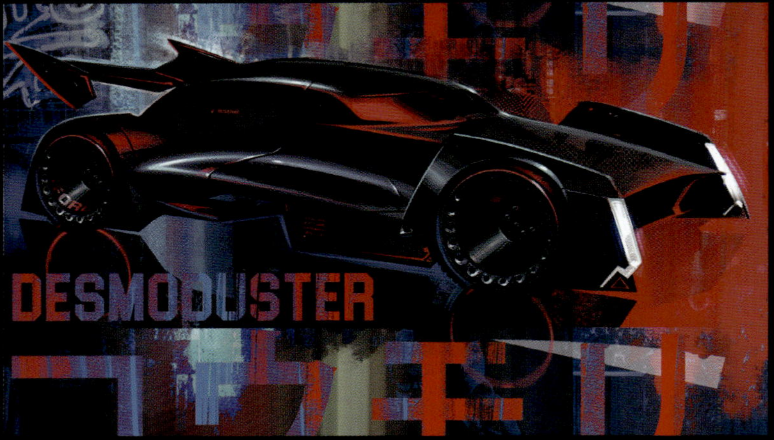

This model has a fairly efficient packaging design, with decent enough headroom for sitting mostly upright, short overhangs for getting into tight parking spaces at the mall, and a large front storage area for groceries. While proportionally not as dramatic as some other offerings in the "vehicle of the night" collection, it still has enough pizzazz from jutting wings and angles to balance out the sensible features

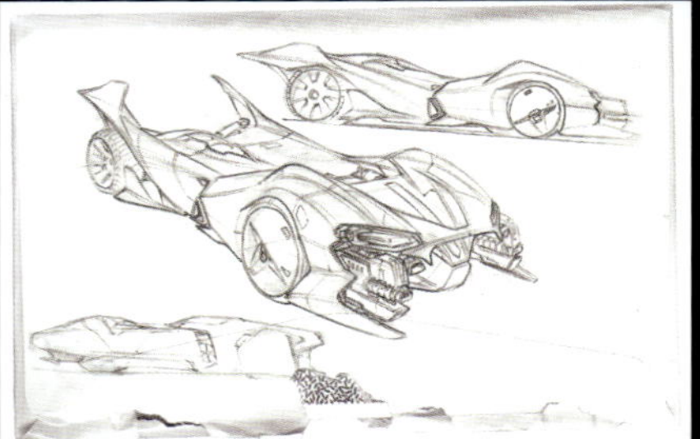

The mail quickly becomes my canvas if I have a pen and there's enough white space.

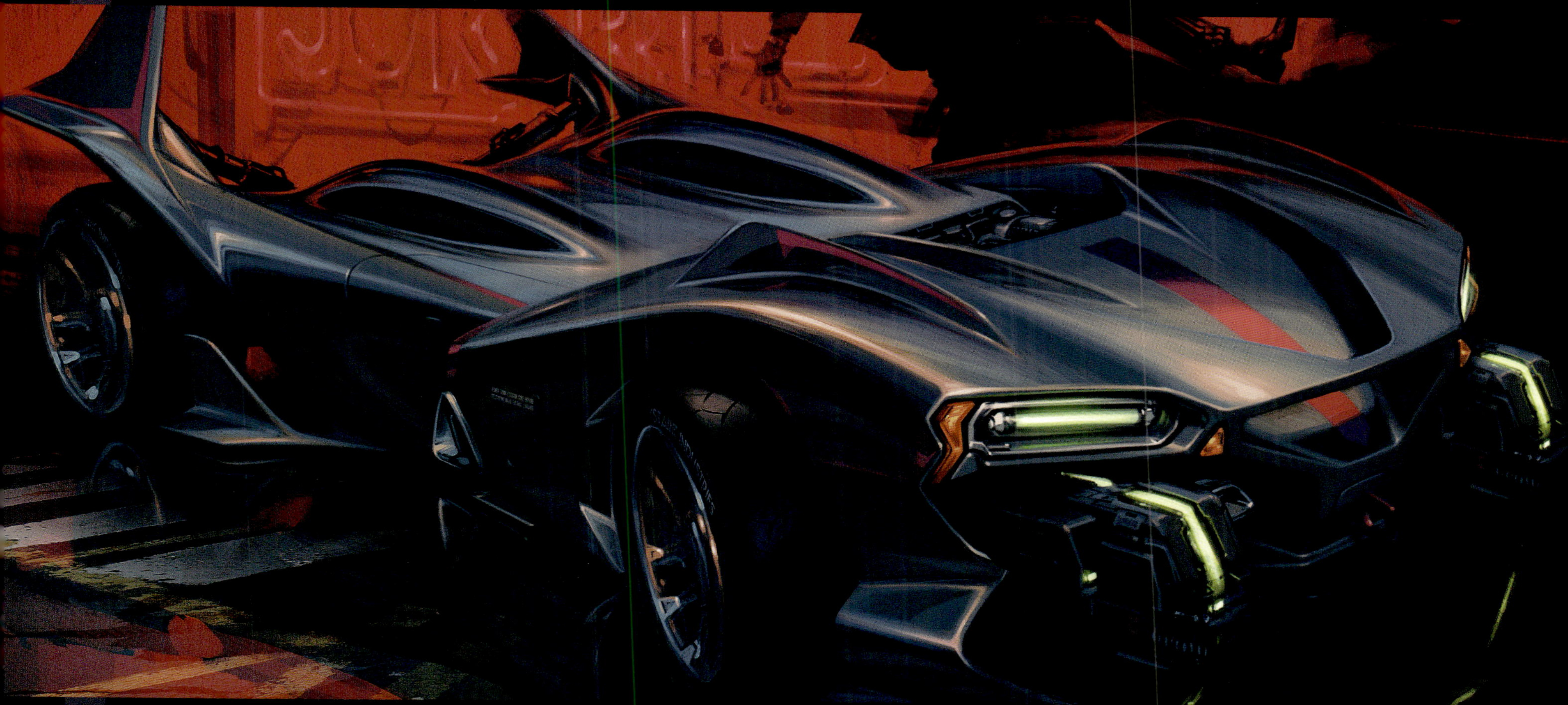

A cobalt-coated carbon road jet arrives in a rain-drenched alley, illuminated by the neon sign of a business that is not one you'd want to be seen visiting. It is a burbling engine of unknown specification, wrapped by a convoluted assembly of winglets, curves, bumps, stripes, and spots of glowing chartreuse.

1992 ROTOXAR 79288

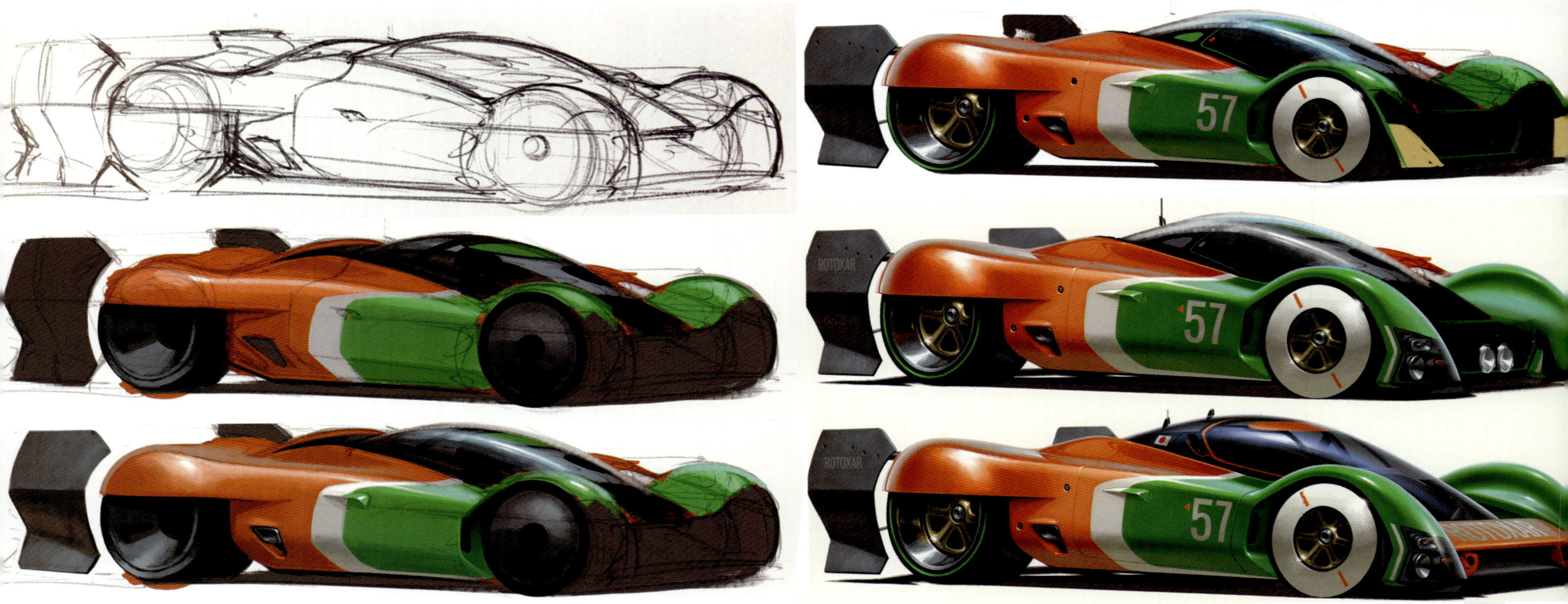

The initial sketch in this sequence is an accurate snapshot of the speed of the thumbnailing phase. Working out a volume and design with the tip of the pen skipping over the paper without lifting is a fast method I used. Some of that connective flow that seems clumsy at first may lead to new detail or surfacing ideas. I do a lot of designs that are optimized for one view that happens in a thumbnail that I take all the way to the final illustration. I feel that most cars have a "best side," or a most photogenic angle. My favorite view is 3/4 to 7/8 driver's-eye-level: an eye-level front angle that shows the length of the vehicle, the expression of the body side design, and the character of the face. This is what I also call the "four-way stop view." From this perspective you should be able to understand the majority of the design without needing to see other views. Think of how you observe the cars around you at a four-way stop; this is the common viewpoint that we're accustomed to seeing vehicles. When you design from that angle of perspective, most of the main character of the vehicle should be clearly expressed with the shapes and details seen from that view.

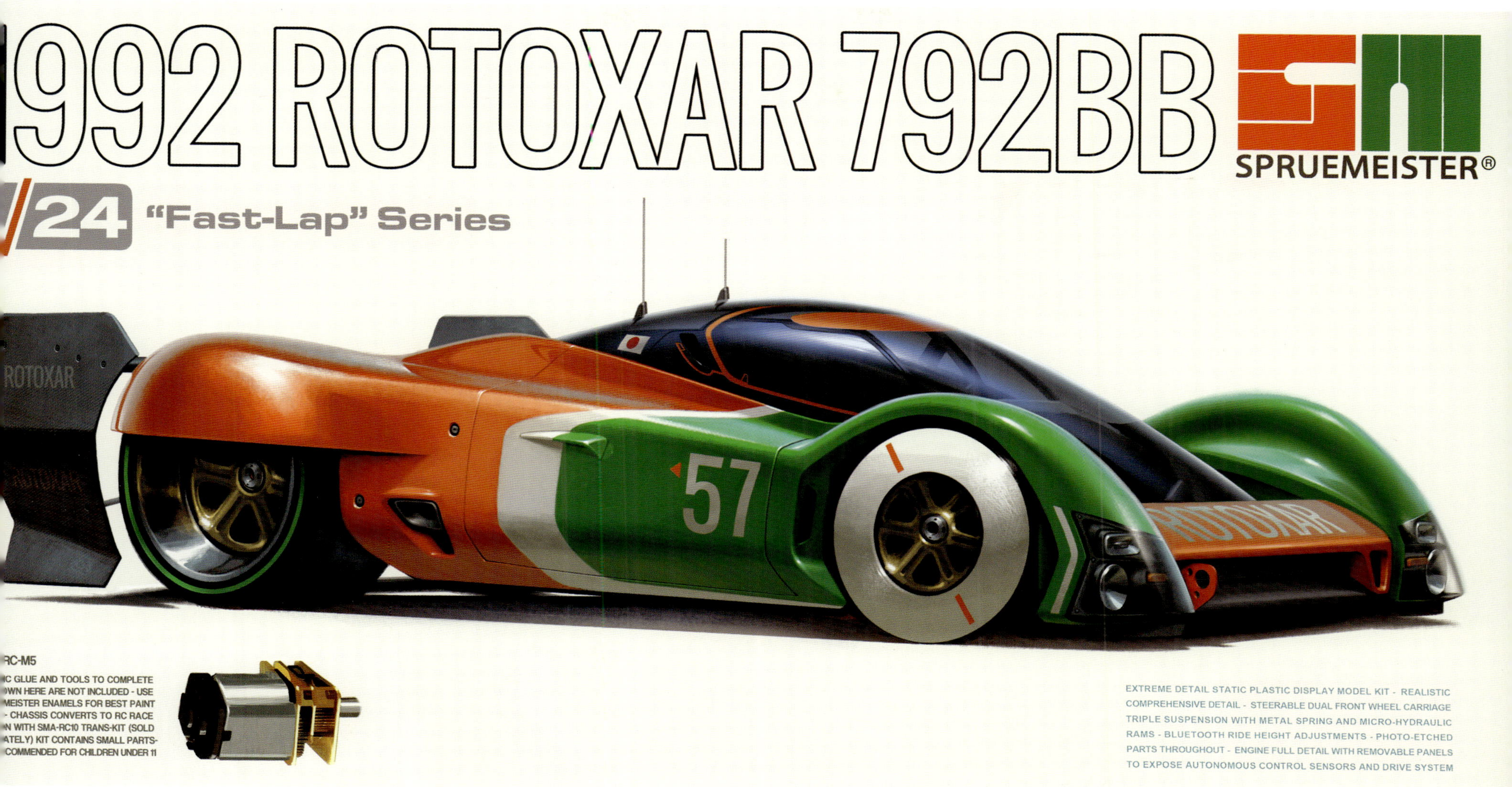

The 792BB could have been shoehorned into the 1990s Group-C race series, or maybe it was and it got lost to history. With some of my car designs, I intentionally make them feel vaguely familiar; maybe you've seen the model before and forgotten about it. If someone asks, "Is this real?" I'm happy with the mystery I've created because people will pause longer to think deeply about something they don't understand immediately. We are encountering such a steady and high-volume stream of visual information from digital sources now, it does take some effort to slow down and look at something carefully, but it has to grab your attention.

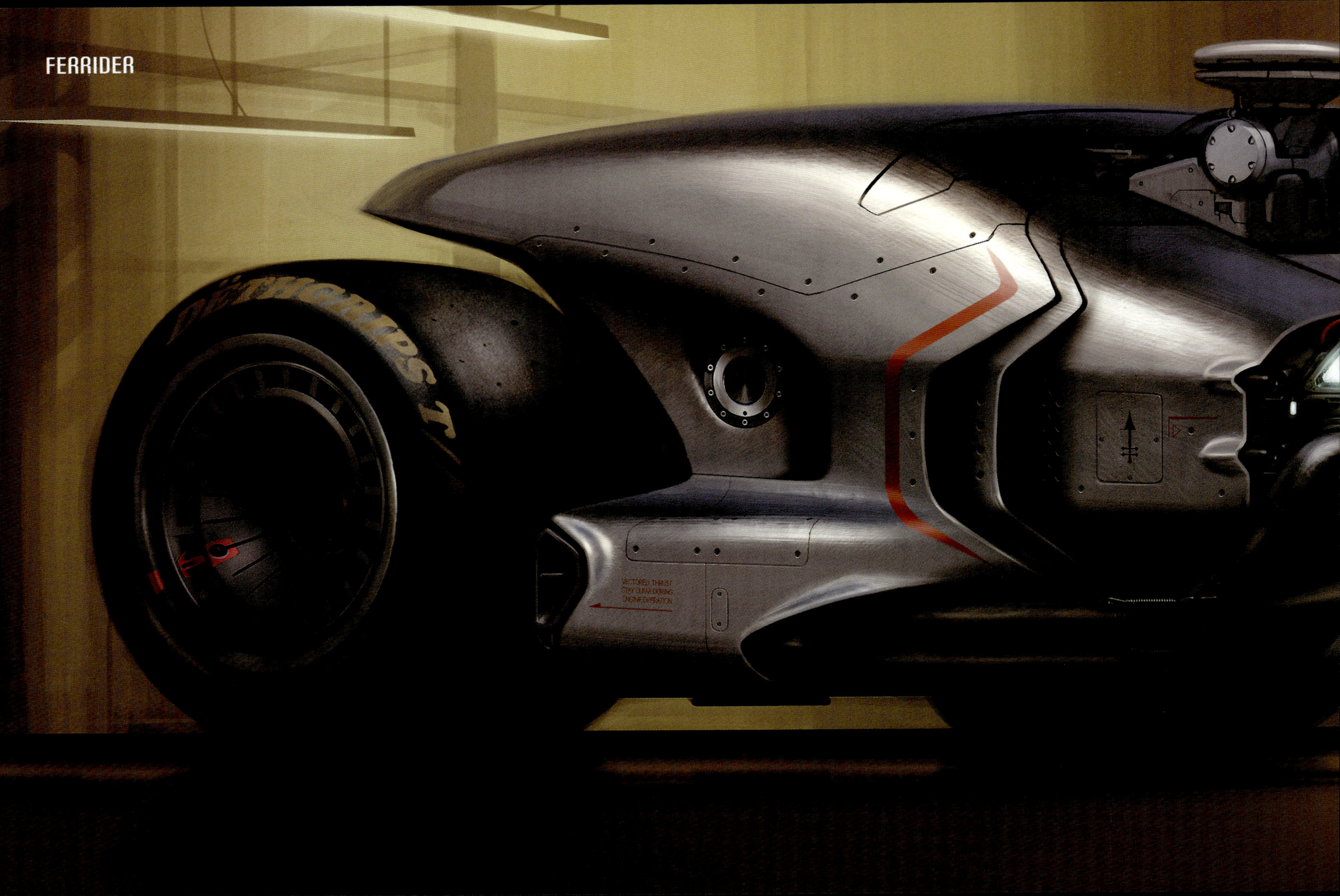
VECTORED THRUST
STAY CLEAR DURING
ENGINE OPERATION

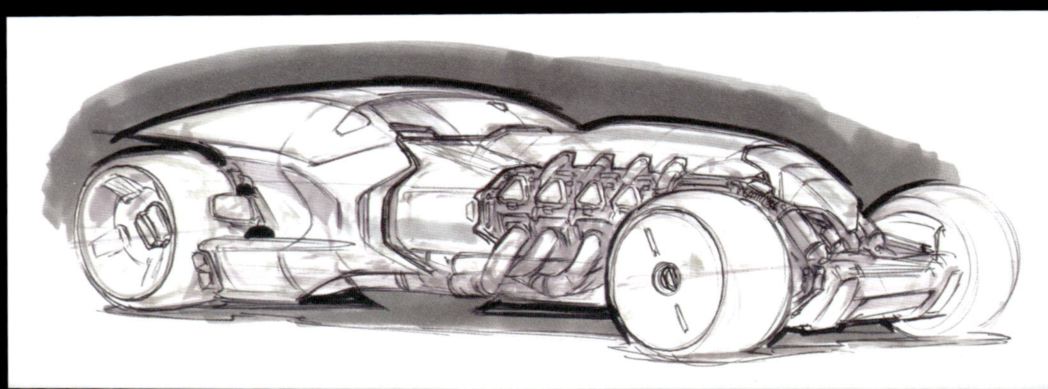

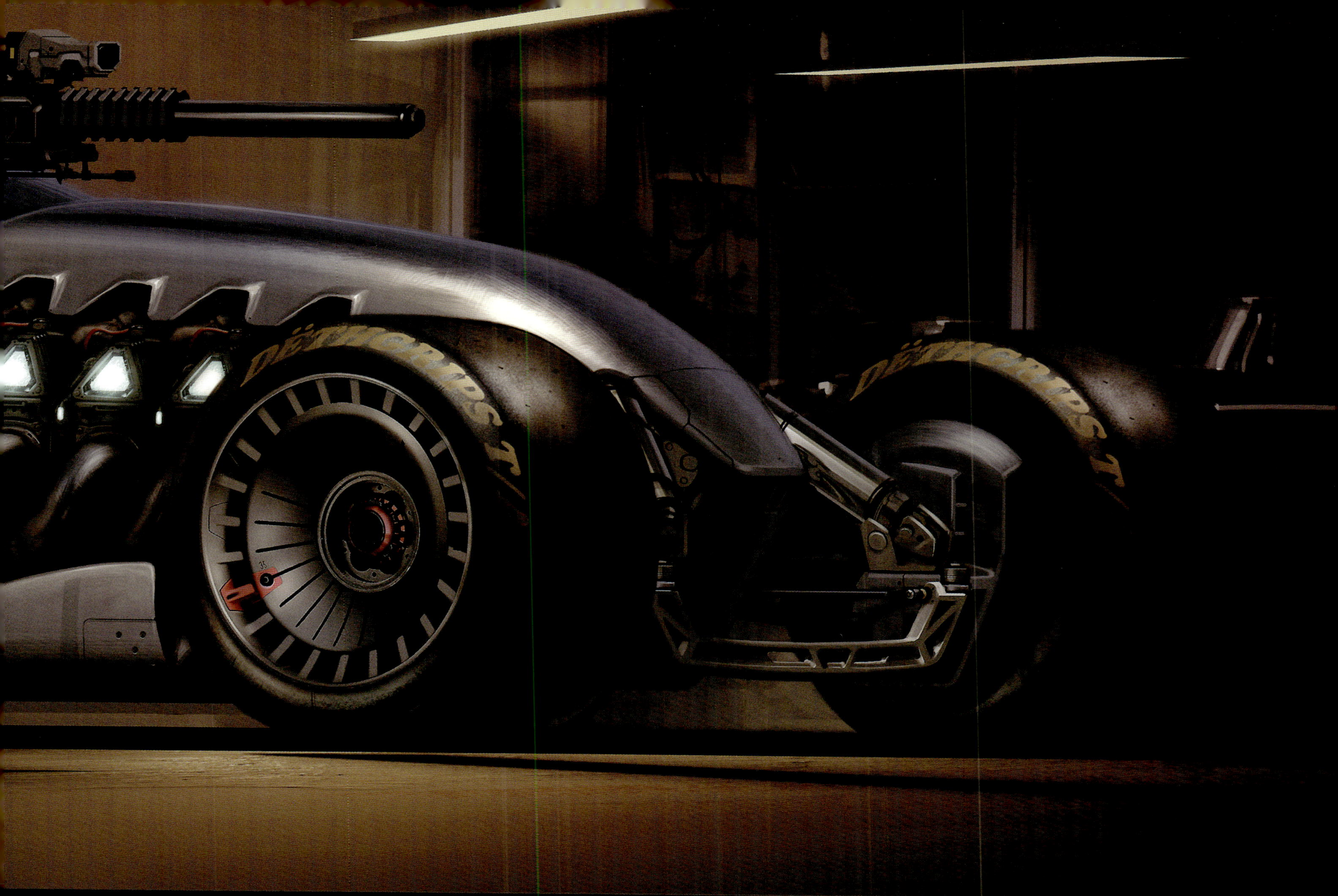

Looks like a hot rod, but it's actually a high-budget airport maintenance vehicle, specifically for ensuring birds and wildlife remain safely away from runways. A good loud blast of throttle, with pummels from eight large pistons, is usually enough to scare the birds away from the tarmac so that jets and planes can safely land. But if that doesn't work, the auto-aim mini gun is guaranteed to clear any avian loafers.

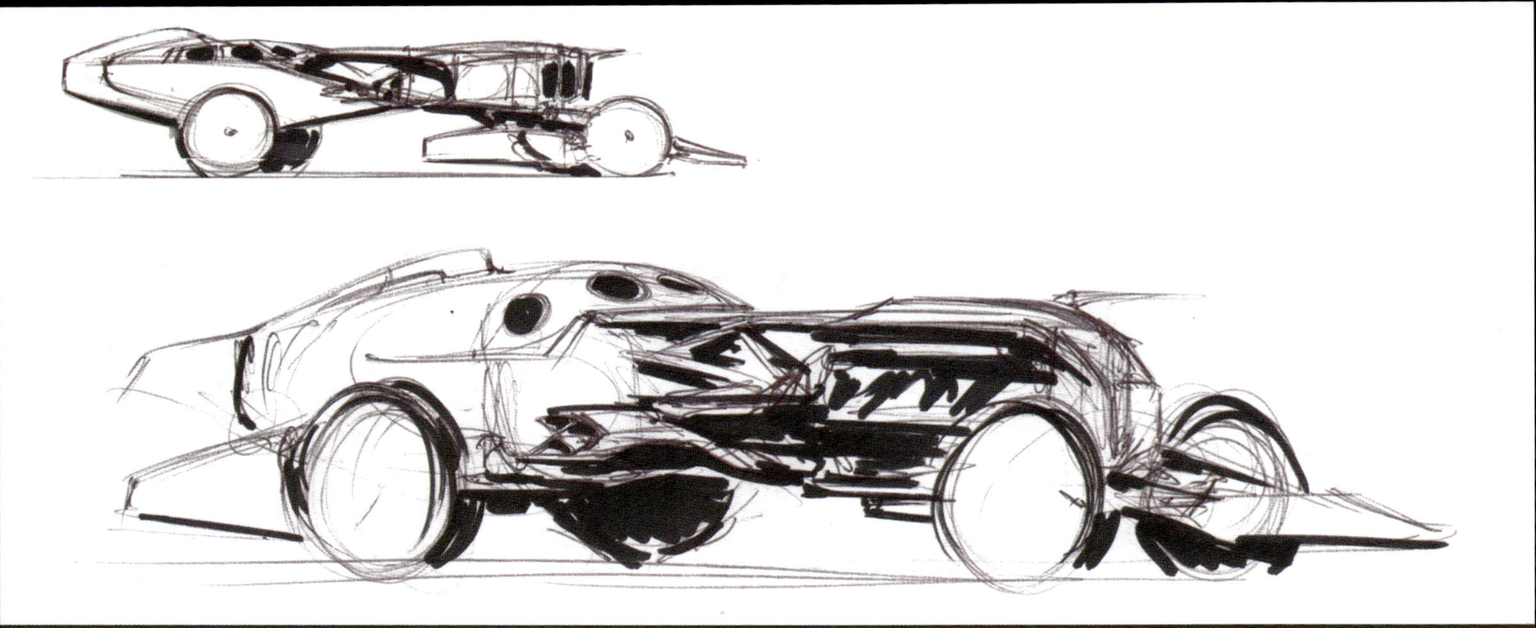

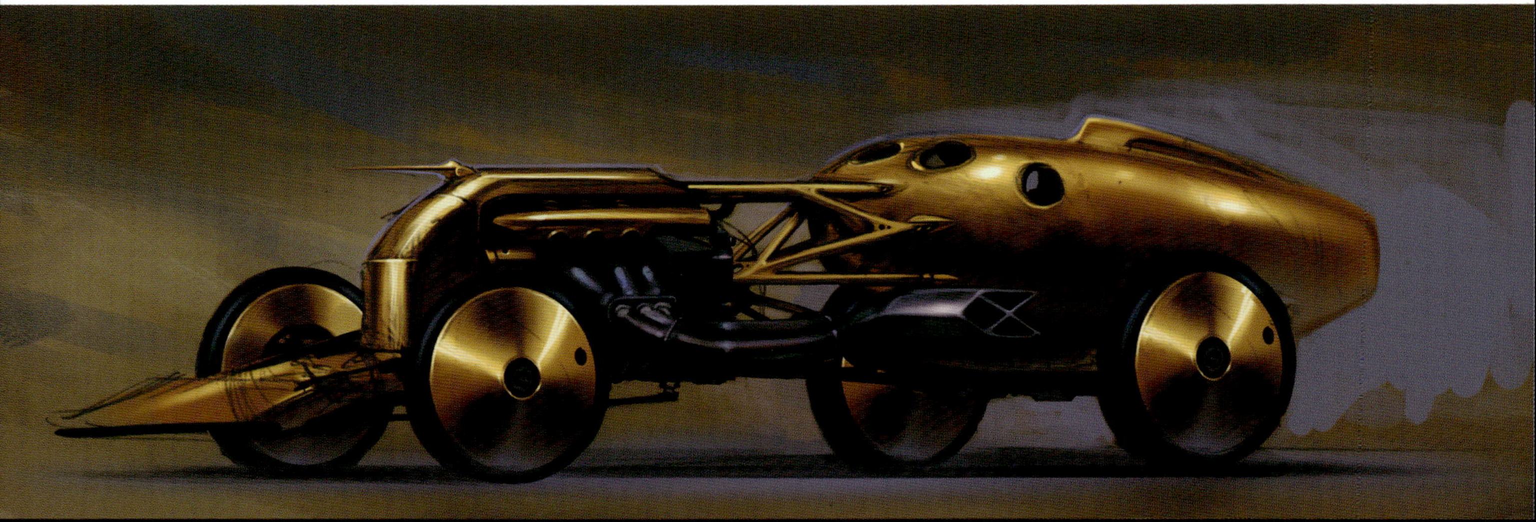

My quickly executed series of early 1900s racers were heavily inspired by Harry Miller's Golden Submarine but also influenced by the dusty old machinery—cars, engines, and mysterious mechanical contraptions—that I would see tucked away in the little local museums I would visit as a kid. Often there would be a tall, spoked-wheel vehicle with cast-iron bits holding the wheels in place, slathered with black gloss paint to cover years of rust. Maybe it was a tractor, a buckboard with metal leaf springs, or a type of proto-auto with carriage body and lead-acid batteries in an oak box under the seat. The items always looked homemade, delicate, obscure, and fading from existence.

The side views of these vehicles were assembled rapidly using digital cut, paste, and distort tools, similar in process to fashion design, where material is quickly cut and pinned to a mannequin in an iterative process of visualizing different ideas before committing to a final design. Sections of the body can be manipulated, stretched, and pulled quickly, followed by some basic sketch over to make it cohesive—a very efficient way to iterate ideas. While there are several ideas in this brief series, none deserved to be taken into a finished illustration, as the name I came up with set a very high bar.

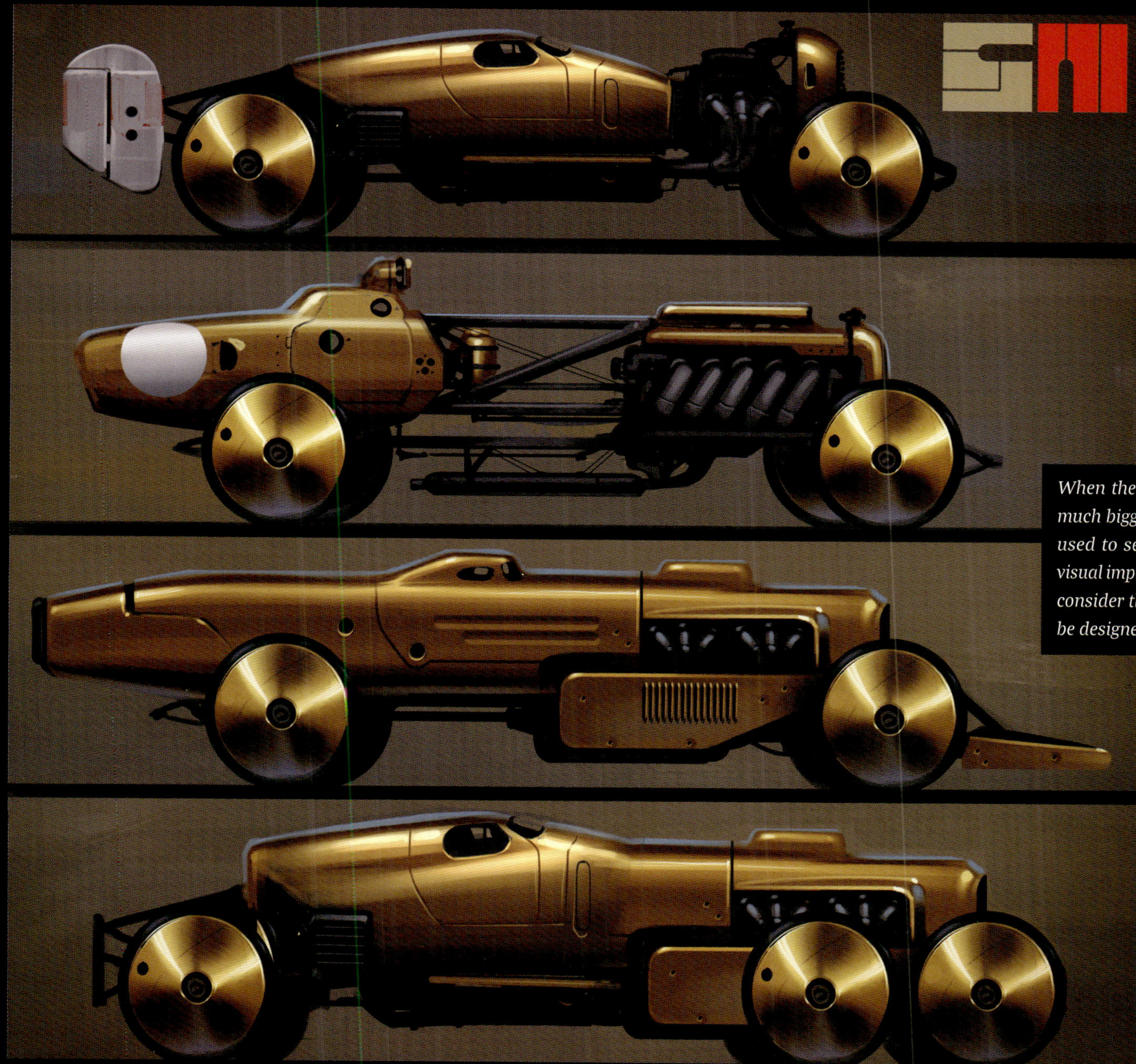

When the scale of a vehicle is much bigger than what we are used to seeing, it has a lot of visual impact and can make one consider the reality that has to be designed around them.

THE SCALE OF VEHICLES

With the most fanciful world building of concept design, I'm able to step away from one of the big constraints from real-world vehicle design and get wild with the size of vehicles. Any vehicle that serves as some sort of transport certainly is more effective if it is large and can haul more volume. But when it comes to personal vehicles, going larger than the average size vehicle is often an expression of wealth. A vehicle of tremendous length, designed to accommodate a huge engine, also consumes gobs of energy, but for the enjoyment of its privileged owner. I can draw massive construction vehicles, too big for our roads, but in a conceptual universe they can find places to fit their heavy, trundling breadth.

DEVELOPING A NARRATIVE TO SPUR NEW IDEAS: THE GP TENS SERIES

Imagine an alternate world history in which Austrian Archduke Franz Ferdinand was not assassinated, and as a result, racing flourished during the peaceful second decade of the 20th century. GP Tens, a Formula Libre, brought together the most gifted and some of the most eccentric automotive and aeronautical engineers of the day for spirited competition, where innovation was the key to winning.

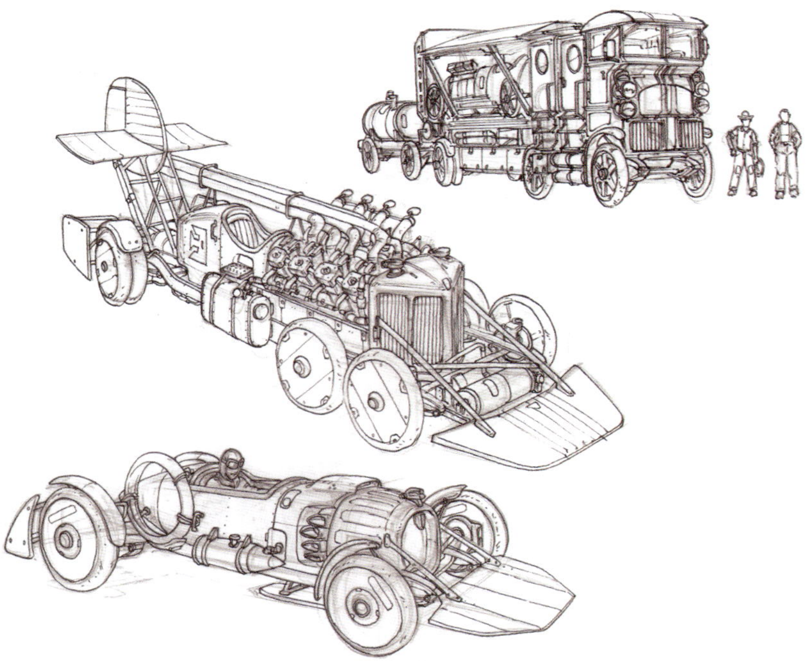

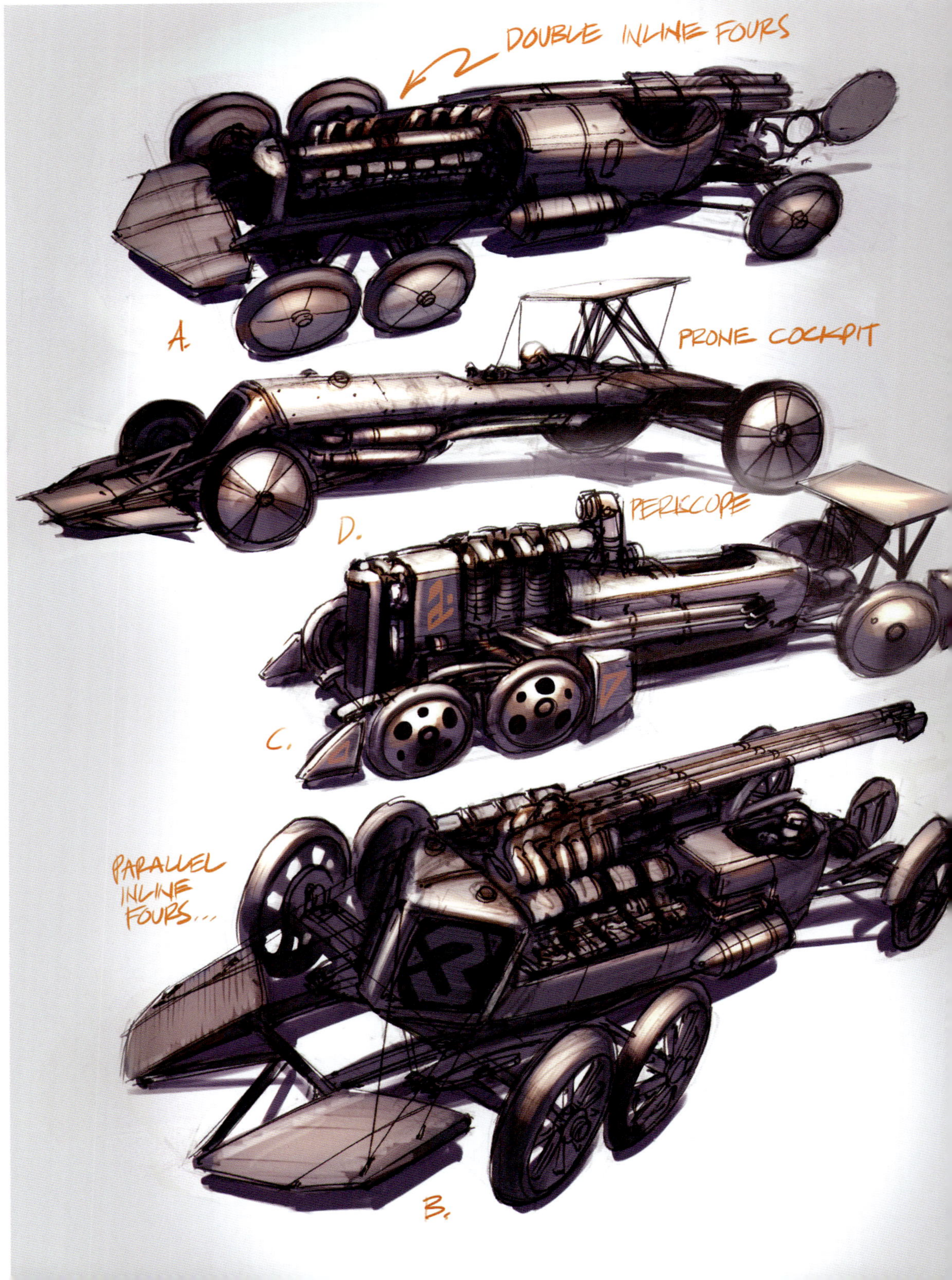

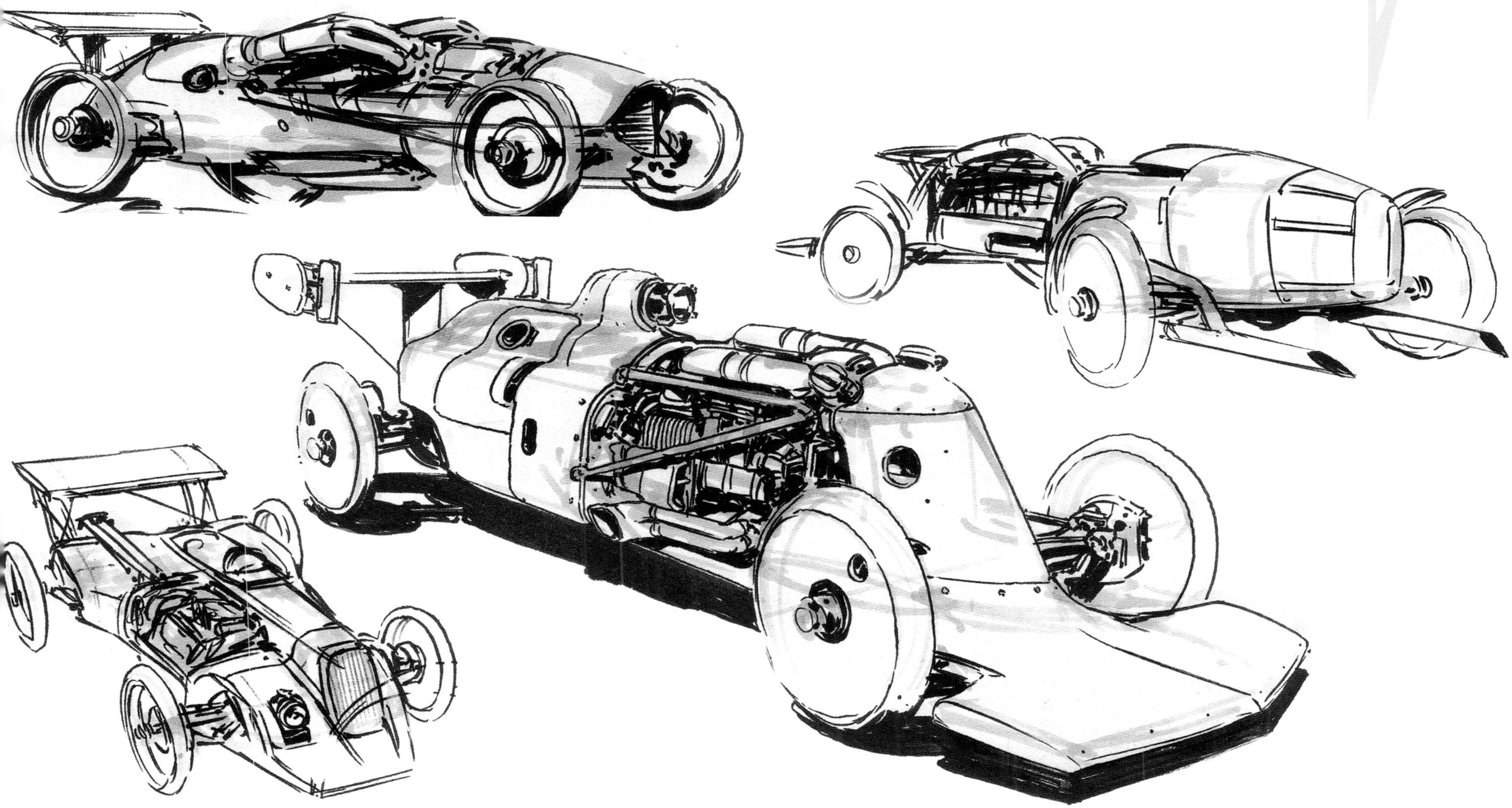

It is fun to come up with a scenario that can spur new ideas, changing the rules of the game for a particular era of design. It's a way to expand the confines of a box that is stifling design. For this series, I combined the aerodynamic know-how from airplane design of the early 20th century with race car design of that time. While aerodynamic devices weren't common features in cars until decades later, rewriting history and introducing wings and winglets on cars much earlier was an exercise that charged up my creative flow. I drew inspiration from early biplane wing technology—stretched fabric material over wood frames, placed thin-gauge aluminum in places, and used an old-style ladder frame—and tall-engine racers, with their tombstone-shaped front radiators, slim bodies, and precariously narrow tires.

Welcome to my imaginary GP Tens race circuit!

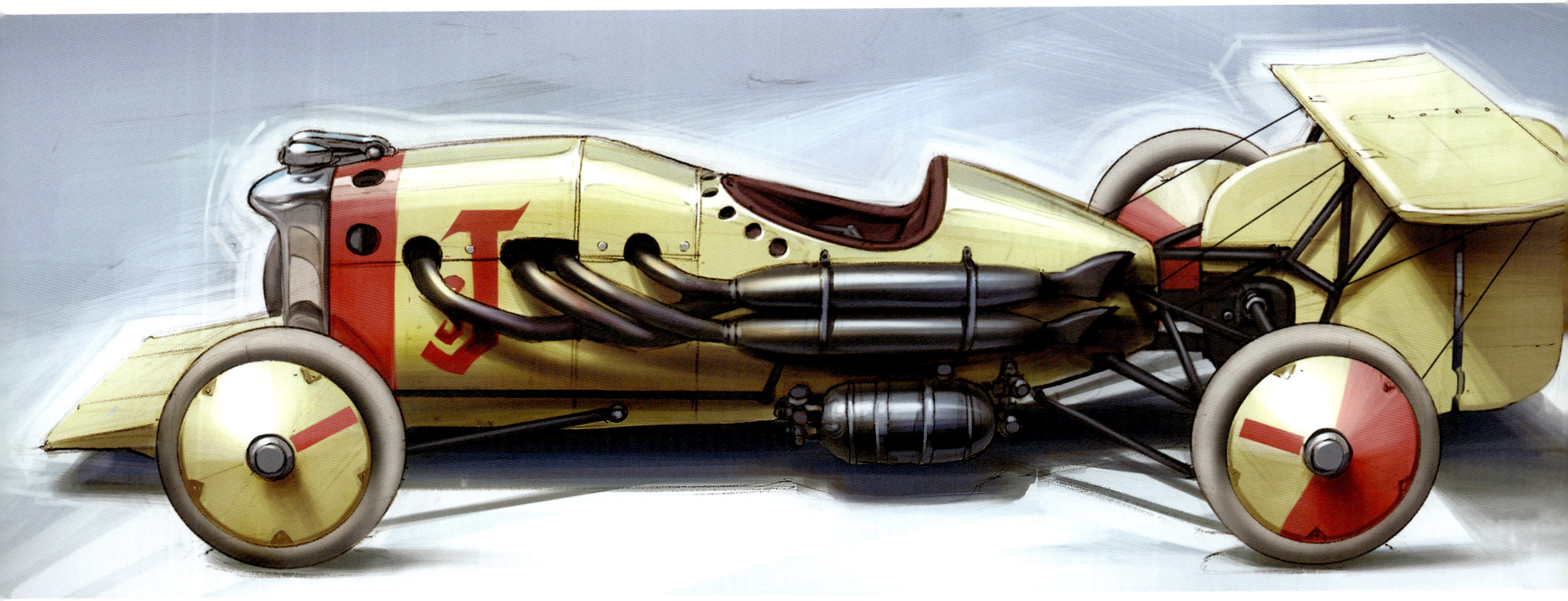

Trouser magnate Samuel T. Y. Jesperson entered the 1917 GP Tens Cup with a unique chassis built around a Brickhouse parallel straight bank 8, two inline four-cylinder engines with a shared driveshaft. A crowd favorite at Jesperson's home-track debut in Dayton, Ohio, the Superflivver failed to deliver, dropping two laps behind the leader in the first 10. Throughout the season, Team Jesperson managed to chase out some chassis issues that plagued its handling performance and coaxed an additional 7 bhp (brake horsepower) out of the 18-liter engine to finish fourth in the overall standings at the end of the season, despite not winning a single race.

The car was put in storage immediately after the last race of 1917 in South Bend, Indiana, in anticipation of running again in 1918. But Jesperson contracted typhoid while on vacation in French Indochina that winter and died miserably without proper care while on a steamship on his way home. The car was unearthed from the coach house of the Jesperson estate in 1952 by his great nephew and is in preserved but unrestored condition, permanently displayed at the GP Tens Museum in Waukesha, Wisconsin.

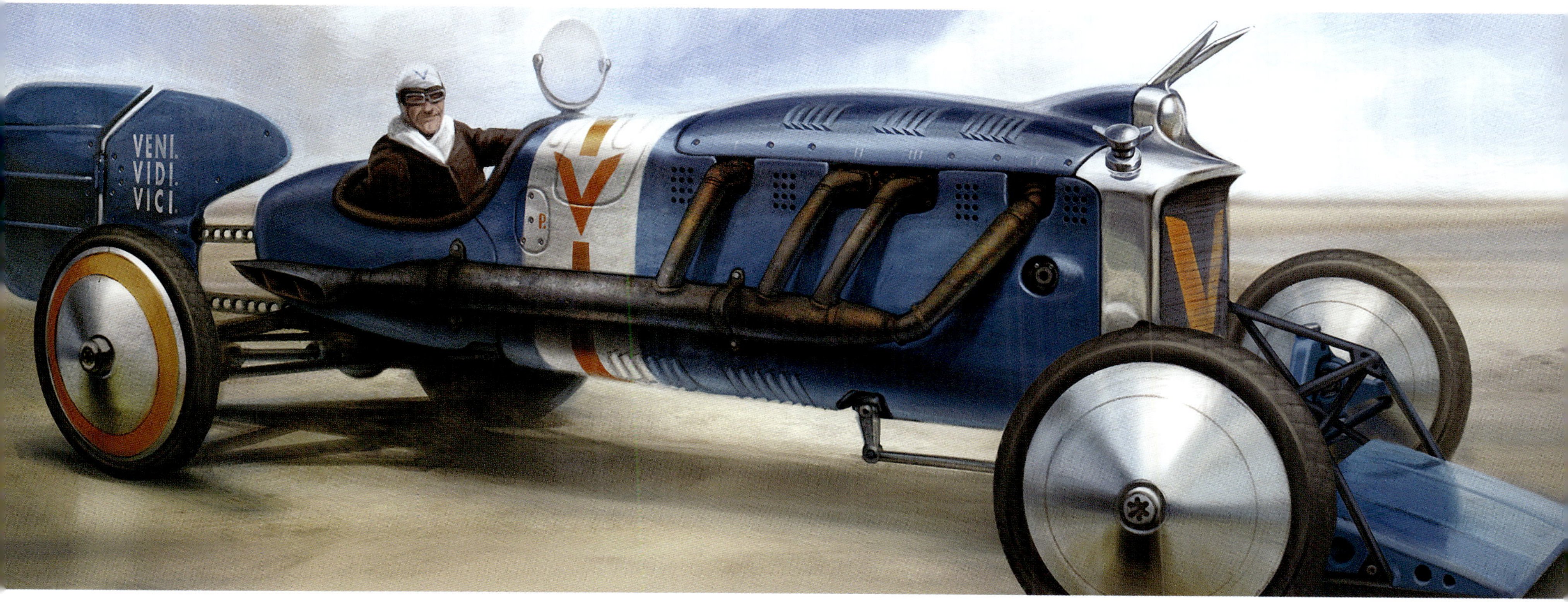

La Victoire Totale "Lapine," shown here in 1917 at Pendine Sands, Carmarthen, during its first shakedown week, with Archie Leabo at the wheel. A straightforward and well-constructed entrant for the 1917 season, it did not make much of an impression, finishing solidly in the middle of the field for most of the races. Later, the optimistic text on the rudder was quietly painted over, headlights and proper bumpers were added, and it was licensed as a passenger car, seen for decades with faded yellow paint, bleached by the sun, navigating the twisty streets on the backside of Paris's Montmartre, engine burbling pleasantly at low rpm and trailing black smoke.

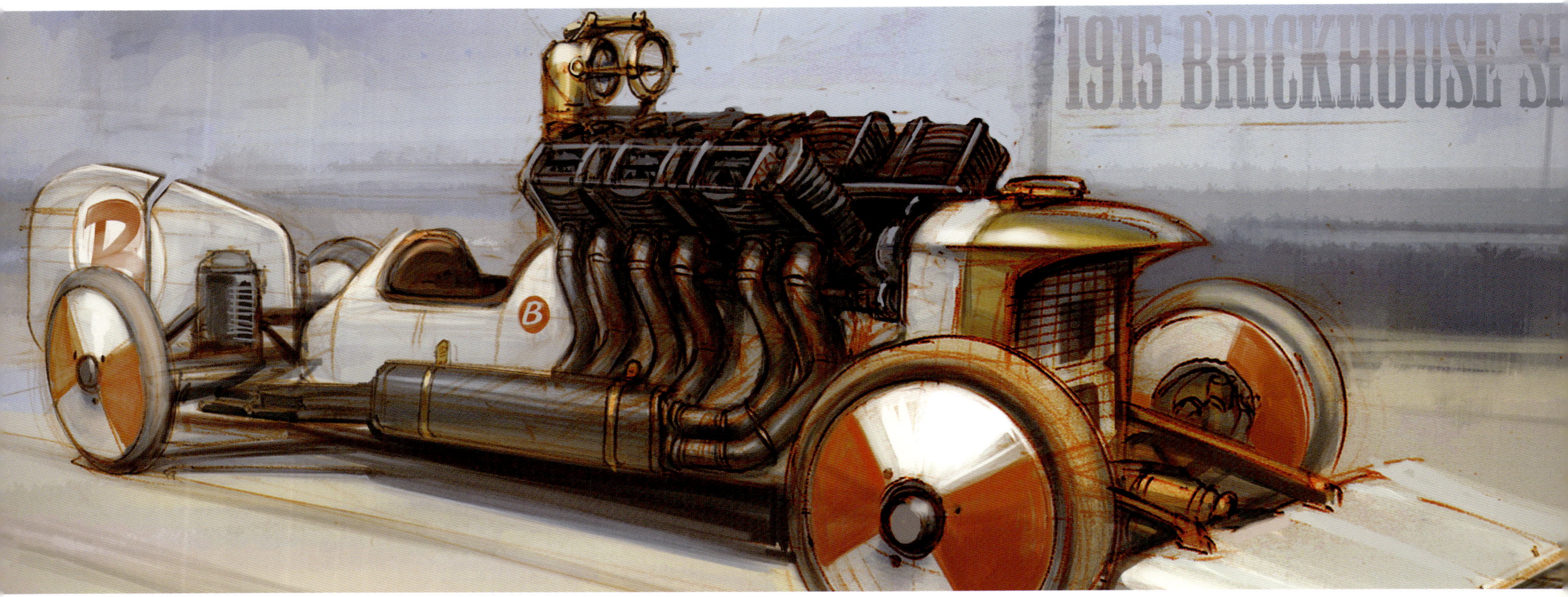

William F. Brickhouse, founder of Brickhouse Mining and Medical, had the 17-liter V6 built for the 1915 GP Tens Cup race in Pennsylvania. Brickhouse managed to finish third at the Uniontown board track. The following year, his brother, Franklin, had the car shipped to England, where he intended a run at Brooklands race track, but the steamship he was on capsized in a storm and sank to the bottom of the North Atlantic. The floatable shipping crate that he had designed as insurance for such an event broke loose as designed, but the crew had survival on their minds, not keeping tabs on the loose cargo. The car was never seen again. The Brickhouse brothers moved on and had success with the 1917 Brickhouse Speedliner, nearly winning the GP Tens Cup that year.

GP TENS BRICKHOUSE TORPEDETTE

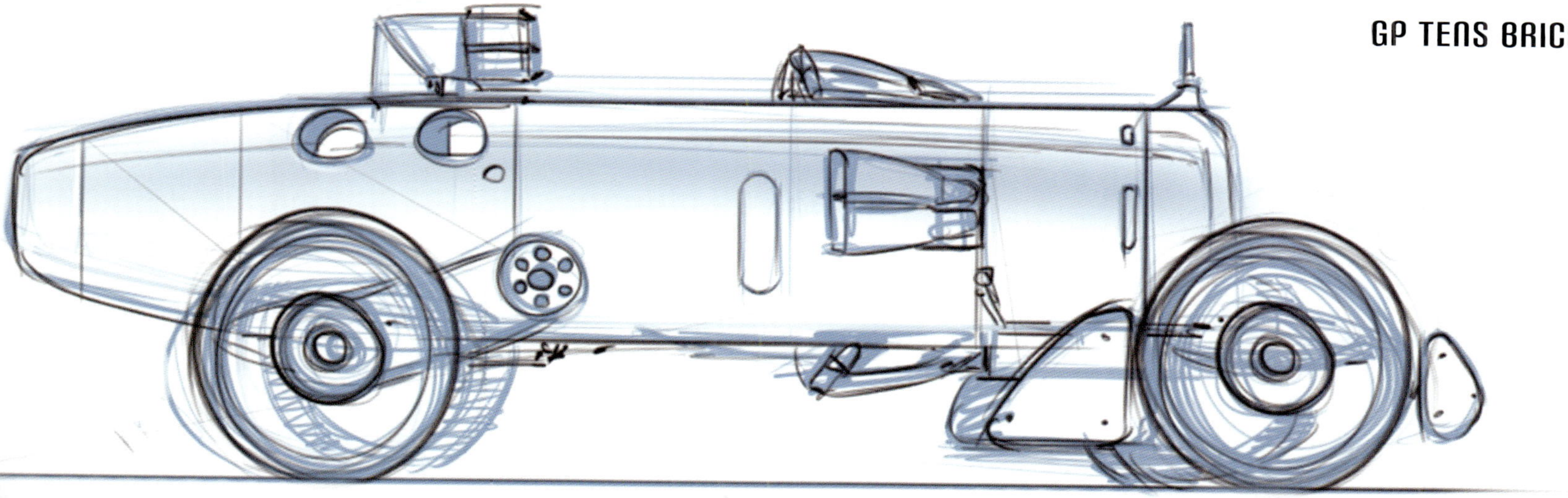

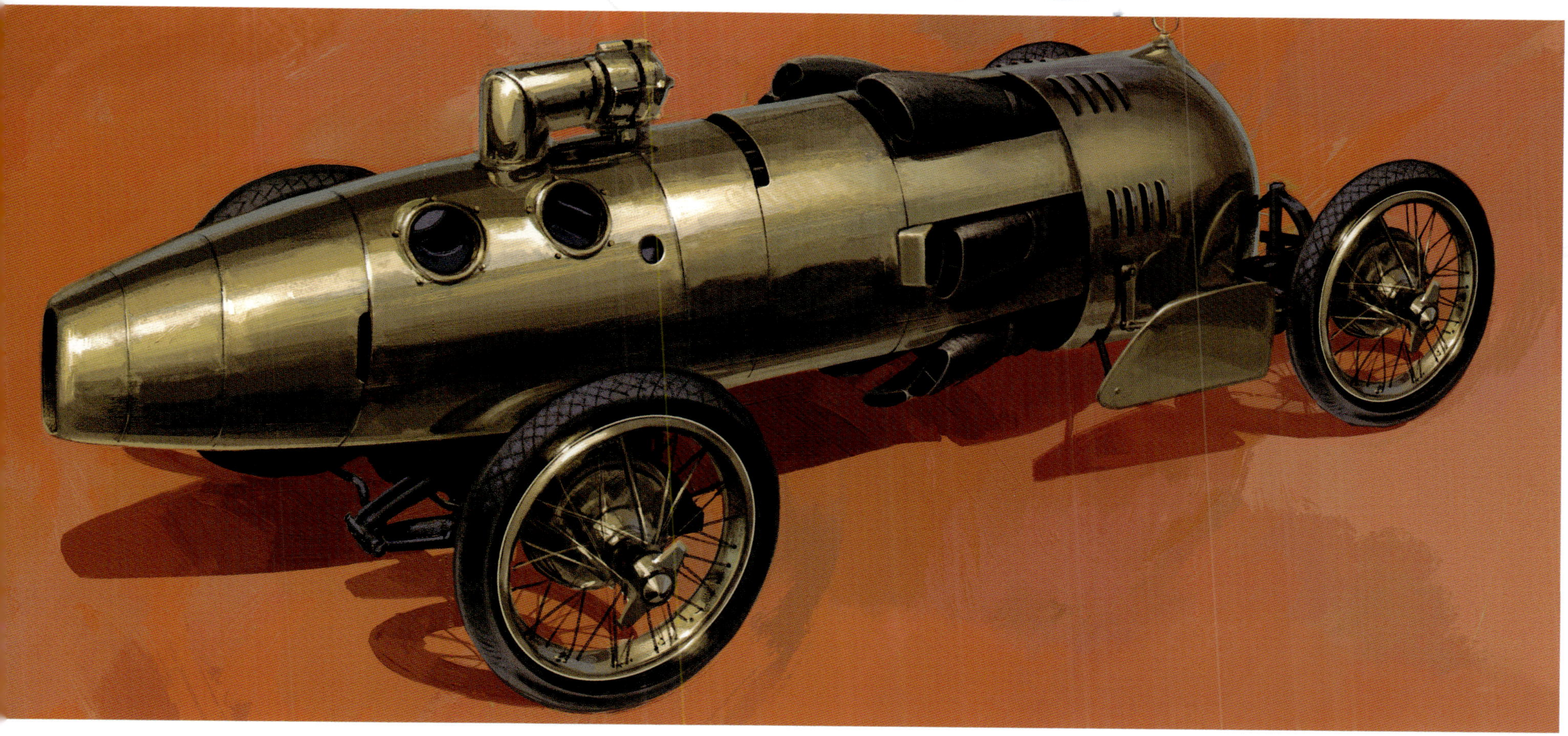

Team Brickhouse's follow-up to its ill-fated Brickhouse Special uses a 12-cylinder radial biplane motor for a lower drag, with trailing in-line wheel spats, no wings, and an enclosed cockpit. With its massive engine and low cockpit, normal forward visibility was impossible, so a Swiss-built Zeickenziss brass periscope was used to view the road ahead from a nearly flat, reclined seating position.

GRAND RAPTOR

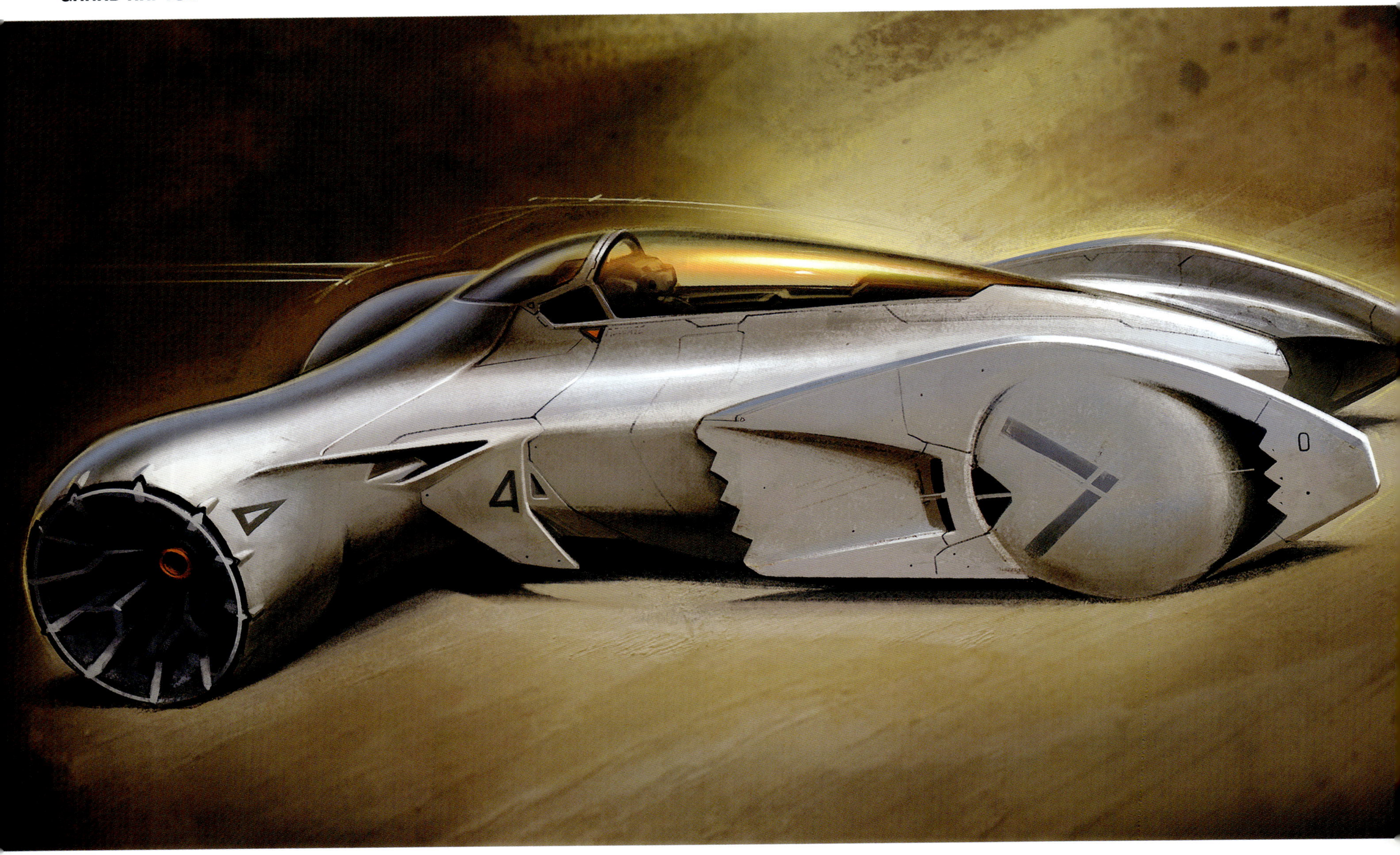

The personal sports car with the DNA of a modern fighter jet went from fast sketch to rapid-fire rendering. Surfacing on a jet and on a car have some commonalities as they are both designed to slip through the wind smoothly, but some components, like a central bubble-canopy cockpit, which are alien to a land vehicle, present good opportunities to shake things up visually. Stealth technology surfacing motifs from jets—the serrated edges on surfaces, flowing titanium panel form wrapping over wheels—brings the two worlds together.

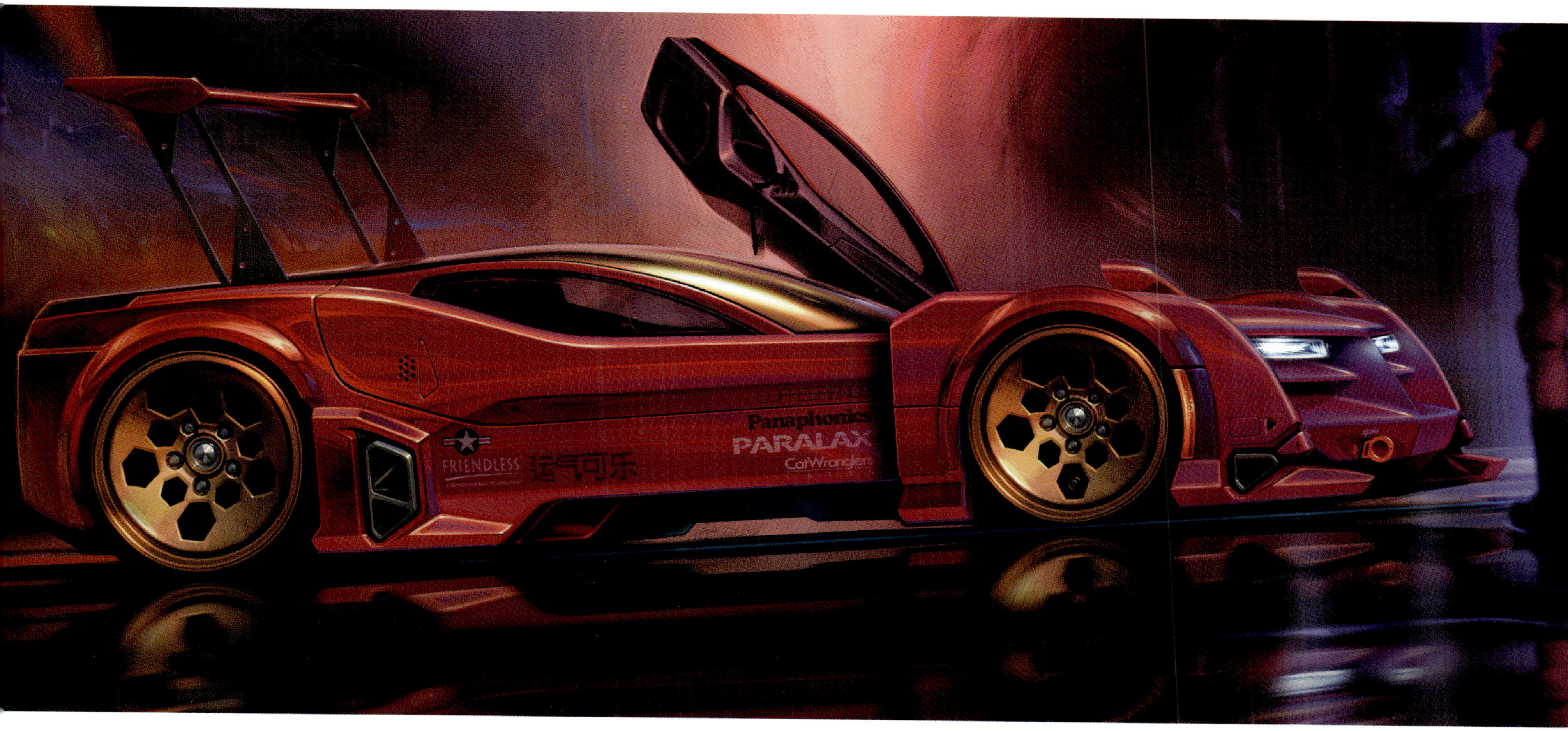

A retro-futuristic, boxy, alley dart optimized to perform well on tight city streets features paddle-shaped scissor doors that look sexy enough when they hiss open but offer little space to climb out of. When a passenger disembarks the small egress, bruised shoulders, lost shoes, ripped pants, and sweaty-brow muttered curses follow.

BATTLE-READY CARS: THE LE MANS SERIES

A brand-new series of vehicles designed with a military aesthetic go to battle on an international vintage sports-car competition. Conceptually, this was an excuse to exercise my love for the look of war machinery with the violent functionality conveniently removed. I have a lot of World War II reference in my mental visual database, but I'm always excited to go to any museum and see the hardware up close and personal in real life.

AGA IKEBUKURO J9E

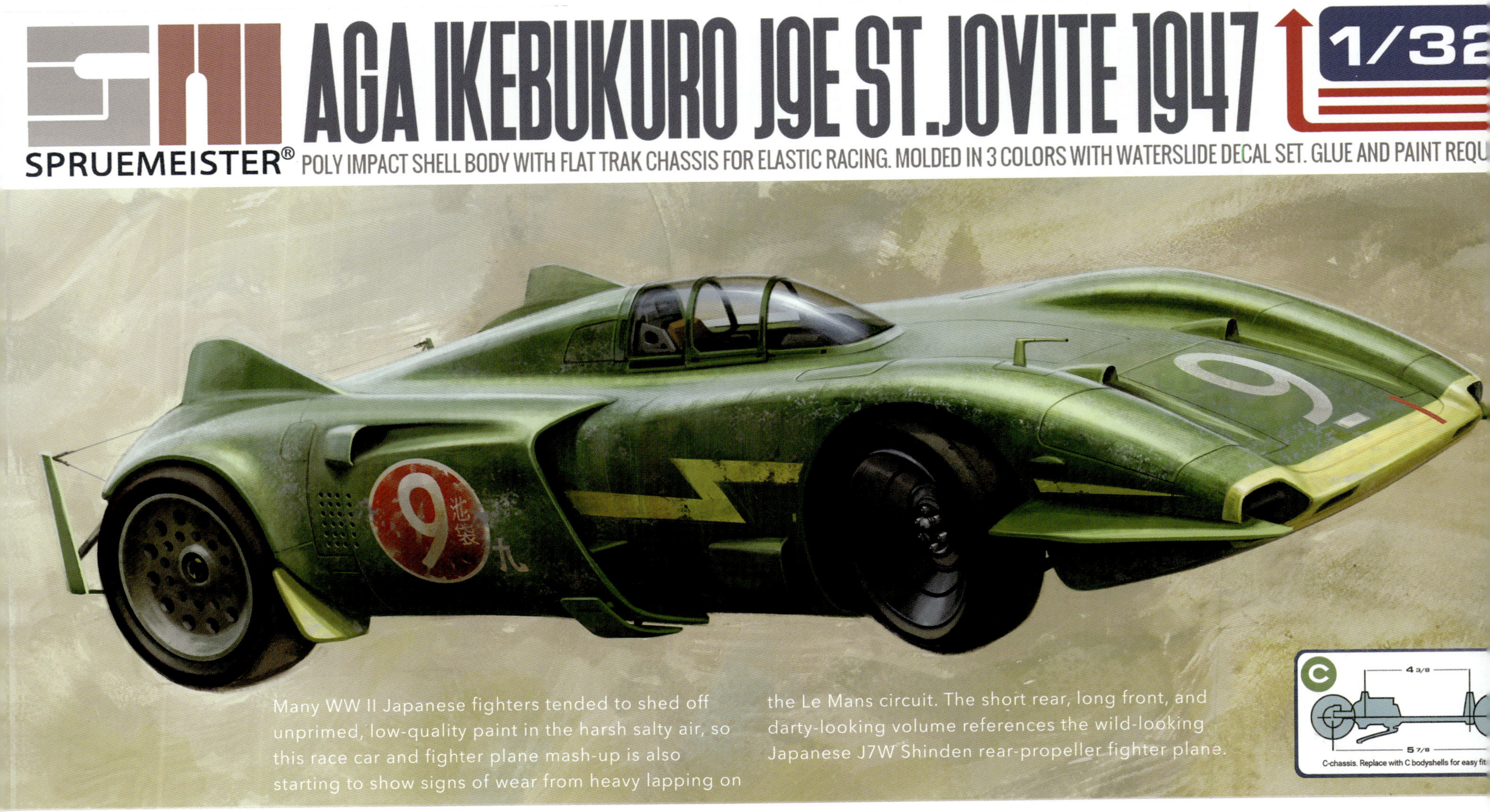

Many WW II Japanese fighters tended to shed off unprimed, low-quality paint in the harsh salty air, so this race car and fighter plane mash-up is also starting to show signs of wear from heavy lapping on the Le Mans circuit. The short rear, long front, and darty-looking volume references the wild-looking Japanese J7W Shinden rear-propeller fighter plane.

TIP: Next time you go to a car (or aviation) museum, look for a vehicle that can serve as inspiration to mix design cues into a new vehicle. Take lots of detailed photos and use them as a palette of design elements you can assemble into a new form.

SPRUEMEISTER® F8B BOLT-THROWER 1/32

POLY IMPACT SHELL BODY WITH FLAT TRAK CHASSIS FOR ELASTIC RACING. MOLDED IN 3 COLORS WITH WATERSLIDE DECAL SET. GLUE AND PAINT REQUIRED.

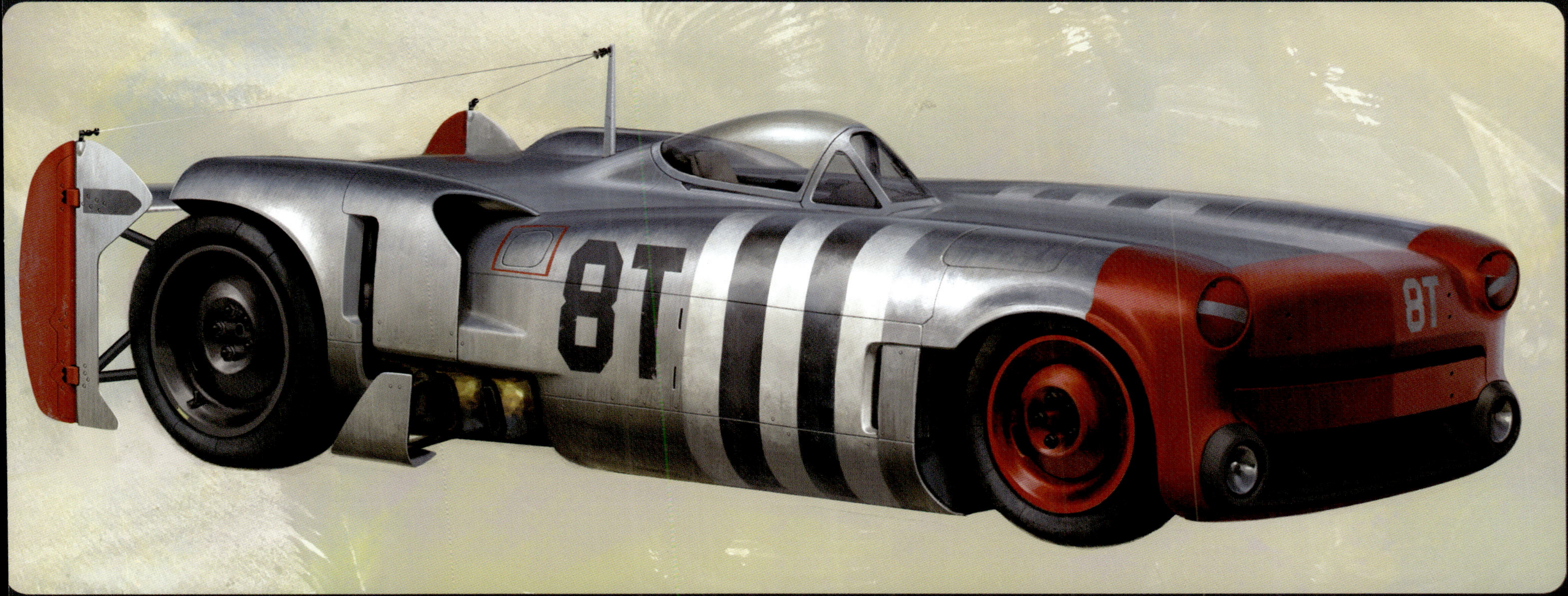

The F8B was one of the most powerful contenders in this race series. The heavy, noisy, American-made sports car possessed brutal speed and presence that had the lightweight fighters pulling aside quickly in a combination of respect and nervousness for the long straightaways. The design is based on the Republic P-47 Thunderbolt US fighter.

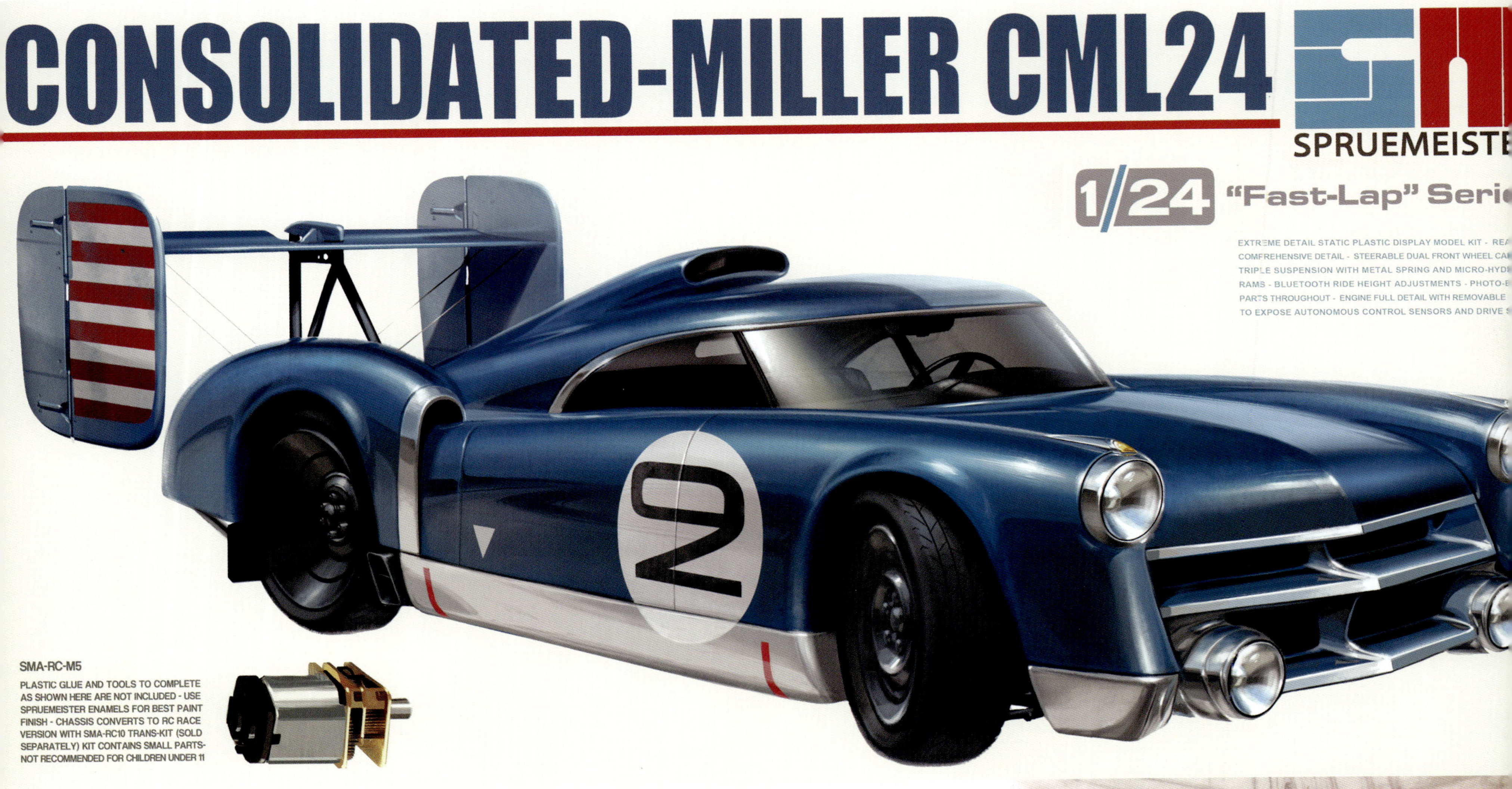

In an alt-reality, the Le Mans American mid-engine, 6-liter, flat-12 contender 1953 Consolidated-Miller CML24 experienced a wing failure in the 20th hour while in 2nd place and was destroyed. Driver Wilbur Shew escaped via ejector seat, unharmed, but walked away from the track without going back to the pits or speaking with his team, and quickly retired from racing. This illustration, derived from parts of the American Consolidated B-24 Liberator bomber, was created by starting with a mechanical pencil drawing on vellum that was used as an underlay for digital color work in Autodesk SketchbookPro.

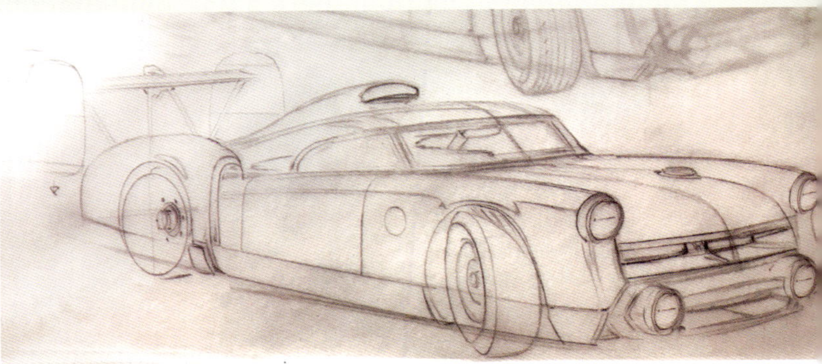

FOUGHT / MINIZ F47U

1/32

RUEMEISTER® POLY IMPACT SHELL BODY WITH FLAT TRAK CHASSIS FOR ELASTIC RACING. MOLDED IN 3 COLORS WITH WATERSLIDE DECAL SET. GLUE AND PAINT REQUIRED.

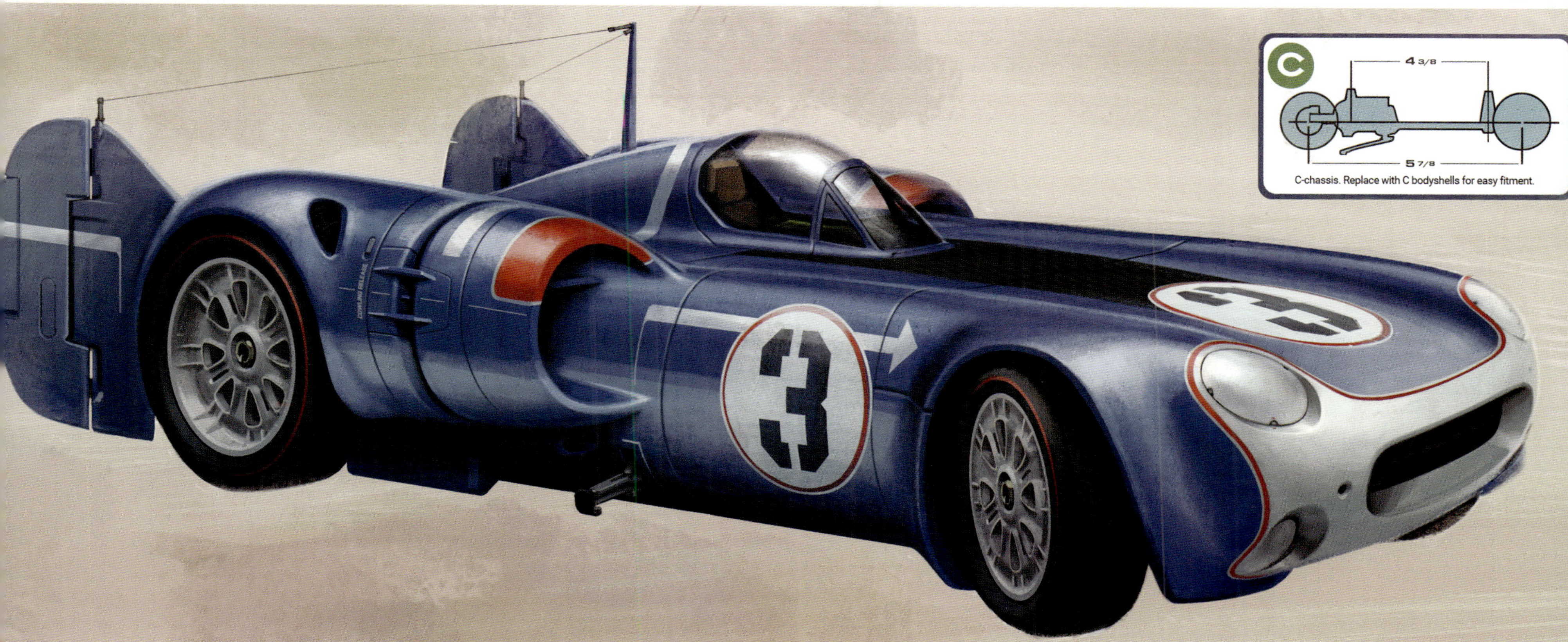

With a body side built off the barrel shape of a radial engine, the F47U's freshly shaved smooth nose provides wind efficiency that is perhaps dragged down by the massive air ducted into the rear flanks. As seen on other vehicles in the series, rear rudder-control surfaces help with handling and getting the car pointed exactly where you need it. This design references the American Vought F4U Corsair, my favorite WWII fighter design.

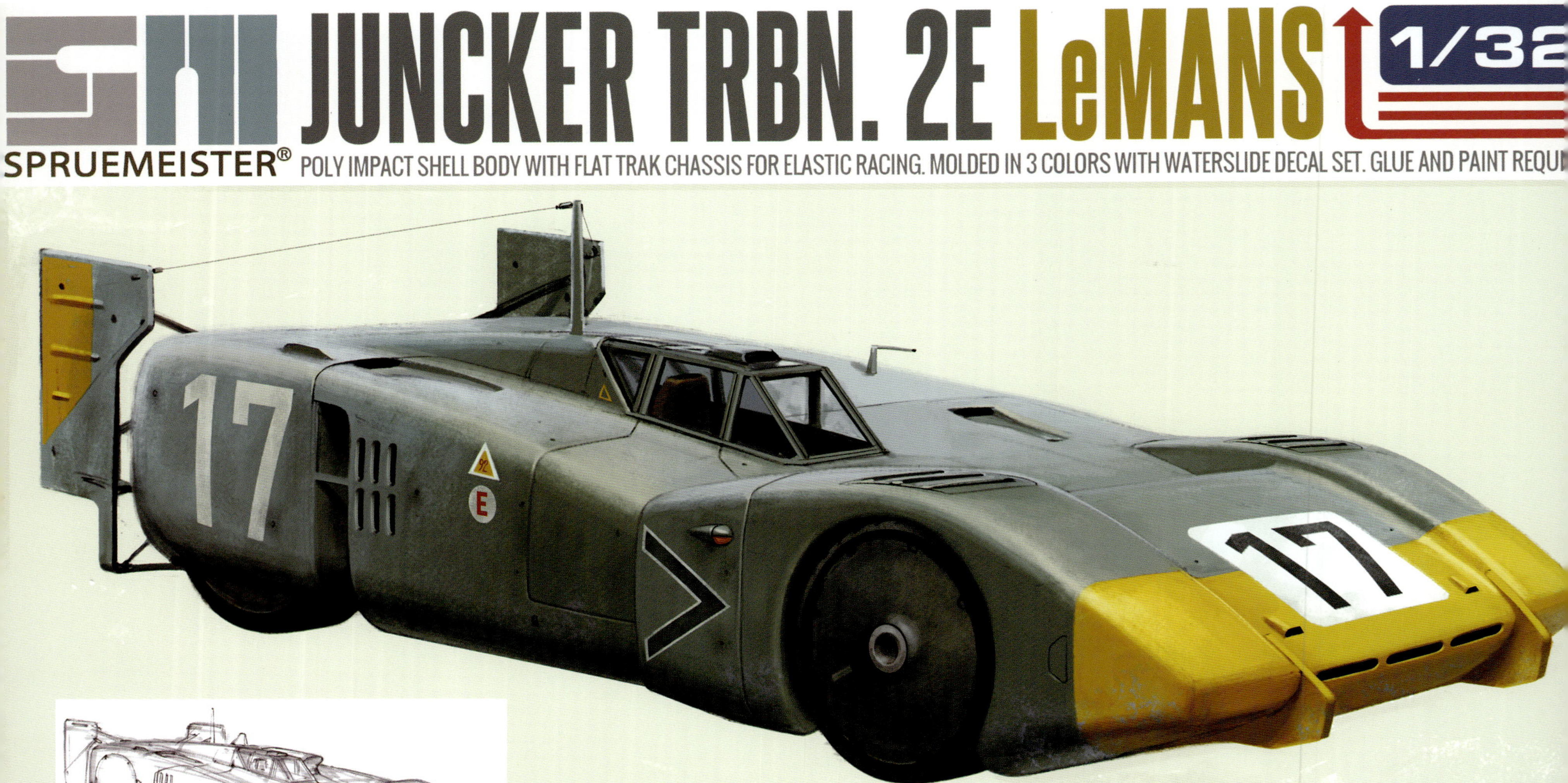

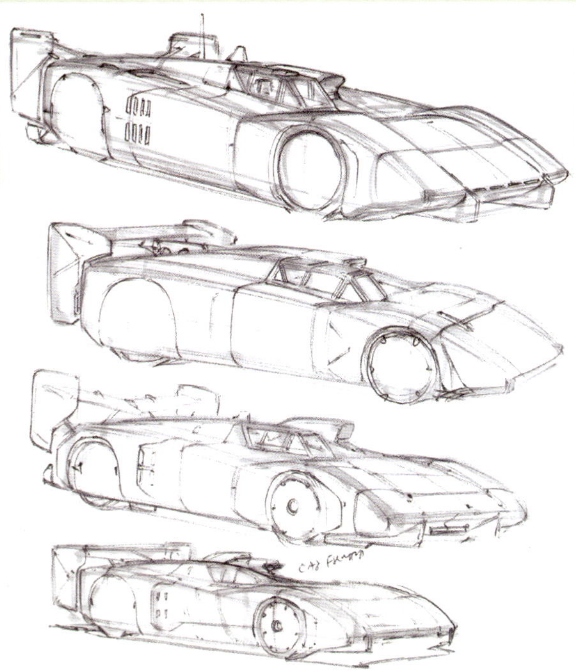

Unique for its departure from the centerline driver position, it is situated as such to permit the packaging of the turbine components. Boxy and heavy, the Juncker 2E was more famous for the high-pitched scream of its engine than the on-track performance. This design takes some design elements and inspiration from the German Messerschmitt BF 109 fighter.

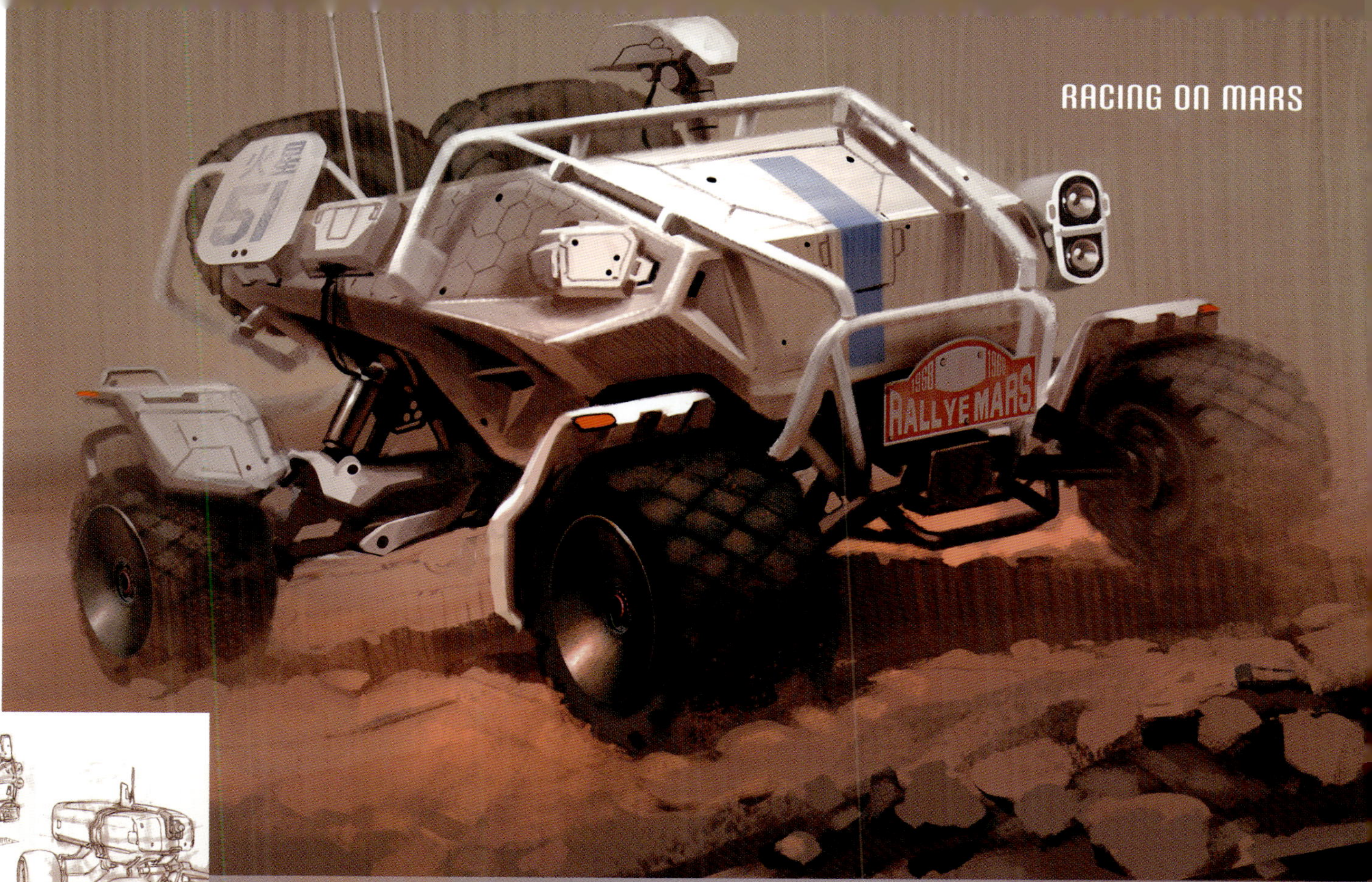

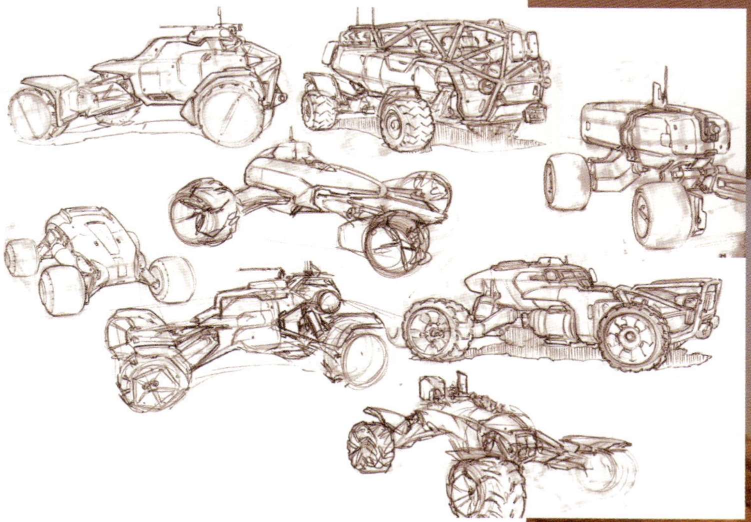

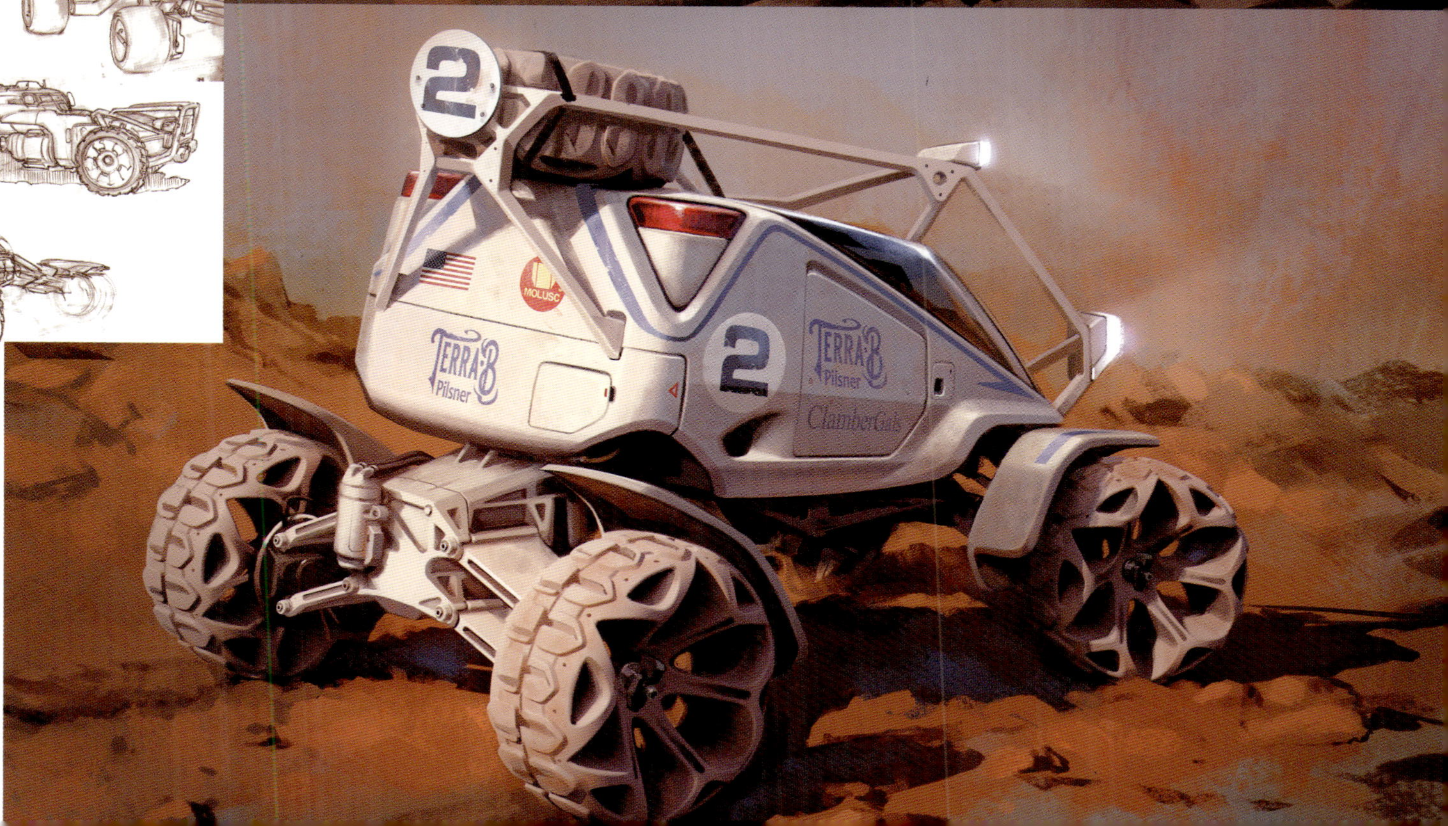

This was spurred by the social-media sketch theme #marsracerchallenge. I'm always interested in developing ideas for something that I hadn't previously given a lot of thought. The red dust and alien atmosphere was fun to try to capture in color as well.

WALCHESTER "BRAMBLESHARK"

The Brambleshark references the British Avro Lancaster WWII bomber with thin aluminum fit tightly over a space frame showing the internal gridded structure.

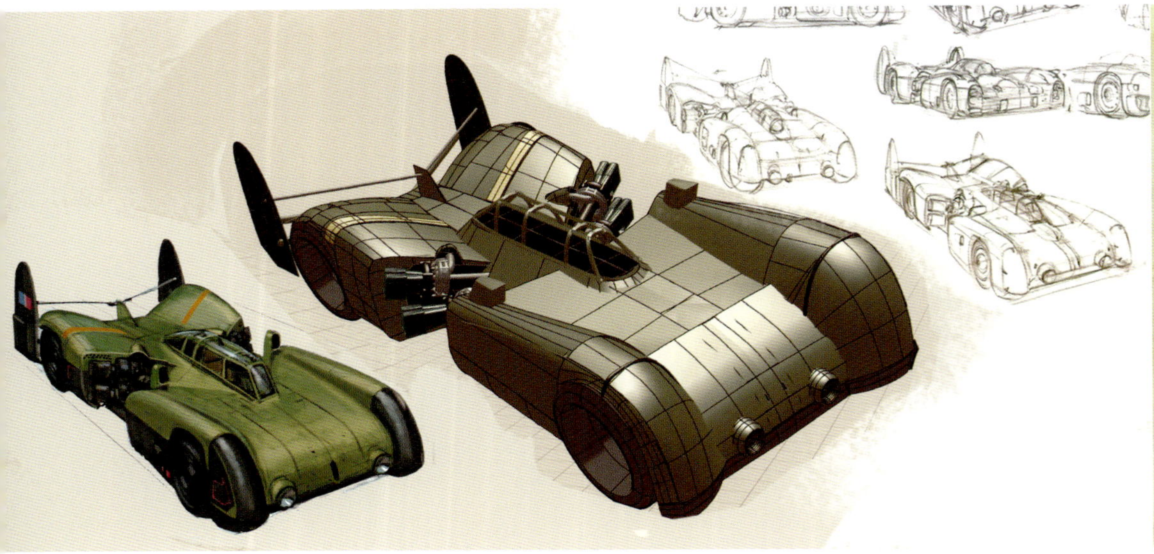

1) Rough it in: ballpoint pen thumbnails and 3D base model.

The initial rough sketches fed into a quick Gravity Sketch VR model. In VR, the mass and turbo exhaust details were fleshed out and camera angles were considered. With a wider car, a high view was best to show much of the design and detail and character of the upper surfaces of the vehicle. The Gravity Sketch model is used as light value multiply underlay. The canopy's scale and positioning were modified from the initial sketch. Scaling the canopy down conversely scales up the vehicle size, while moving the canopy back increases the drama of the hood and implies power.

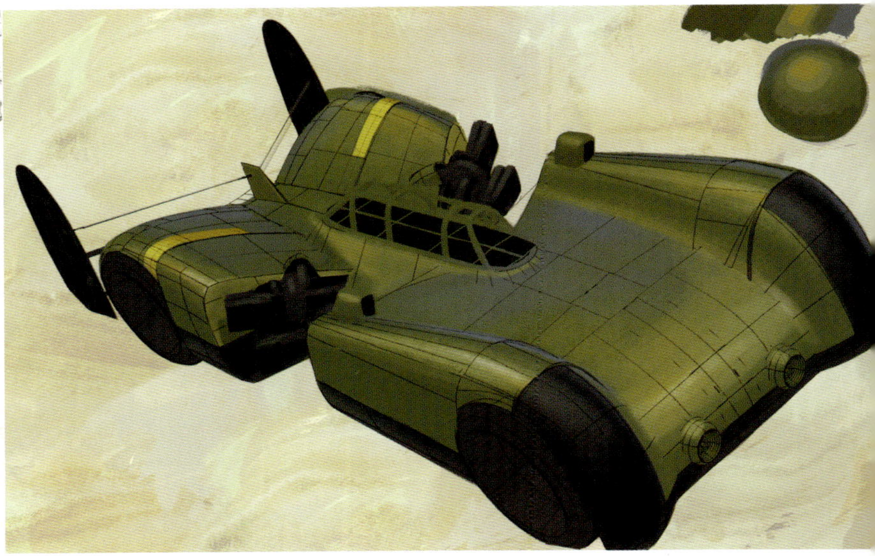

2) Create color comp: establish lighting, material, graphics, and overall color.

I blocked in color in the next step: a drab green main tone with golden highlights and bluish Fresnel effect (reflection increase) on surfaces that angle away from the direction of our sightline. Surface paint that isn't high gloss can still have quite a bit of color character and show volume with value changes. Sun-beaten paint often acquires a warm hazy highlight from oxidation and weathering.

The scale and feel of any vehicle is achieved by understanding the human reference. Where the driver sits and how big the cockpit is will dramatically impact the overall feel of the vehicle.

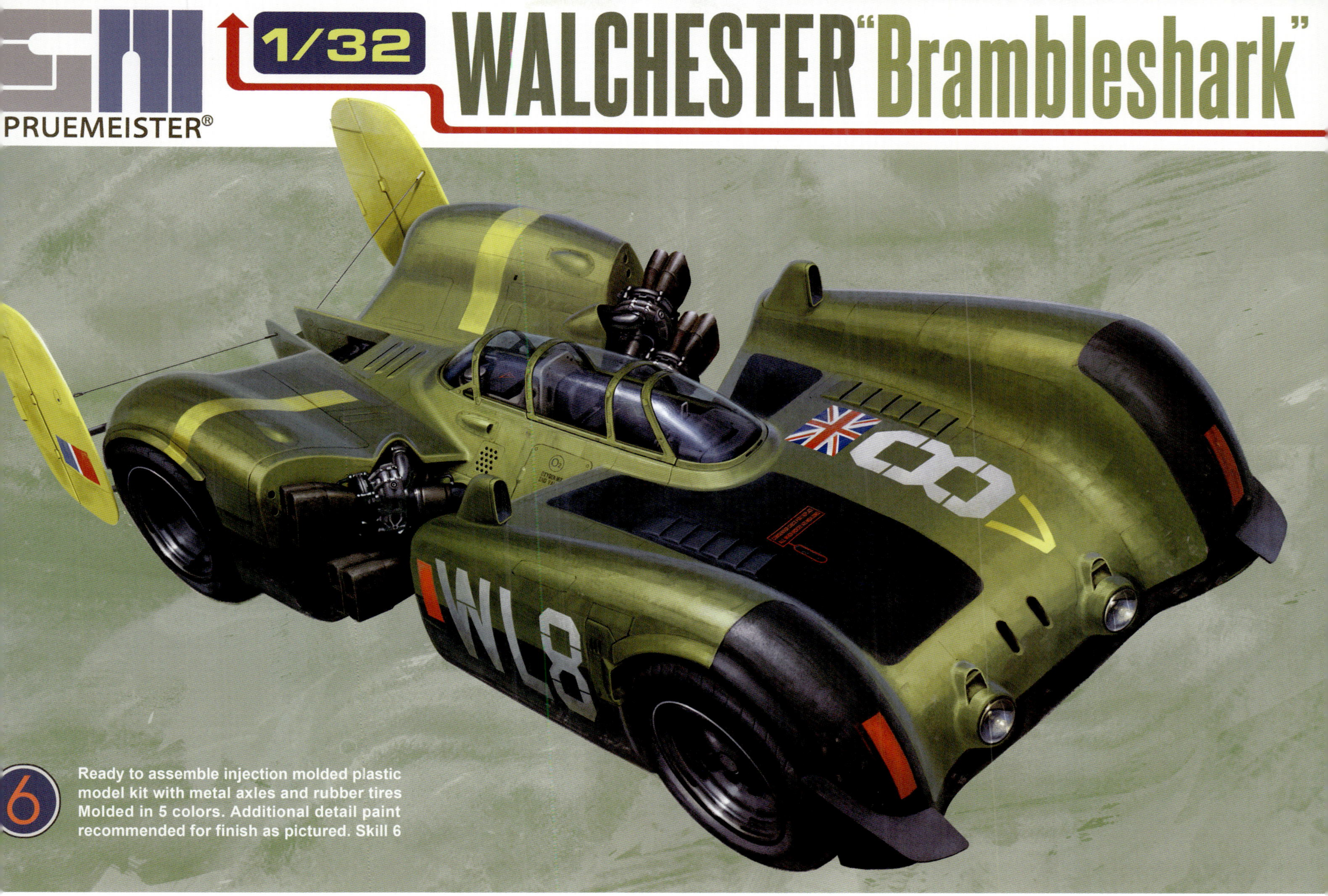

3) Finalize illustration: clarify detail, tighten it up.

Generally, I focus the biggest value expression on a part of the vehicle near to the camera so it comes off the page. The front near fender has the hottest highlight. The final illustration almost always has a separate background layer that I can tune in hue and value as the car is rendered. A lot of these have a broad-brush paint texture created with layers of scanned in grey gouache that has been color-tuned. With this illustration, I played around initially with a pale yellow background to give more contrast to the green, but sometimes the general overall feel of the image supersedes the logic of the color. Green on green seemed to just work best, by working simply with decent value contrast to the car and a touch of blue, so the warm green bits of the car would come out stronger.

BOX-CHUCK

This design goes back to my youth as well. During the 1970s, a fuel-efficient vehicle was of great value. While most Americans were driving their massive boats around our town, our family had a small, somewhat delicate but well-packaged compact French Renault R8 with a rear engine, unique style, and gobs of character. Not long ago, my mind wandered back to that car and reimagined it with aggressive race-style box fenders and diamond-shaped endplates on a high rear wing.

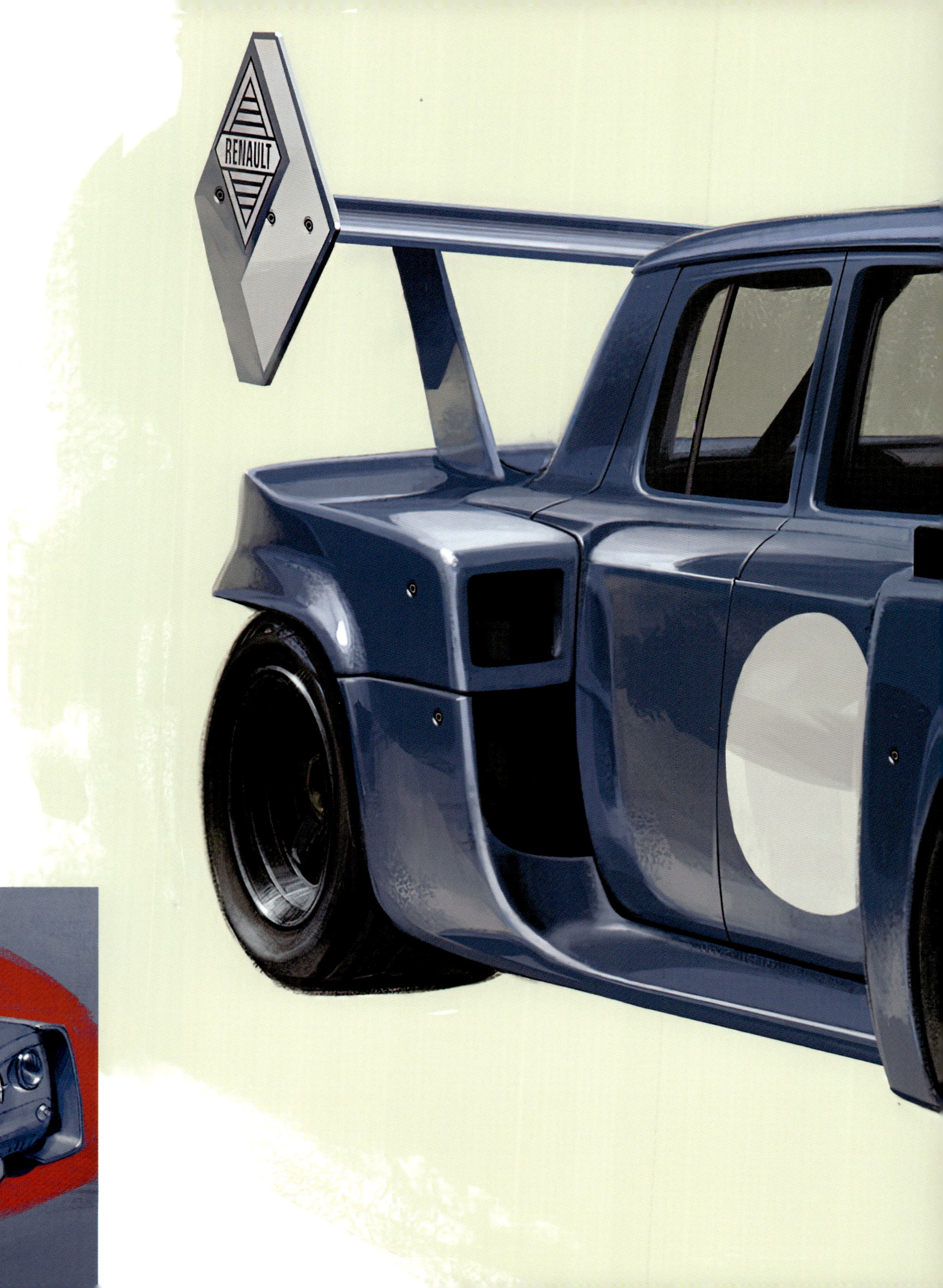

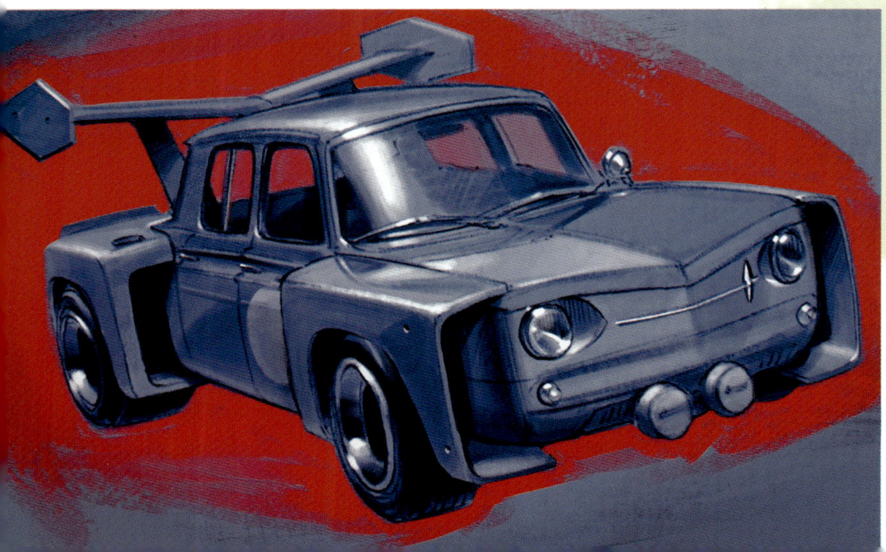

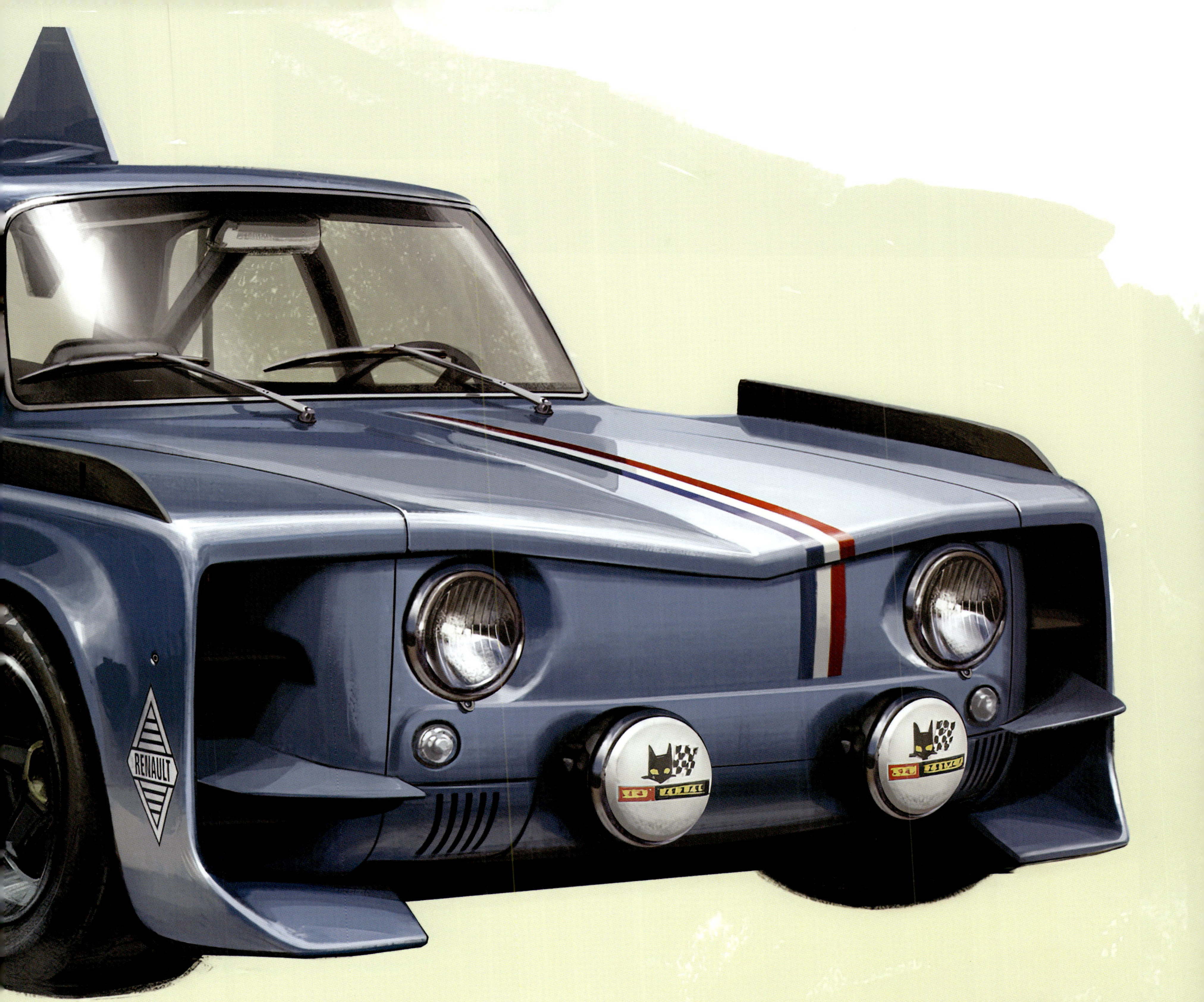
RENAULT

MEAN GREEN BEAN

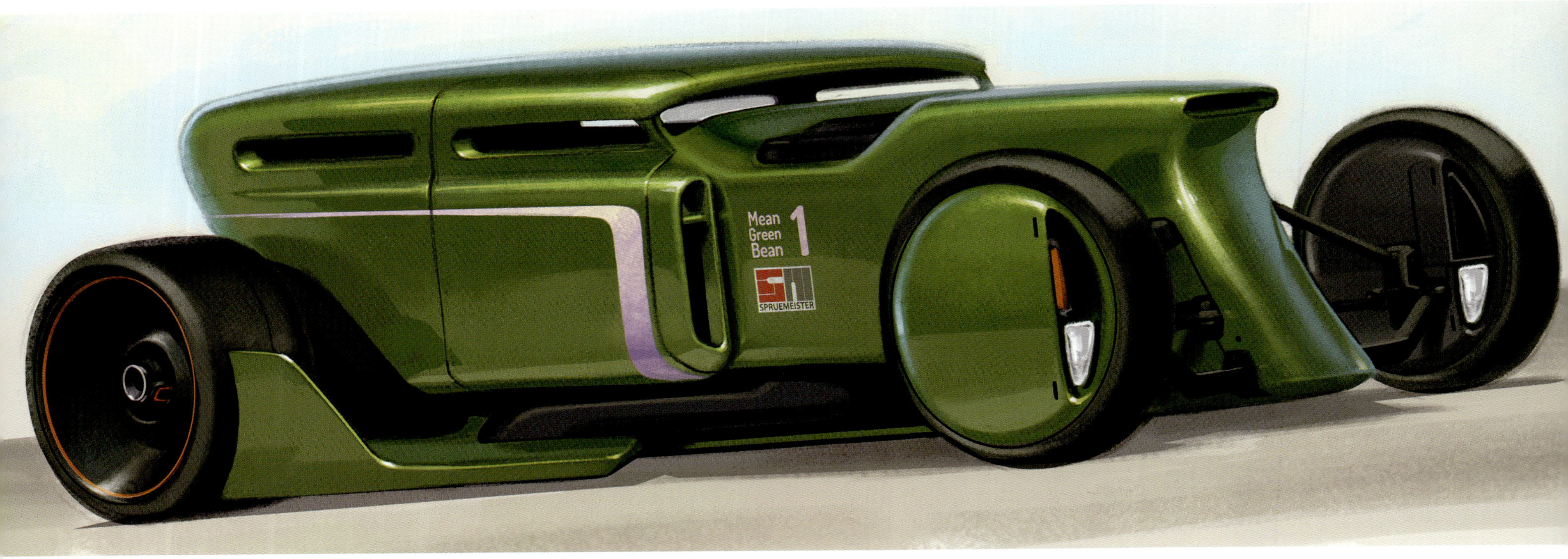

A modern tech iteration of a 1932 Tudor body, I painted it green with a little gold flake, one of my favorite colors. As this one got the dusting of paint, it gave me childhood flashbacks to a pile of cooked green beans—not something I enjoyed! What sounds tougher on the streets than a ride named after a reviled vegetable?

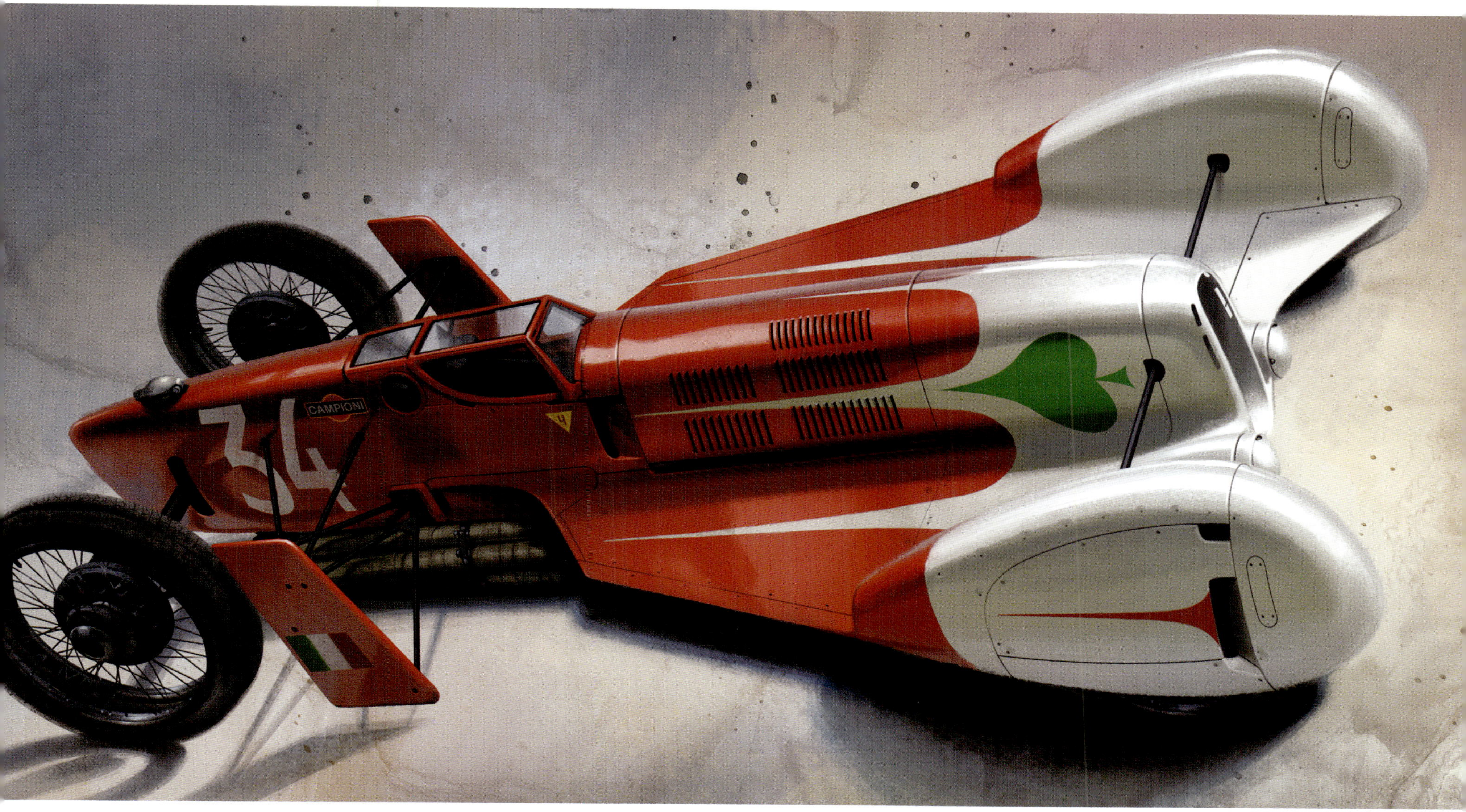

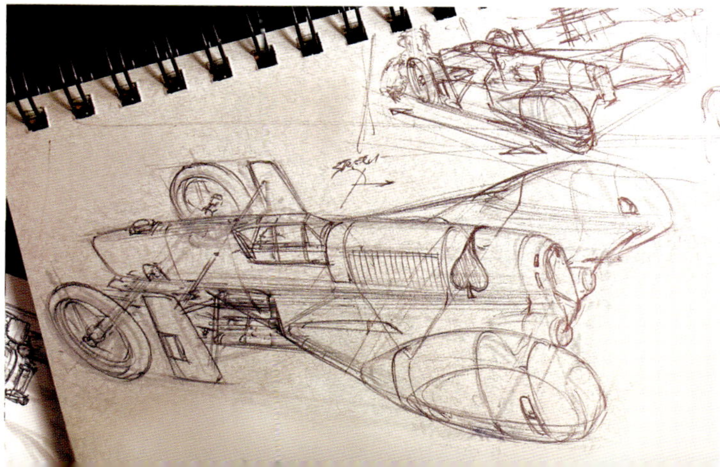

I imagined this to perhaps be a 1930s competitor for the dry lakes, **demi-streamliner**, land speed record. It features early auto tech: flat plane glass, leaf springs, narrow tread-wire spoke wheels, aircraft aero bits, and a riveted-over frame aluminum body.

RALLI-MORPHOTIK

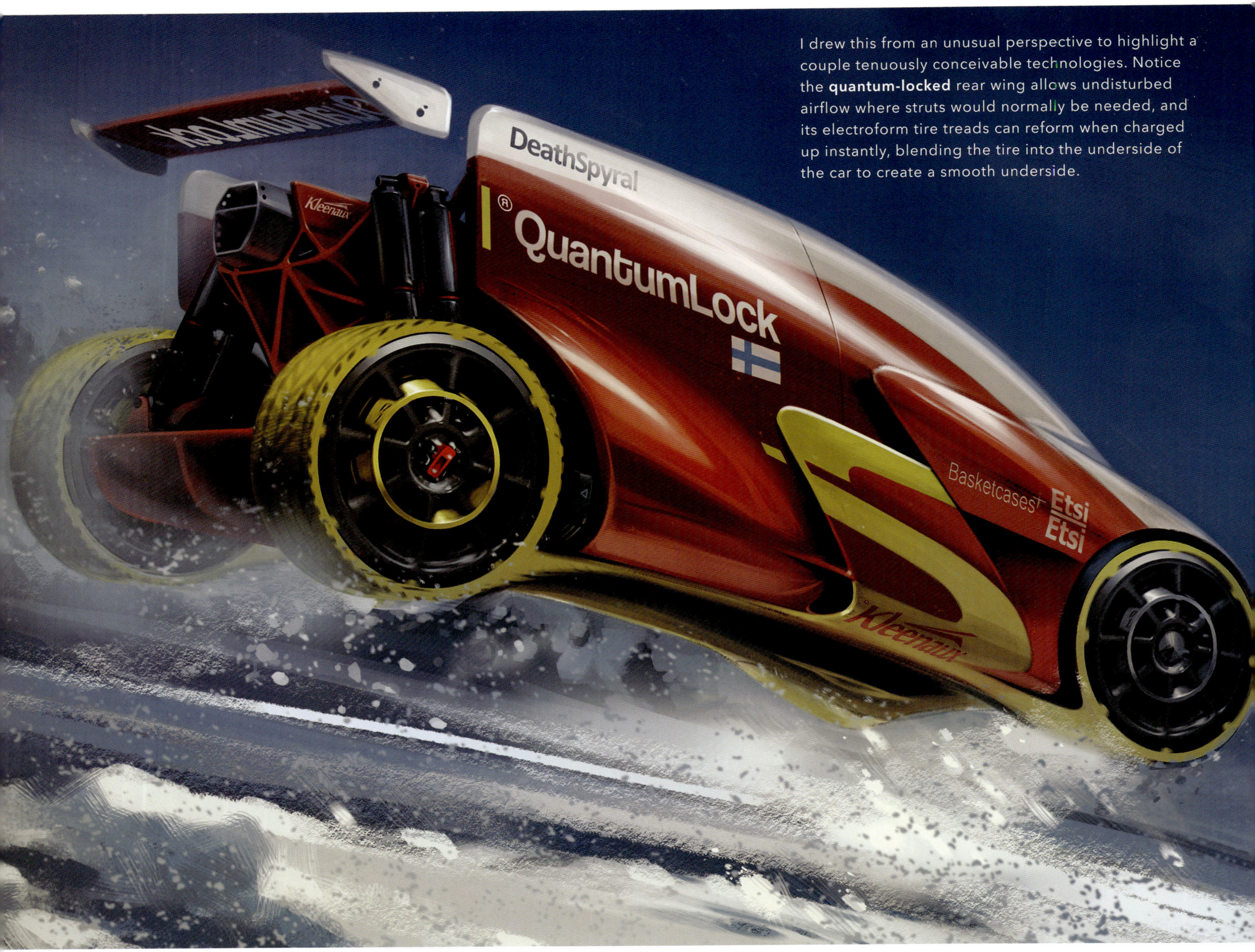

I drew this from an unusual perspective to highlight a couple tenuously conceivable technologies. Notice the **quantum-locked** rear wing allows undisturbed airflow where struts would normally be needed, and its electroform tire treads can reform when charged up instantly, blending the tire into the underside of the car to create a smooth underside.

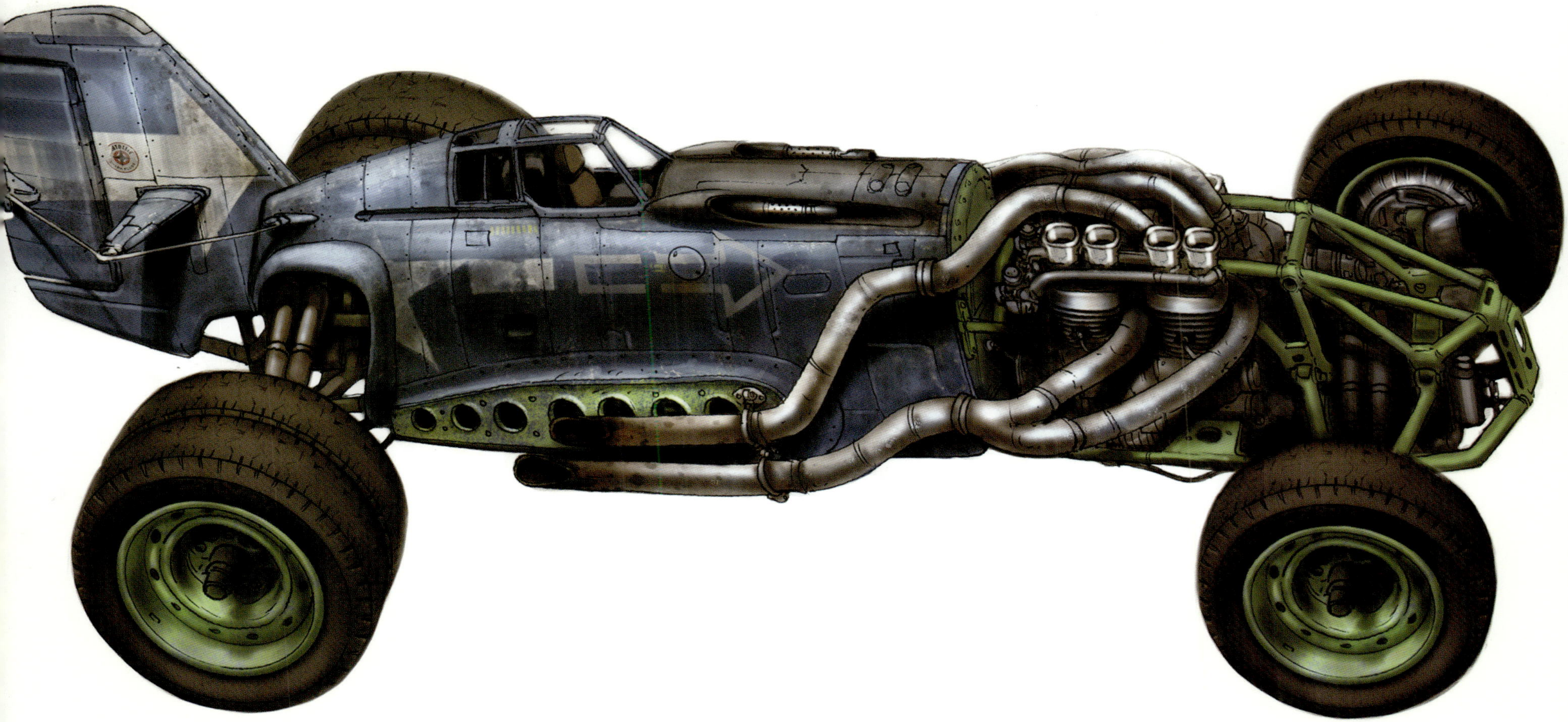

I liked to imagine this homebuilt car would be from a member of a war-surplus hot-rod club, customized in a garage in Reseda, circa 1952, and that it set a land speed record with rudder steering and a tubular front chassis.

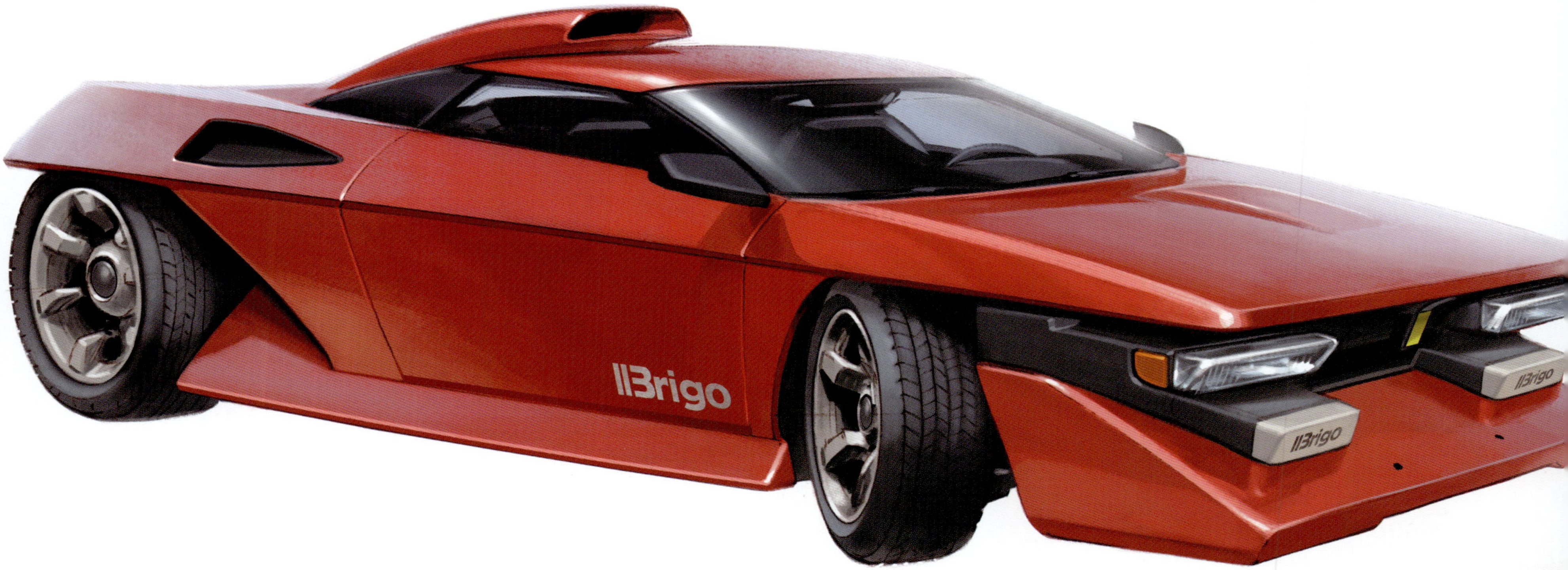

It was in 1986, at the crescendo of a pulsing and rumbling Italian techno soundtrack. While revolving slowly on a polished marble disc elevated above the stadium floor, a thin metal cable whisked away a shimmering white silk cover from the hard-cornered mystery car. It revealed what cannot be denied by any of the auto show coverage as simply "wedgy" and, for the most part, unusual. Two dozen sets of hands on worn pencils and miniature steno pads quickly summarized the blood-red sight while cameras' auto-focus motors whirred and shutters snapped shut in sync with flashes of bluish light. Within 10 minutes, the tiny northern Italian auto studio's earnest and optimistic work had been noted on paper and film, and the cigarette-huffing throng of writers and reporters took their cue and turned their backs to move onto the next press reveal.

Zagadini Model 1, a fiberglass and plaster mock-up in the form of a car was a dream with enough of a budget to get it to this point and no further. Its design was not quite pretty enough or familiar enough to find confident interest from a wealthy benefactor. Zagadini Model 1 was pushed out of the hall, up a ramp, and into a lorry late at night, and was never seen again, becoming nothing more than an obscure piece of automotive trivia.

I have issues with wheels! They are absolutely critical to make the vehicle look realistic, exciting, and sit well. This means a lot of work needs to go into this part of the illustration.

Often, it takes a lot of time to draw an expressive, fresh, and attractive wheel that suits the car well visually. It can be a bit laborious to have to draw the exact same design in a slightly different perspective for the rear of the car. When the wheels are done, however, and done right, the vehicle really starts to have life and a connection to reality; the rest of the vehicle can come together in relation to the wheels.

The term *wheel* is frequently used to describe an assembly that constitutes two parts: the metal wheel rim and the rubber tire. The relation between the two is not arbitrary. A thinner sidewall tire is more often seen in high-performance sporty cars, while a taller sidewall and smaller wheel-rim combo is more common in heavy-duty and off-road vehicles. Tire technology has changed this ratio as well. Sports cars in the 1960s had taller sidewalls than the sports cars of today.

The following series shows a process to illustrate one of the simplest designs: a spun metal disc wheel. The simplicity of the design means that it has applications in the past, present, and future. Disc wheels also can be very aerodynamically efficient, so, functionally, they are useful in competition vehicles and vehicles where fuel efficiency is important. Considerations need to be made in regard to brake cooling, but if your design universe is fantasy, you can always disregard some things, like being able to actually stop your car!

Drawing the wheels, as opposed to cutting and pasting from photographs, will ensure your finished vehicle is cohesive and also represents your own design creation as a whole.

I draw the wheel completely with the major axis (the long dimension) of the ellipse straight up and down, as I can more easily draw other shapes and modify in this regular axis. When the wheel is complete, it can be rotated and placed into the vehicle illustration so that the minor axis lines up with the axle in perspective.
(See Scott Robertson's *How To Draw!*)

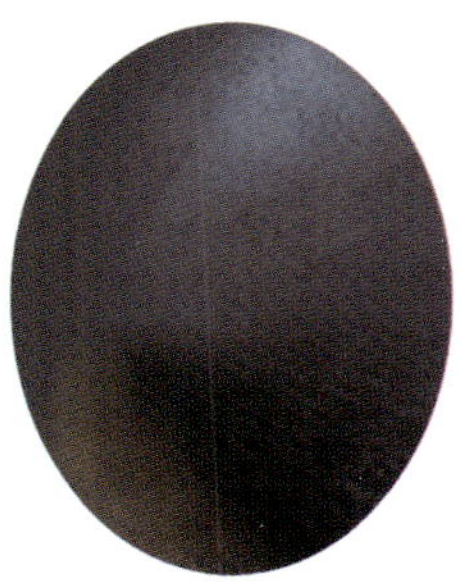

1) Draw the sidewall of the tire, a convex rubber dome.

The sidewall of a tire is rounded to evenly distribute the internal air pressure and also direct the deformation of the tire outward as it compresses under the weight of the vehicle. As this rounded shape curves around, it essentially becomes a torus shape, like a donut. This is a challenging shape to shade, as light is changing in multiple curved directions. Simplifying the rounded section torus into a beveled shape makes it easier.

Begin with a domed rubber disc. While tire rubber is essentially just black, I usually add some tinting to the shading—sky tone and warmth from ground-reflected light. I use my favorite chalky brushes in large scale to get some rougher finish.

I always start with the tire sidewall, so that I can establish the rubber-to-metal ratio.

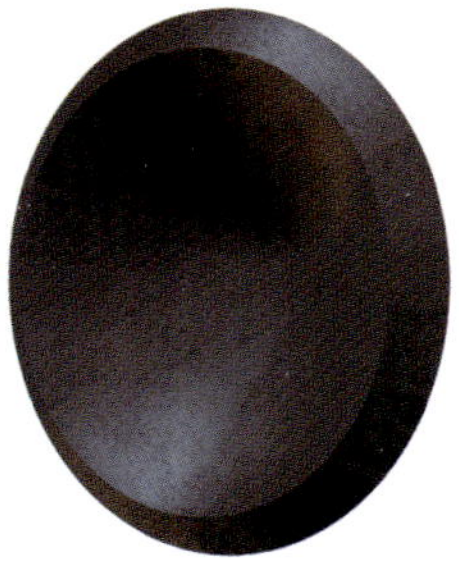

2) Continue sidewall of the tire, concave inner bevel.

Copying the sidewall disc, rotating it 180 degrees, and scaling it down quickly gives the sidewall some form. We now have an angular bevel at the edge of the tire visually. The dome shape that pushes in will become the inner chamber of our beveled torus once the wheel rim is added in the next step.

The process of cutting, modifying, and pasting is something you definitely should take advantage of using digital tools.

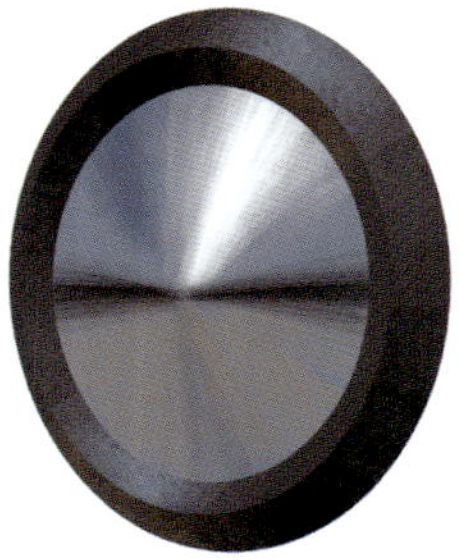

3) Machine-turn metallic disc.

The wheel rim disc is illustrated in its basic form. The lighting here is comfortable and ordinary, around noon with the sun high in the sky and over our shoulder. Machine turning or circular brushing on the face of the disc results in cone-shaped, somewhat diffused reflections that radiate out from the center. Upper-facing surfaces reflect the sky tone—I pretty much always use a slightly purplish and neutralized blue for the sky (here, my RGB values are 92, 115, 42). If you work in the oversaturated colors to show chrome or metal, it tends to look artificial. Downward-facing surfaces get warm earth tones. The bright and lively white highlights work best when they contrast relatively duller surface finishes.

I like lighter tones so that between the earth and sky reflections I can create a dark horizon line that represents distant mountains or buildings. Subtlety in value and color is effective when everything is finished, so use restraint.

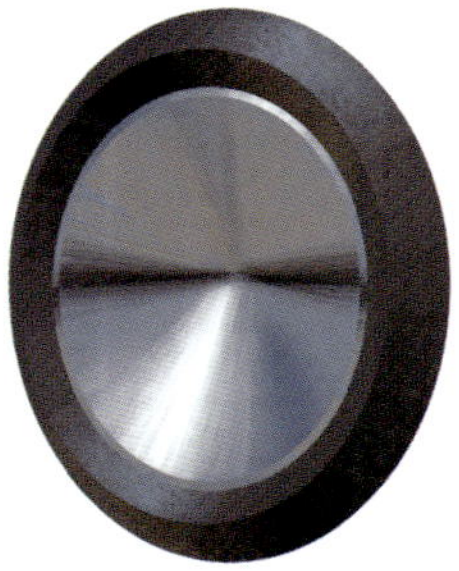

4) Add a beveled edge to show metal thickness.

Much like we did with the tire, rotating and scaling a copy of the wheel disc creates a concave wheel with a beveled lip. As this is a concave surface, our reflection logic is the same, but note it is the upper surfaces of the disc that are facing downward toward the warm earth, while the lower surfaces face upward toward the sky. Notice that we are not simply flipping the disc vertically but rotating it 180 degrees, which is like flipping it vertically and then horizontally. This is important to make the concave disc look correct.

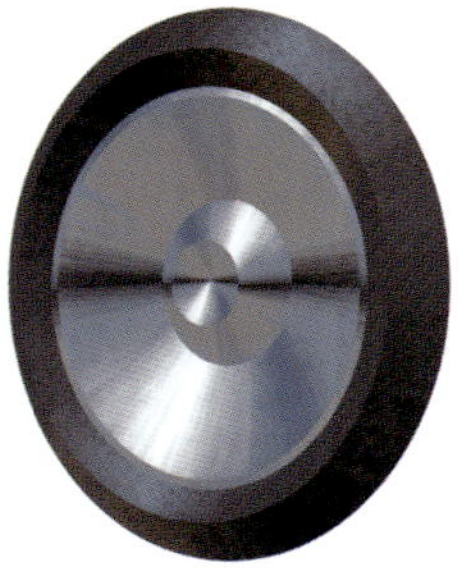

5) Push and pull the disc shape by copying, scaling down, rotating, pasting.

You can push and pull the shape of the wheel visually by repeating the scaling and rotating process quickly and easily.

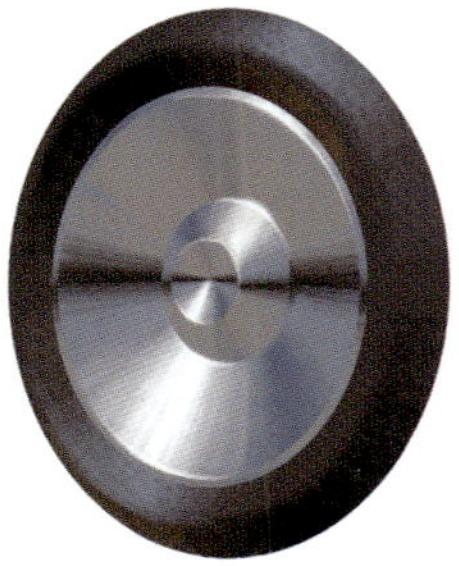

6) Catch highlights on edges to indicate circular fillets.

As the discs stack up, the sharp-edged transitions are harsh in appearance and do not represent the subtle shapes of an actual manufactured wheel. By softening the edges between each disc, they become cohesive. The logic of shading these transitions is done by understanding that the fillet will stretch and pull the reflected area, so where a white highlight hits, that white highlight gets lengthened and stretched along the fillet. We also need to soften the beveled corner on the tire sidewall.

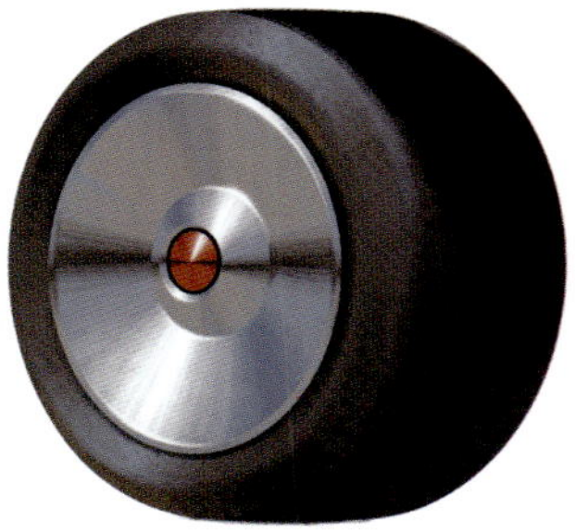

7) Complete the tire by drawing the cylindrical depth.

Adding the rest of the tire completes the mass of the wheel assembly. Much of this will likely be in shadow, tucked under the wheel well of the vehicle's body.

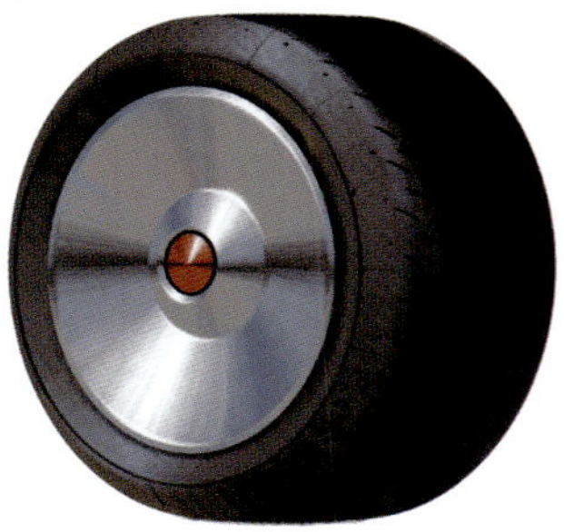

8) Add detail to the tire for realism.

Detailing the tire tread can be a lot of labor, so look for ways to simplify the pattern. The logic of the grooves (known as sipes) on the tire should match the vehicle. Sports cars get small grooves, while trucks and off-road heavy-duty vehicles get knobby tires. Racing cars may often have completely smooth tires, though the sidewalls should still show some detailing.

Use reference to understand the typical markings, lines, and grooves on tires until you are familiar with their appearance and can design from your head.

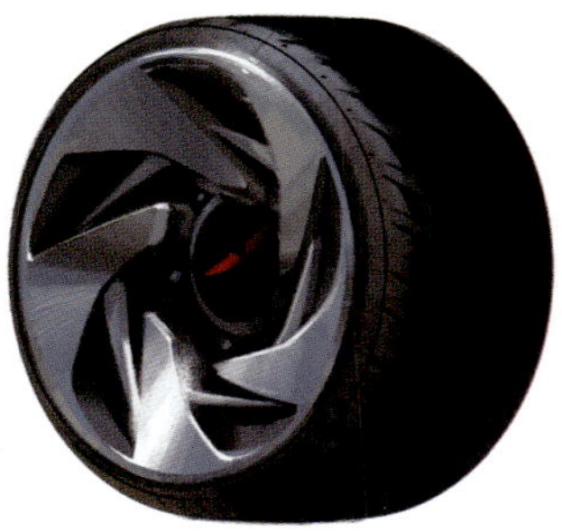

9) Modify the wheel surface and resize the wheel relative to the tire.

You can use the spun metal disc to create more complicated wheel designs. In this variation, I've cut away holes into the disc so that we are left with a twisted turbine blade design and modified the tread with an aggressive repeating sawtooth notch. Scaling up the wheel rim makes the tire sidewall smaller and the overall wheel sportier. A loose, rapid execution of the sketch and a lively splattered highlight bloom and dazzle. They emphasize the metal finish of the wheel and help make the image feel more as if it was accomplished through a painterly process instead of a more clinical digital one. The level of detail and style of rendering of the wheel should match the rest of the vehicle.

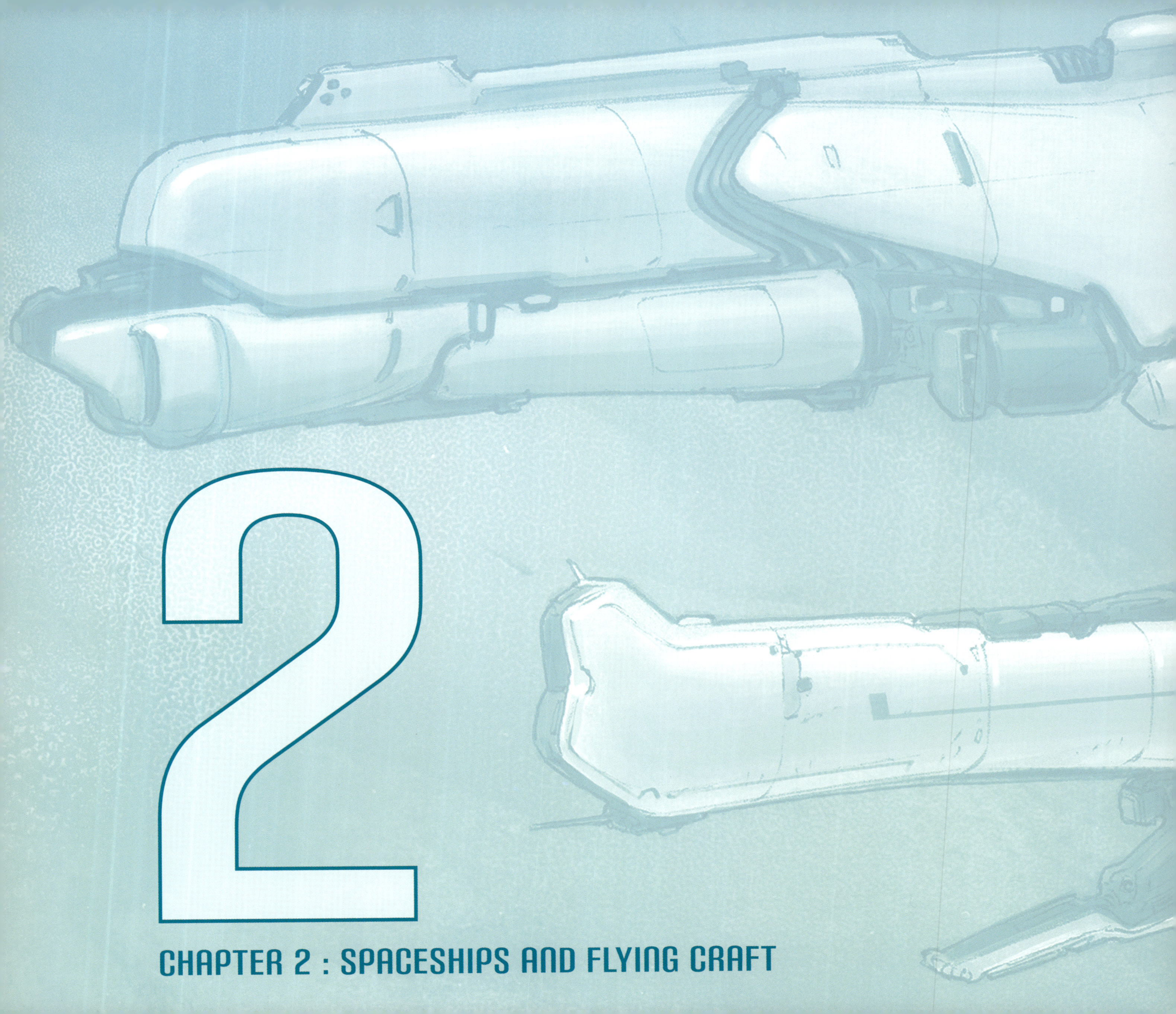

2

CHAPTER 2 : SPACESHIPS AND FLYING CRAFT

Sometimes I don't have a conscious plan when I start to draw vehicles. Absent-minded doodles on paper are like a quiet message from the subconscious—*let's explore this area today*. When it doesn't start with a wheel, the form that appears on the paper very likely sprouts winglets, thrusters, and bubble canopies. A lot of these details may very well make their way onto wheeled terrestrial craft, but when I can, I take a different route than the last sketch exploration. If I just completed a rendering of a race car or giant industrial truck, chasing that with a dram of spacecraft is a refreshing next course. As with my other vehicle explorations, I like to consider a variety of designs that draw their form from vehicles with specific purposes, such as garbage removal, construction, vessel towing and repair, medical, and transportation of goods. Such vehicles add variety to a concept-design world heavily populated with warships and fighters, so I feel I trod fresh turf when I can depart from that genre.

In this chapter, I enjoy stretching my legs with silhouettes and shapes that are much more dynamic than most wheeled vehicles, as flying vehicles have wings and winglets that spread away from the fuselage, and spaceships of the far future can really be inventive forms with completely alien outlines. Using the shape of one ship drawn on the page as the negative space to suggest the outline of the one I draw next to it is one of my favorite creative exercises. I also enjoy using colorful fluid and textural backgrounds to suggest an alien world and provide a strong contrast to the metal surfaces of the vehicles.

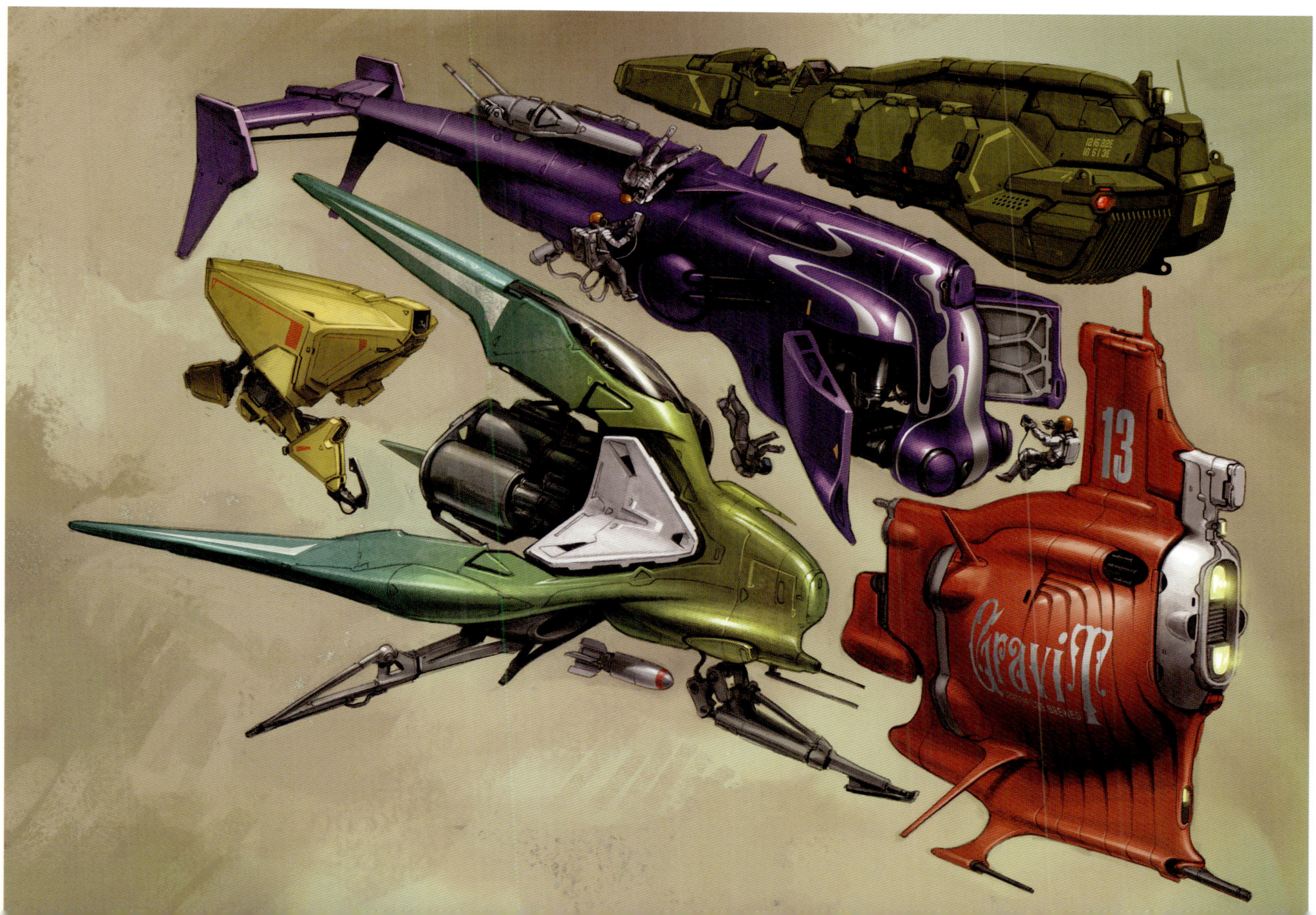

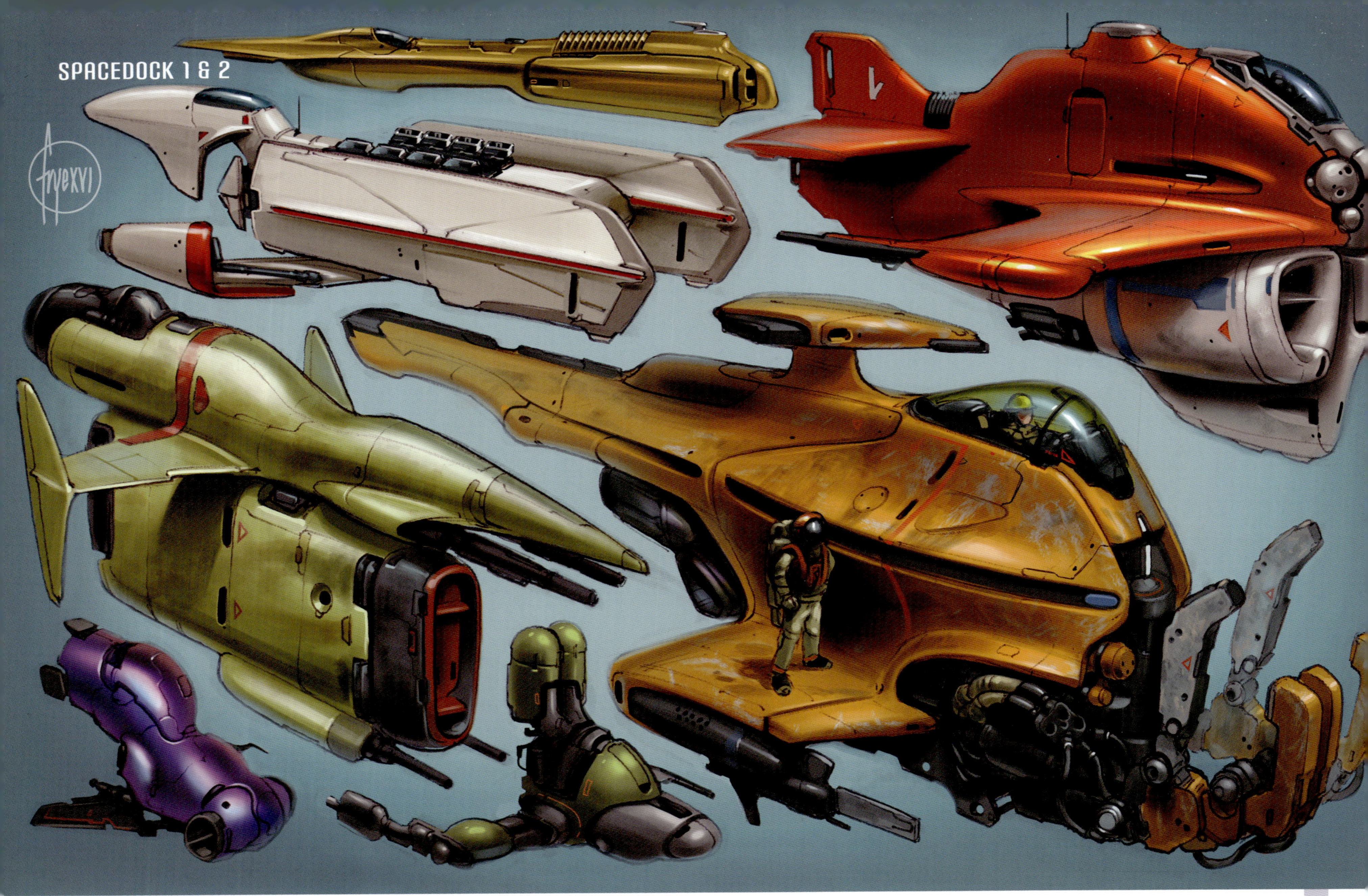

It's a busy day at the dock, with ships packed in tight. As with any of the negative spaceship exercises, creating new shapes from the outline of the neighboring ship is the idea, but pushing each ship in a different visual direction with color and graphics also encourages creativity.

By taking one shape and drawing the one next to it in the space formed by the outline of the first, this introduces some creative randomness and produces forms that I may not normally sketch by themselves.

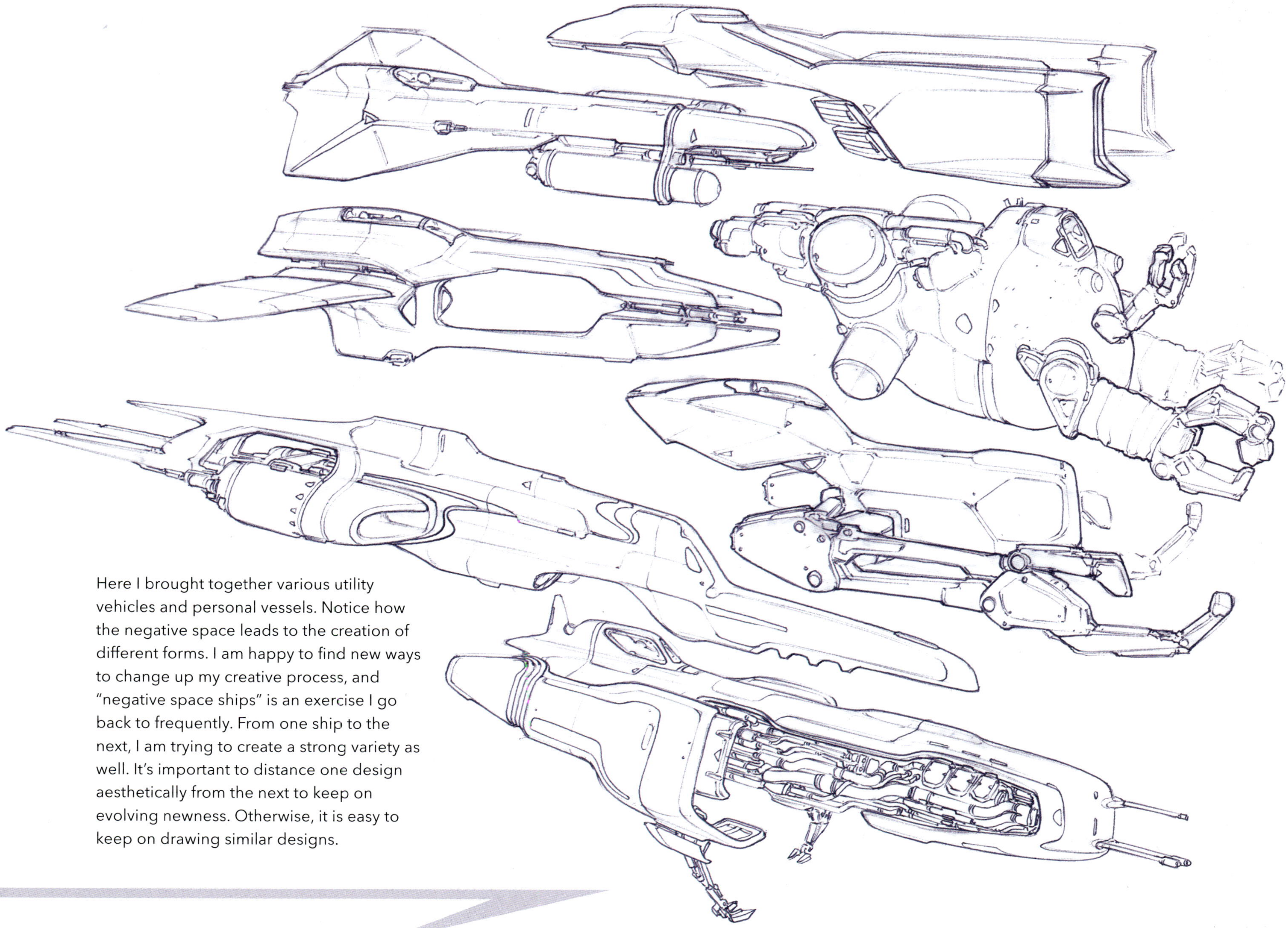

Here I brought together various utility vehicles and personal vessels. Notice how the negative space leads to the creation of different forms. I am happy to find new ways to change up my creative process, and "negative space ships" is an exercise I go back to frequently. From one ship to the next, I am trying to create a strong variety as well. It's important to distance one design aesthetically from the next to keep on evolving newness. Otherwise, it is easy to keep on drawing similar designs.

PIT STOP

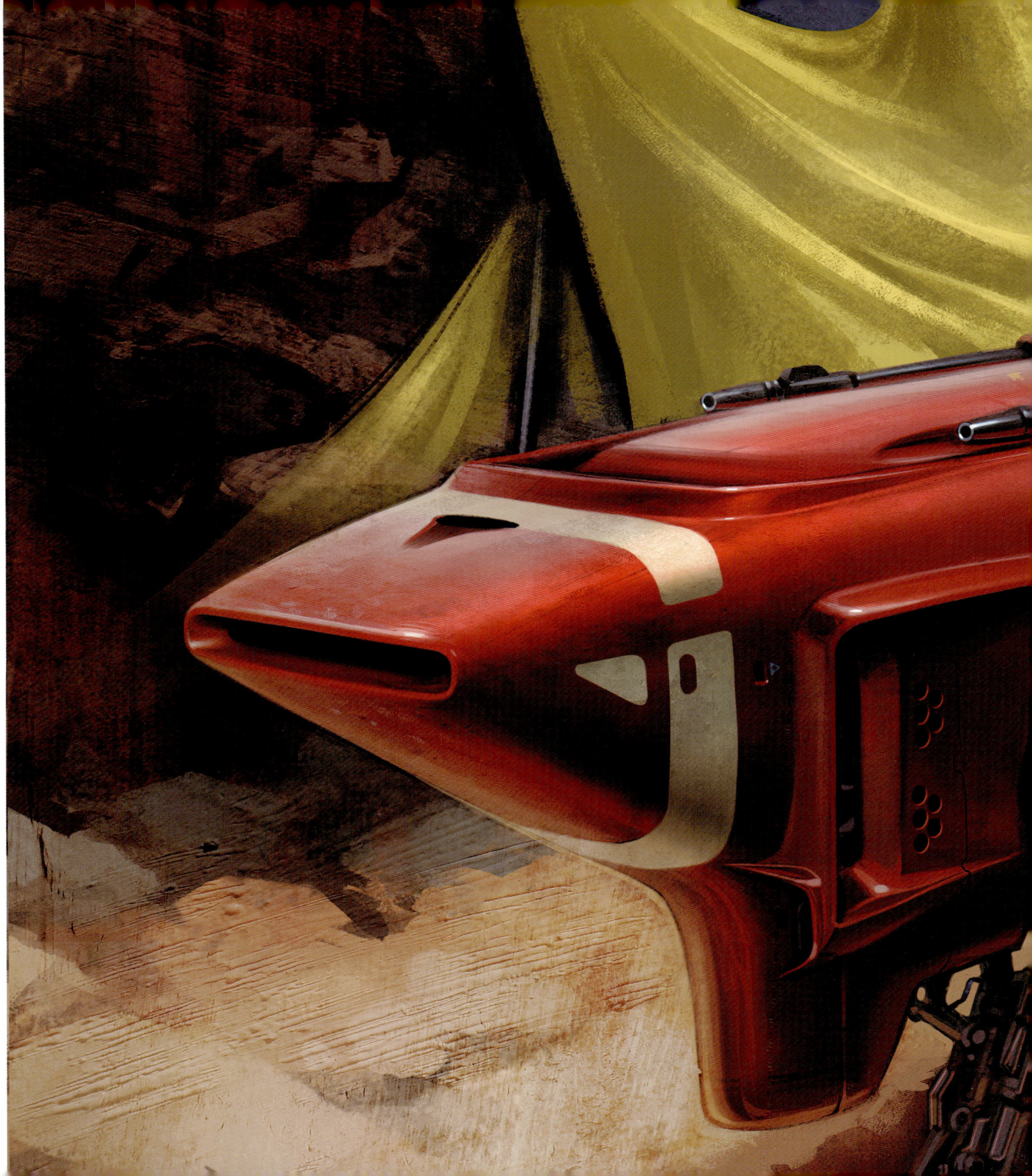

The blue spark from the outlet means that the spacecraft is charged. The pilot just needs to unplug from the solar collector, pack up their gear, and get a move on. The month-long rally has a tight schedule.

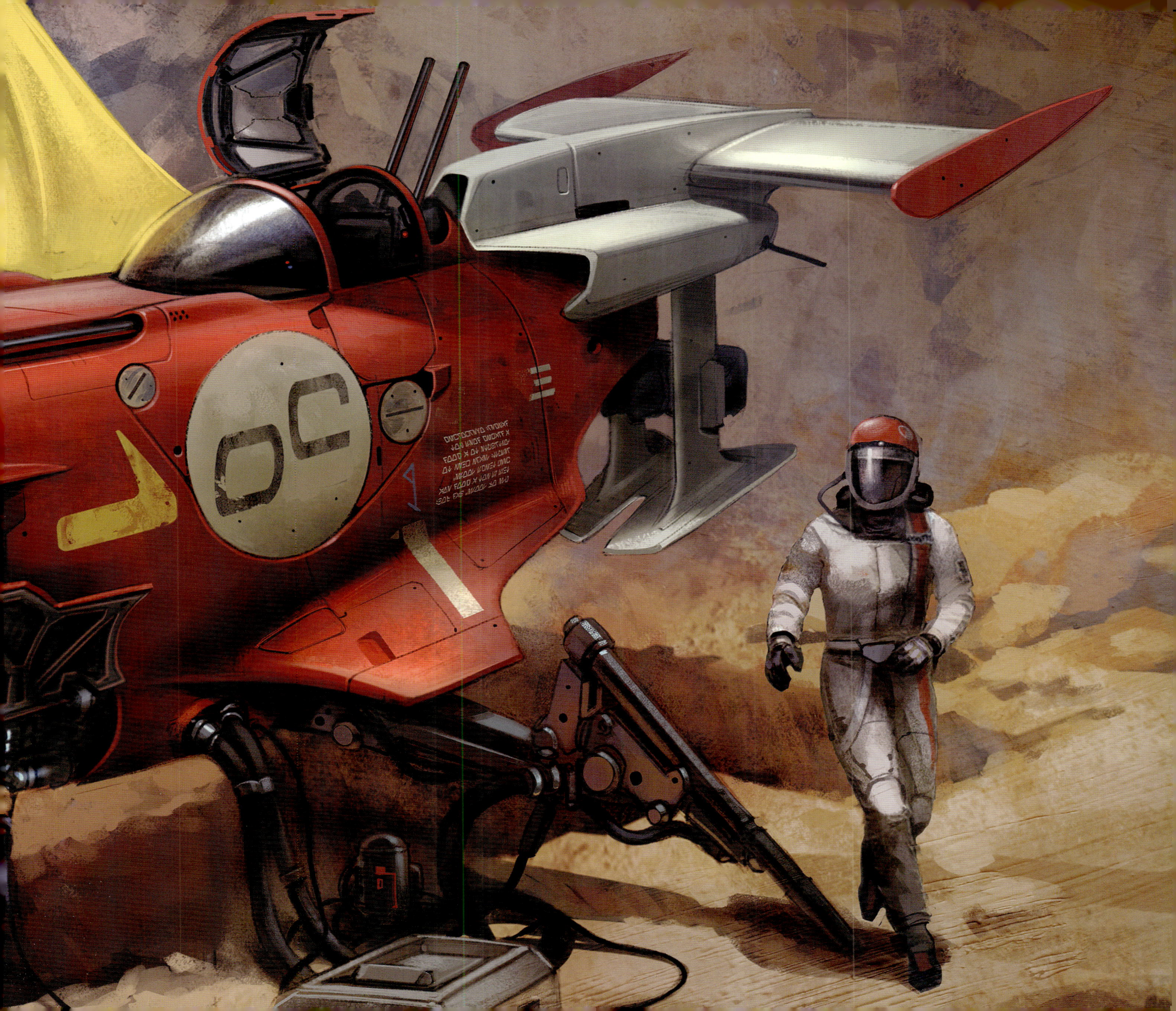

SALT BYKER

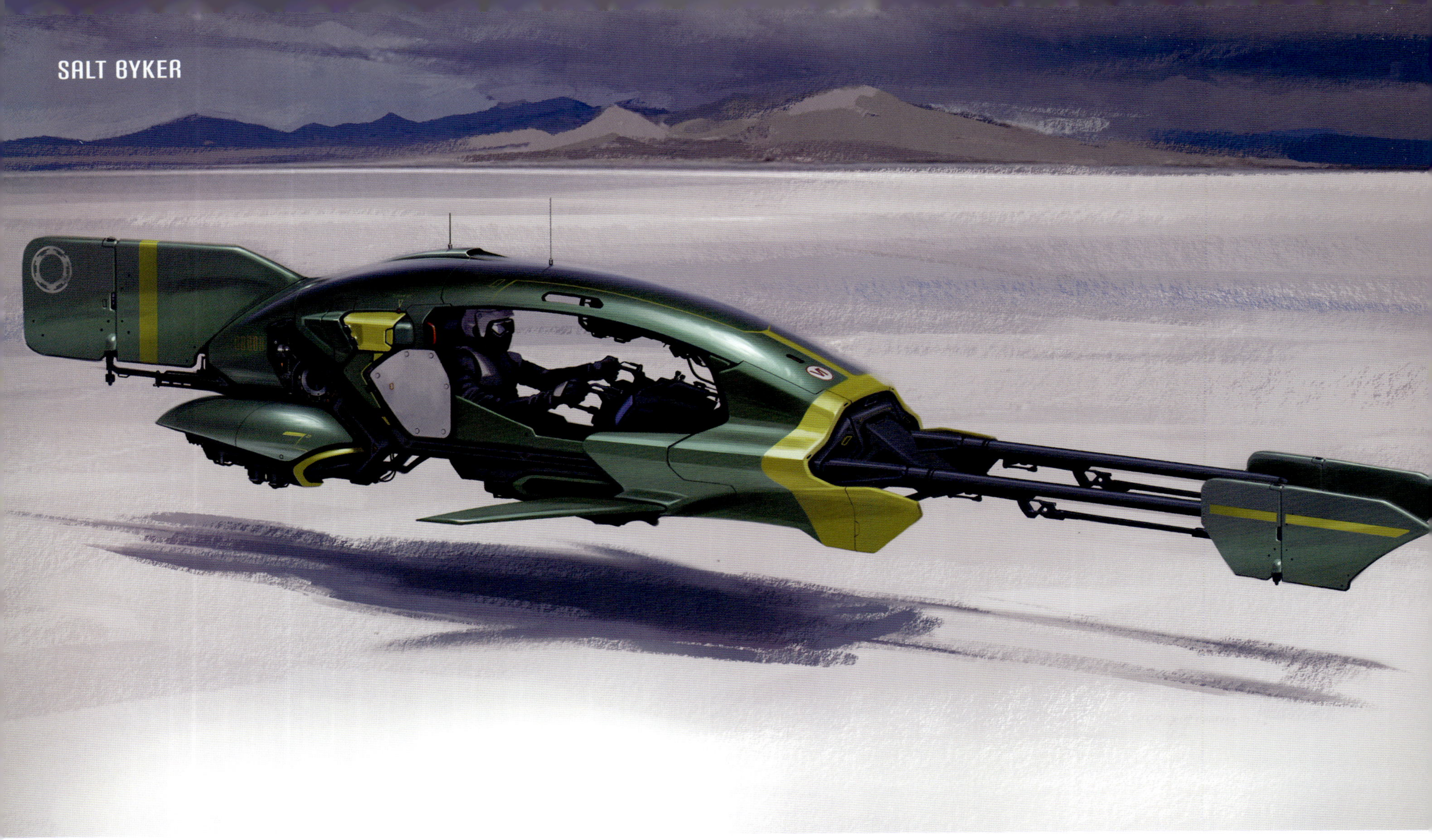

Over the crusty salt flats of a not-too-distant copper-core moon, temperatures can get up to 250°C at high noon, so hastily making one's way from the shaded safety of one spaceport to the next is critical for one's survival. Speed is essential; style is just a bonus.

Many years ago, I visited the Bonneville Salt Flats, an enormous dry lake bed in the Utah desert. During summer, the water recedes and a hard-packed floor of salt stretches for miles, and high-speed enthusiasts from all over the world come to test their vehicles in a straight line timed run to the horizon. The pure, white salt surface is otherworldly. In this illustration, I went back to my photos of that trip and tried to match the blue-violet colors of the shadow, the distant mountains shaded by an approaching storm cloud, and the texture of the salty surface, indicated rough with chalky digital brushes in Photoshop. A looser environment provides a visual energy and textural contrast to the tightly rendered and manufactured hard surfacing of the vehicle.

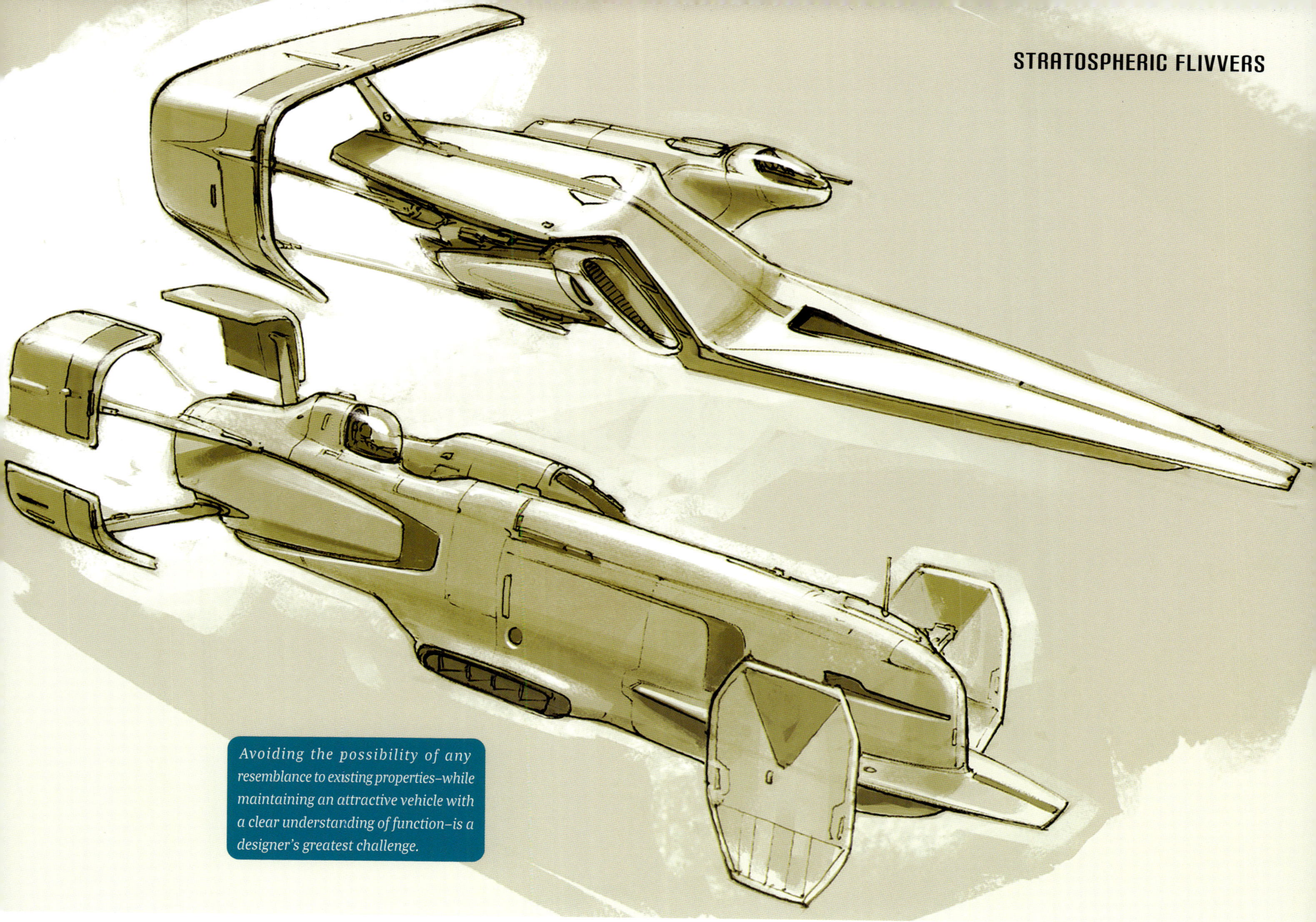

Avoiding the possibility of any resemblance to existing properties–while maintaining an attractive vehicle with a clear understanding of function–is a designer's greatest challenge.

Here are a couple of my thoughtful asymmetrical-form considerations, searching for newness and surprising myself with some quite different designs through my creative sketching and encouraging myself to explore with little self-restraint. The brain likes to categorize things into familiar folders to understand and manage the tremendous amount of visual input. All too often I get the "that looks like . . ." comment, referencing some video game or anime series that I've never seen. Sometimes it's easier to not worry about creating a comfortable-looking design and to instead push into the realms of weirdness.

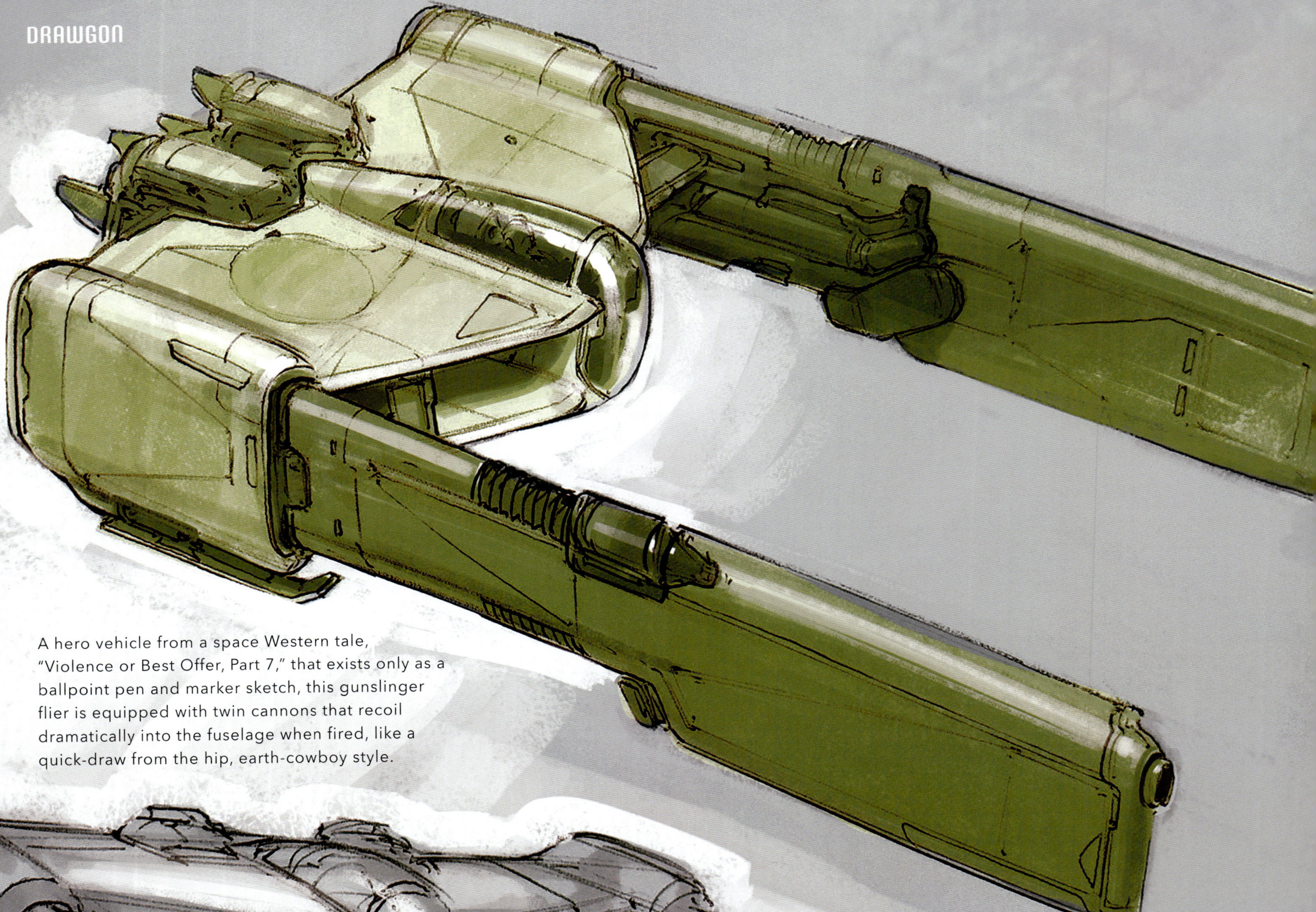

A hero vehicle from a space Western tale, "Violence or Best Offer, Part 7," that exists only as a ballpoint pen and marker sketch, this gunslinger flier is equipped with twin cannons that recoil dramatically into the fuselage when fired, like a quick-draw from the hip, earth-cowboy style.

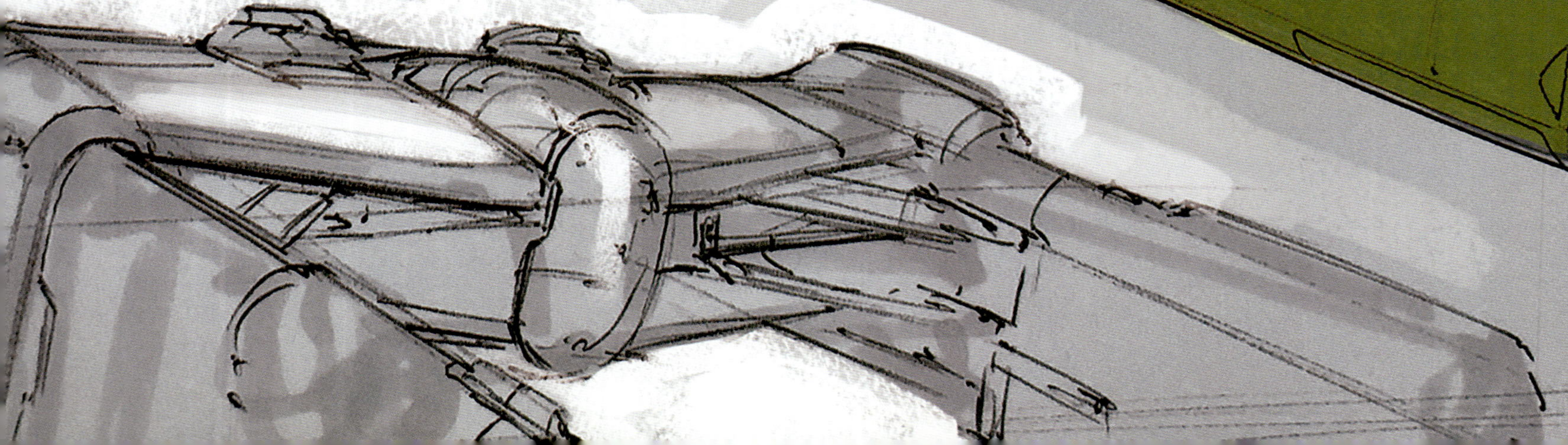

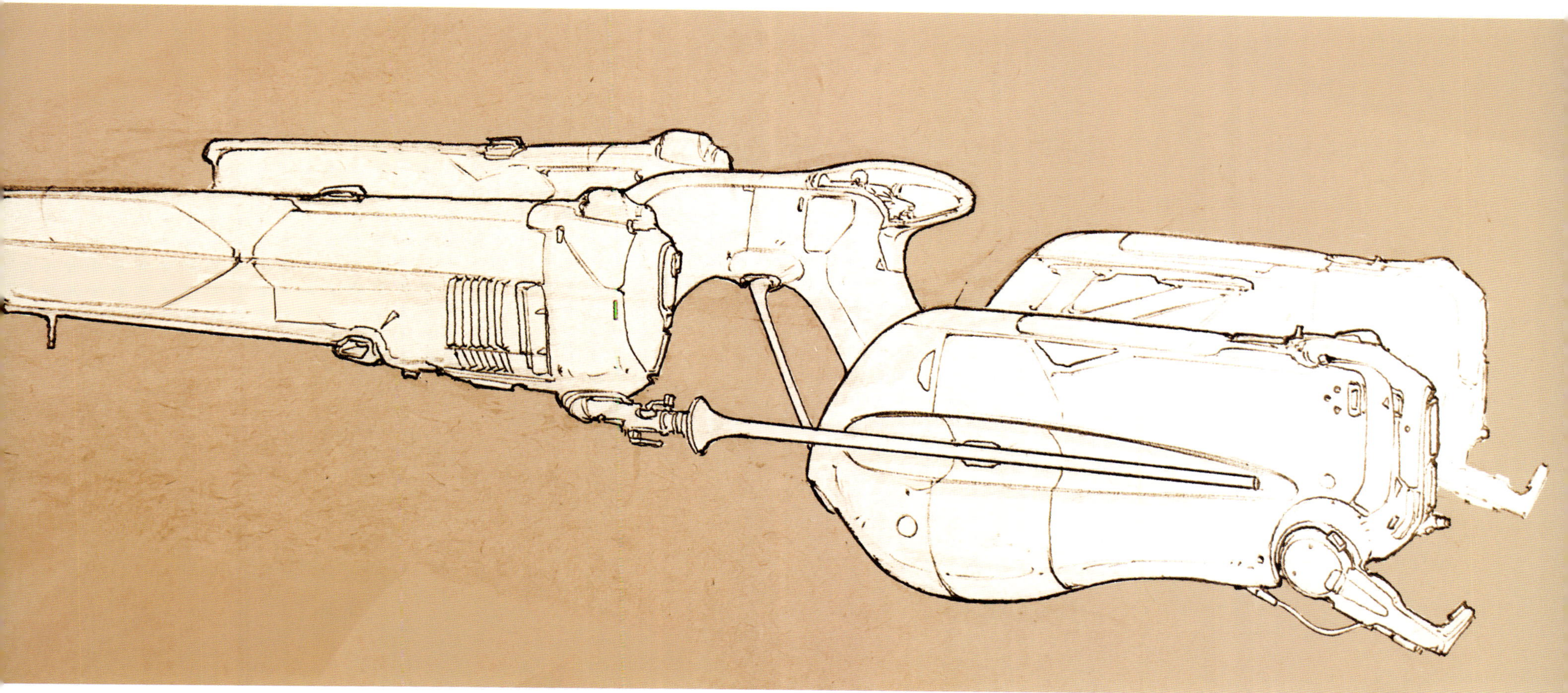

Another space-vessel shape exploration using ballpoint ink on paper and toned in Photoshop. An odd design with four corner masses and compact central cockpit with the suggestion of space jousting and a retractable lance in its stowed position, flush against the fuselage.

A SMATTERING OF SHIPS

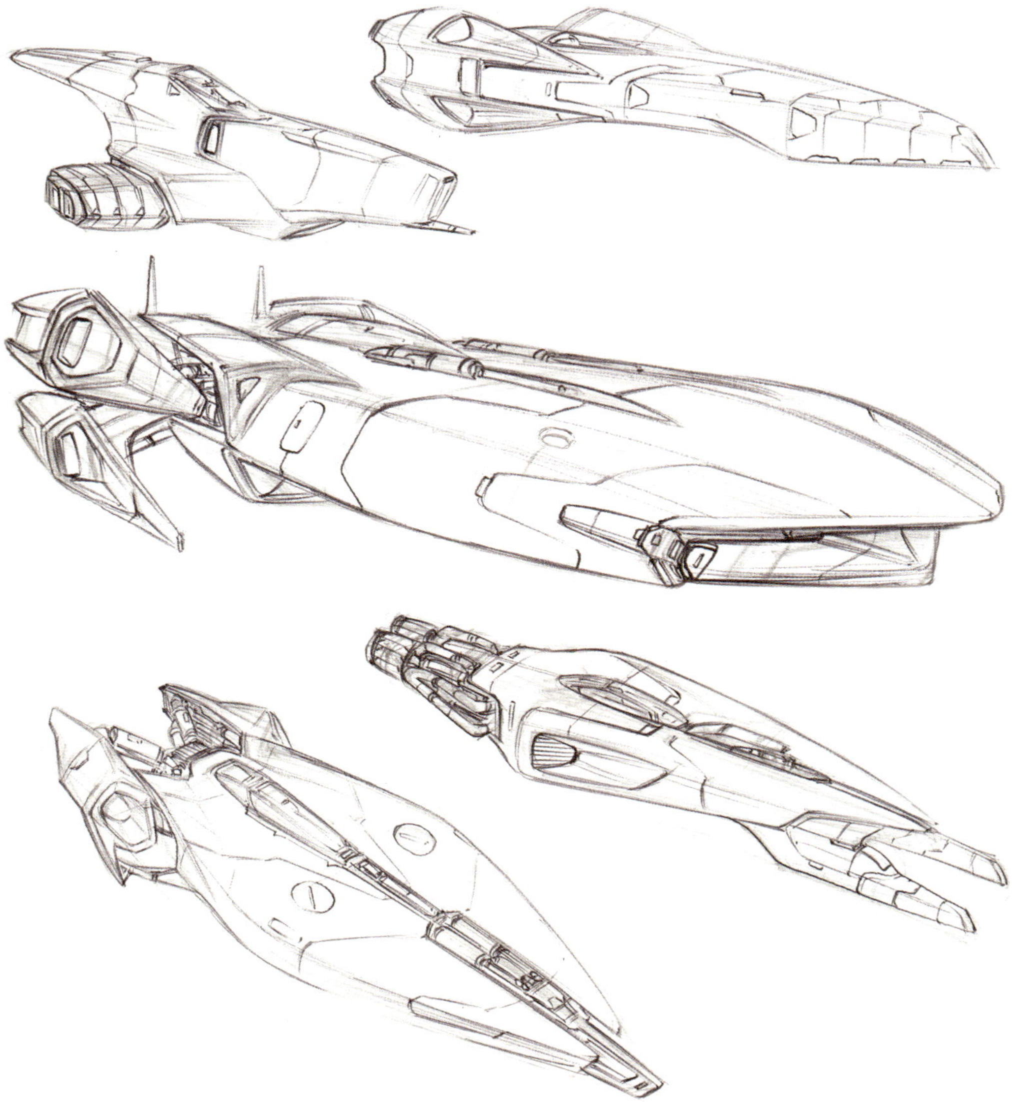

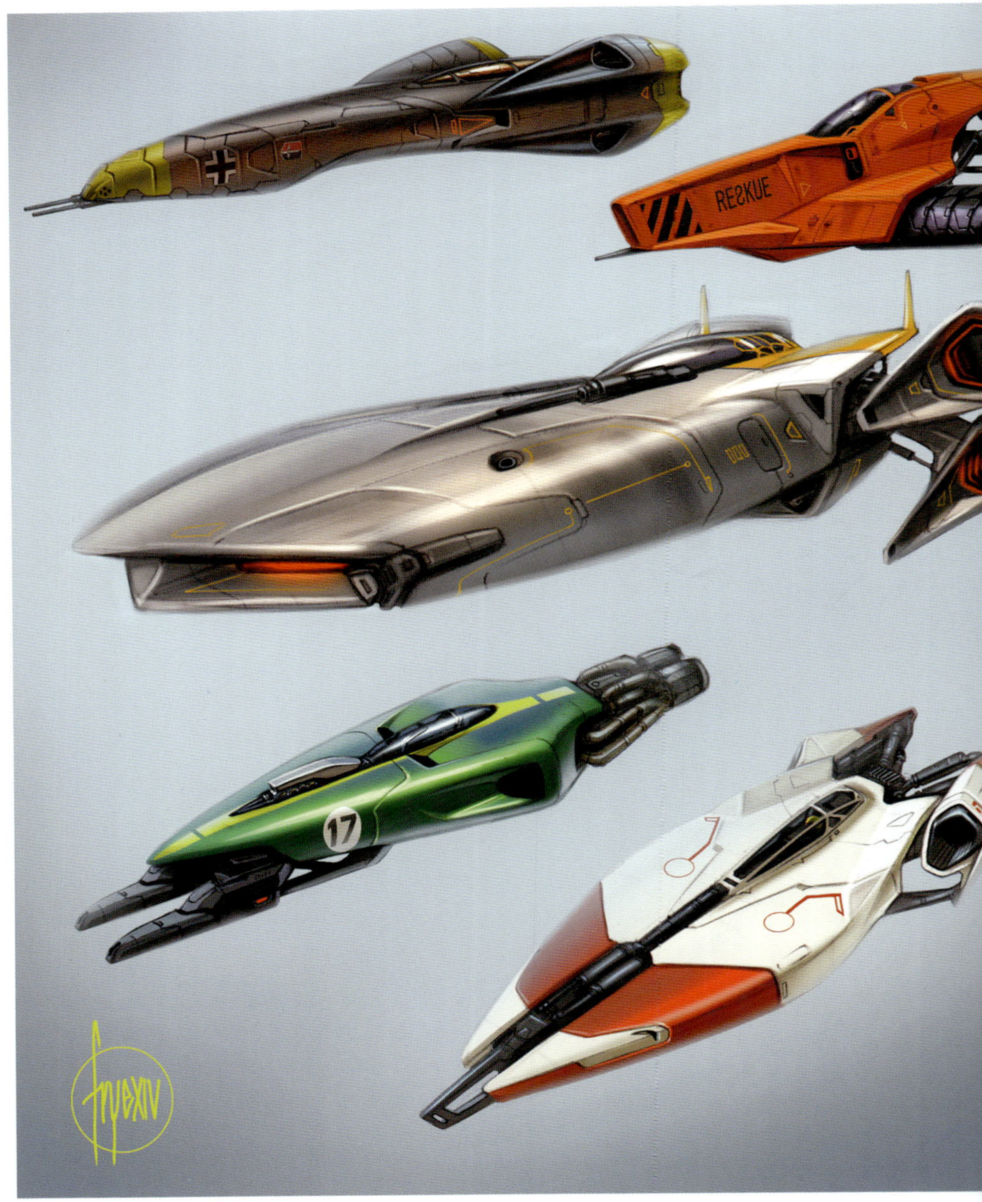

A page of sketches emphasizes a variety in overall appearance and purpose of flying craft. This is one of my first attempts at a single-page variety of ships from many years ago. I first drew them all with a fine mechanical pencil on letter-size copy paper, and then scanned the sketches into Photoshop to add color. I am always interested in speeding up my process, but also retaining quality in my work and not letting the process disrupt my creative flow. For much of the work in this book, analog (pen, marker, pencil on paper) precedes digital work as my personal optimized process. I like the tactile interface of hand on paper, as I feel like I can get my idea out directly. When I get to the stage of applying color, digital tools let me test different applications of graphics on vehicles, try color combinations, and explore the surface appearance of my designs. Being able to test blue, click undo, and paint something yellow as an option is a fantastic ability that only digital illustration can offer so quickly and easily. Shown here are a tow ship, a military recon ship, a couple of sports cars for space, and a competition race ship. Can you guess which one is which?

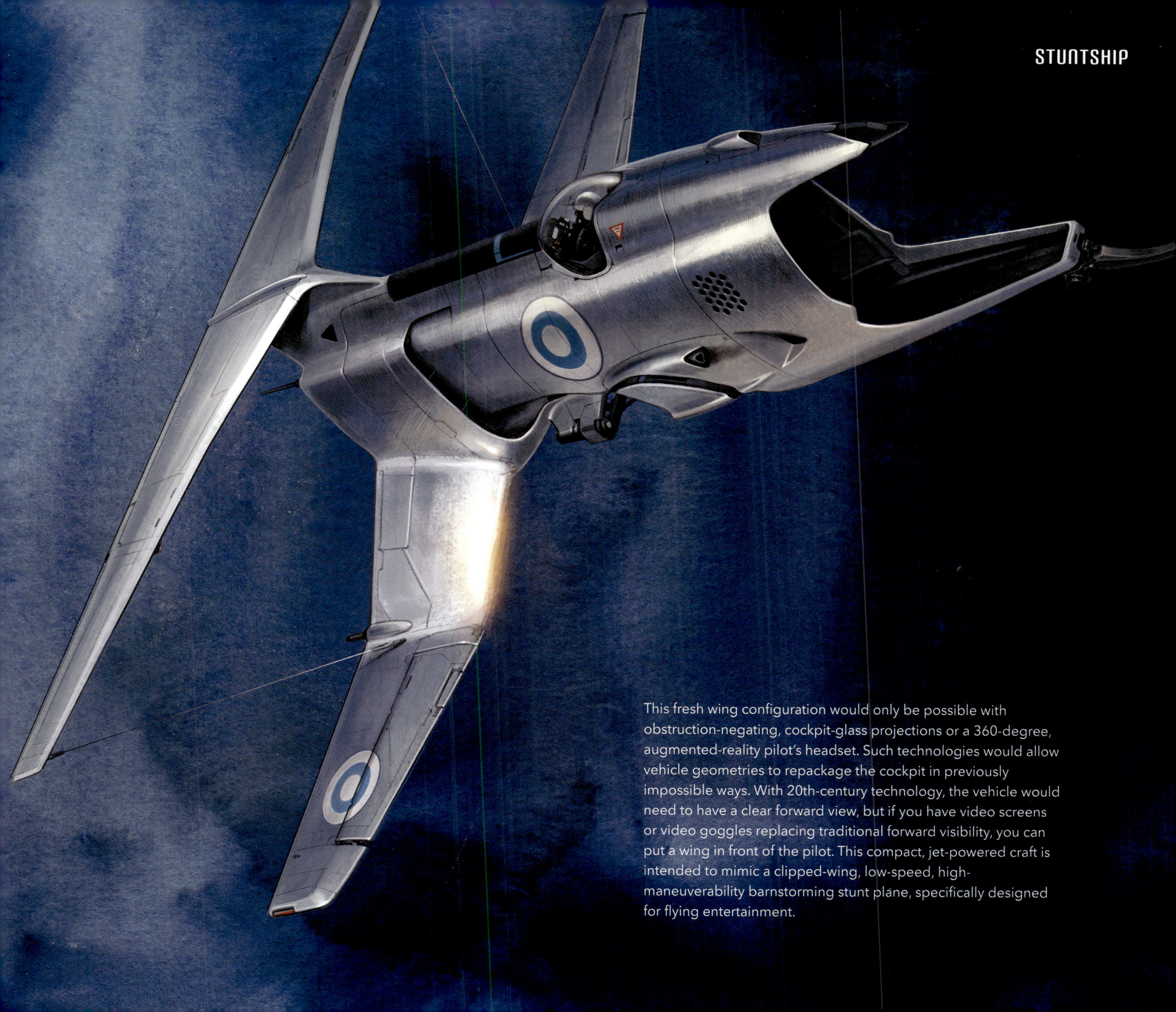

This fresh wing configuration would only be possible with obstruction-negating, cockpit-glass projections or a 360-degree, augmented-reality pilot's headset. Such technologies would allow vehicle geometries to repackage the cockpit in previously impossible ways. With 20th-century technology, the vehicle would need to have a clear forward view, but if you have video screens or video goggles replacing traditional forward visibility, you can put a wing in front of the pilot. This compact, jet-powered craft is intended to mimic a clipped-wing, low-speed, high-maneuverability barnstorming stunt plane, specifically designed for flying entertainment.

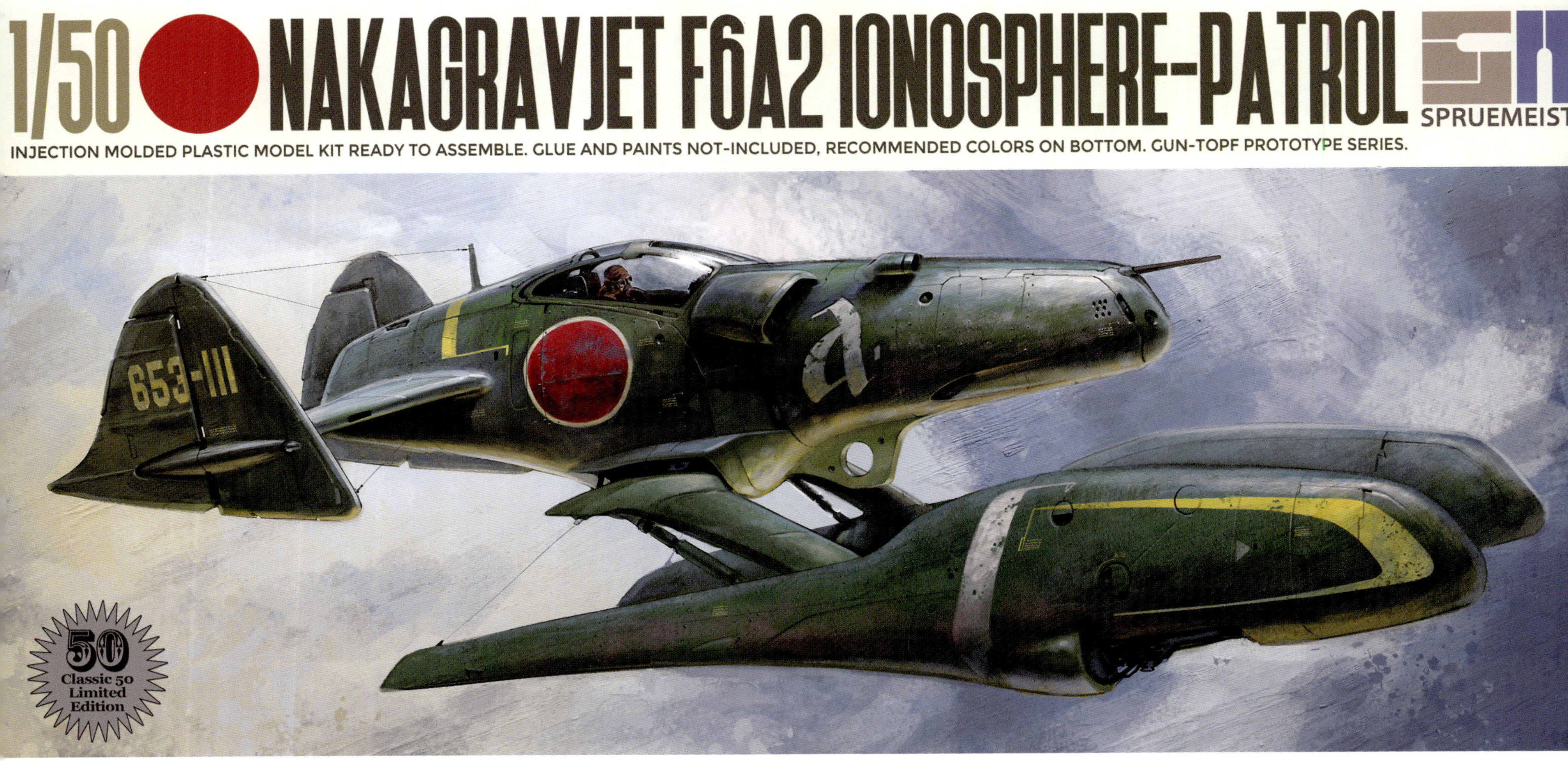

Illustrated deliberately in a more frenetic and textural style than my usual fare, this antigravity flying machine cribs its coloration and graphics from WWII-era Japanese fighter planes, replete with de rigueur flaking paint, exposing battered bare metal underneath. The contrast of yellow striping gives it a nice pop. The pontoons visually reference the mass of prop-driven seaplanes, but in this instance, imply some technology that provides antigravity lift and propulsion. This painting style was an attempt to pay tribute to the work of Japanese illustrator Yoshiyuki Takani who created hundreds of fantastic illustrations for mechs, tanks, and airplane model kits. His paintings are very passionate, with pronounced, strong brushwork, dramatic composition, and backgrounds made up of roiling oceans and storm clouds. This particular design got a lot of love on my Instagram page, so I am working with some friends to build a limited-edition kit to bring it to reality.

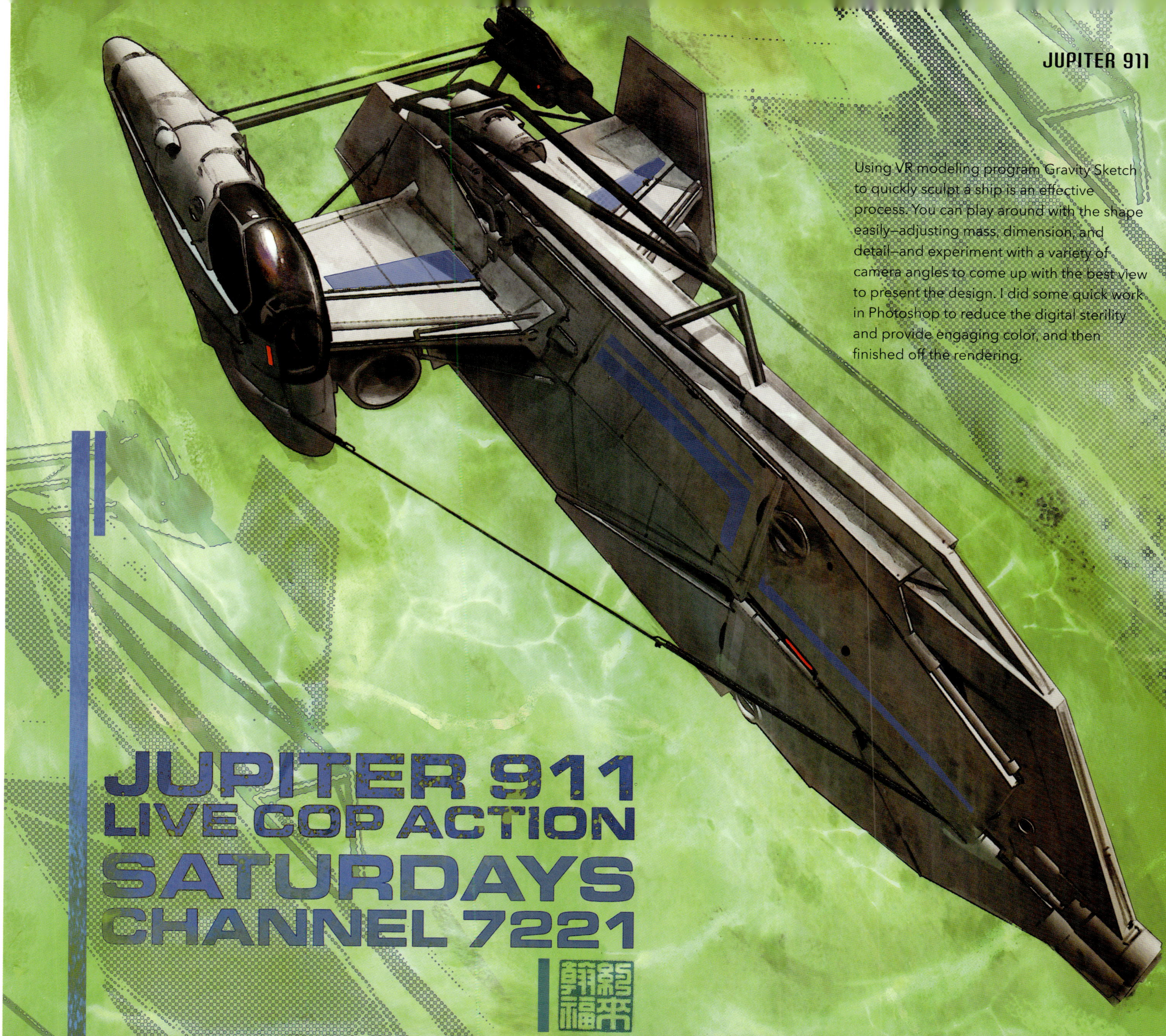

Using VR modeling program Gravity Sketch to quickly sculpt a ship is an effective process. You can play around with the shape easily—adjusting mass, dimension, and detail—and experiment with a variety of camera angles to come up with the best view to present the design. I did some quick work in Photoshop to reduce the digital sterility and provide engaging color, and then finished off the rendering.

GUN TOPF 3

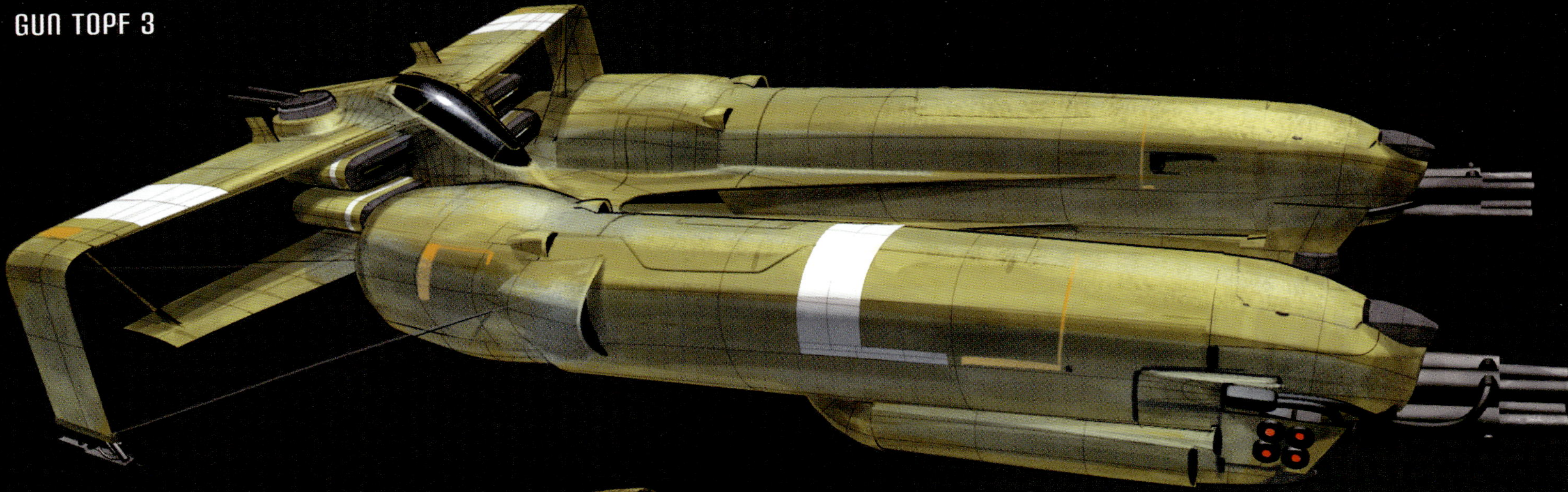

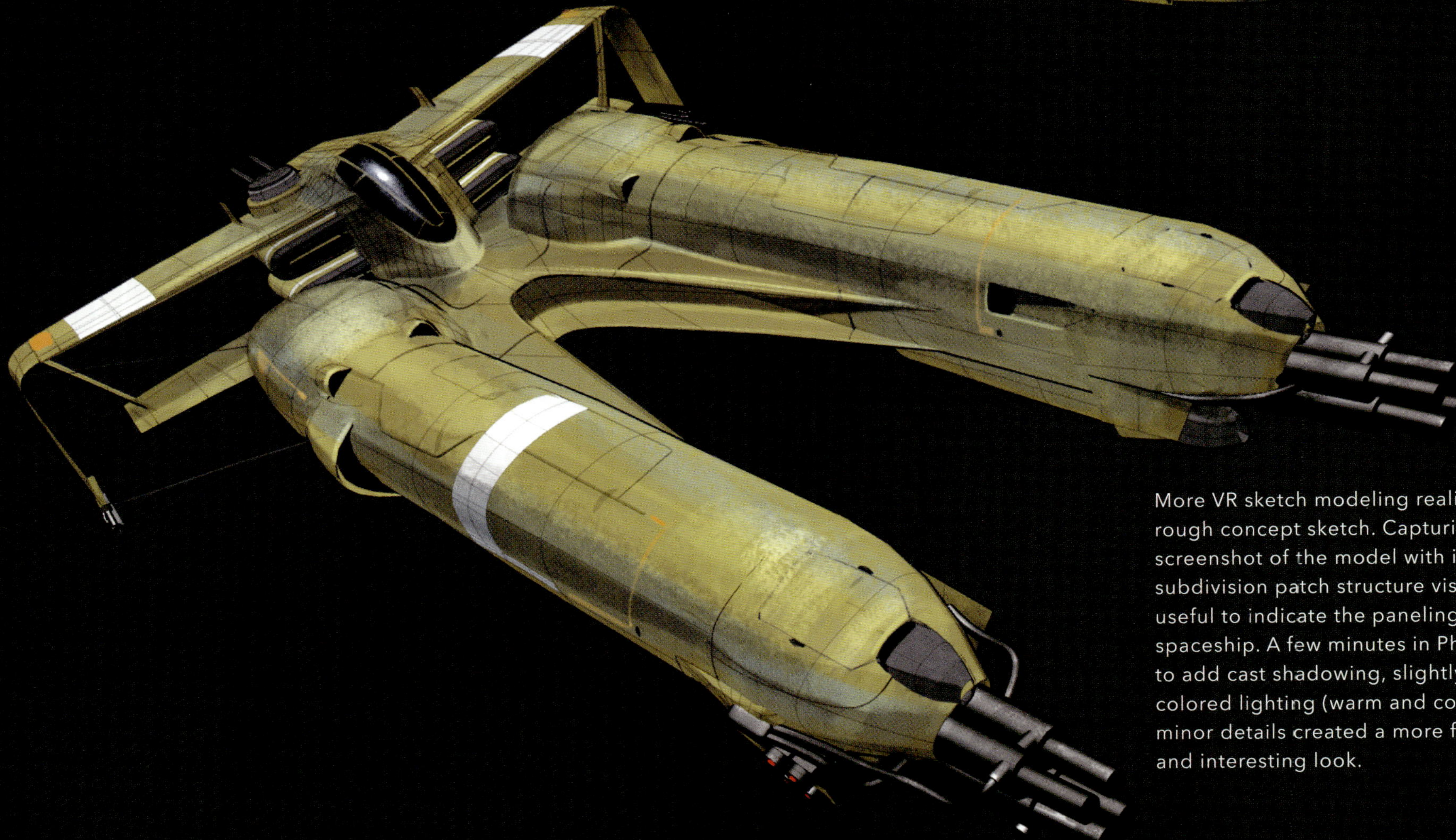

More VR sketch modeling realized this rough concept sketch. Capturing a screenshot of the model with its subdivision patch structure visible was useful to indicate the paneling on the spaceship. A few minutes in Photoshop to add cast shadowing, slightly colored lighting (warm and cool), and minor details created a more finished and interesting look.

F9W FURYWHIP 1/48

1/48 Scale Full Advanced Detail Plastic Kit With Metal Parts

SPRUEMEISTER™

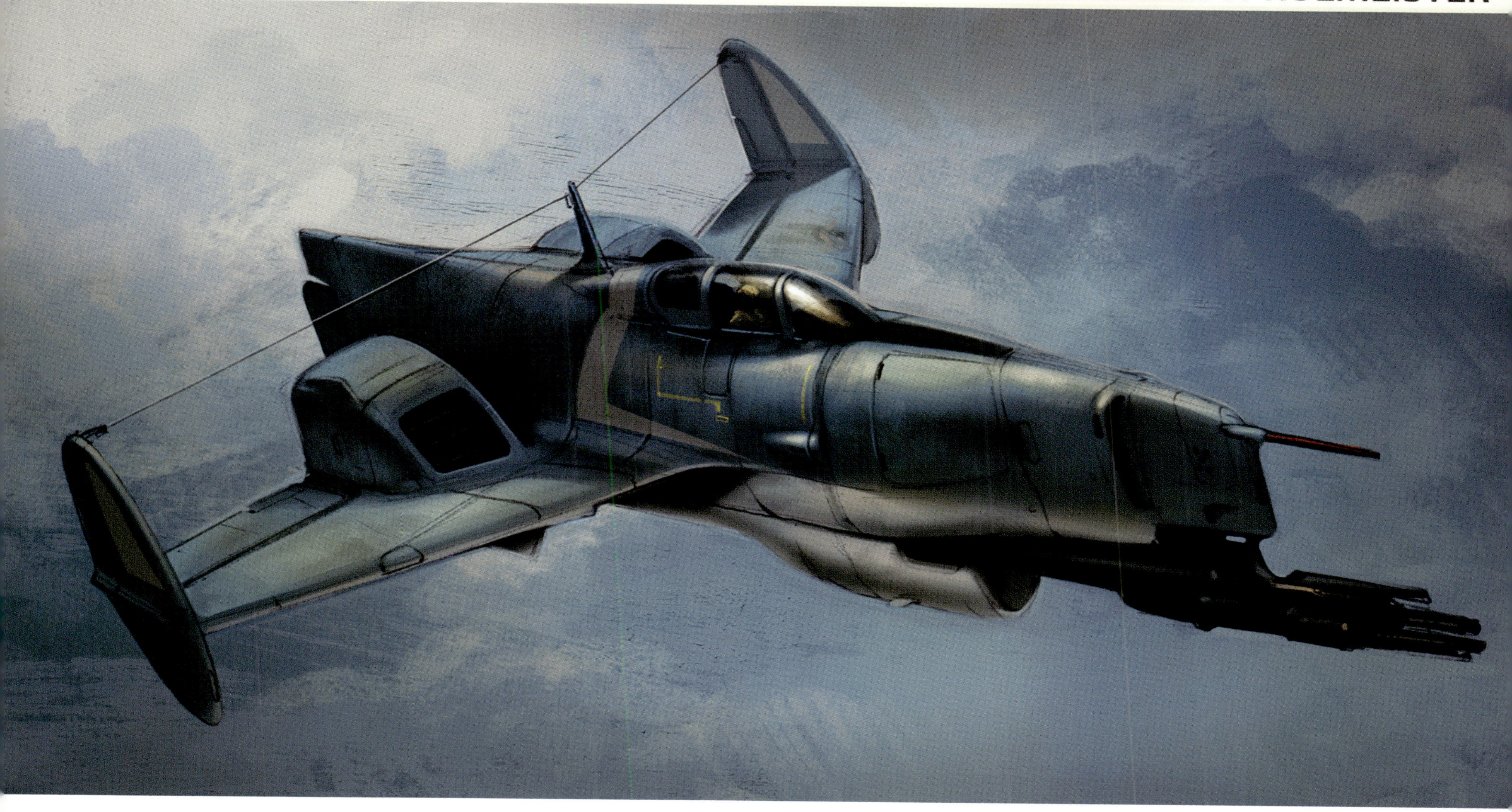

A thick and stubby atmospheric space fighter, the F9W with naval camo and fuselage mass is reminiscent of American WWII fighter planes of the Asian-Pacific Theatre, the term for the Asian Pacific geographic region of the war. American fighter planes in that region were distinct from planes used over Europe, partly because of the specific needs of range and landing/takeoff capabilities. Asian-Pacific Theatre planes were mostly carrier-based, so they had to have folding wings and short runway takeoff capabilities. European theatre counterparts enjoyed taking off from large grass fields and had shorter range requirements, as they did not have to fly over large areas of ocean to get to their engagement points. Also, relevant visually, American Asian-Pacific Theatre planes were colored blue to blend in with the color of the ocean, while planes in battle over land generally had olive, brown, and tan camouflage.

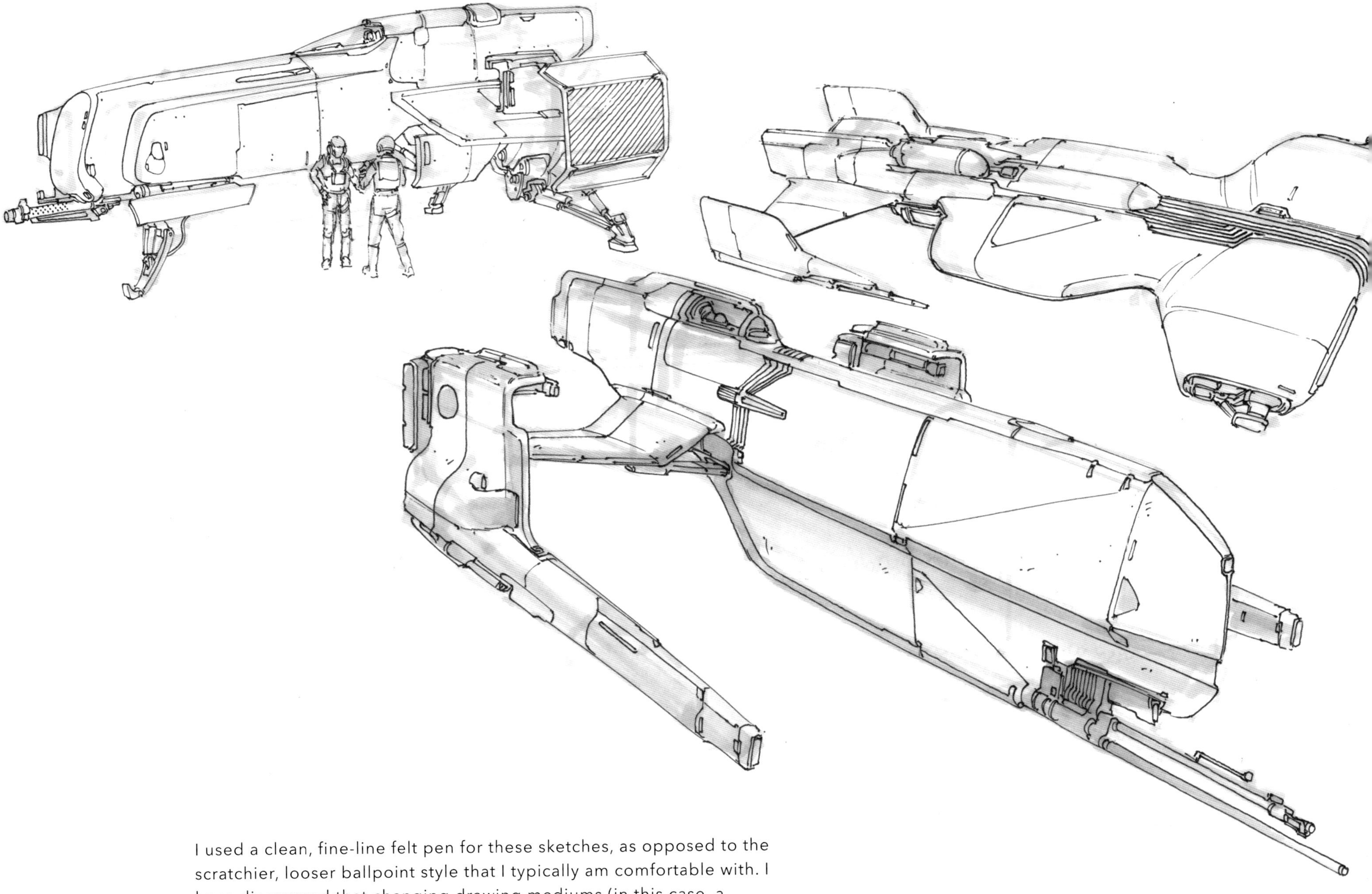

I used a clean, fine-line felt pen for these sketches, as opposed to the scratchier, looser ballpoint style that I typically am comfortable with. I have discovered that changing drawing mediums (in this case, a different type of pen) instantly produces creative results, as the brain tackles each differently.

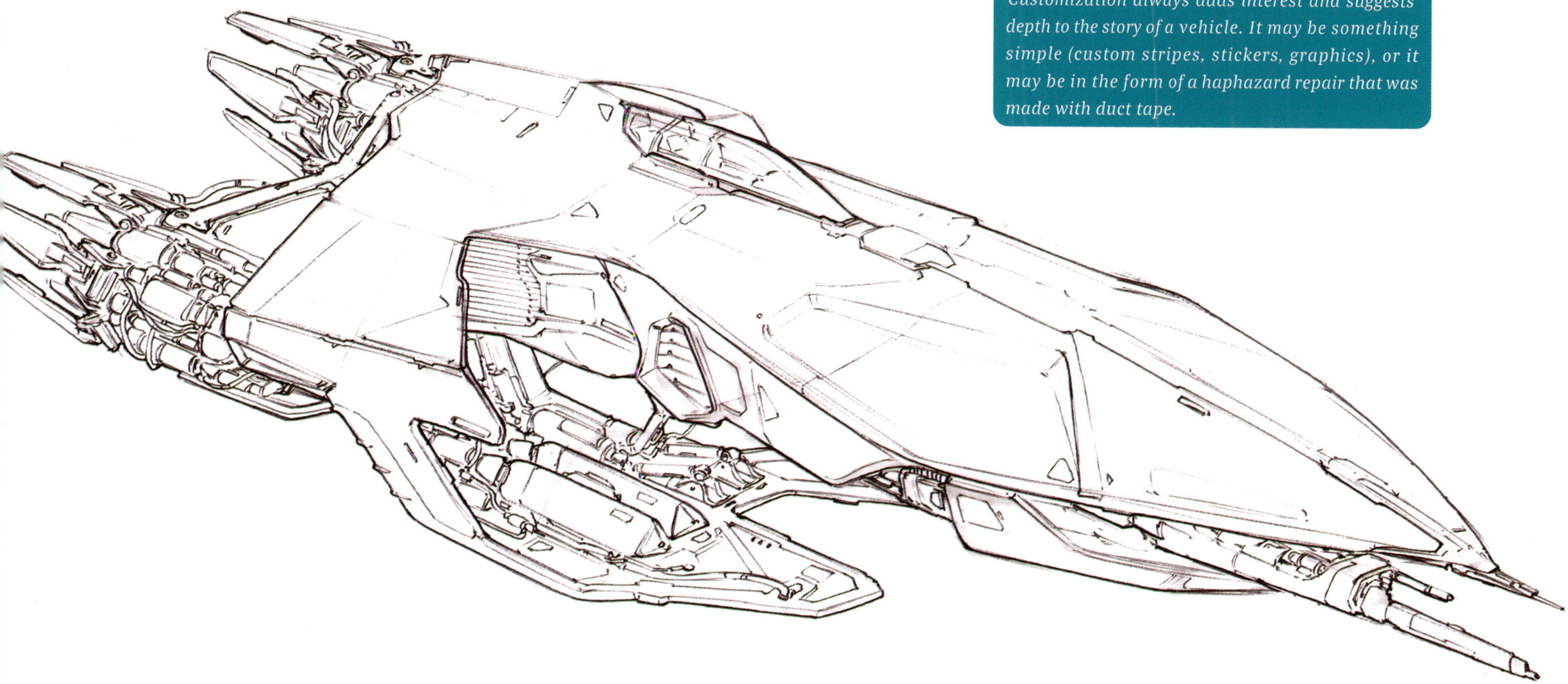

Customization always adds interest and suggests depth to the story of a vehicle. It may be something simple (custom stripes, stickers, graphics), or it may be in the form of a haphazard repair that was made with duct tape.

A somewhat plebeian spaceship, it was brought to life with expensive hot-rod modifications: paneling removed and mechanisms tweaked and exposed. Often, it is a mechanical upgrade to the engine, a process of hot-rodding to eke out more power. With cars and spaceships alike, to be able to modify the engine, sometimes you have to remove bodywork because the extra parts no longer fit under the original panels, but other times, the panels are removed to show off the beautiful custom work, passionate investments of time and energy.

SWEEPY WING BOMBER

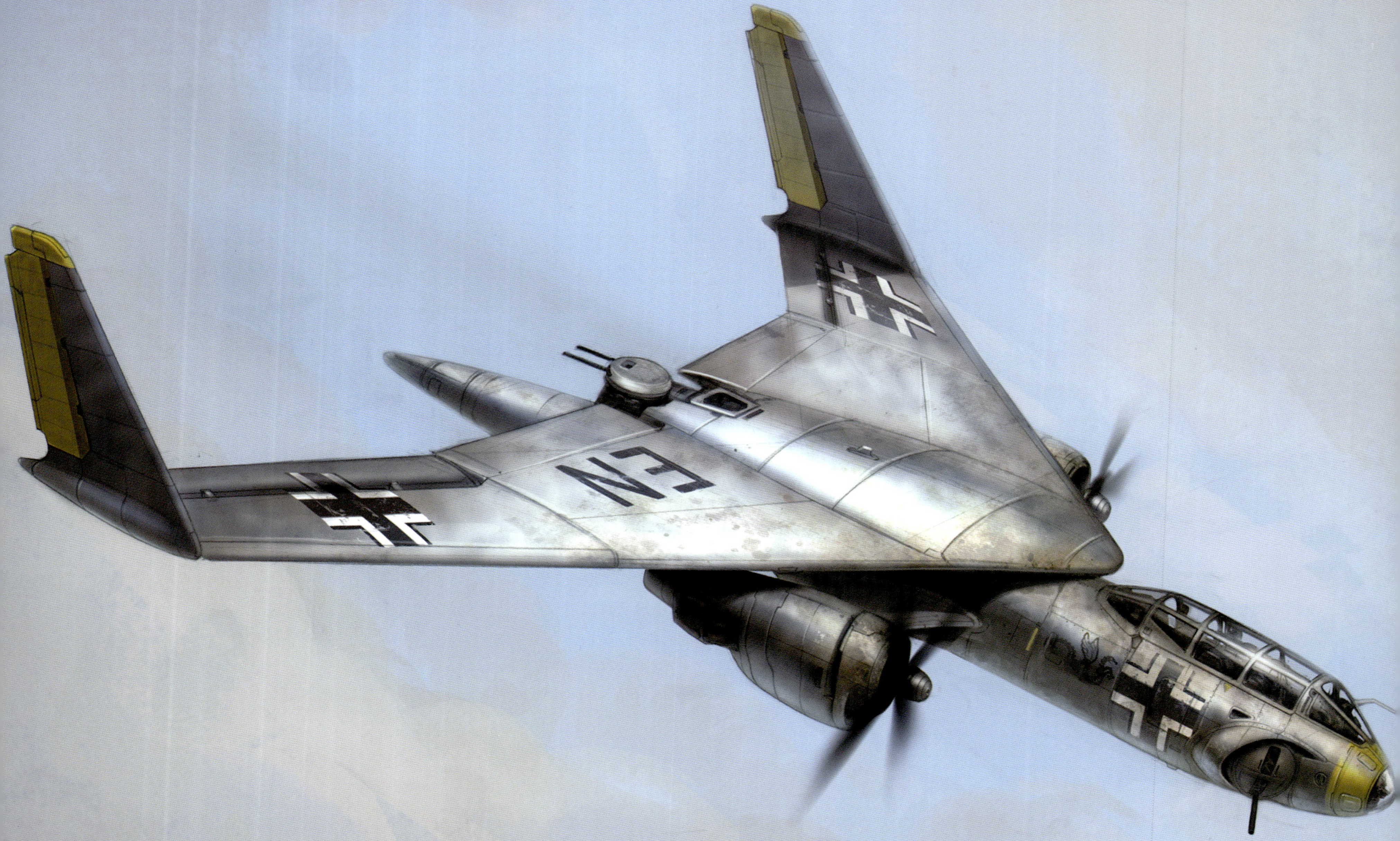

Flying wing concept merged with a more typical WWII-era tube fuselage. One of the oldest illustrations in the volume, the drawing style is what I was doing around 2004—tight ink line drawing with color underneath, preserving the line drawing in the final image. Detailing and implied technology in concept design can be imaginative and fanciful, but at the same time, you have to ensure there aren't any glaring anachronisms by being familiar with the era of design and the materials, manufacturing technology, and aerodynamic ideas around that time.

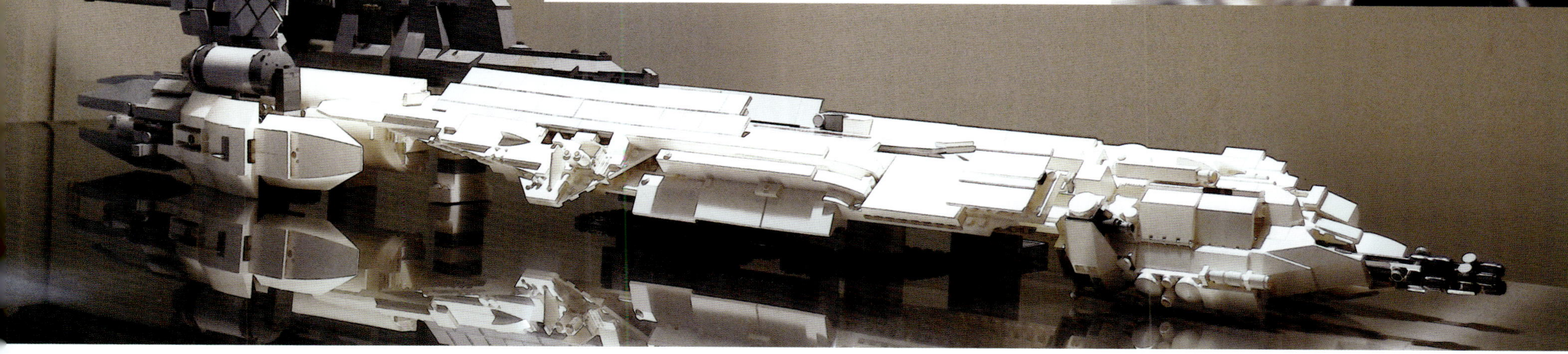

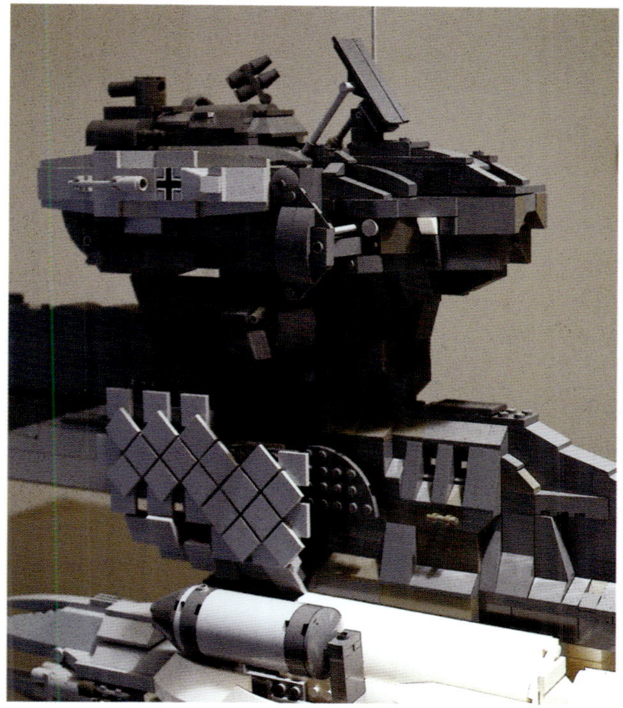

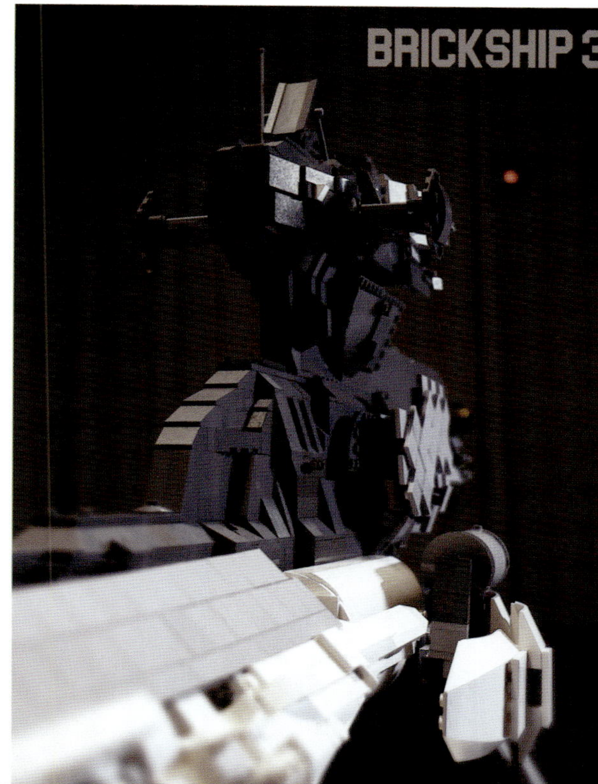

I wanted to try using Lego bricks as a different medium for creating new forms and designs. I started to buy a variety of white and gray bricks by the pound and ordering specialized finish bits like smooth plates, antennae, and other **greeblie** details. My original idea was to create a basic shape, photograph it, and then render more detail over the photo, but the level of finish I was getting brick by brick presented a design that in itself was complete. While certainly not a fast medium for ideation (and undoubtedly the loudest from the incessant digging through piles of plastic bricks looking for the right one), like 3D data form development, you are able to see your design in different perspectives and angles, and capture views to show the design at its most dramatic. I recommend trying out Lego when you need a break from difficult perspective construction, or you want to spend some time away from screens.

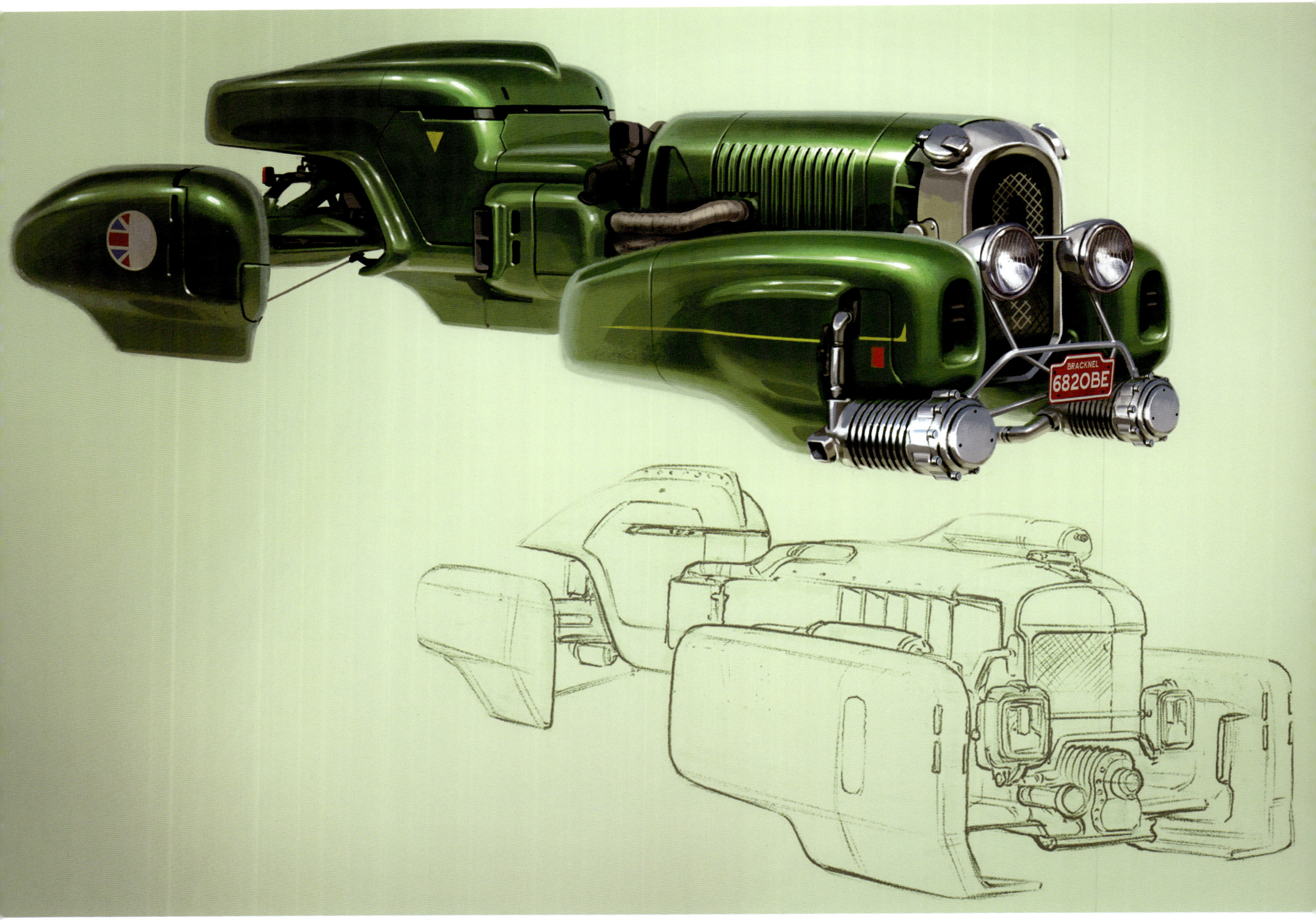

A couple of pencil sketches from many years ago, I used a vintage-car form and detailed set of ingredients to make a retro hovership. The exposed mechanical bits and interplay between chrome and pure-hued paint is a familiar and classic combination, British racing green and polished metal, that always seems to work so well.

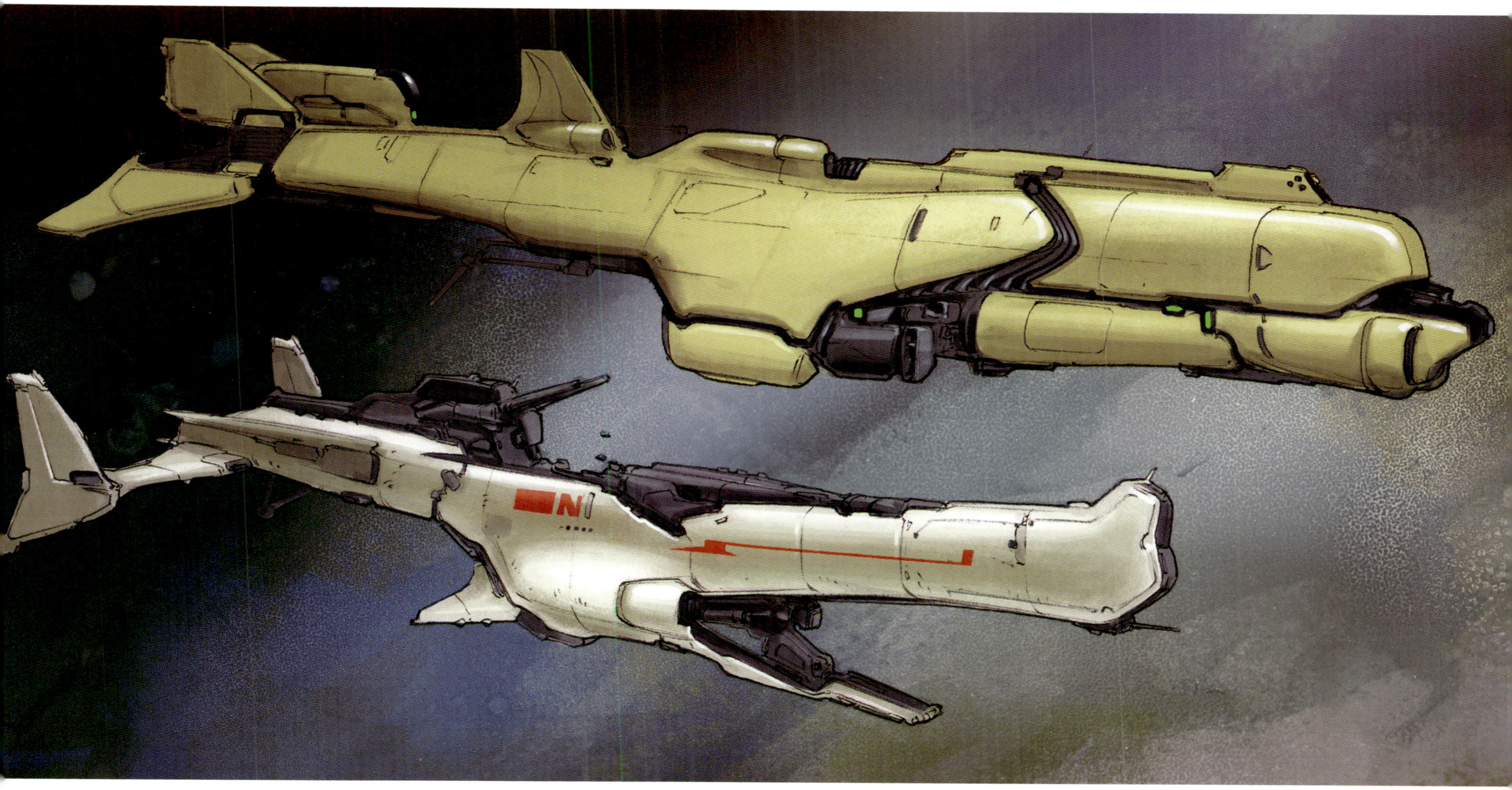

Both ship designs came from looking at the odd-looking basking shark. These are quickie ballpoint sketches with some color and value to indicate form. Shapes and form language have controlled chaos intent; beauty is not expected, but interest is.

LEYNNWOOD-HUXLEY RAFDF BR-52 "HUT"

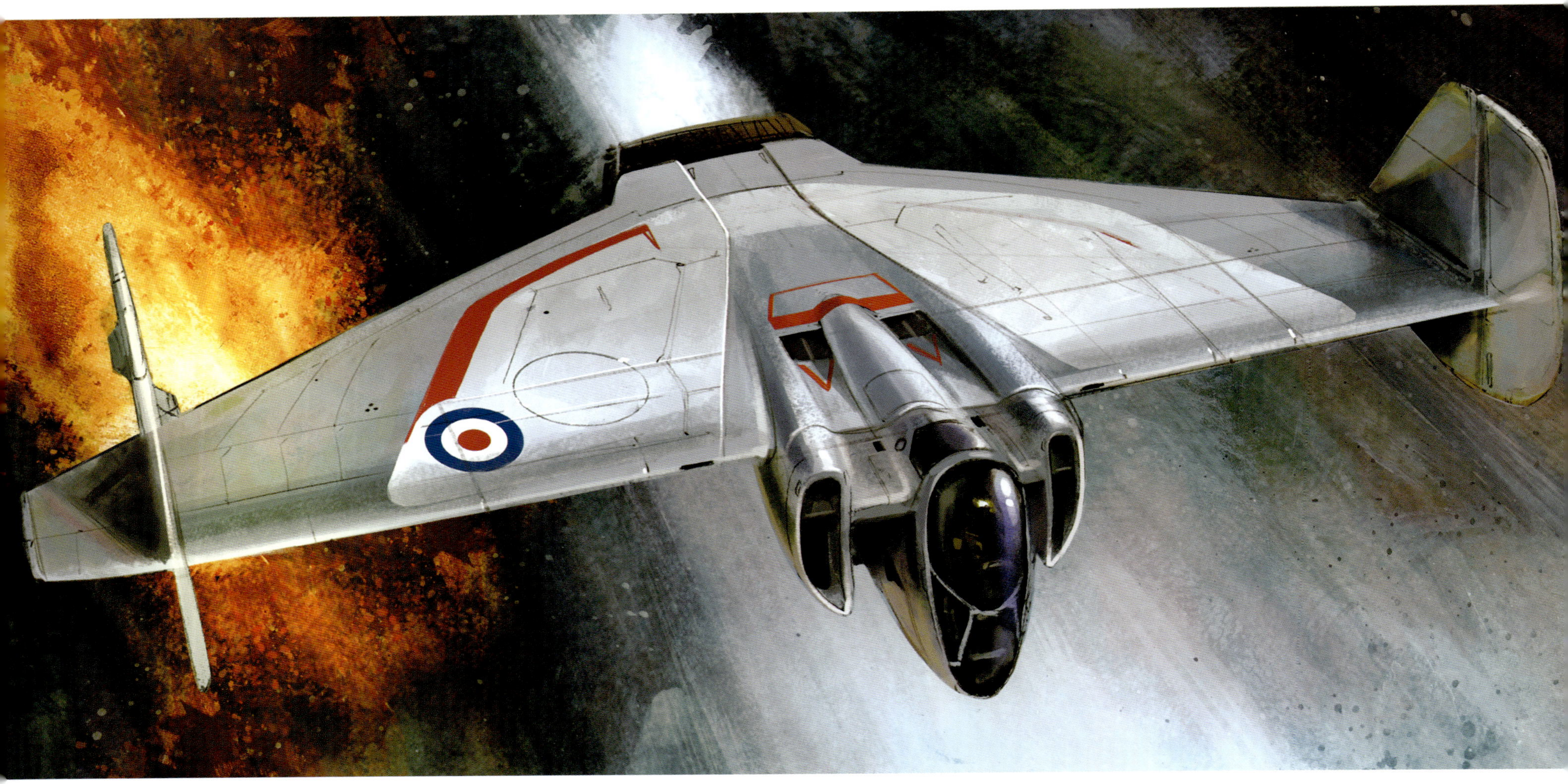

A retro-improbable design and rendering exercise, the Hut is a compact, 1960s flying-wing jet bomber. The zooming background texture, blooming explosion and colored reflections and shadows in the metal surfaces on the wing tips made this a particularly enjoyable illustration to create. Many of my energetic and textural backgrounds, like the one here, are produced by photographing ink and paint applied to paper or illustration board. I can then import the photographs of paint brushwork, paint splatters, and ink blooms into Photoshop and tweak color, contrast, and layer effects to create the appearance of land, sky, space, clouds, and explosions.

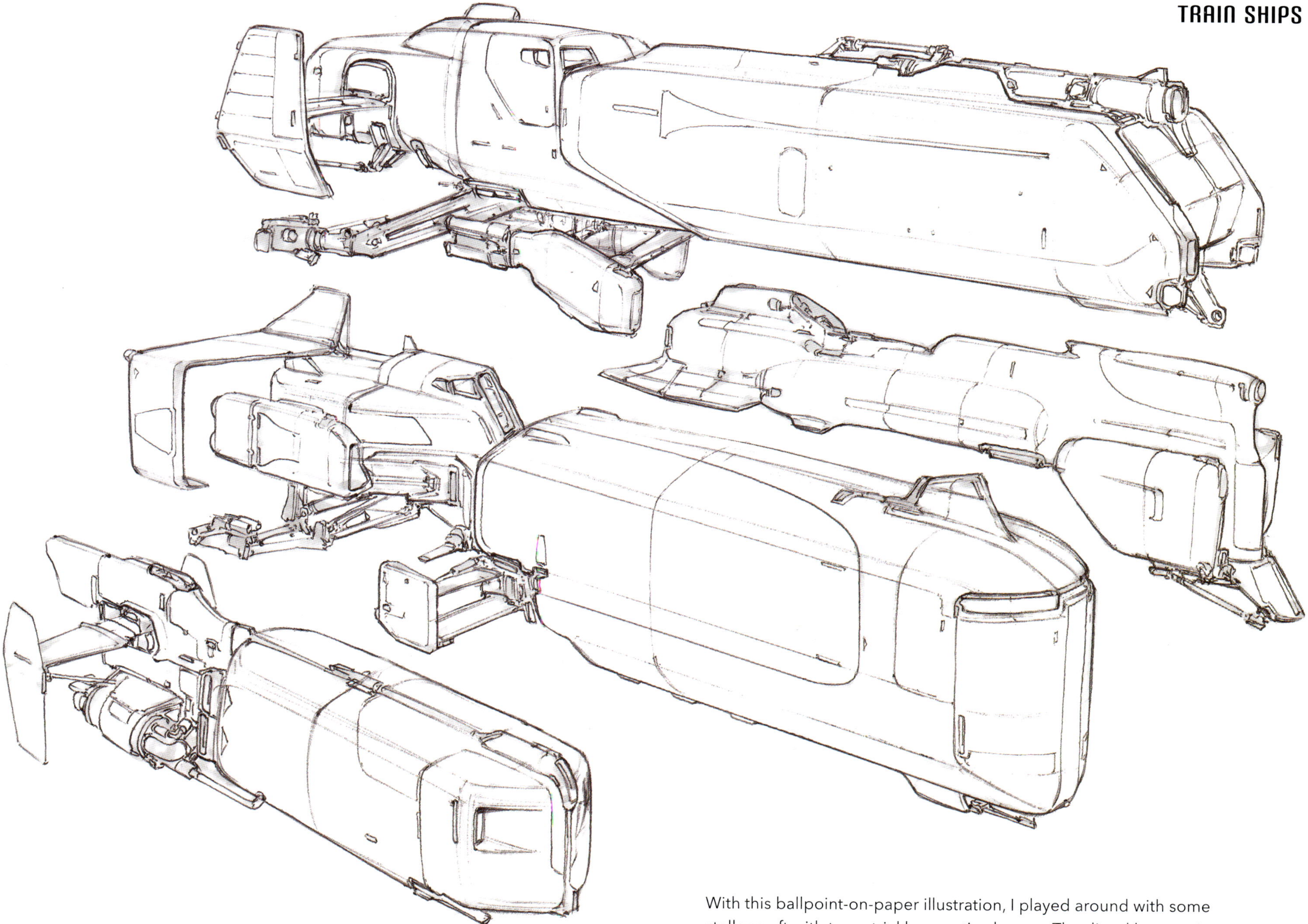

If everything in a design is new, it can be hard for the viewer to relate to it. Adding parts of the design that are analogous to designs in our own environment make them more accessible.

With this ballpoint-on-paper illustration, I played around with some stellar craft with terrestrial locomotive bones. The diesel locomotives most of us are familiar with generally have a very large blocky engine mass with a little cockpit snuggling on the back. Adding other train-like details, like the high mounted central headlight on the front, is enough to suggest some rail riding vehicle genetic link. I often achieve some fresh solutions that retain a comfortable familiarity by mixing different themes together.

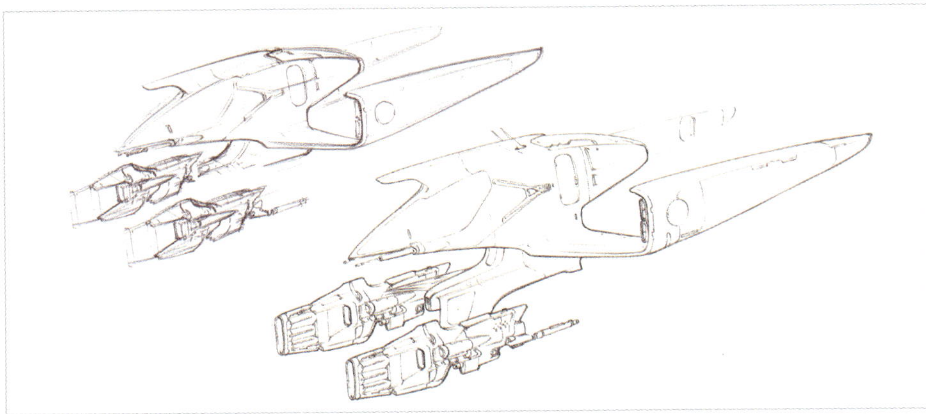

On occasion, I'll take a second look at a sketch that I created, and then put it aside, as I didn't have a vision of taking it into a color illustration. I had taken this rough sketch to a fairly tight ink-on-paper line drawing that was all ready to render up, and then I forgot about it. Upon seeing it in a file folder years later, I thought it was worth revisiting, and had an idea to render it up as bare-metal finish. There were some design elements and perspective issues that got some minor adjustments, but in this case, it was kind of nice to just focus on rendering, as all the design work was already wrapped up.

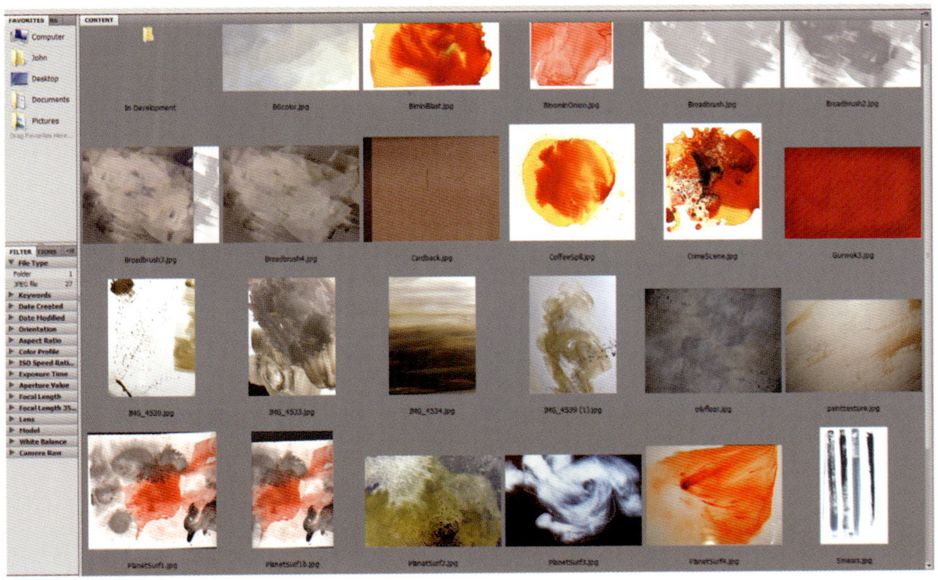

1) Create an analog texture collection.

This is a look at my analog texture folder. These are scanned-in images of paints, dyes, and foodstuffs (milk, soy sauce, olive oil, angostura bitters, food coloring, chili oil, etc.) applied to paper or plastic film that I use to create a visually tactile and lively digital drawing surface. The hue, saturation, and contrast get adjusted. I invert the values sometimes and use the variety of layer treatments—often soft light, overlay, screen, and multiply—to get various effects. Textures are also used to apply over the surface of the vehicle to indicate weathering or mimic the built-up paint from brushwork of gouache-illustration technique.

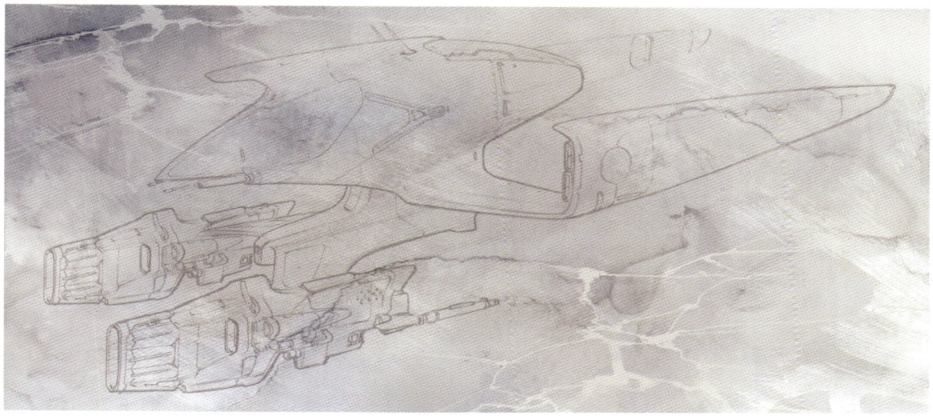

2) Apply the background.

The background is applied through layering of textures. Color and toning is carefully considered to contrast my planned value and color of the vehicle, but usually adjustments have to be made as the vehicle gets laid down in the image. While essentially abstract, there is an implied icy-planet surface with frigid, liquid-filled fractures. Reduced value contrast in the background allows the foreground objects to come forward on the page.

Background Development: Create a Texture Collection

The focus of my artistic drive has been on the vehicle itself. This means that the background and environment are less interesting to me from a creative perspective. I would prefer that someone look at a car or spaceship that I design and imagine the world it must inhabit. To create a finished-looking piece, however, it does look best to have some color and texture to provide a backdrop for some of the vehicles I render. It was very common to have an ink-dye type of background for vehicle illustrations created in the 1960s and 1970s. This was done with toxic dyes that are no longer available. Artists like Syd Mead would create a suggested environment by combining marker dyes with elements of rendered architecture. Automotive stylists would simply create a bleeding blob of color to contrast a metallic vehicle, sometimes letting the background color reflect into the subject car's shiny surfaces.

I have been experimenting with alcohol dyes on Yupo paper, which lets the dyes sit on top rather than be absorbed, creating interesting psychedelic blooms and bleeds of color. I also collect textural images such as rough brushwork that I can use to make an image appear to be created using traditional painted media like gouache and swirling liquids that I photograph as they blend into each other that I can use to imply distant galaxies for space images. These chaotic and fluid-looking textures contrast the tight and precise surfacing of manufactured vehicles. I have some favorite textures that I tend to reuse frequently, such as a large resolution photograph I took from a ladder, high above of my garage floor, which has the stains of oils and liquids from 75 years of cars. The spattering of subtle rusty reds, browns, and dusty smears is a fantastic texture that I can use to overlay on top of the vehicles themselves to indicate the marks that appear with age and heavy use.

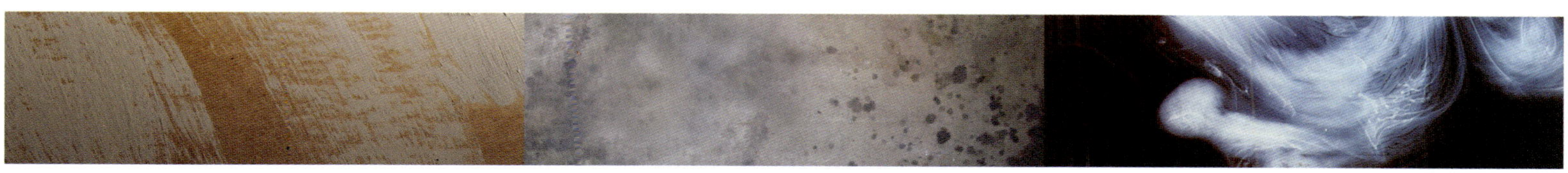

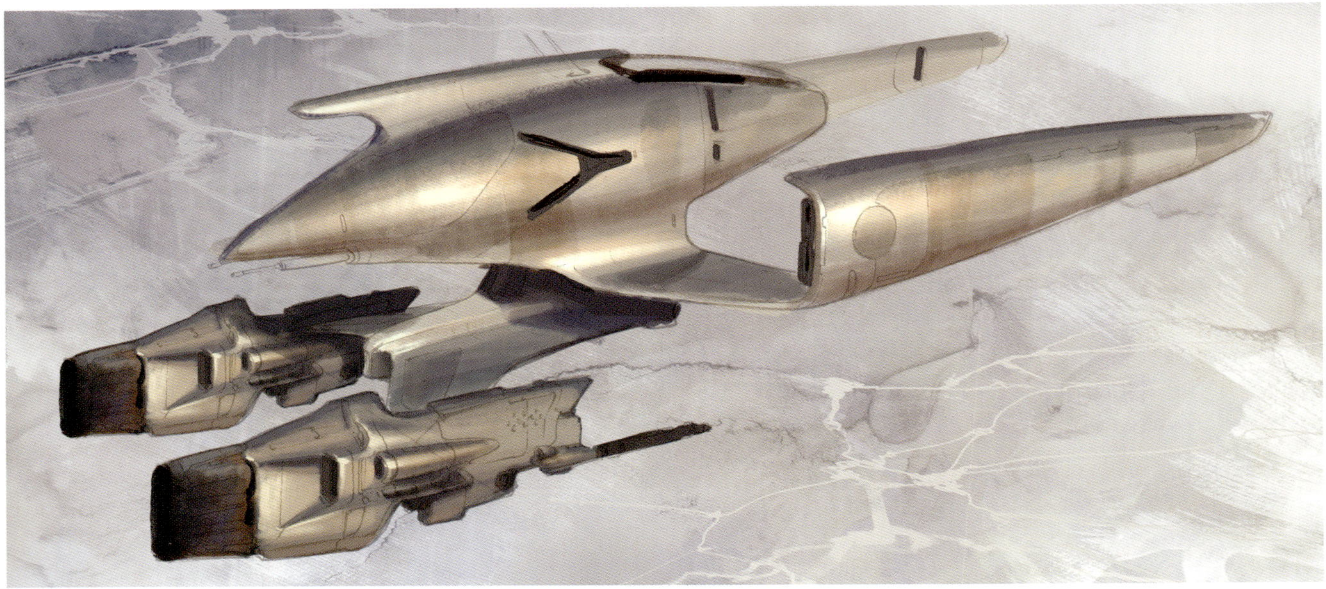

3) Apply color to the ship.

A quick application of color to the ship allows me to get a sense early on of what the impact of the final image will be. Here, I am looking to make sure the ship pops, or comes off the page. This ensures that the general forms feel like they have volume and that I am seeing good definition of the object relative to the backgrounc I'm always looking to confirm that the background crawls around the outline of the vehicle in an interestin way and that parts overlap to promote perspective depth and are easy to read or understand. The colors I chose are akin to sunrise lighting: light orange and low on the horizon while the sky transitions from turquoise to darker purple tones at the top of the sky dome.

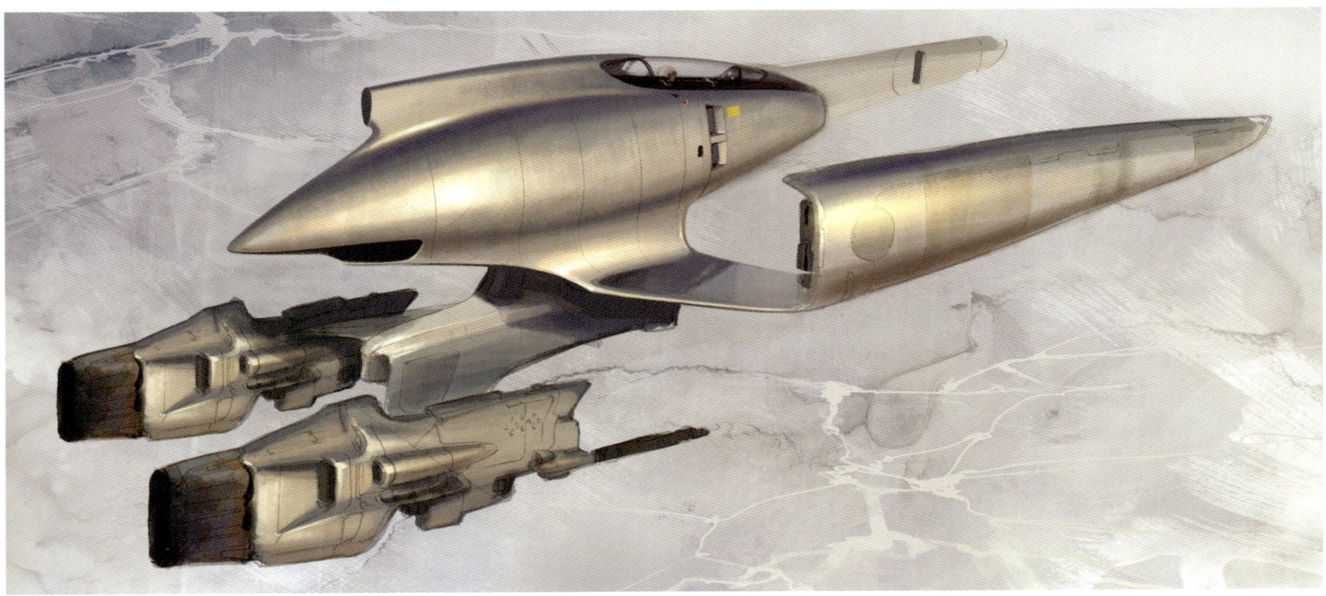

4) Establish the focus area.

I begin with the cleanup and clarification of the image in the primary focal point area—that place that I want the viewer to focus their attention. This area gets enhanced value contrast, the splashiest highlights, and the most delicate detail usually. In this step, I've carefully applied color and value to describe the form, and I've also tuned the fuselage shape a bit, bringing the largest, fattest section of the teardrop body farther toward the rear. I clipped off the crest shape on top, which had given the ship the character of a leaping rabbit. The reflected shadow color on the downward-facing surfaces has a general warm color, but above the wing, where that surface is blocking the color reflecting from underneath the vehicle, the color is briefly more bluish.

The upward-facing surface of the wing reflects the sky and also the fuselage itself. I darkened the fuselage reflection into the wing to enhance the feeling of metalli shininess. These "cheats," to make things look better tha what would be physically calculated with actual geometry, are what make an illustration more visceral than a straight photograph or CG rendering of 3D geometry.

When you are able to break or bend the rules with light and color, you can make the object "look its very best" without being restrained by the limitations of optical reality.

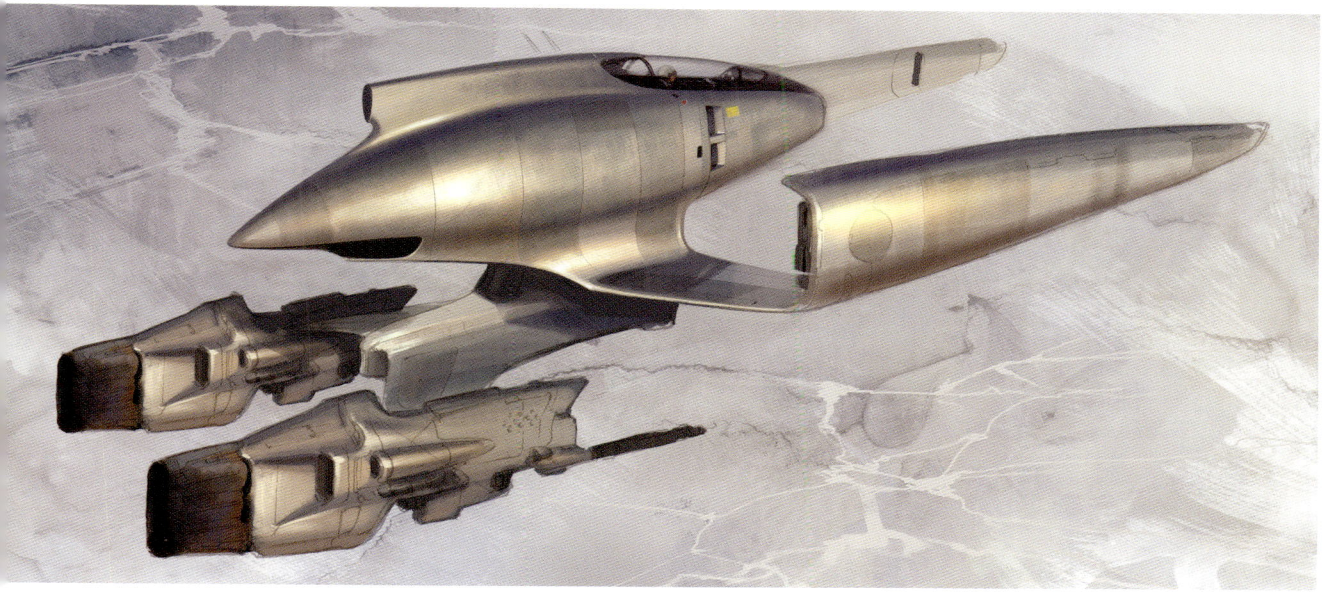

5) Adding realism to the metal surfaces.

Minor work is shown in this step, but it's important in the expression of manufactured bare-metal surface application. Aircraft fuselage exteriors are essentially thin metal-skin panels that are formed and attached to a ribcage space-frame structure underneath. Where each panel is attached to the frame member, you will often see a subtle difference in the appearance of the metal-skin panels. Using a light-color toning overlay, different from neighboring surfaces, enhances the feeling of an assembled set of surfaces, each reflecting light in a slightly different way. Part of the reason for this is that metal has a grain direction as it comes off of a roll, and if panels are cut to shape and applied in different directions, the way the light bounces off will be somewhat different. Additionally, the material may indicate pieces of the airship that have been replaced in some sci-fi storytelling illustrations.

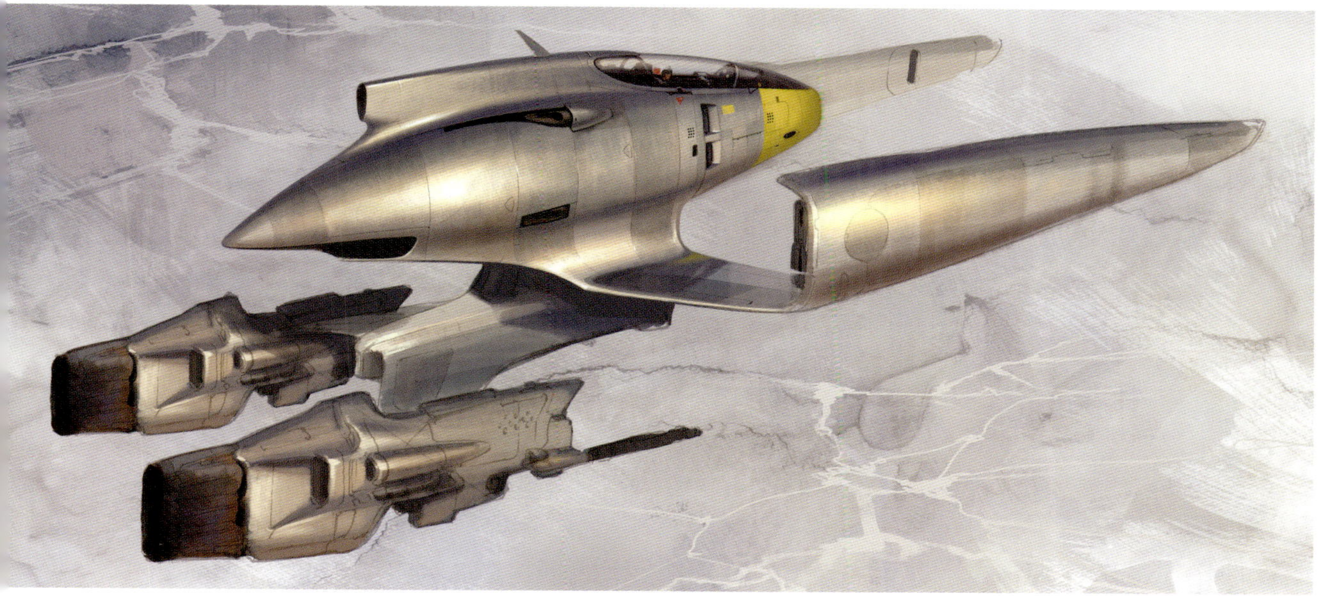

6) Apply detail to the fuselage and cockpit area.

The strong contrast between the black-exhaust cut-out areas and the metal skin keep the eyes on this general area. I wanted to bring in some pure color to get some spots of playful interest and to express the difference in material finish on the vehicle. Yellow worked well against the greenish-blue metal, and it also referenced real-world, jet-fighter identification markings. I considered the form of the vehicle, the areas that I wanted some additional focus of attention and enhanced that with detailing and shapes that push in and pull out to break up broad surfaces that need more character. The scaling of the canopy, cockpit, and visible pilot allows the viewer to understand the direction, operation, and size of the vehicle.

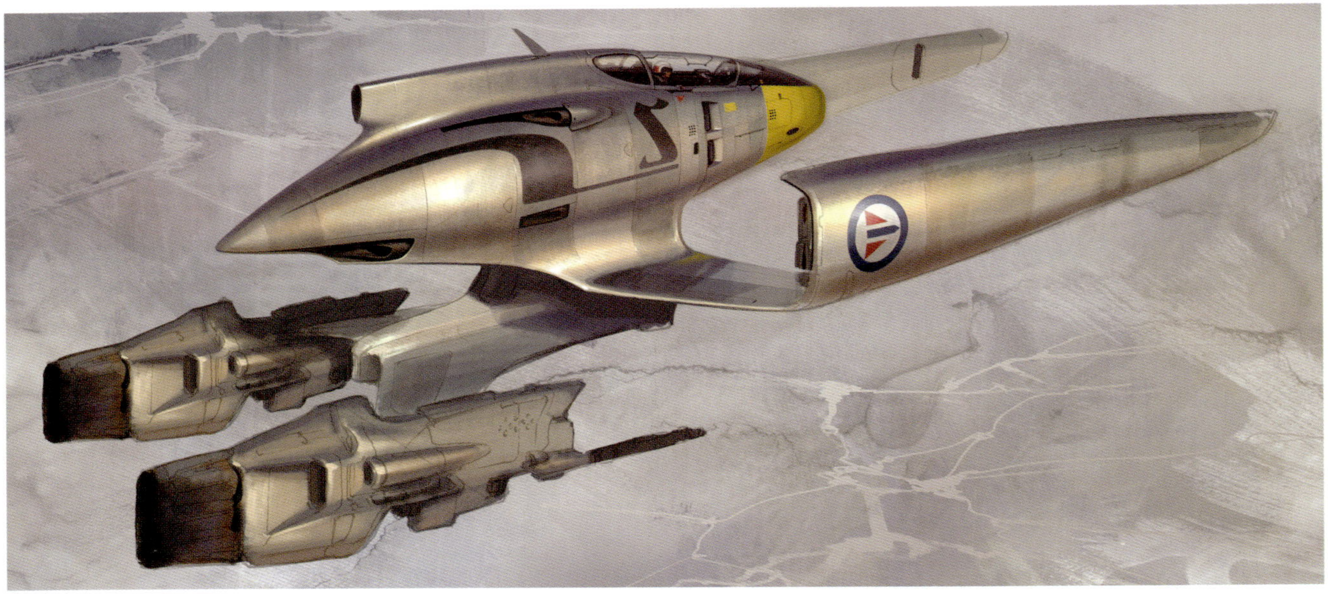

7) Retone the illustration.

In this stage, I've retoned the whole image, darkening it so that the environment feels more like dawn and less overexposed. Again, with the key focal area being the fuselage, the flanking pontoon shape on the right had a bright highlight that was pulling too much focus, so the application of a blue-white-red roundel graphic on top of the white/orange sunglow knocked back the attention. On the main fuselage, black-painted graphics curl over the surface—relating to the motion of the vehicle and its overall form—and around the upper-exhaust cutout. Treating the optical properties of the graphics differently, such as reflecting the light with cooler and less lively contrast, helps indicate that the graphic is created with a semi-matte paint applied to the metal surface.

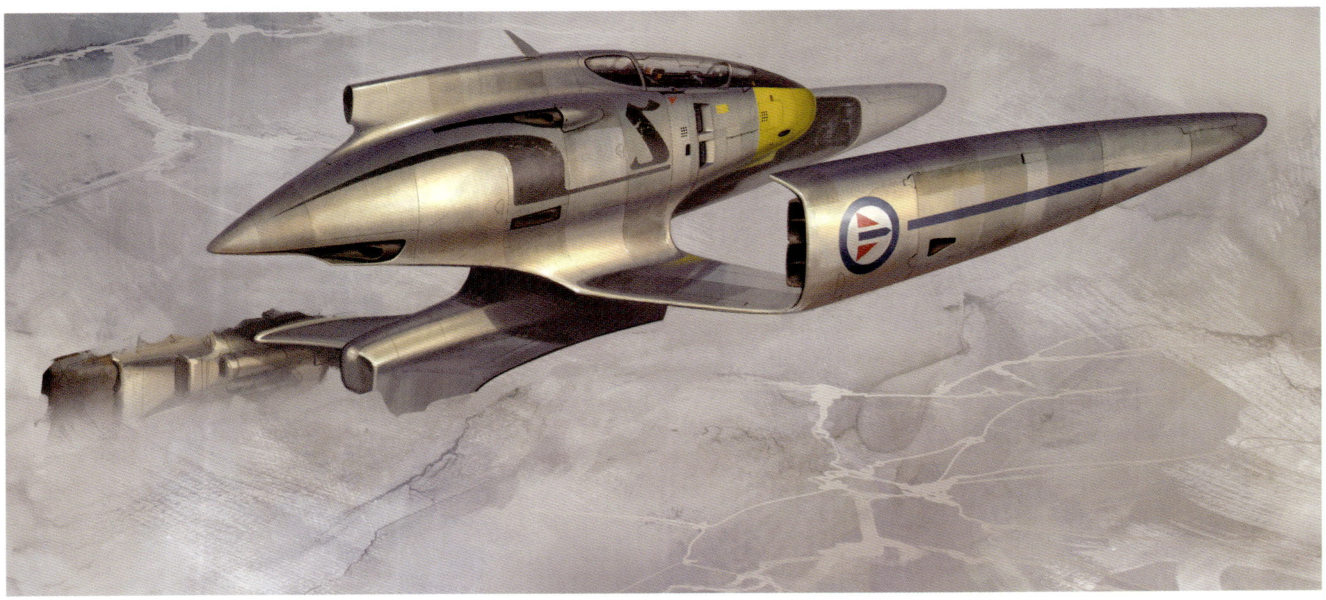

8) Refine shapes.

The far-side, fuselage-flanking pontoon shape was an issue from the beginning of the sketch, and it is here that I finally address the overlap with the cockpit. Since the pontoon center of mass was lined up exactly with the cockpit, the two shapes started to visually merge into one. By moving the far pontoon shape down and reducing the length, it becomes more apparent that it is well beyond the cockpit, not part of it. Again, this is a cheat from the actual perspective construction, but one that goes essentially unnoticed in the overall image. During this stage, I begin to refine the platform shape under the fuselage that the engines hang off of. I pushed the darkness of the cast shadow to give more visual depth to the fuselage. I also wanted to be able to relocate and resize the engines to fine-tune the perspective, so they will be drawn on a separate layer in the next step.

Graphics should always enhance the form, tell some functional story, or direct the viewer's gaze.

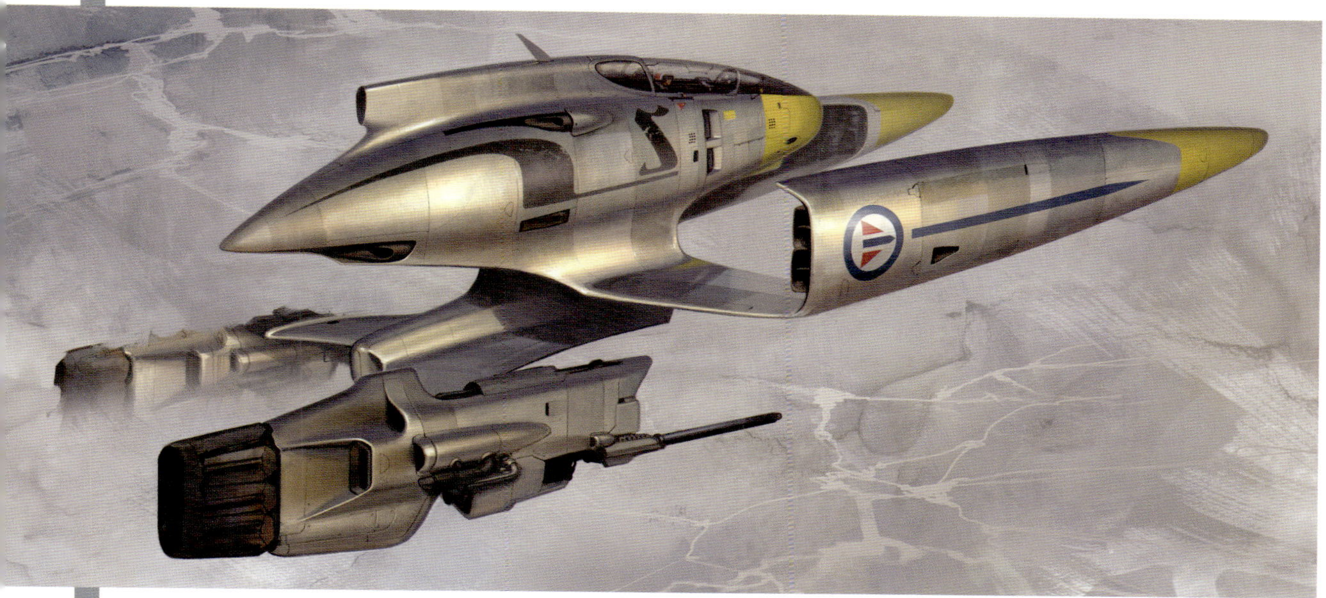

9) Illustrate an engine on a separate layer.

The near-side engine gets illustrated in the step. Tones are darker to imply less atmospheric haze, which makes the fuselage appear closer. Additionally, the metals are cooked and broiled a bit with warmish exhaust weathering to show heavy usage and functionality. I experimented with painting the tips of the pontoons with the same yellow as the nose on the cockpit, but I was not happy with the way it was drawing my eye to the right and looked unnecessary. With the completion of the engine on a separate layer, it was simple to duplicate, scale, and modify slightly to appear as the port-side engine in the final image. It is important to change both the shading and detailing of a duplicated object so that it doesn't look simply digitally copied.

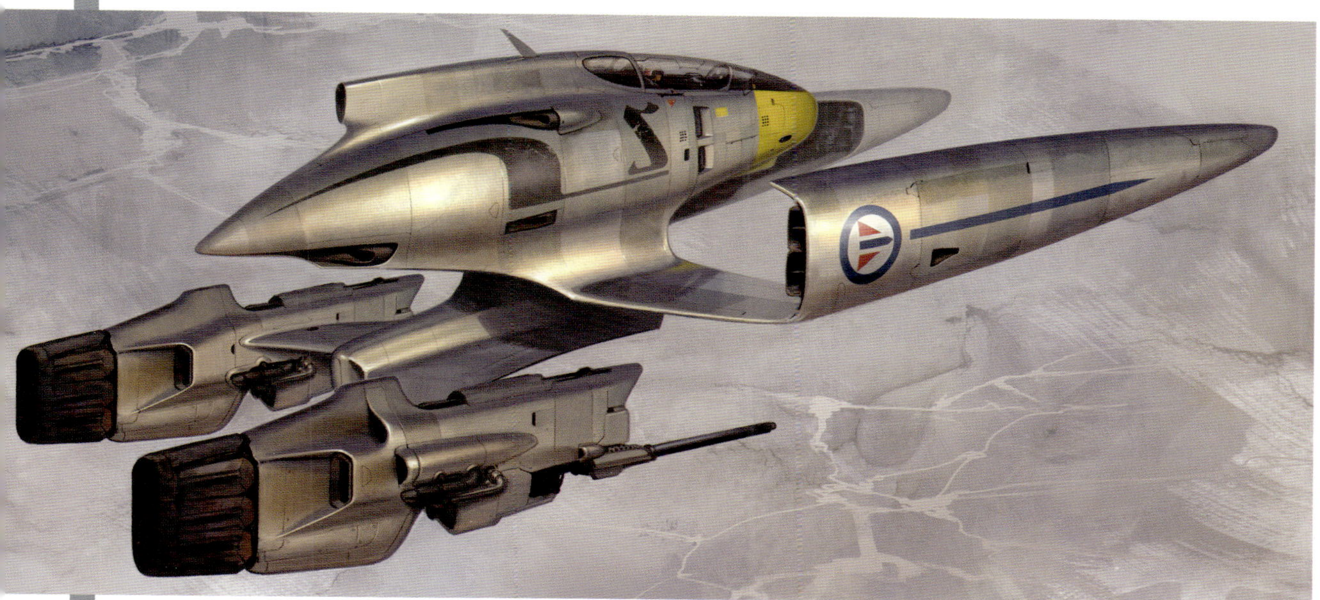

10) Finalize image.

Adding the last little bits of detailed drawing, adjusting overall toning or contrast, tuning perspective, and all sorts of cleanup activities happen at the end of a drawing. And calling it done is no easy task. You need to look at the feeling of the image as a whole; the details are not as important as the overall read of the image.

Can you see the vehicle clearly on the page? Does it look three-dimensional, solid, lively, and does it feel like it exists in the environment that has been created? If you haven't been taking care of the overall image, there is a sense of unease that something just isn't right, and you'll unsuccessfully keep on adjusting little details trying to fix what "feels" wrong. If you have done well throughout the image-creation process to manage good composition, perspective, color, and value, then the last steps of finishing a piece are much easier.

I find that it's important throughout the process to look at the overall image from different distances–both by moving far away from the desk and by scaling the image down–as one can easily get overwhelmed with the details of an image.

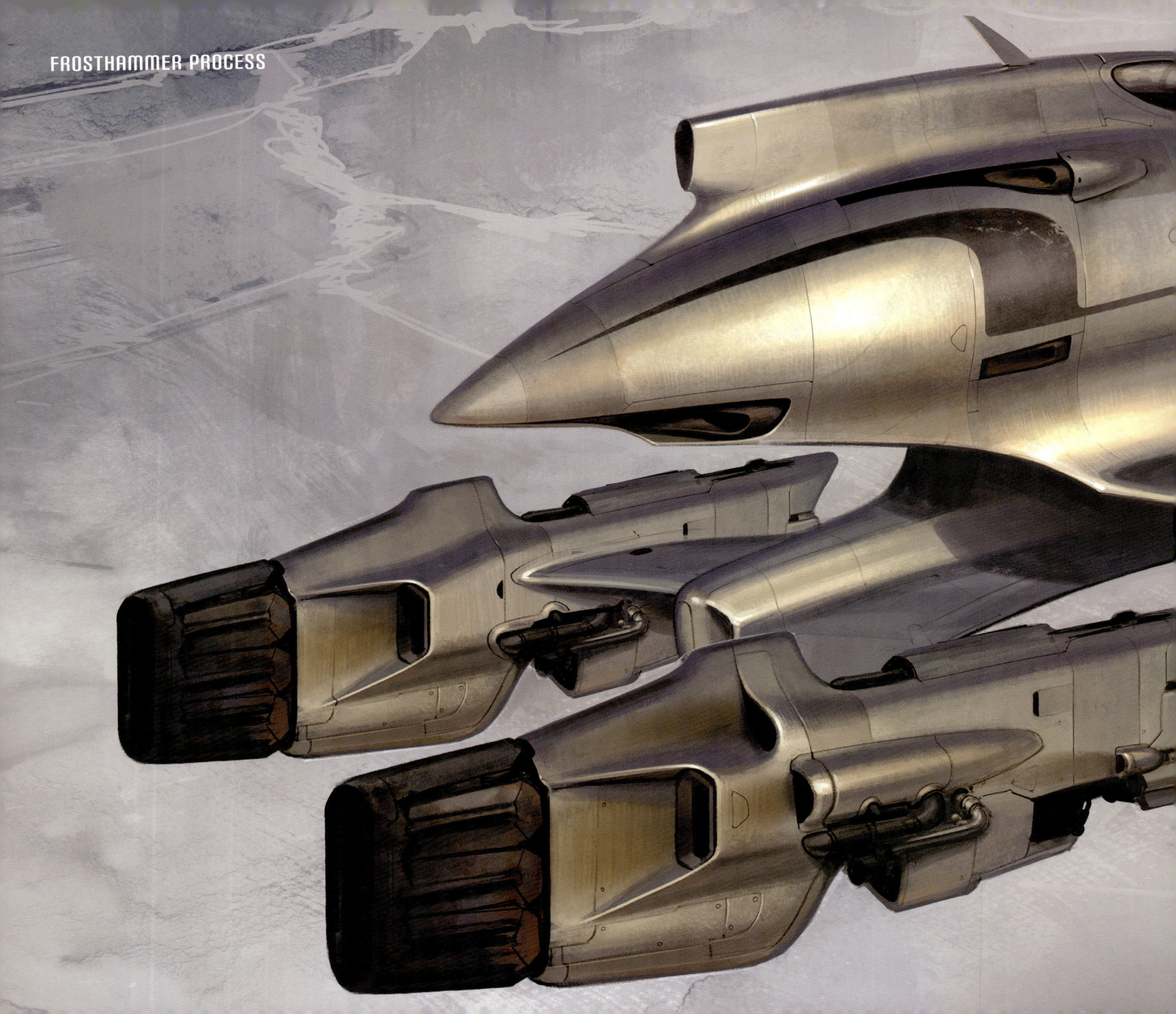

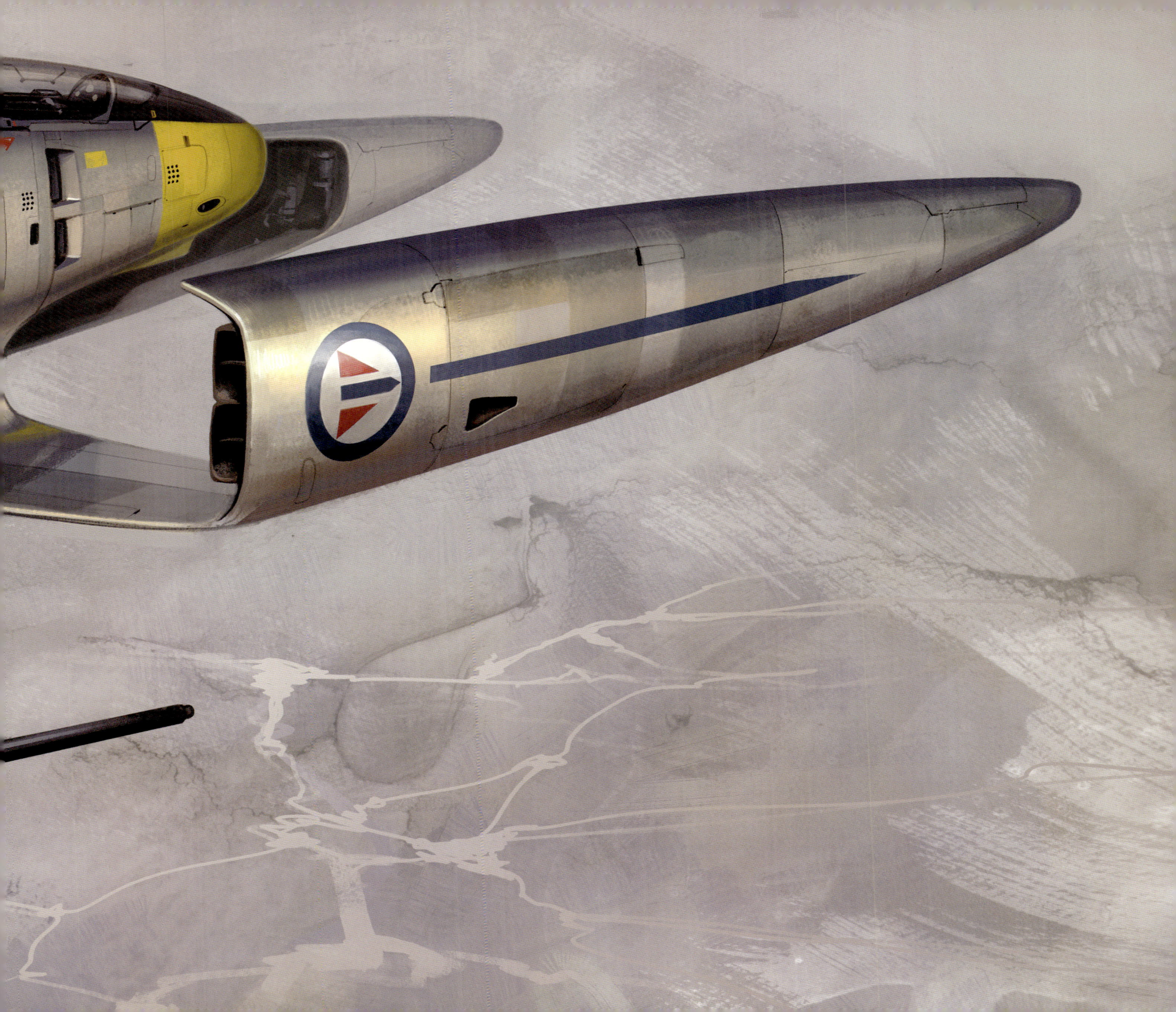

3

CHAPTER 3 : AUTONOMOUS RACING

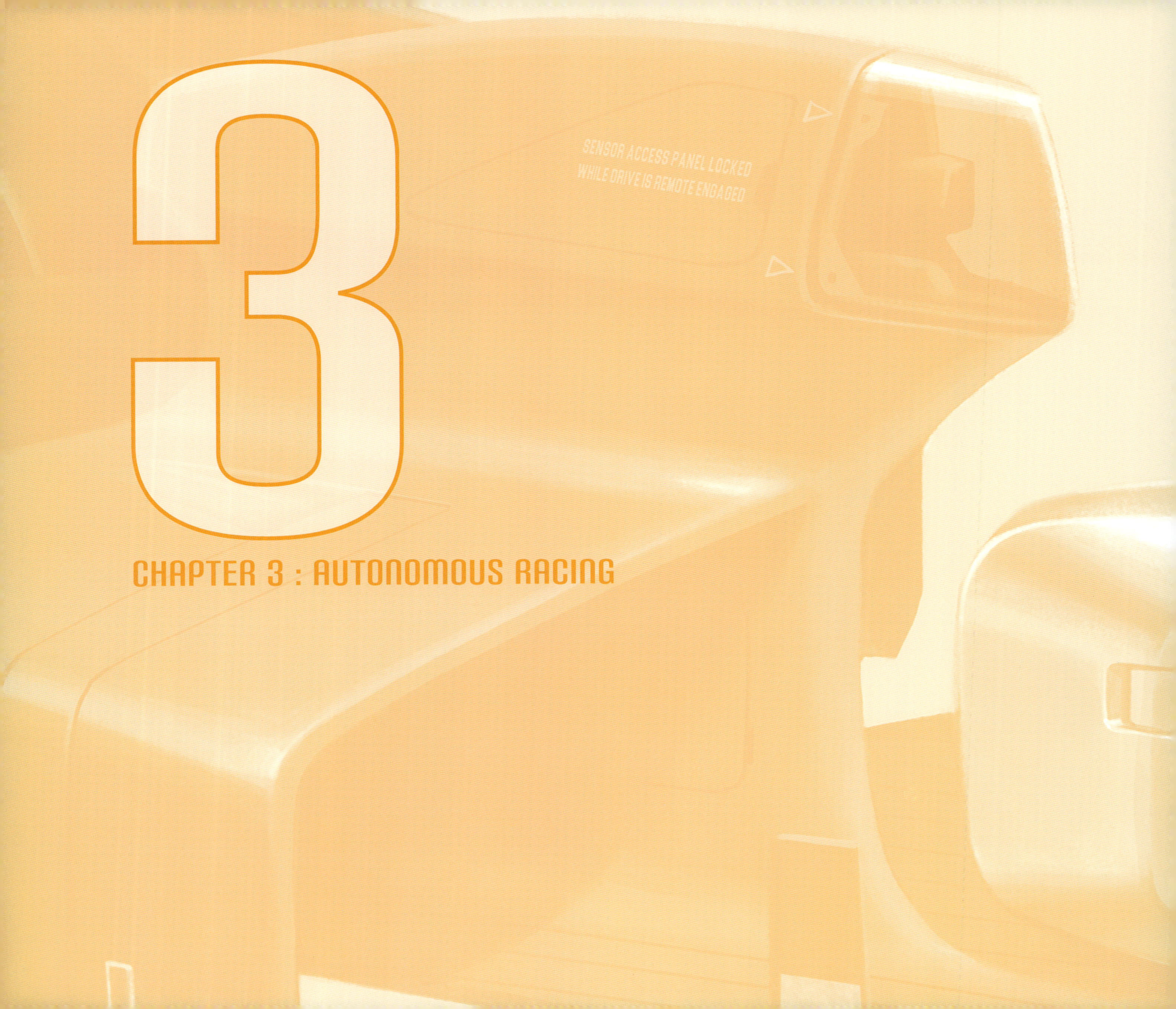

One of my favorite ideas to explore is autonomous racing. Surely, as I write these words, the technology is already advancing, and these ideas will be well out of date in the near future. We will be passengers, fully reclined, in what was once the driver's seat, eyes closed, and relaxing with our favorite music. Perhaps it was agreed that auto racing could only continue if the vehicles were driverless. In the 1960s, transistors, radio, maybe radar or other primitive auto-navigation systems would have been needed, maybe even punch-card programming for each circuit.

For this series of cars, I devised an arbitrary set of rules to suit a particular appearance of the cars, as racing rules tend to develop and dictate what cars can look like from one generation to the next. In addition to eliminating the driver, I decided to dictate a neutral downforce regulation: no wings for anything beyond straight-line stabilization. Wings are normally added to race cars to direct air pressure that acts upon the vehicle to push it down onto the road. This has been a Pandora's box of sorts because aero development adds more complication and expense to vehicle designs. A neutral downforce regulation would try to eliminate the wild mess of winglets, oddly bent surfaces, and ugly twisted body forms, simplifying the cars and reducing the investment of competition. The result? All bodies that allude to prewar racers and a jarring imbalance of front and rear tire size. This is a nod to a hot-rod aesthetic and also conceptually dictated so that the cars would be forced to powerslide their way around the track, lighting up the rears to keep from understeering.

The series picks points along the conceptual history, such as 1960s simple cigar-shaped bodies and the 1970s boxier carbon-chassis designs, and even some closed-wheel ideas. Throughout, the designs visually emphasize the absence of the driver, removing mass specifically where the driver compartment would be with the specific intent of creating an alien and unusual mass and silhouette in its place. Referencing actual liveries makes the brain feel somewhat comforted by the familiarity of something seen before. And the sponsor names and race locations spelled out on the hypothetical model-box packaging remind one with a good knowledge of the history of motorsport that this is something outside of the one that we know. As for naming the cars, I generally try to trigger a sense of familiarity with references in colors and words used for many of them. The names often call back aurally to specific cars but remix and reimagine the words in a way that's off just enough to be funny sounding.

Competition through organized racing has always encouraged new technologies and optimized existing ones in the pursuit of victory. What if the driver were removed from the equation decades ago, put into action by a governing board after some raceway tragedy?

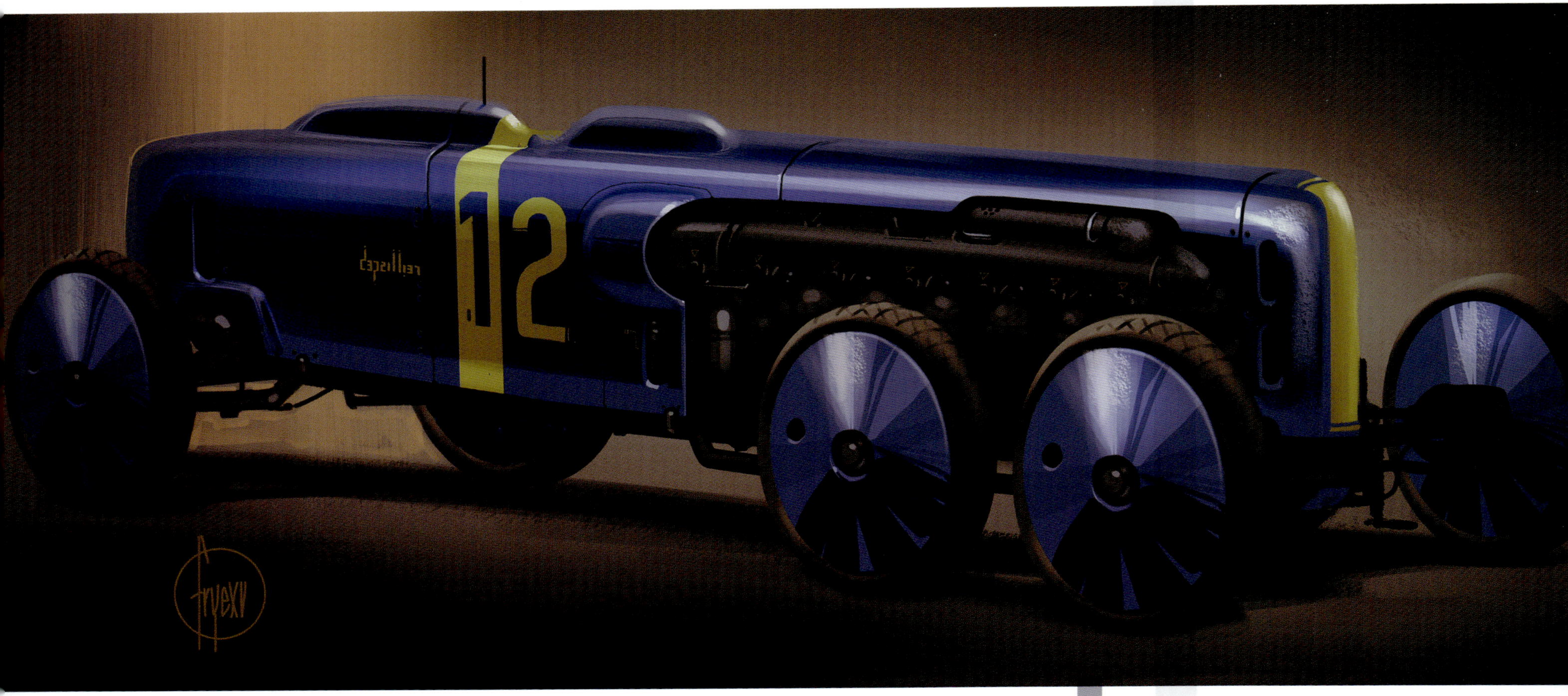

This sketch brought together my love of early 1900s race cars with the six-wheeled 1975 Tyrrell P-34. Autonomy as a concept allowed me to drop any concern about human packaging and sculpt the fuselage in any clean shape I wanted. This sketch was the impetus for all box art I designed for the open-wheel, autonomous model kits.

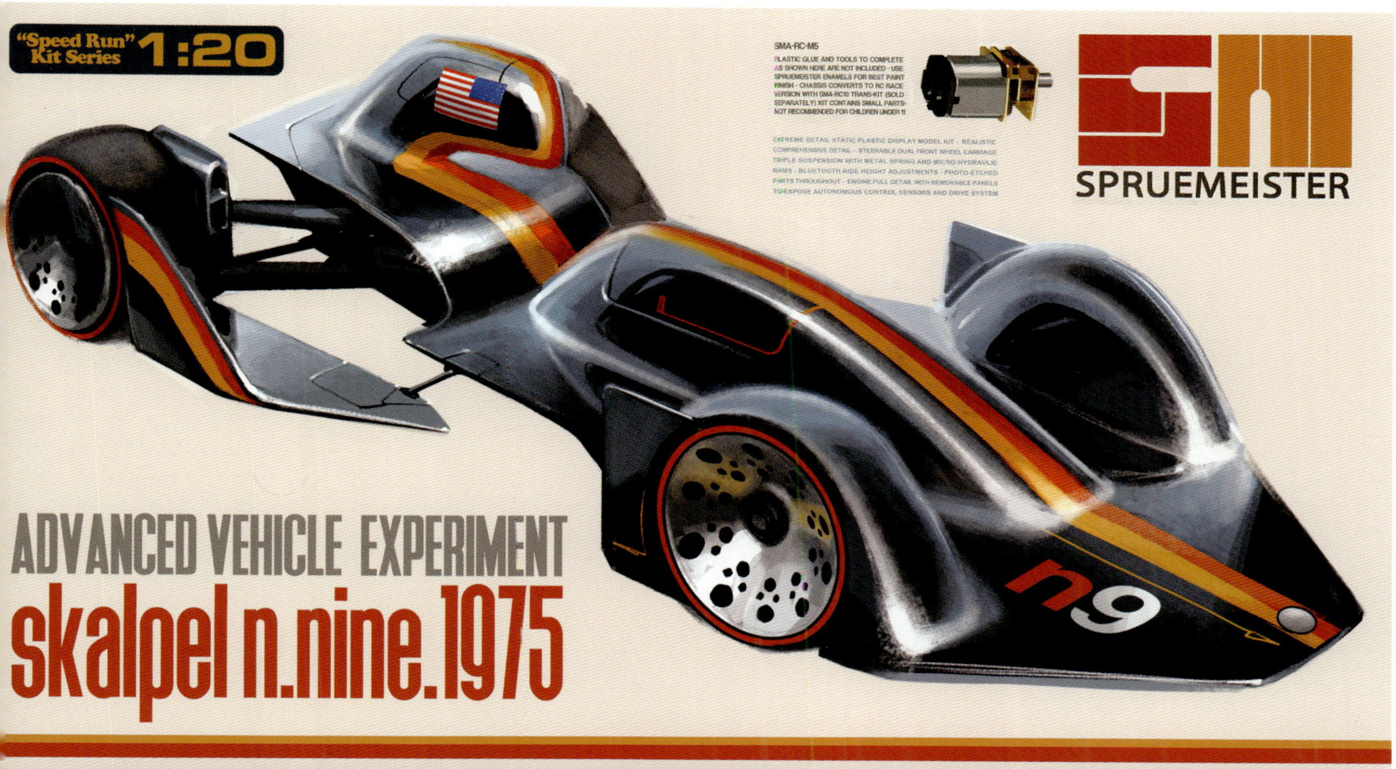

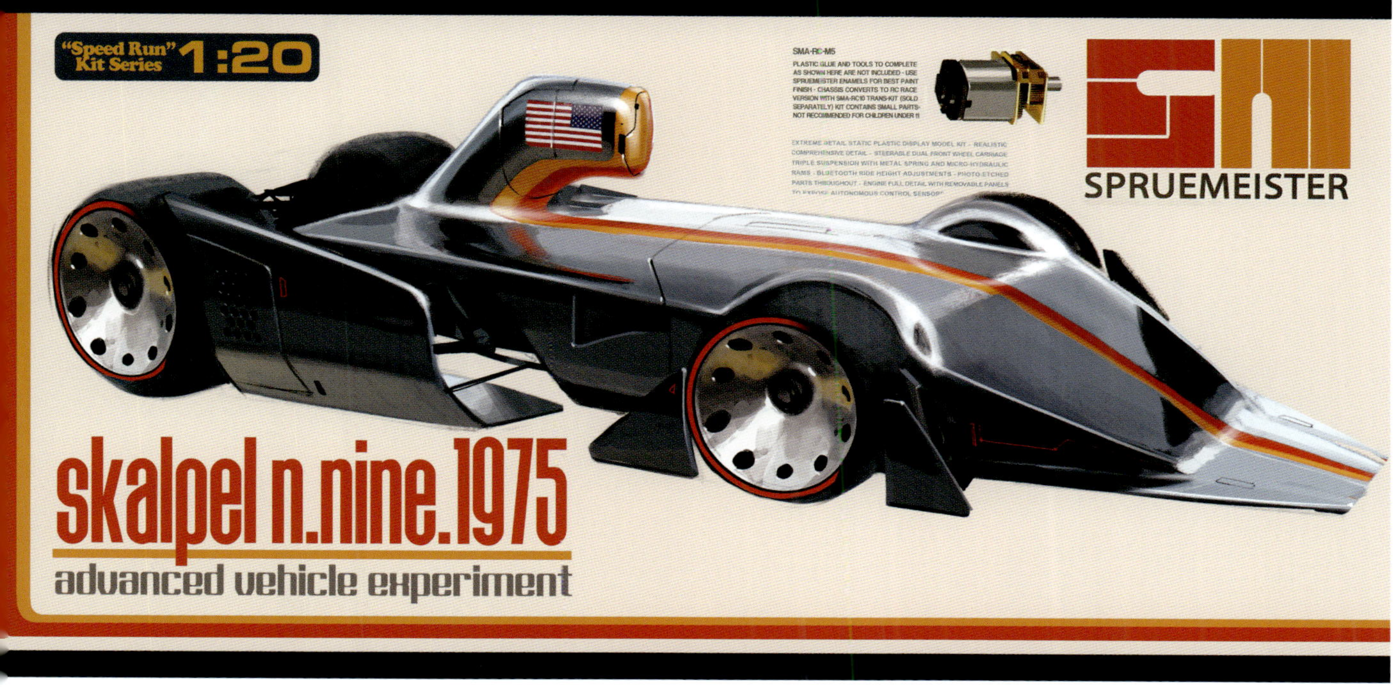

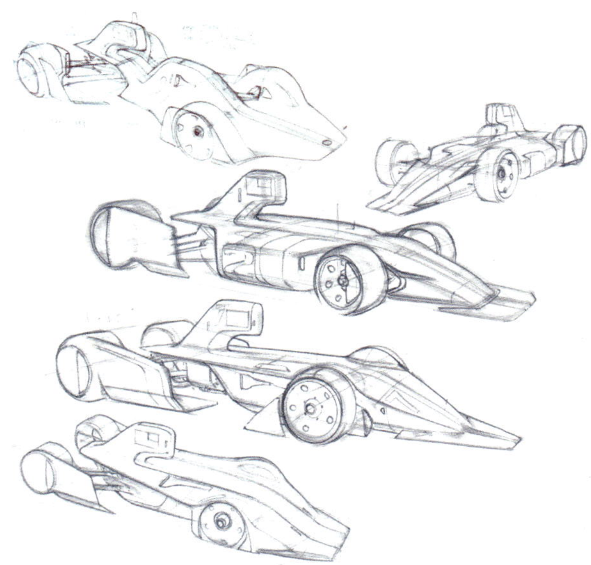

Referencing the ultra-low Shadow Can-Am race-car concepts from the early to mid-1970s, the wheels and engine box are draped with a blanket of melted bodywork that flows to the ground. As always, stripes make it appear faster, but here, red and orange against black specifically sets the era. The color work was for a quick comp only; the illustration was taken no further than this stage.

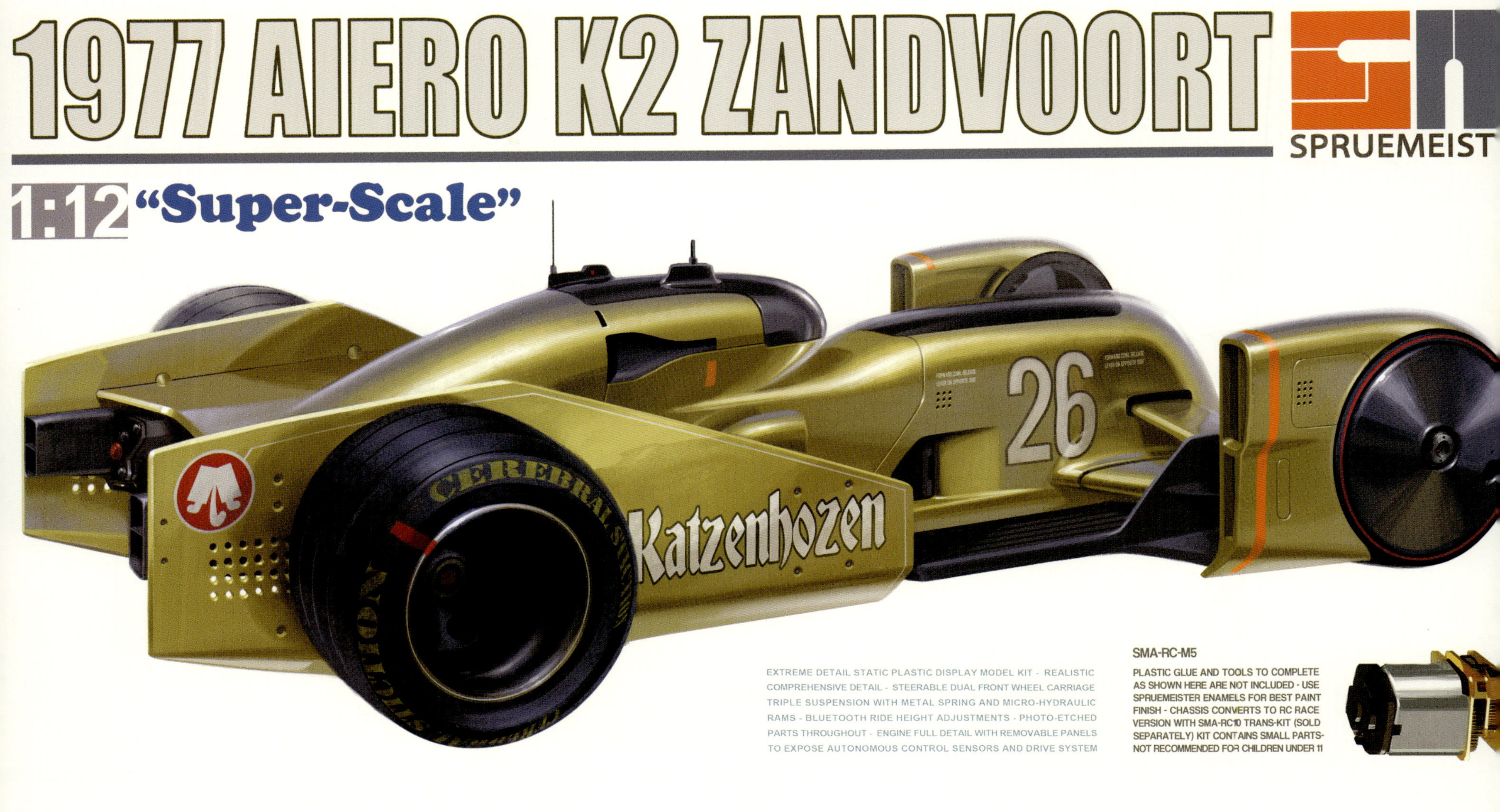

A vision in gold, wingless and stuck to the track with outrageous fat rubber and ground effects, the Aiero has long side panels that serve as wonderful space for sponsor branding. Upper-rounded fuselage surfaces were helpful to play up the lovely color shifts that happen when metallic gold paint wraps over a surface in the sunlight.

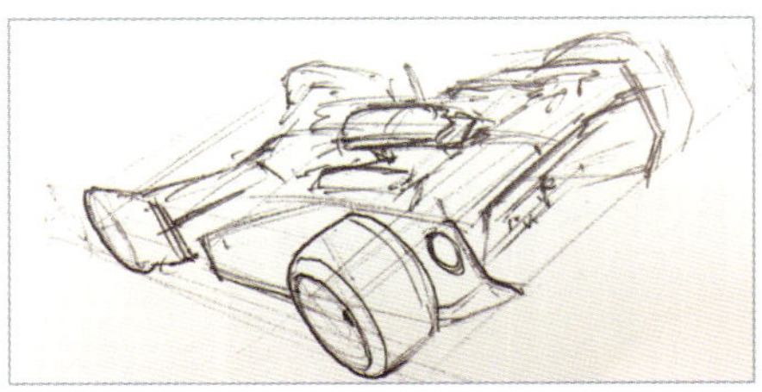

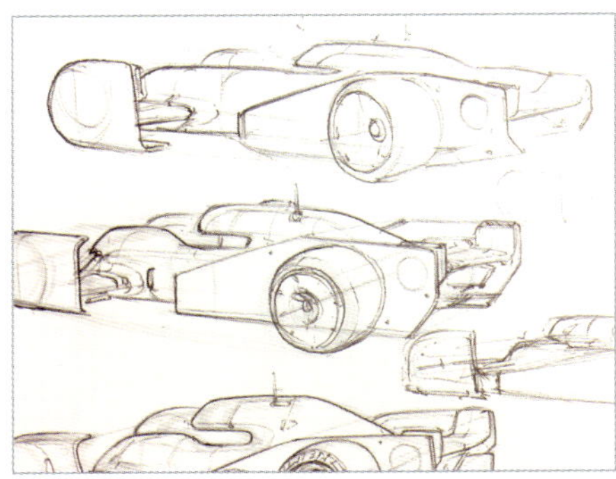

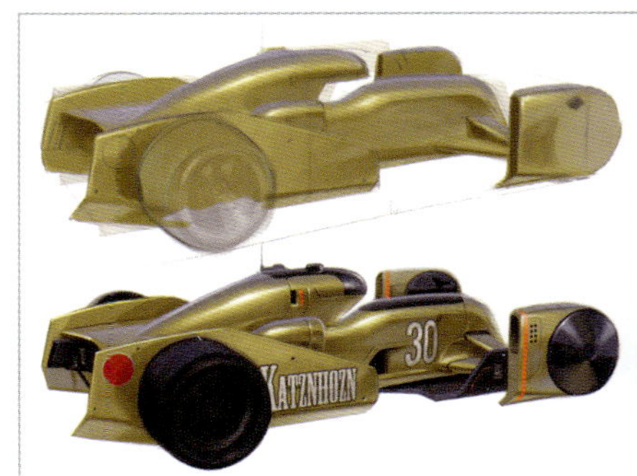

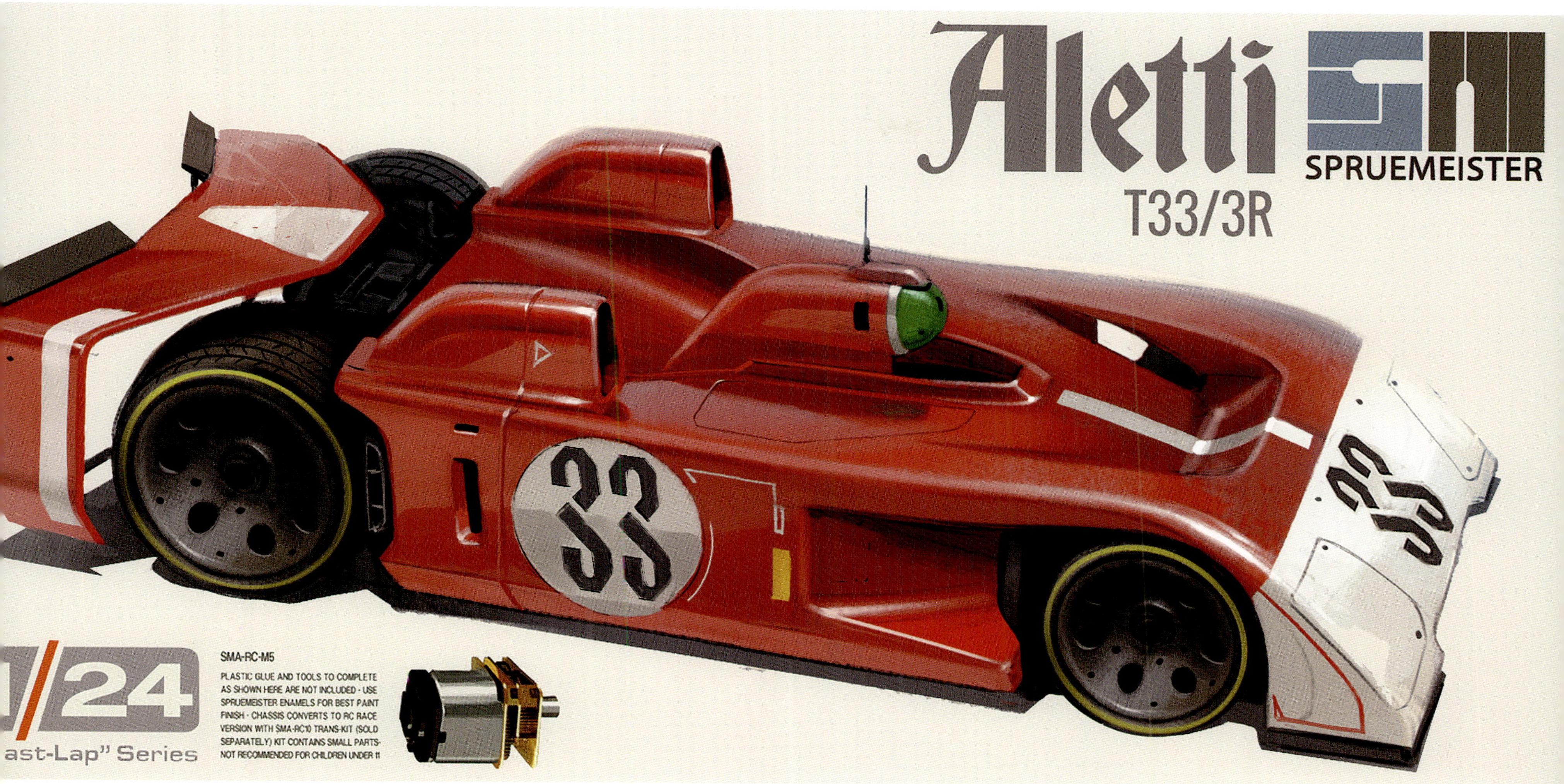

The broad-stroke graphics used to differentiate teammates on race cars are as attractive as they were functional. A nose dipped in white was enough to make the Aletti memorable. Cars of this era were often smoothed and refined based on best-guess aerodynamics, while the rears of the cars were just left to nature, open and exposed, as it was assumed the airflow in back didn't matter so much.

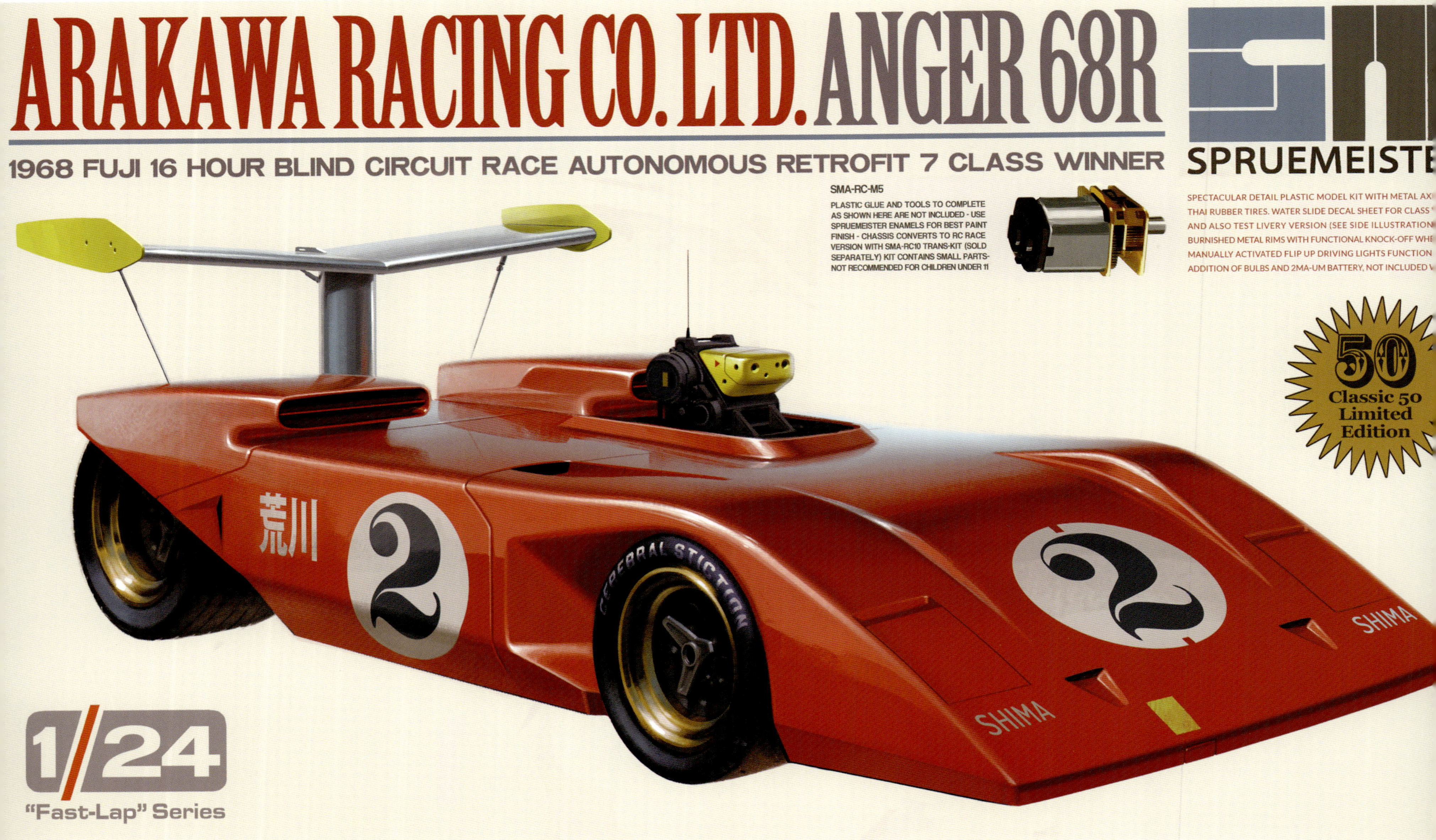

Another period Can-Am doorstop, the 68R is pure in form, with interest in the treatment around the wheels and a tensioned high-mounted **dihedral** wing with Day-Glo endplates. The colors are a nod to Pete Brock's famed Hino Samurai design. This design sketch indicates an autonomous retrofit with a sensor pod installed in the human-driver position.

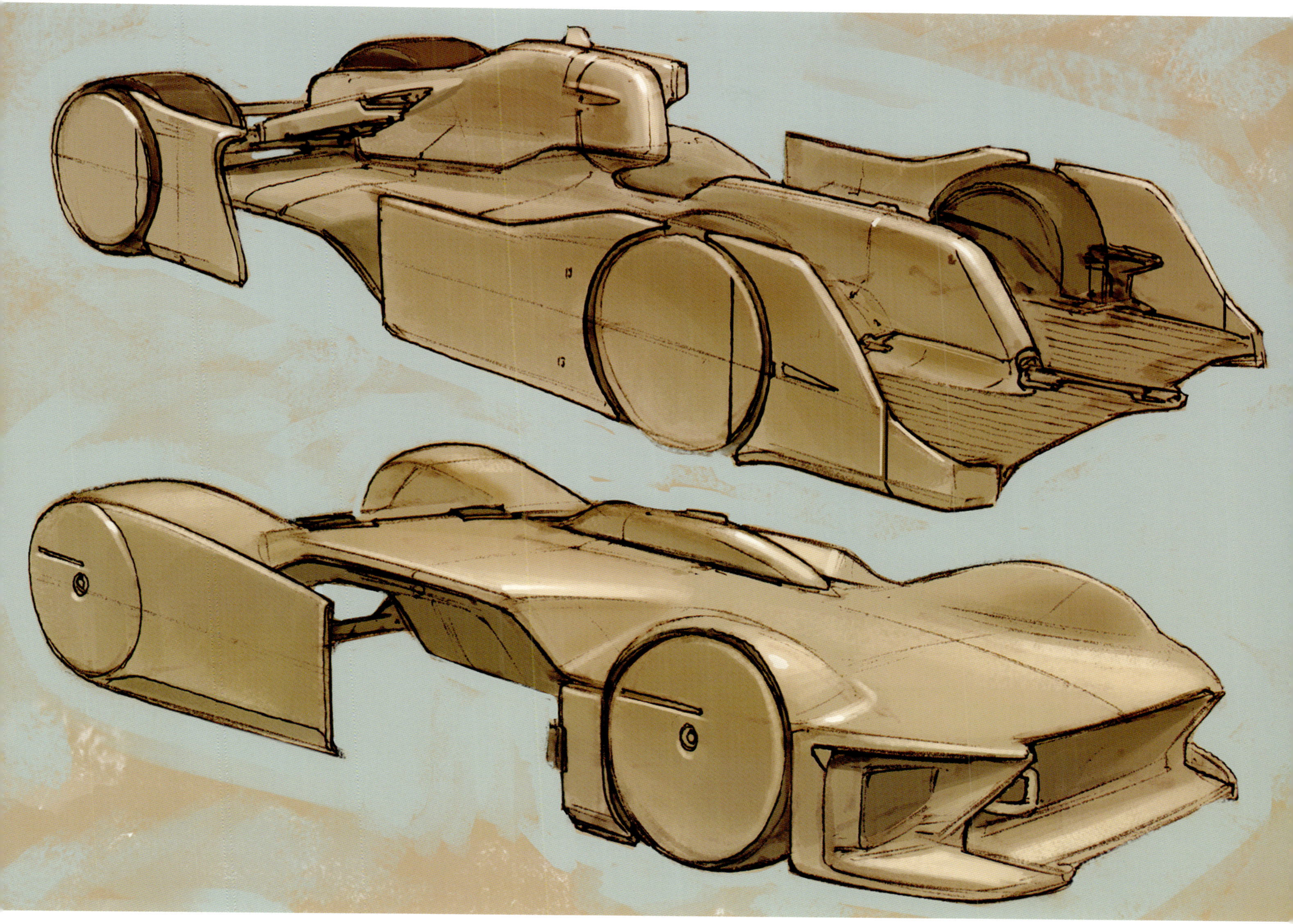

Doodling autonomous race bodies, I cut away mass in new and unexpected ways, using a strong turquoise background to highlight the silhouette of the shape.

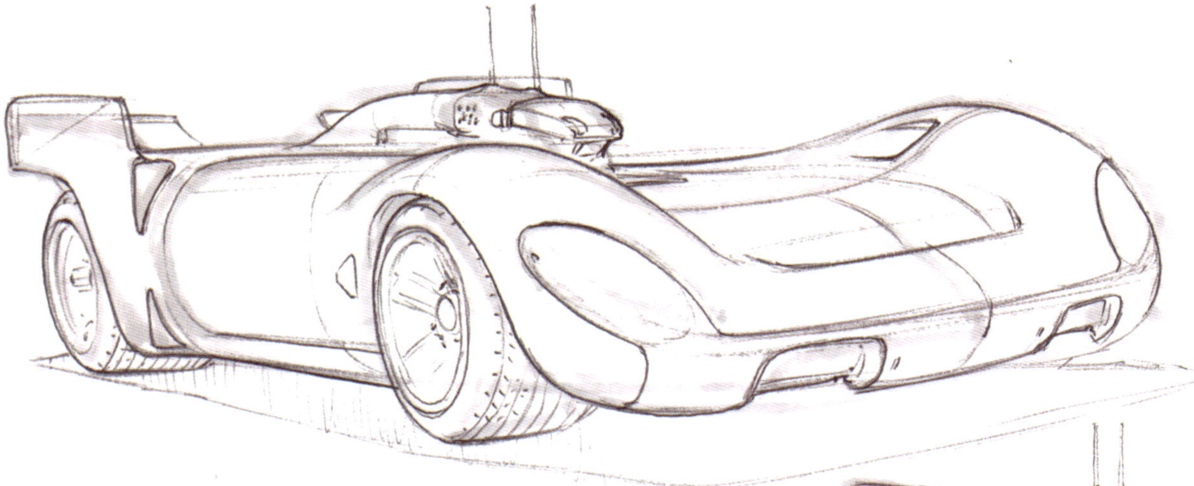

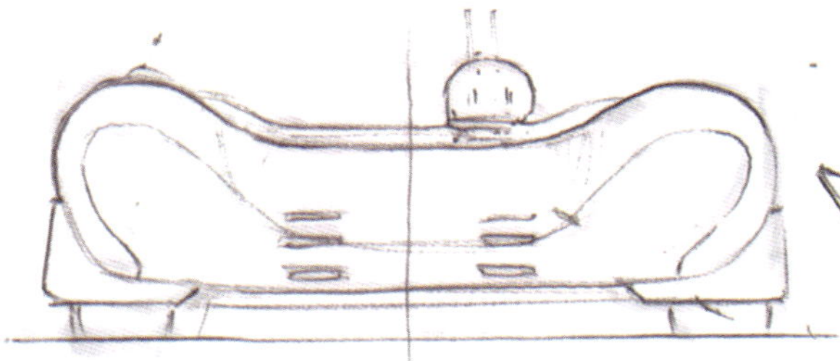

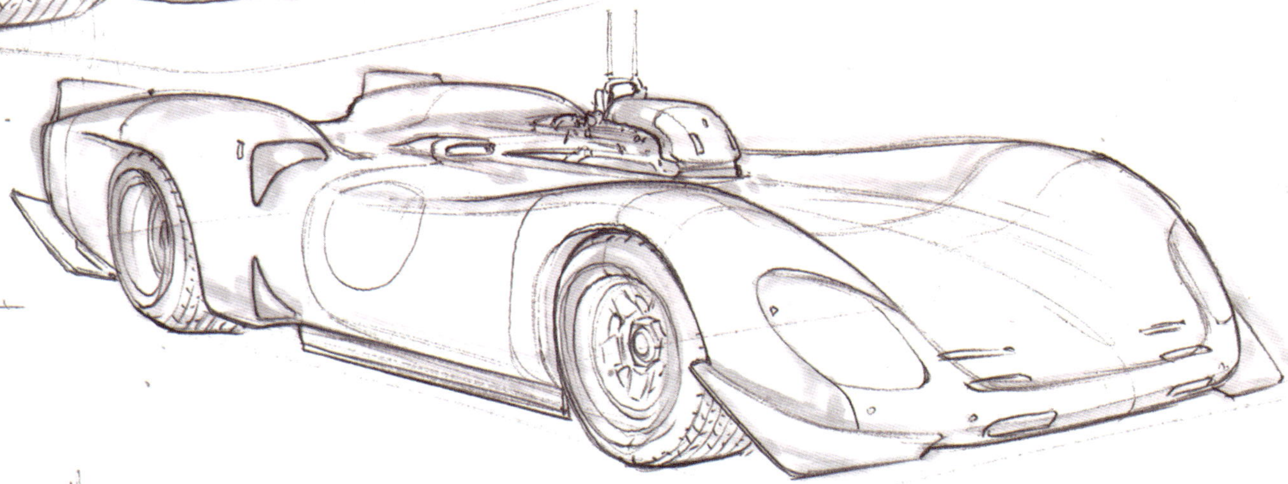

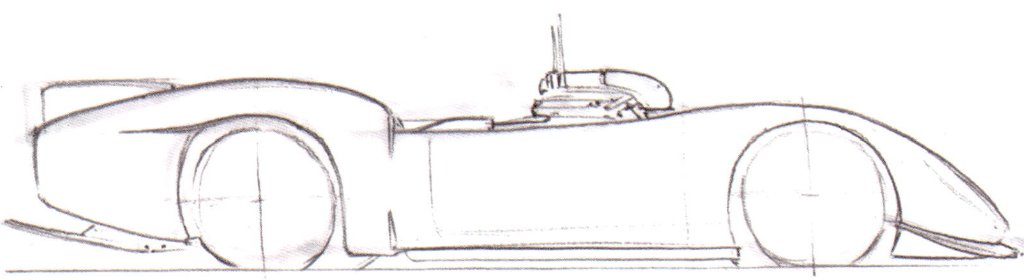

Liquidy 1960s form language and thoughts of Porsches shaped these expressive studies. While colorful graphic options were infinite, maybe my indecision on where to take it is why the sketch was never illustrated completely.

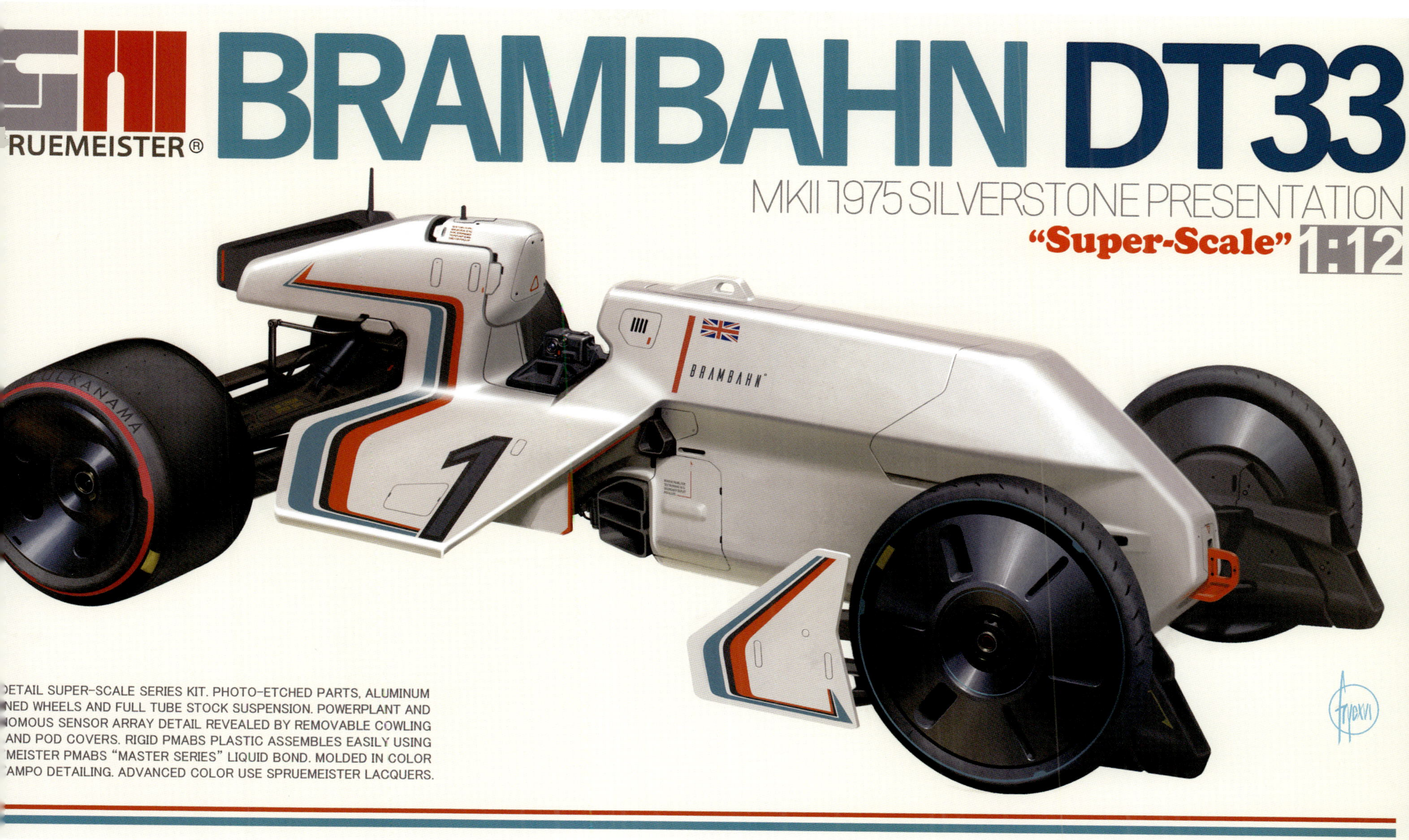

White-pearl paint, a trapezoidal structure, and solid black wheels define the strong base in this minimalist design. The color details seem to allude to the selling of a beverage, but the overall graphic balance is simply classic.

TEAM MODENA-CYBER TYP. L1-AUTONOMA

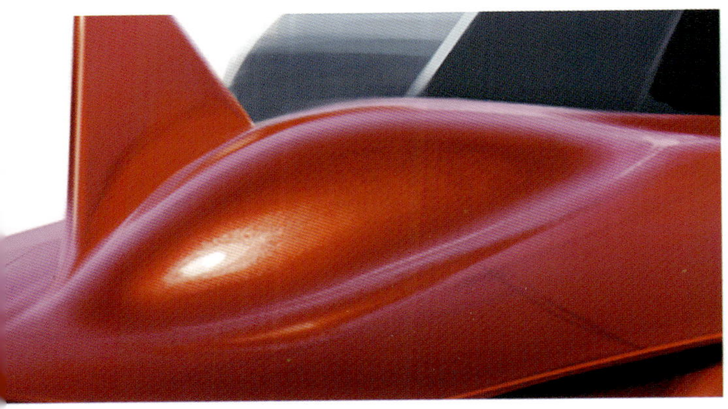

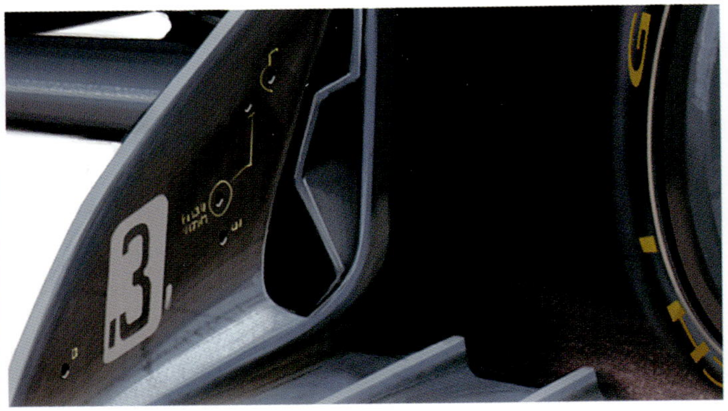

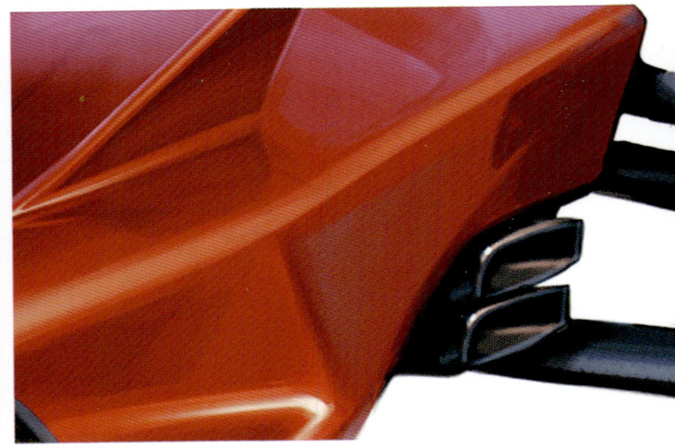

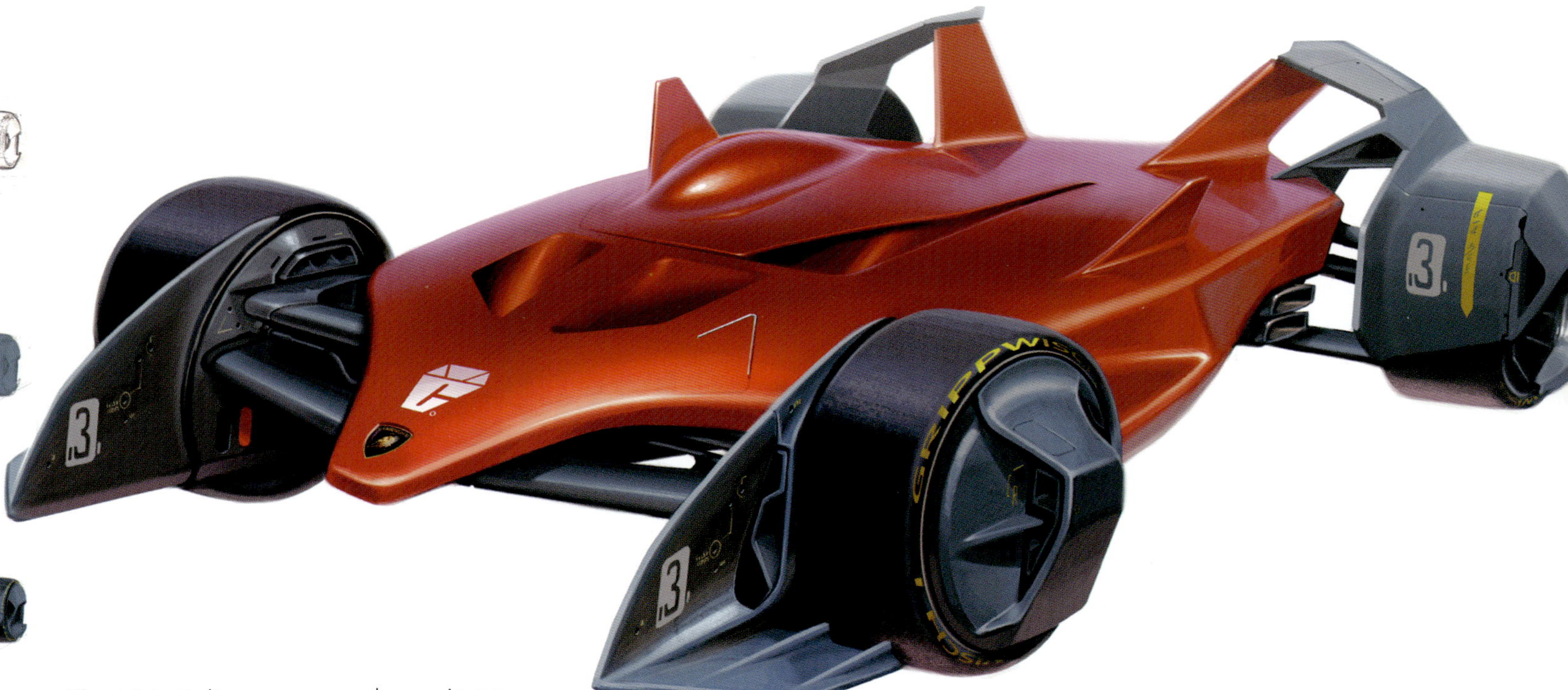

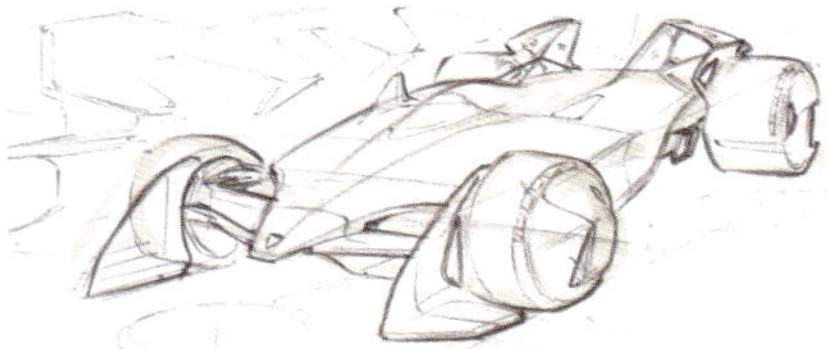

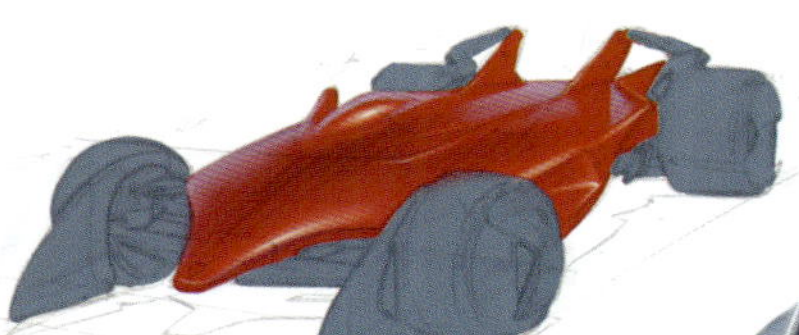

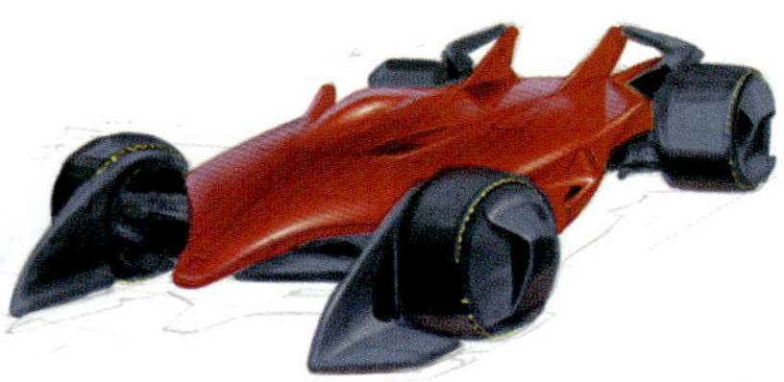

The L1 is Italian supercar drama in an open-wheeled autonomous wide shape. One of the most modern designs in the autonomous series, the rubber is fat at all corners, and the sensor equipment is fully integrated into the design, eliminating any need for a tall sensor pod.

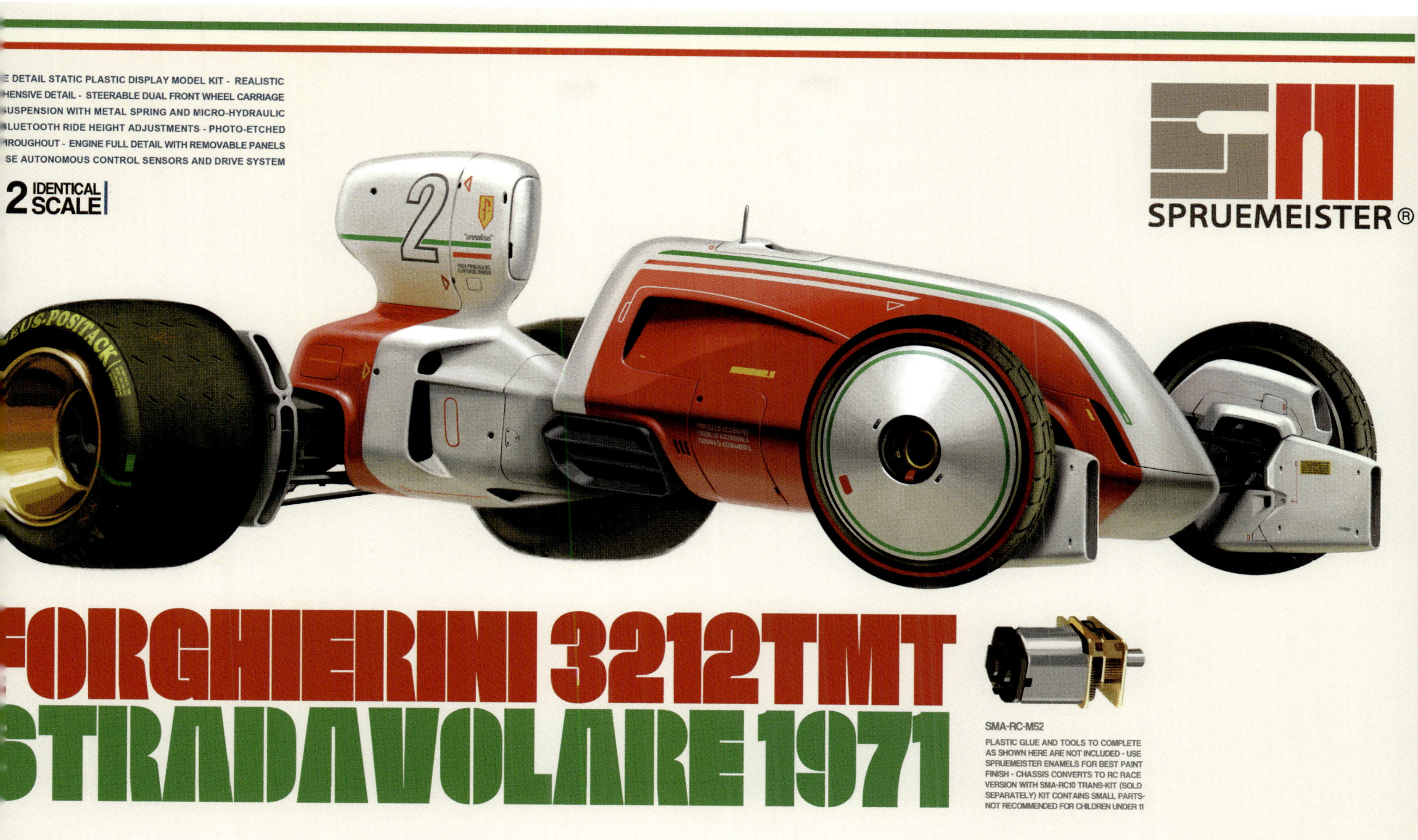

This model represents the iconic shape expression of the open-wheel, autonomous race design series. The tall and narrow front area suggests an unusual but undefined powertrain technology, and then the shape drops down to highlight thematically the absence of a driver. The negative space is possible only by the elimination of human-packaging constraints. Large sensor pod dominates the profile and alludes to the tall air-box generation of Formula 1 cars. T-bucket-style hot-rod elements collide with the F1 references, raked chassis, fat rear tires, and skinny fronts. The polarizing tire concept functionally suggests a computer-controlled lighting up of the rears would be needed to negate strong understeering and produce better on-track action for the spectators.

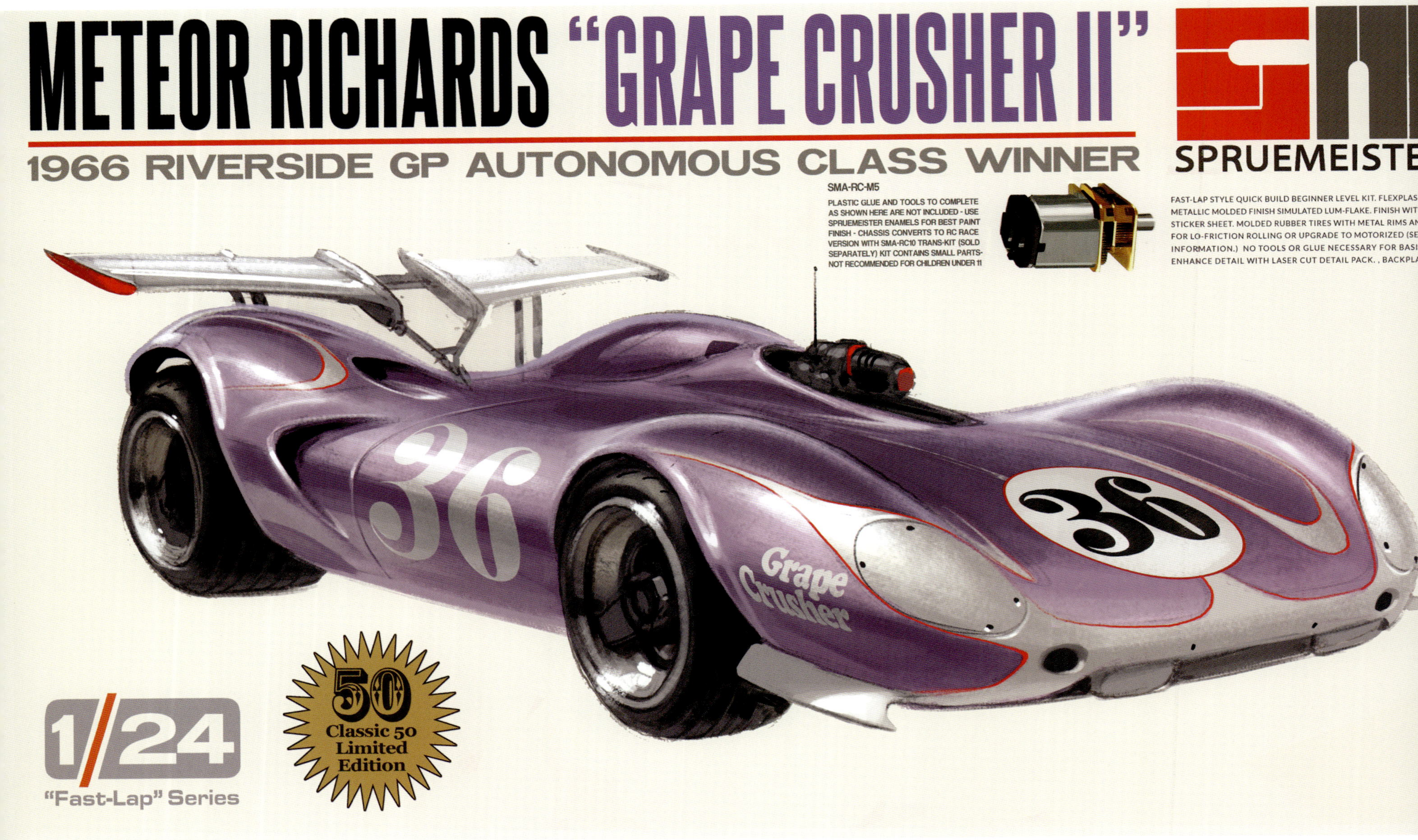

Painted metallic lavender, the Grape Crusher II features hand-formed, mid-1960s aluminum bodywork with old-school garage pinstriping. With independently adjustable rear wings, they were quickly reigned in by rule makers,who sought to clamp down on dangerous aero experimentation. The car's overall impression was heavily inspired by the late 1960s Paul Newman-sponsored Honker II Can-Am car from Ford and Holman-Moody.

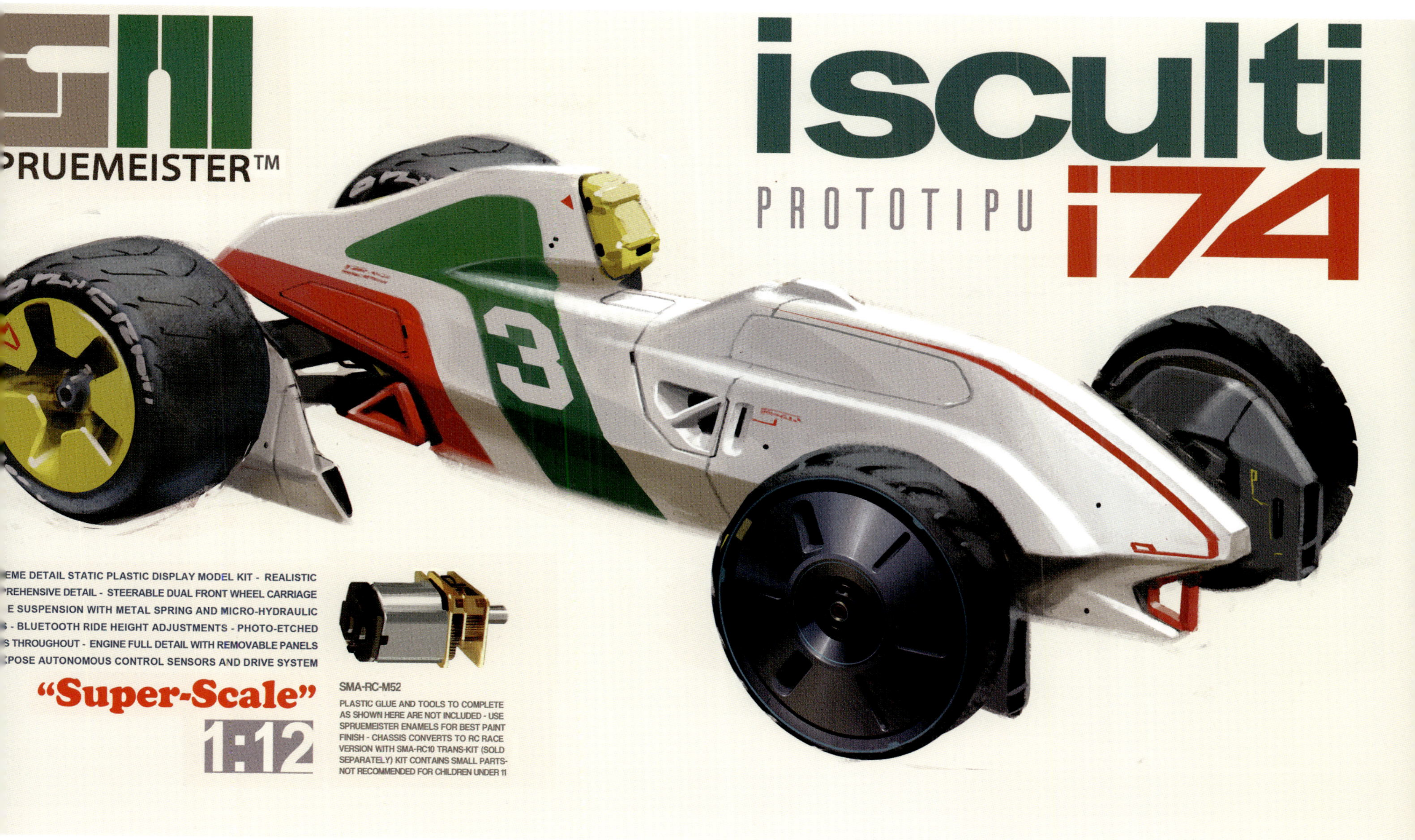

Compact proportions and an Italian rally-car genetic structure define the i74. The iconic colors of the Alitalia Airlines make an appearance here as a nod to the unforgettable Lancia Stratos rally car—one of my favorite automotive designs of all time that made its debut at the Turin motor show in late 1971.

LOTRON 77SP "JONES PLANAR SPECIAL"

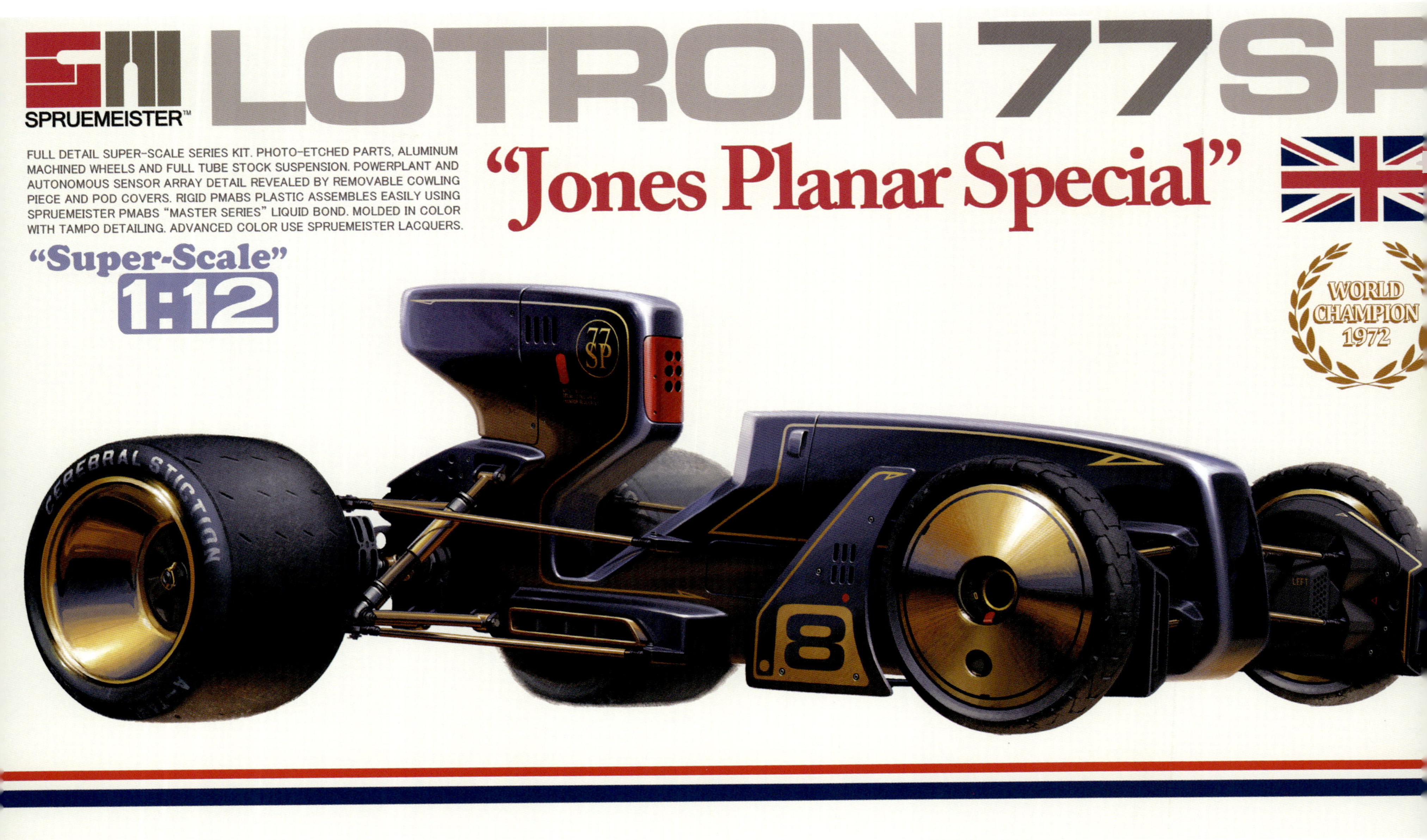

This was a livery I was obsessed with doing and doing right. Gold and gloss black can have a lot of color coming from the environment: purply blue, orangey ground tones. I added a couple spots of red detail to the vehicle to balance it all out. The crudely boxy, but deliberate and hot-rod posturing, design is accentuated by the thin pinstripes of gold and detailing on the piano-black bodywork. Matte-black wheel covers are a secondary key material to add interest and depth. Working from the rough-color comp, the colors evolved into warmer rose gold.

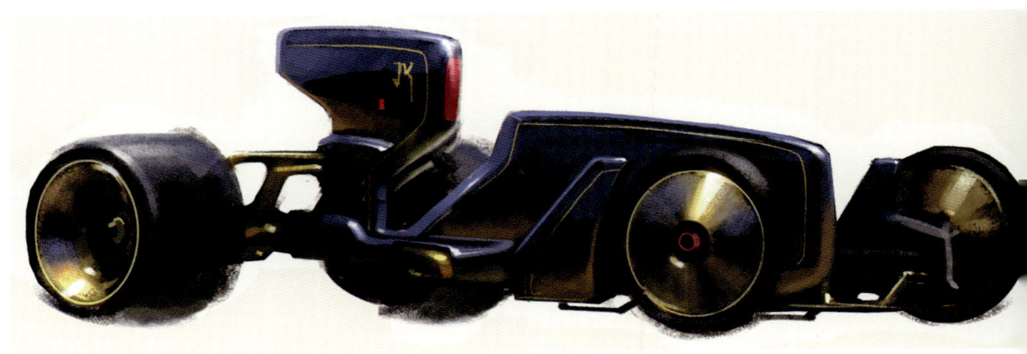

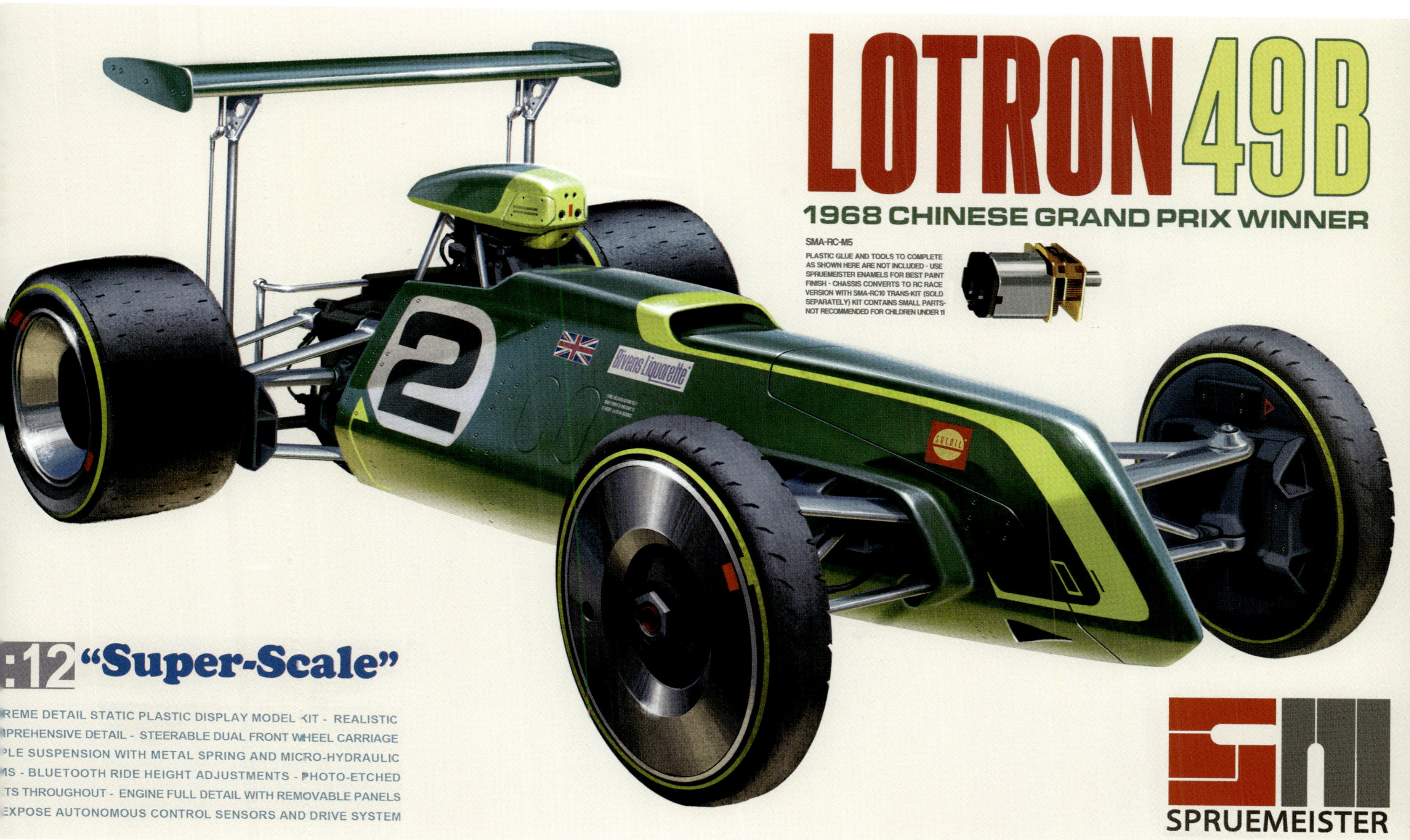

A minimalist design with spindly tubular suspension elements suggests careful attention to lightness and period-correct vulnerabilities. Cars in the 1960s were usually designed to be as light as possible, meaning safety was not considered as a serious priority. Parts often broke as they were built to last only for a race—brutally powerful but delicate. Notice that the race venue and year would be unlikely in our historical timeline, but designing within alternate realities allows for a world with fewer political tensions and more diverse competitive sport.

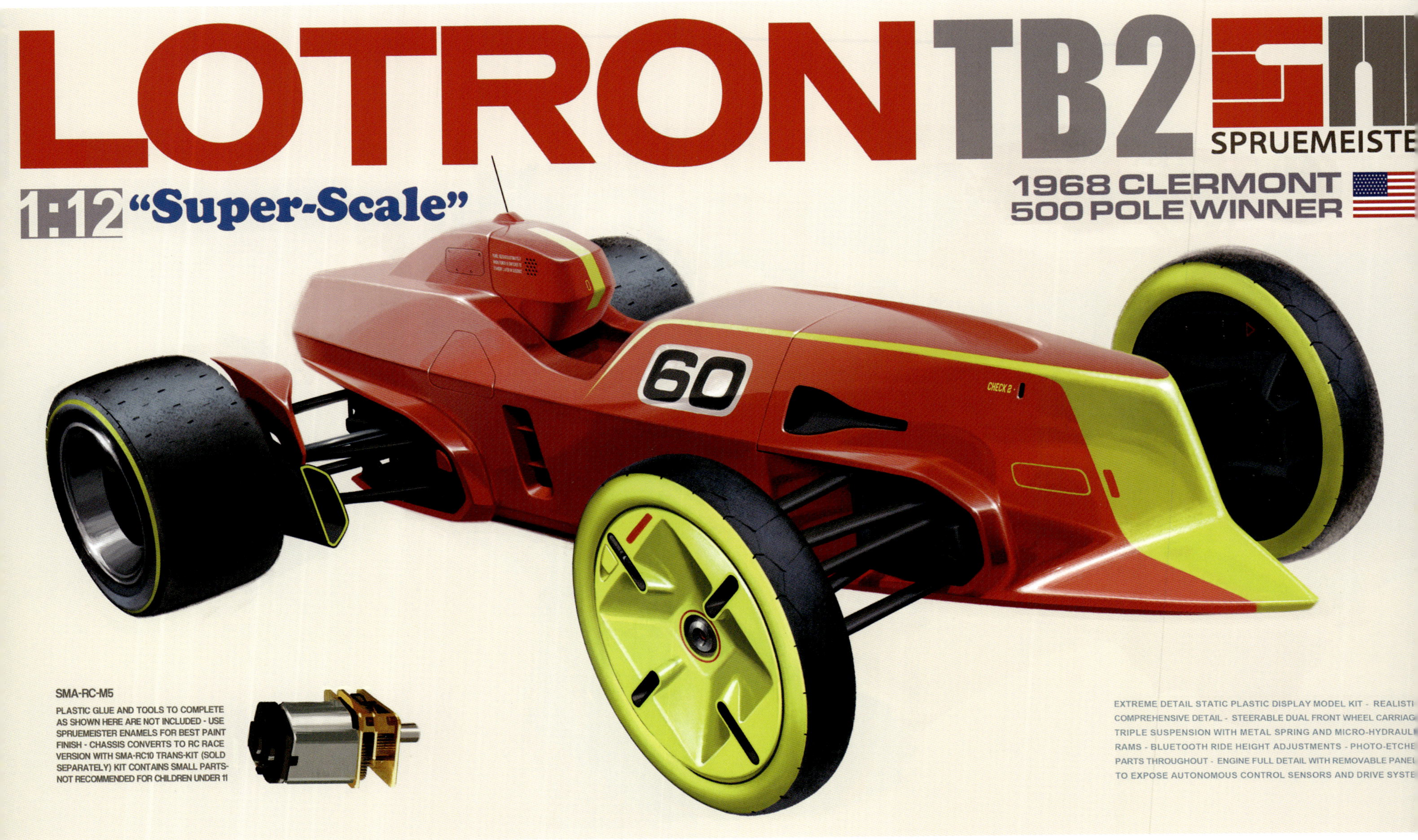

The Day-Glo yellow edged axe blade is designed to cleave the air and the competition on the massive 12-mile triple radius Clermont oval track. Its color and form are inspired by the STP Lotus Indy car driven by Joe Leonard.

KOI 33

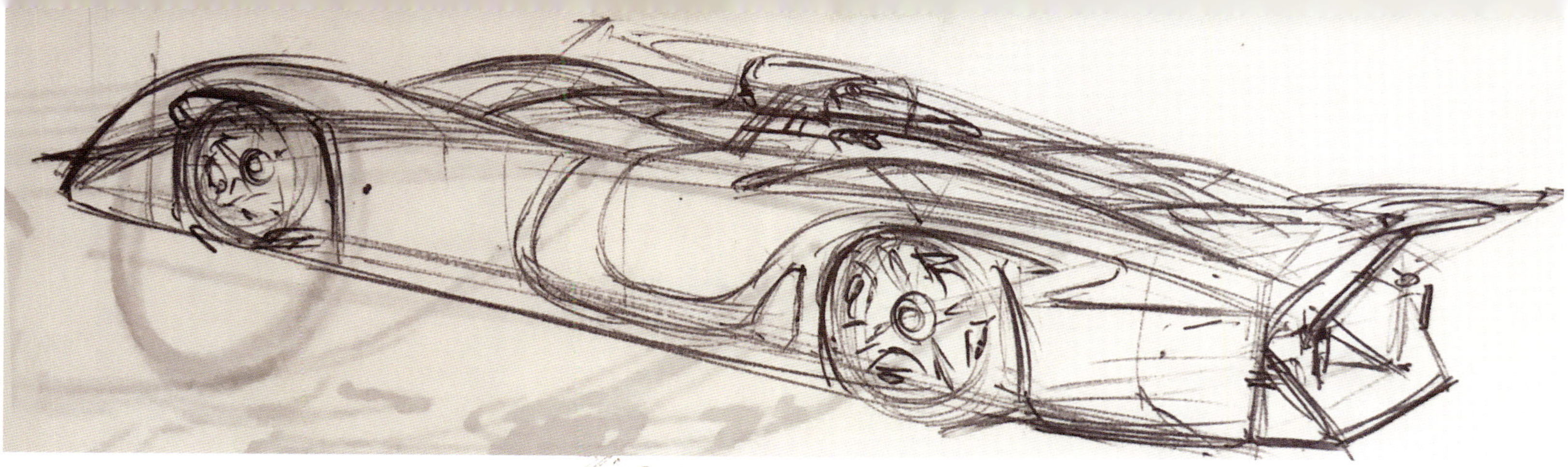

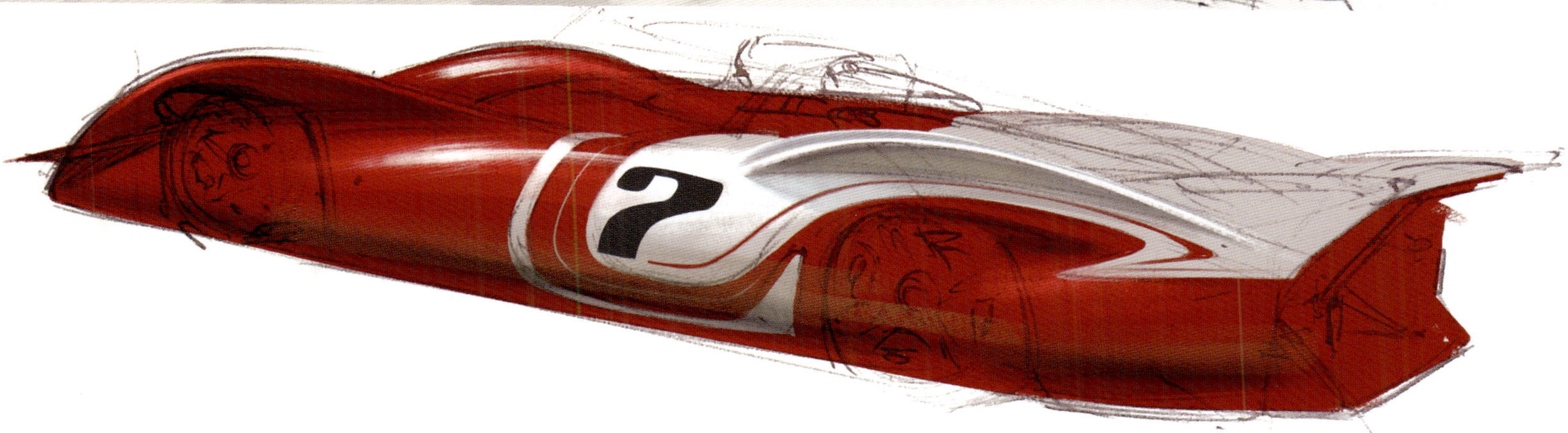

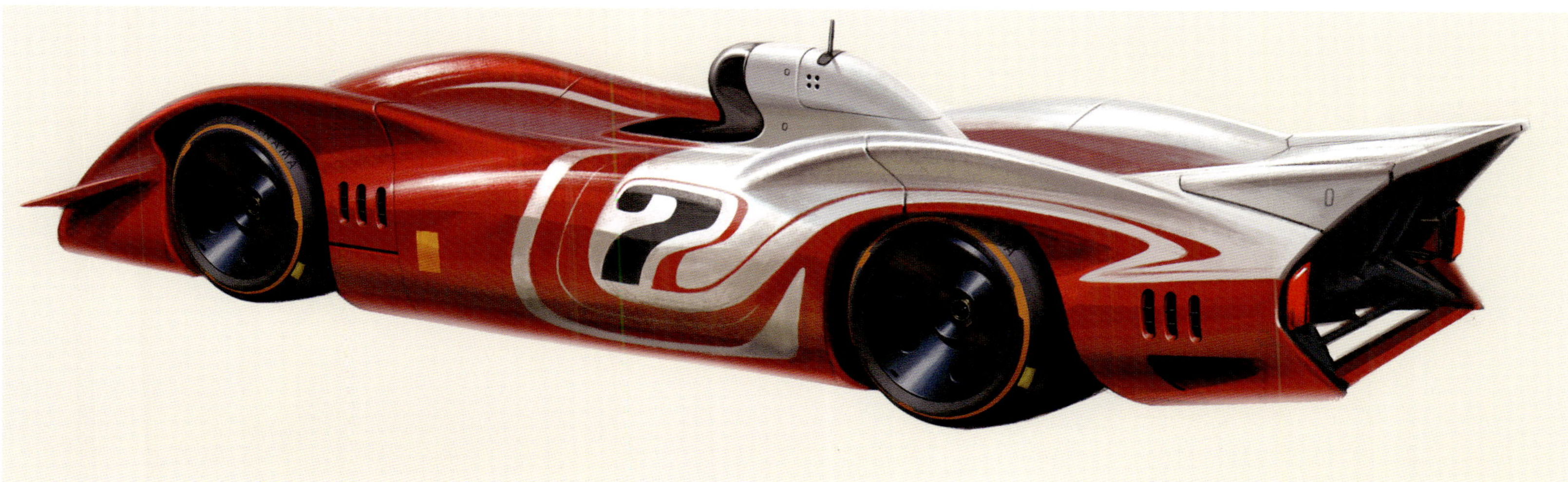

Care for something fishy, but pretty? This has Group 6 vibes, circa 1968. My three-step sequence shows the vigorous ballpoint on paper sketch, shot with my camera phone and sent to my computer to color up in Photoshop. Sometimes I won't have time to take a design much further than a quickly colored sketch, so I will grab some parts of previous sketches, but I refrain from using anyone else's work or photographs. I work hard to complete the illustration with elements drawn by myself. For this particular one, it was a late night and I was getting tired, so I grabbed the wheels off of another car that I had illustrated.

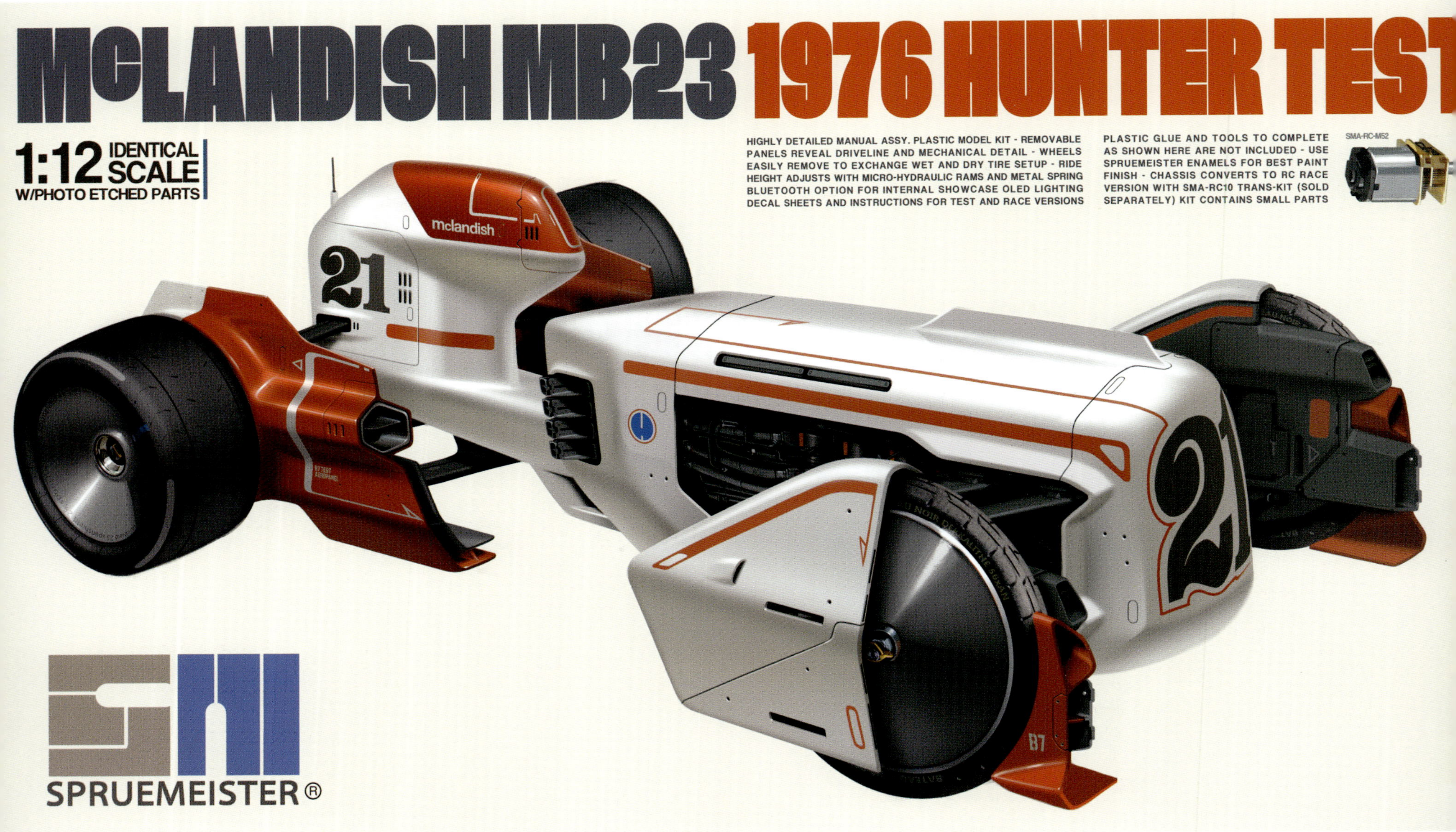

The MB23 is not at all a svelte design. In fact, the aero work around the wheels imply some desperate but misguided attempt for improved performance during the test. Engine side panels removed for the test session illustrated give a glimpse at the vertically proportioned mystery power plant.

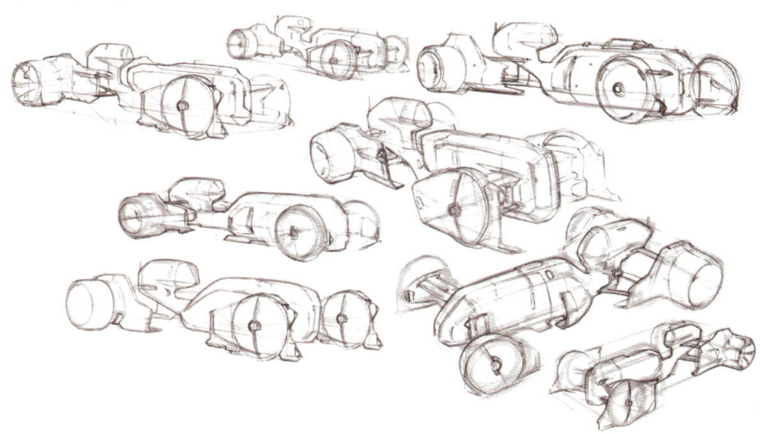

McLandish Profile NZ4/2 GP 1983

SPRUEMEISTER®

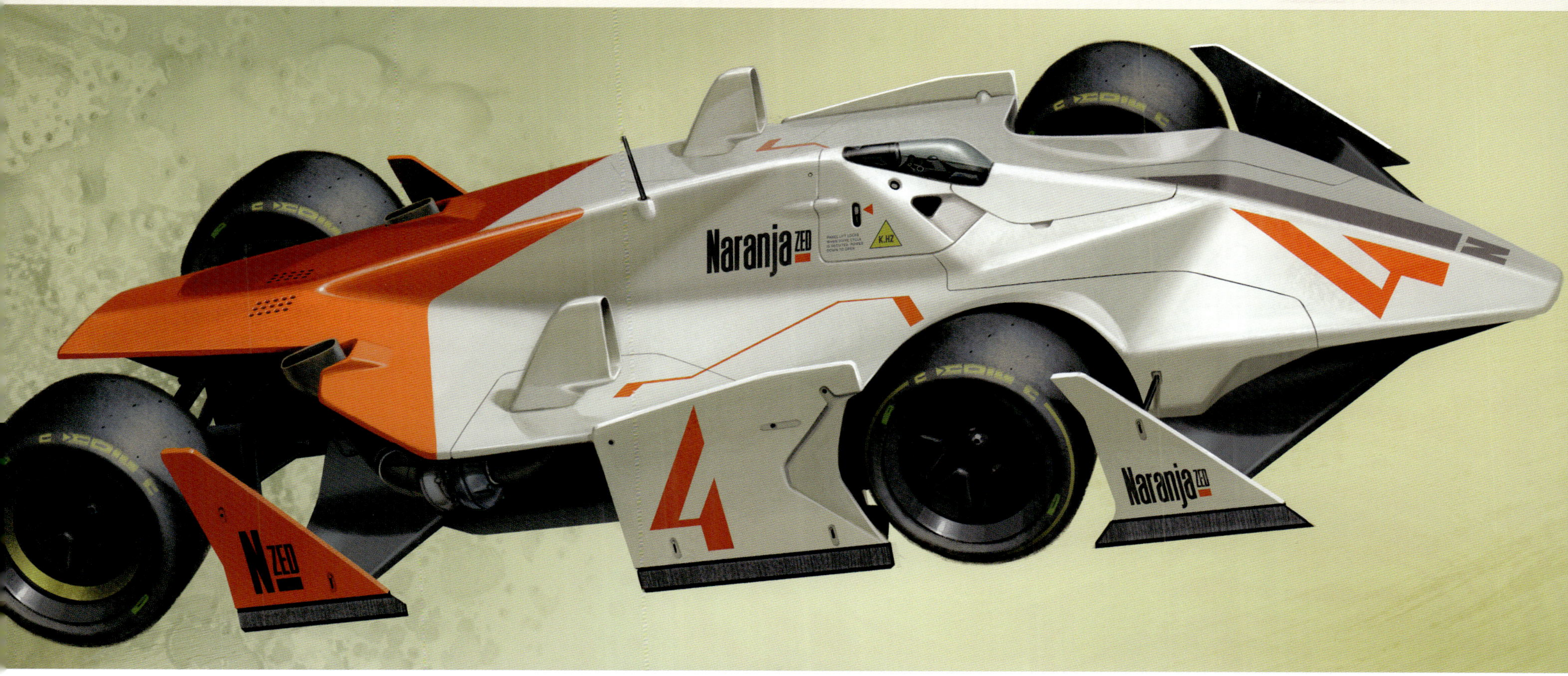

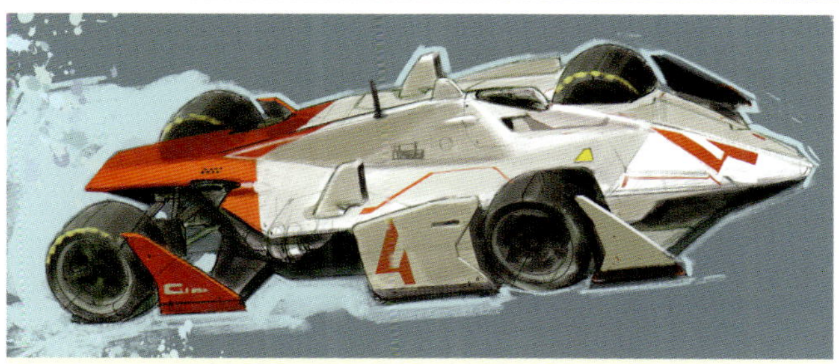

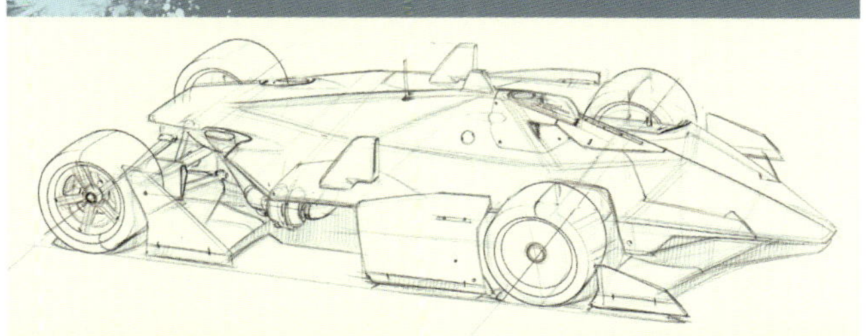

A few generations removed from the McLandish MB23, the NZ4/2 shows a very different aesthetic and set of rules. It is an autonomous alt-reality spin on the oddly bulky and cab-forward 1983 Formula 1 season, the last period where cars had exposed engine elements. The livery is familiar to attract nostalgia, but is a critically different aesthetic.

NAKAMA KUROYAMA NK302: WINNER 1966 MEXICAN 24-HOUR GRAND PRIX

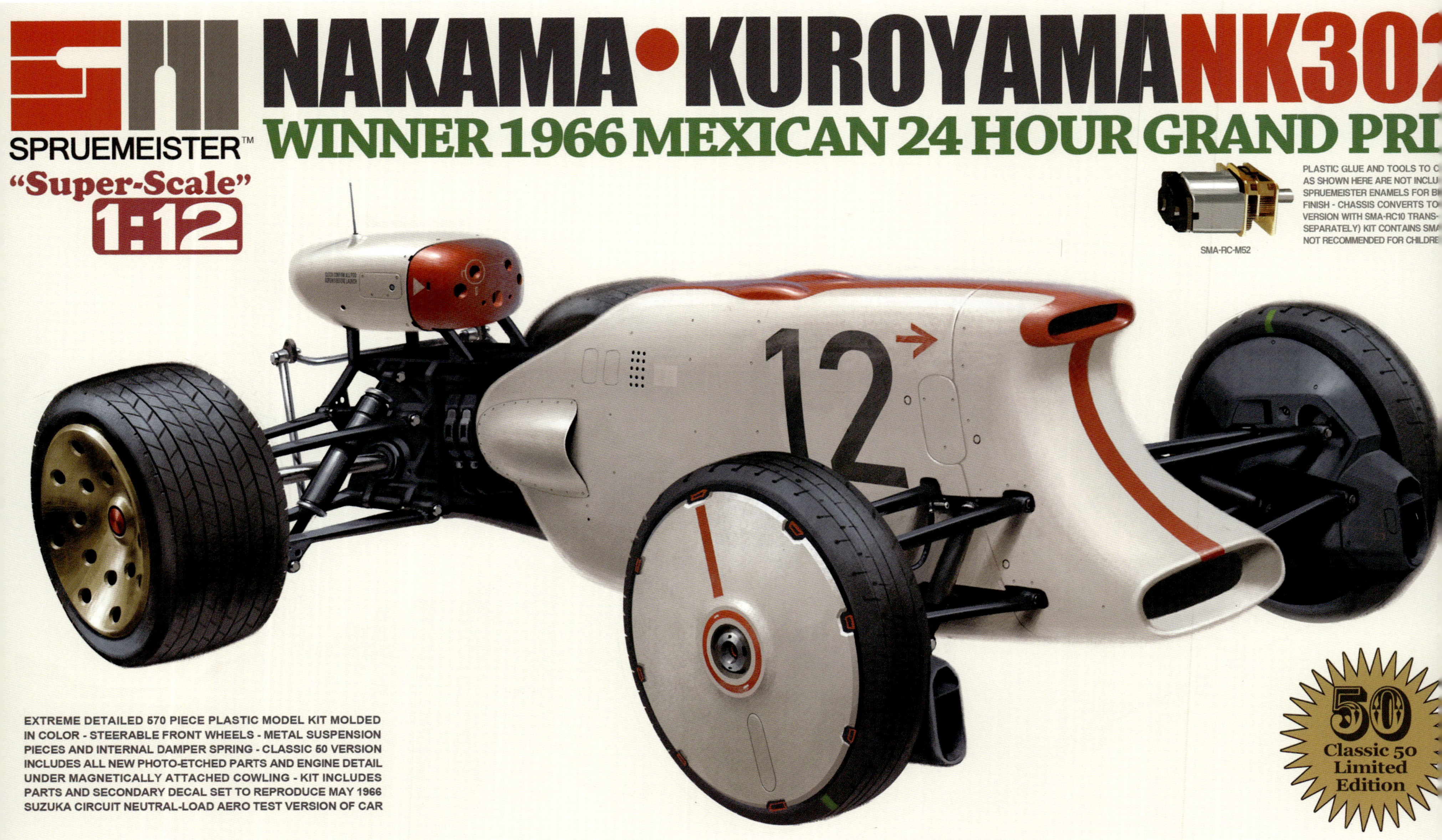

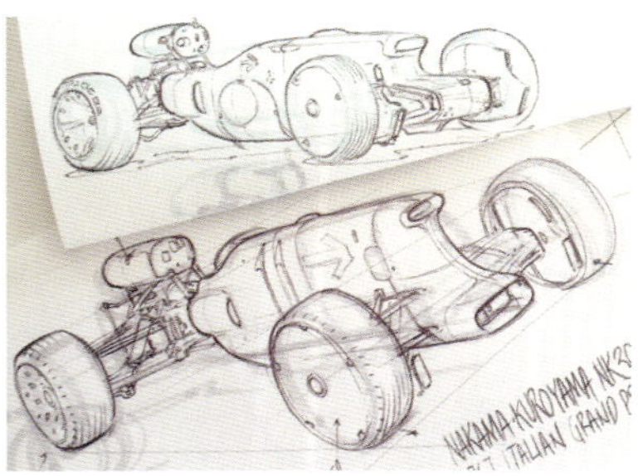

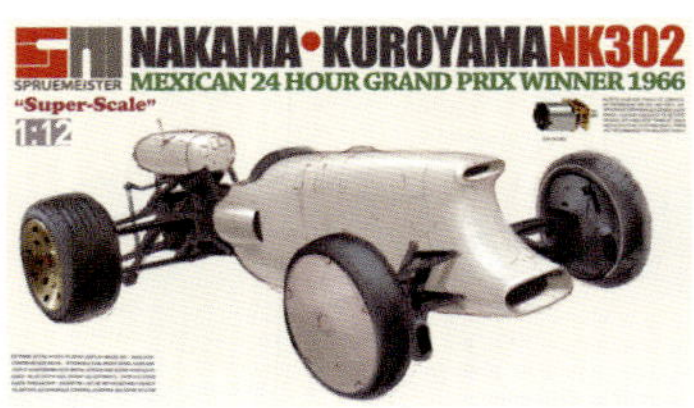

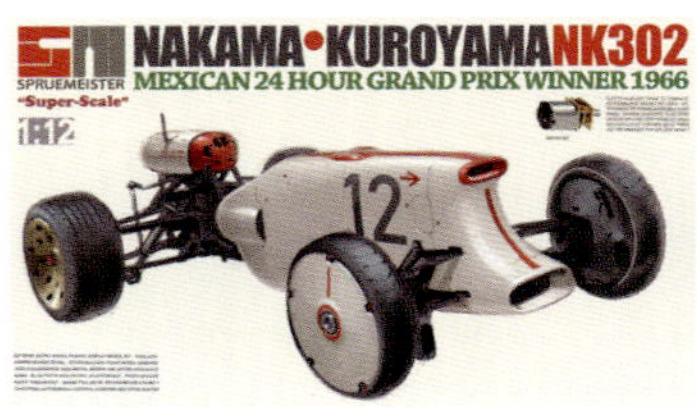

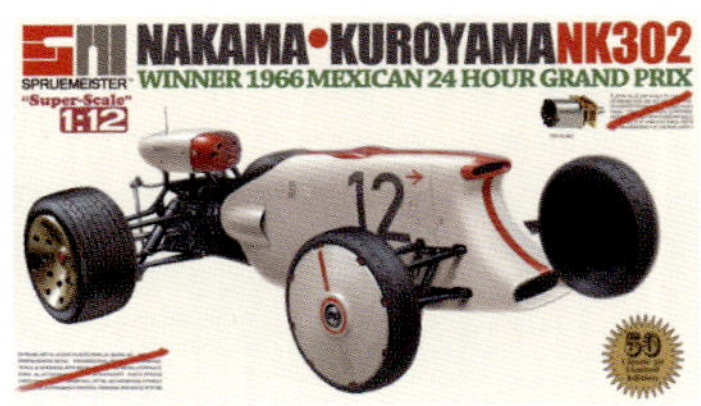

One of the earliest of the open-wheeled autonomous designs, it is distinctive with its infrared rear section, simple teardrop sensor, and control unit pod. The main body is more like an odd, exotic fish than a race car, but on the track, the car came together as needed, winning the 1966 season-ending 24-hour autonomous race in Mexico.

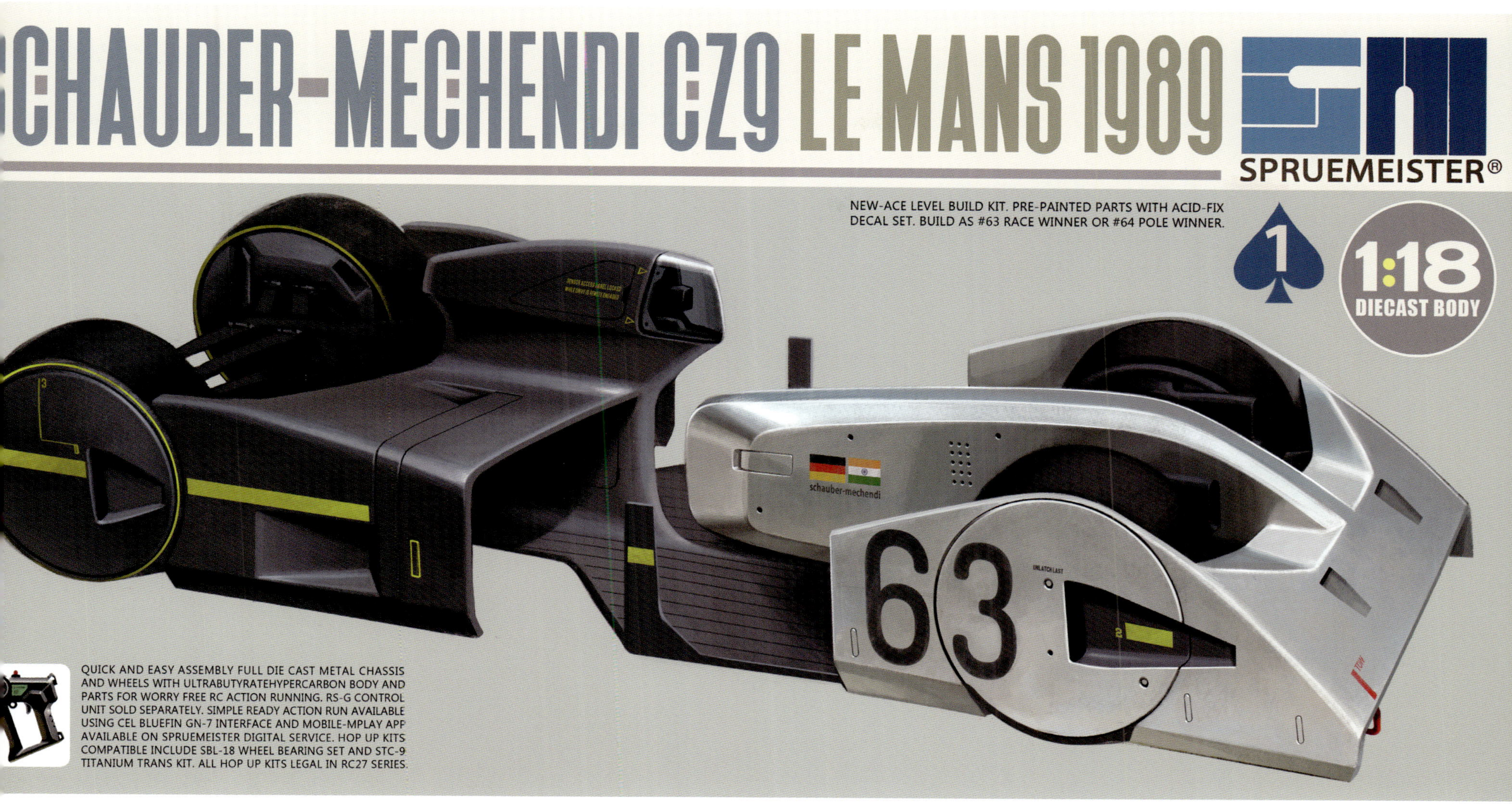

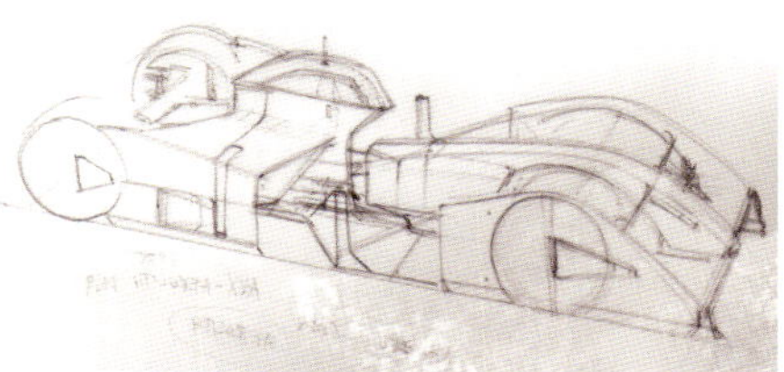

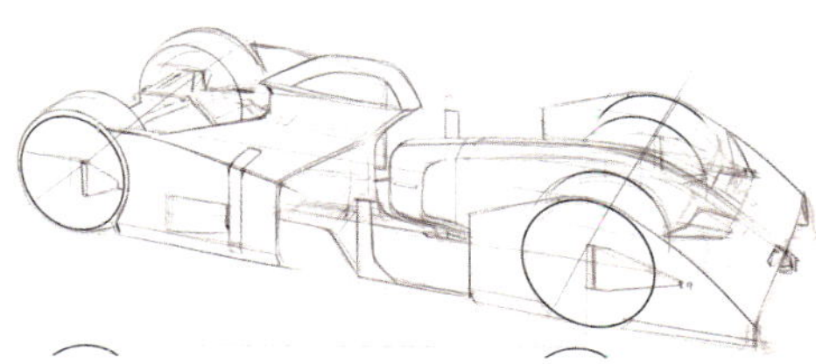

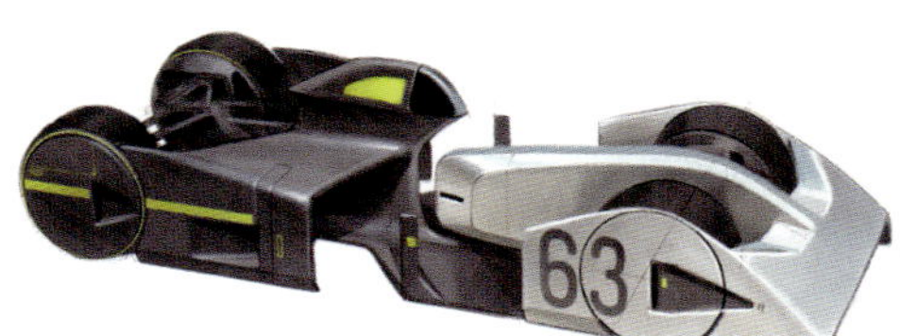

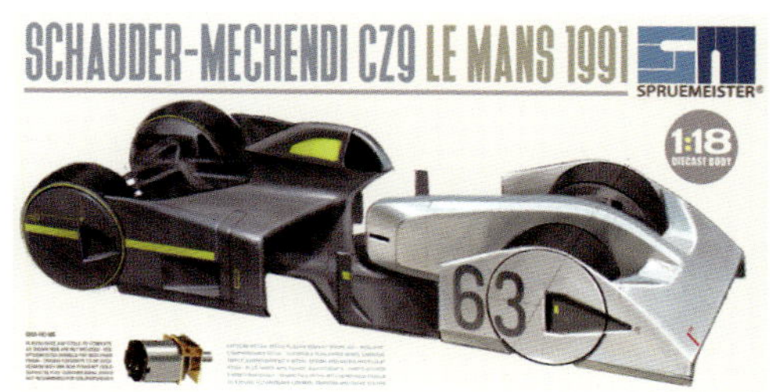

Impossible lightness and strength from alternate-reality materials allow the designer to go wild with mass and structure. This vehicle's front and rear forms are connected by only the thinnest of floor plans. Its flexibility offers some impact-absorbing suspension when needed, or complete chassis stiffness. Again, the elimination of human packaging is emphasized visually and seized upon as a design opportunity.

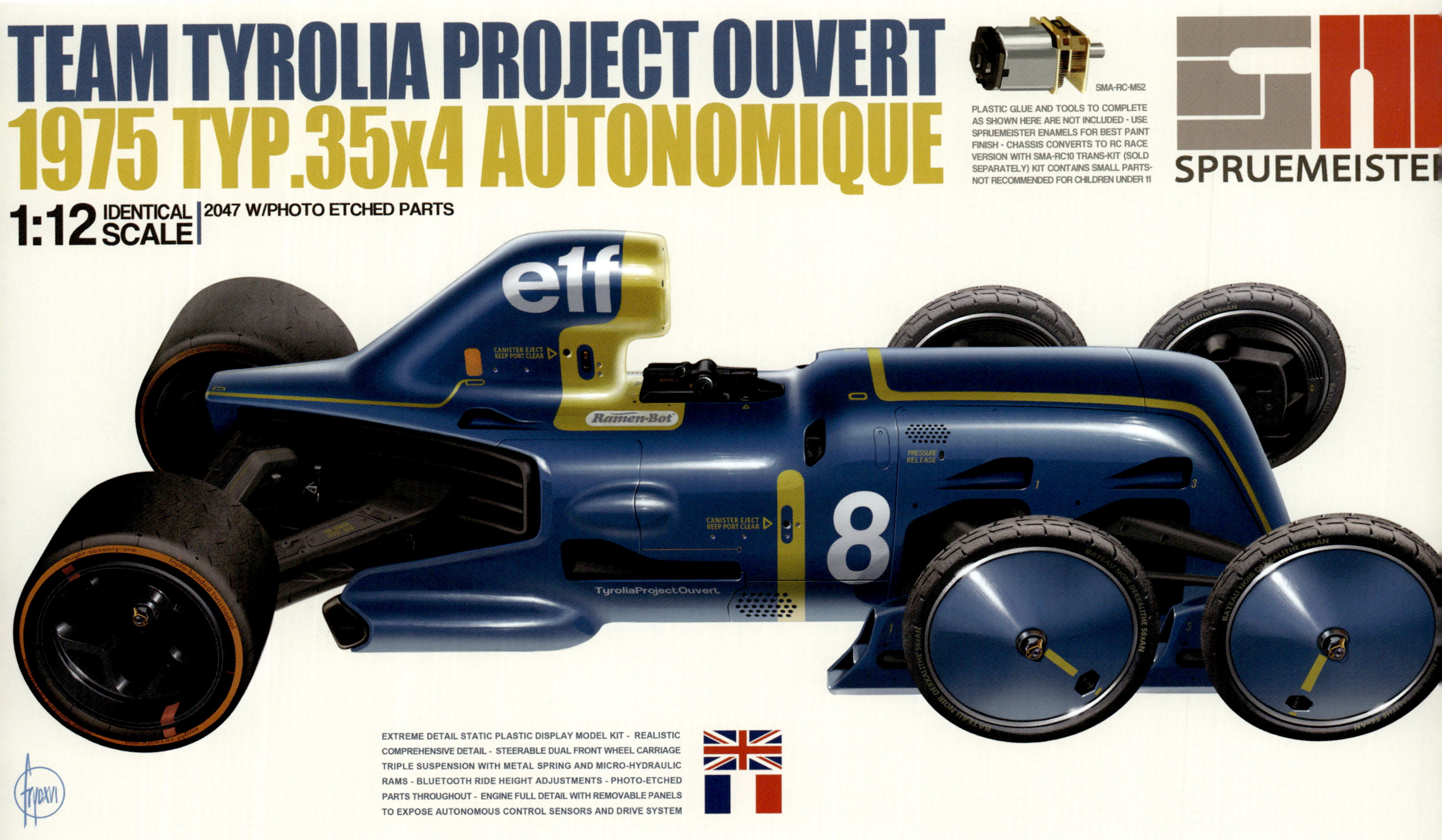

I'm a gigantic fan of cars with six wheels. This was one of the first in the retro autonomous racing series that I illustrated. And it's still a favorite of mine for the details, colors, finishes, and all those wheels!

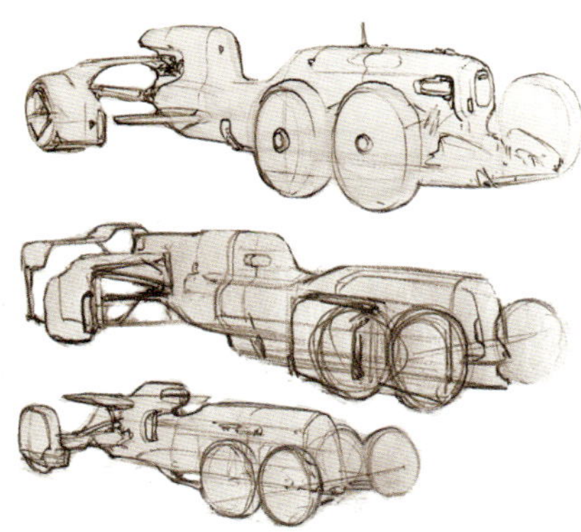

MARSCH AN/991 1988 TRACK MODE

SPRUEMEISTER®

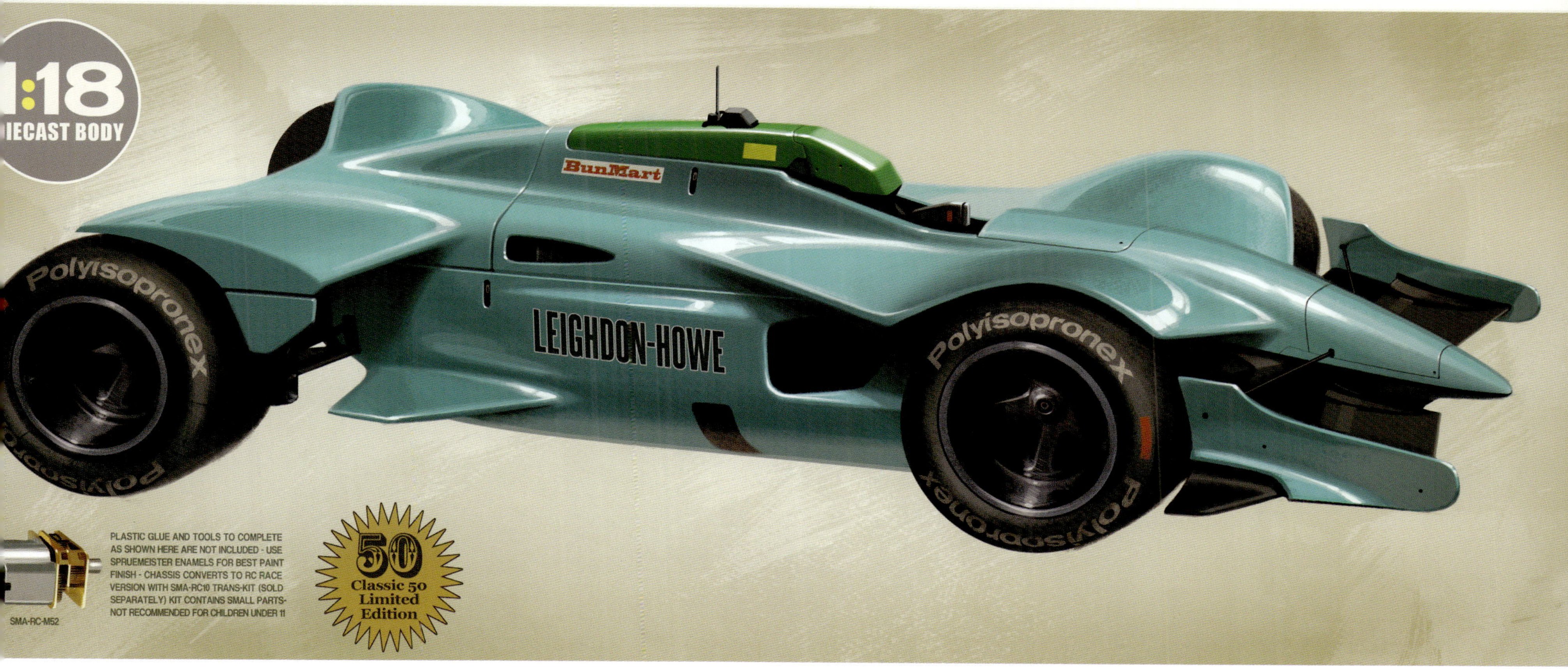

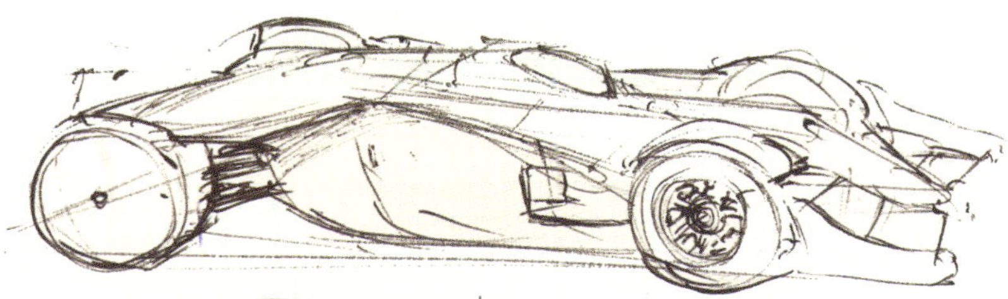

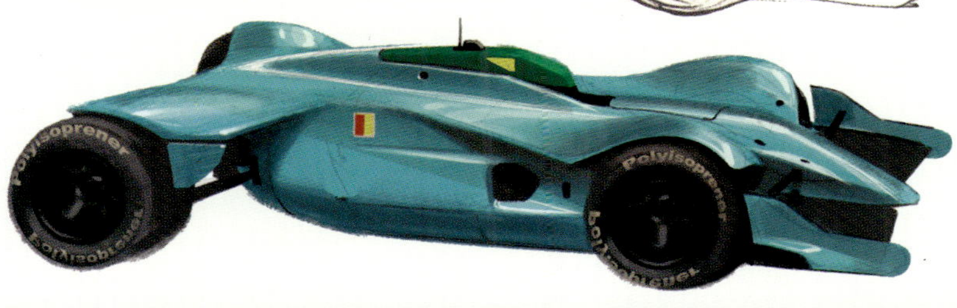

One of the notably unique liveries of the early 1990s was that of Leyton House Racing. In this inspired illustration, I made sure to carefully present the undulating surfacing in all its turquoise beauty by using an indoor strip lighting reflection. It snakes over the surfaces in a way that's quite different from single sunspot light source rendering.

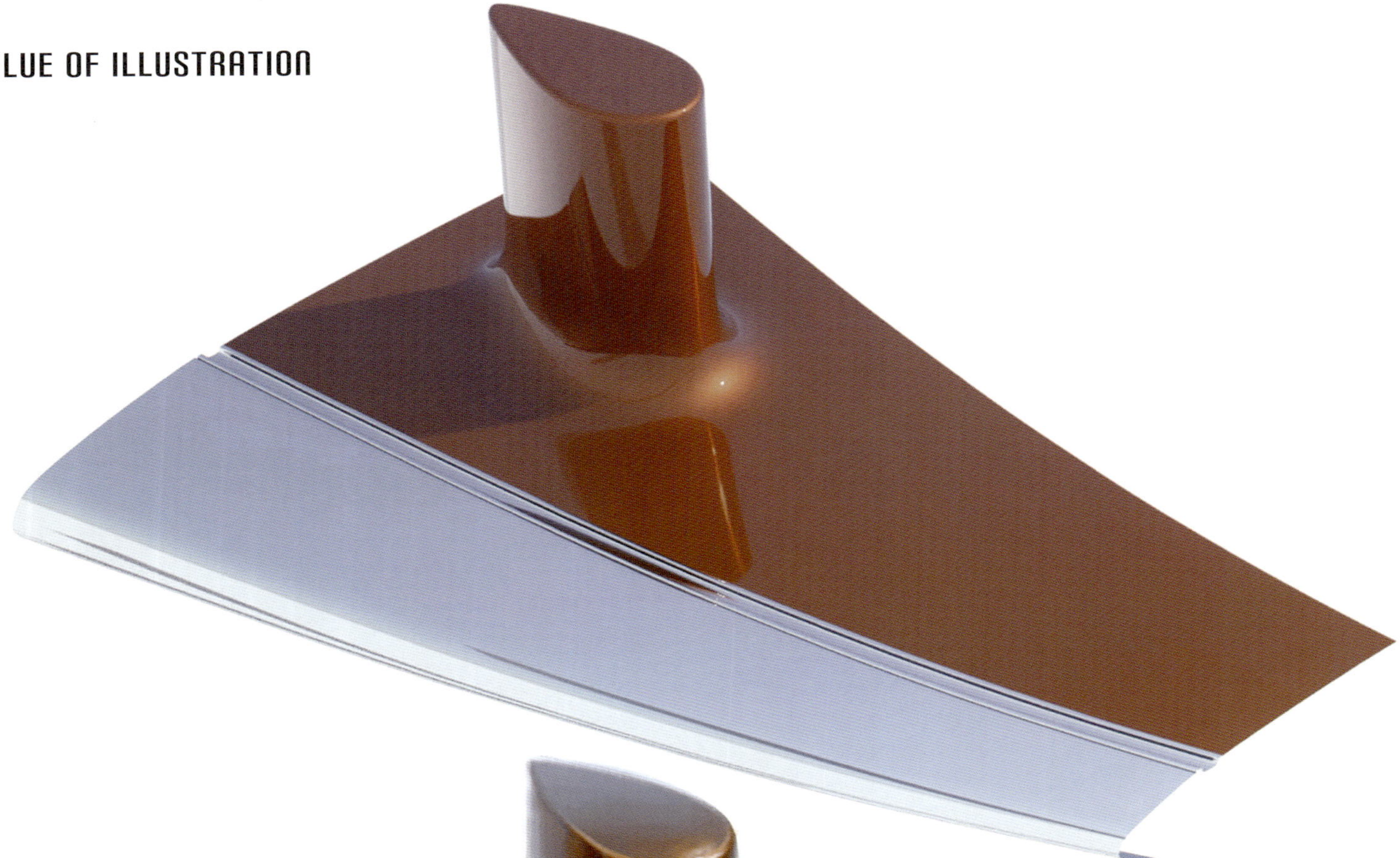

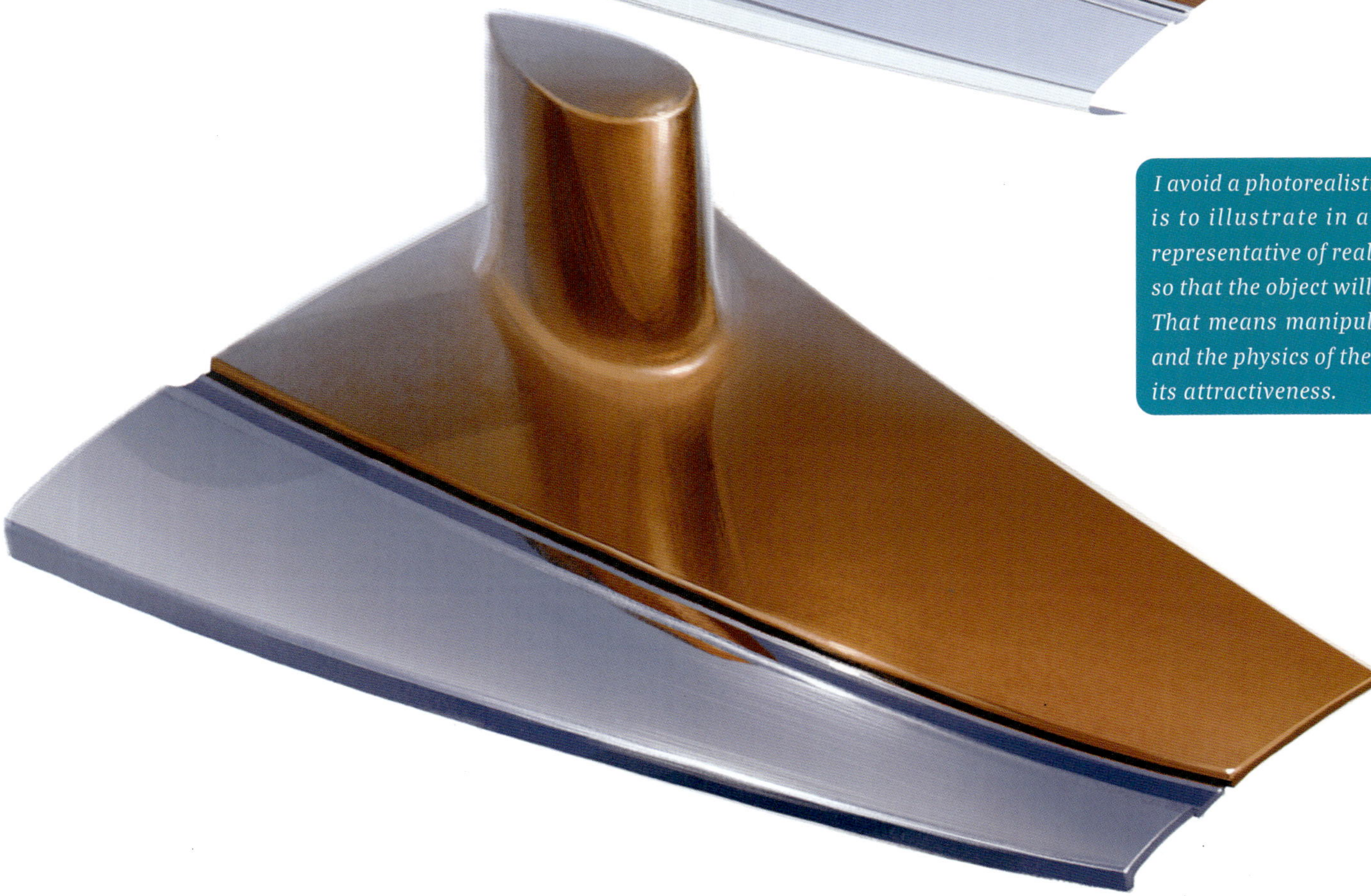

I avoid a photorealistic style, as my aim is to illustrate in a style that looks representative of reality, but enhanced, so that the object will look its very best. That means manipulating light, color, and the physics of the image to heighten its attractiveness.

A design-school discussion I remember from long ago reflected on this question: If a shadow falls on a chrome surface, can you see it? If you make a digital model and ray trace an image, you will get a technically correct image. With the top image, perfectly clean chrome does not collect a visible shadow. I could illustrate it that way, but is it important to be technically correct when it comes down to optics, such as lighting, value, reflection, and color?

When illustrating anything from my mind, I can cheat calculated optic reality and make it look however I want, as long as it's somewhat believable and that the changes I make enhance the appearance of the object—making the shape and material clear and legible. In this case, a light shadow on chrome "looks right," as it doesn't end abruptly at the edge of the paint, making it look more natural. I also added more volume to the paint by increasing the sky-blue Fresnel effect toward the back and juicing the orange metal flake. Running a thin bright highlight along the edge of the painted surface, where it meets the chrome, with some linear highlight effects, makes things pop more. Simplifying the soft fillet between the vertical shape and the main copper form helps the understanding of the surface transitions.

There's no way one lighting setup in CG would give you all that; it couldn't have all these things in reality in one single-lit view. Making CG models does allow you to create multiple camera angles of the object and make quick changes to color, material, and graphics.

Does a shadow visibly fall on chrome? It does when I need it to.

Creating a 2D illustration gives you the flexibility to eliminate technical optical limitations to produce a more engaging image.

4

CHAPTER 4 : TRUCKS AND BIG RIGS

I've noticed that I find a lot of comfort in sketching trucks. I think that's because it taps into my halcyon childhood sketching memories, when I spent many hours sketching army trucks and tanks. Even more than race cars, military vehicles were my favorite vehicles to dream about (that is, until the first Star Wars movie came out). Semitrucks, delivery trucks, utility trucks, and vehicles with obscure and unidentifiable purpose are scattered throughout any pile of sketches close at hand. My favorite ideas get more thought and development in color illustrations.

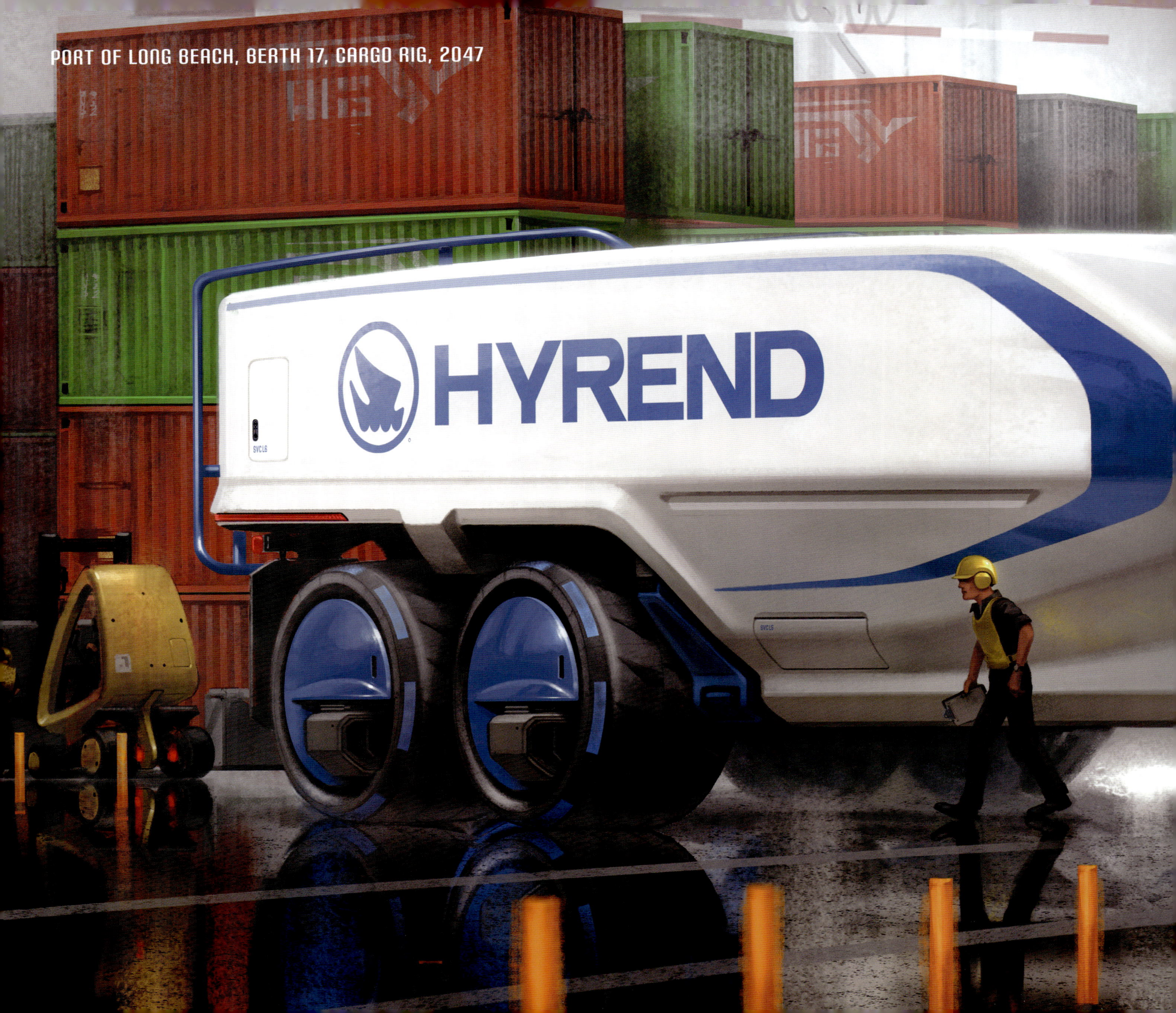

PORT OF LONG BEACH, BERTH 17, CARGO RIG, 2047

While the safety benefits of autonomous vehicle control were impossible to ignore, certain aspects of human drivers were difficult to replace. A careful balance of autonomous accident avoidance and traffic optimization coupled with the security monitoring and site work (loading/unloading, recharging) ensured the prolonged careers of drivers throughout the remainder of the 21st century. Electric battery technology made great strides in the late 2030s, while vehicle drive and regenerative braking and steering was wheel-centric, allowing miraculous small-space navigation with six-wheel steering and parallel **scrub crawling**.

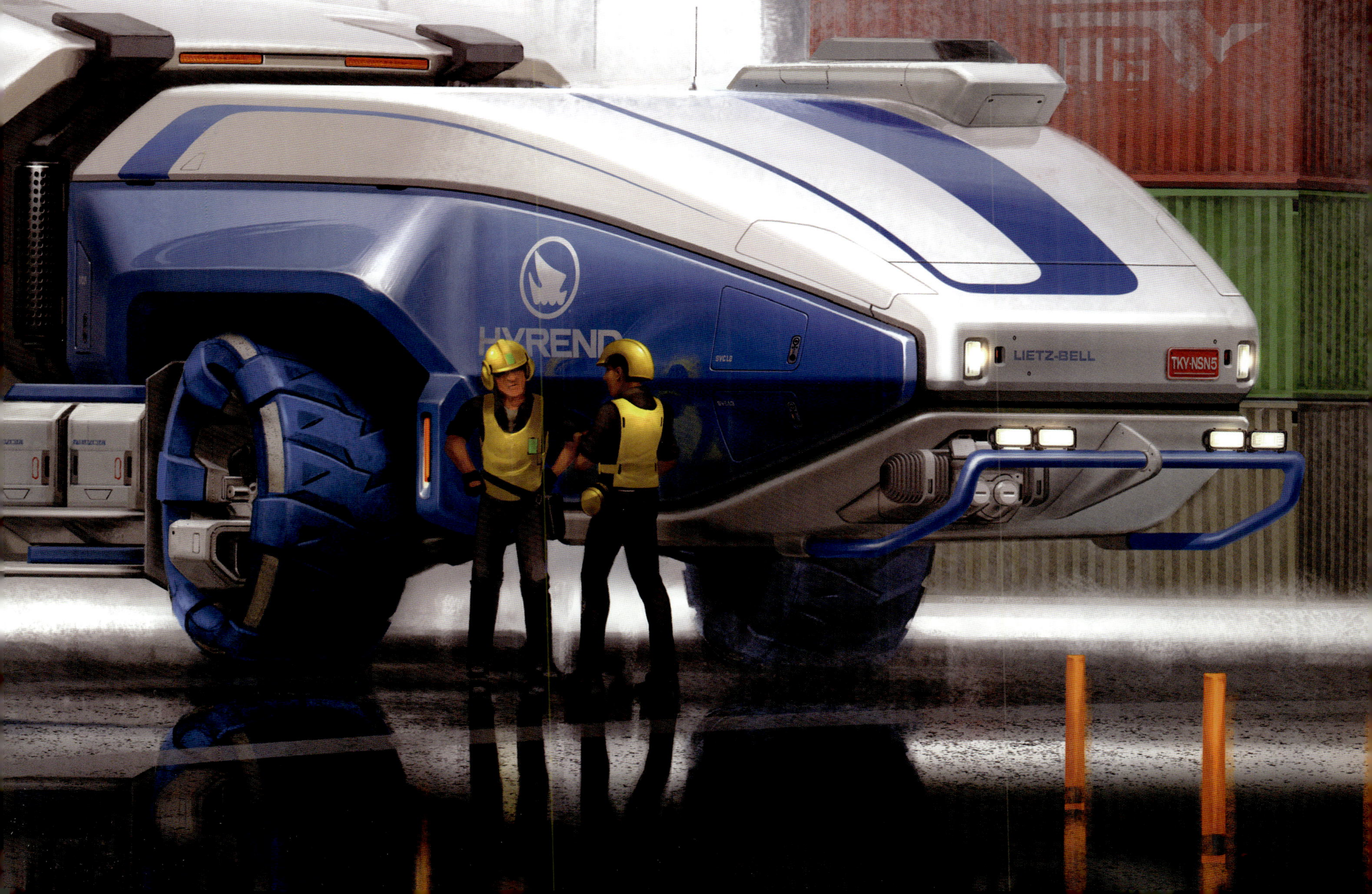

FYRETRUCKS

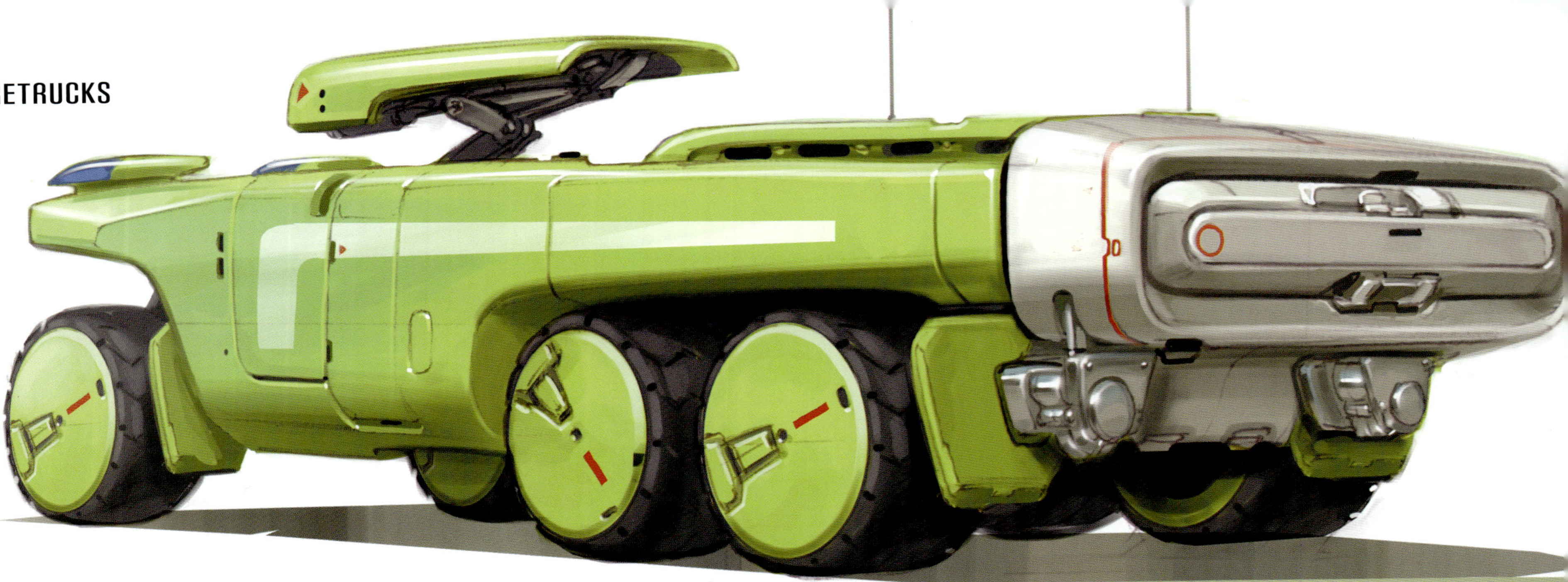

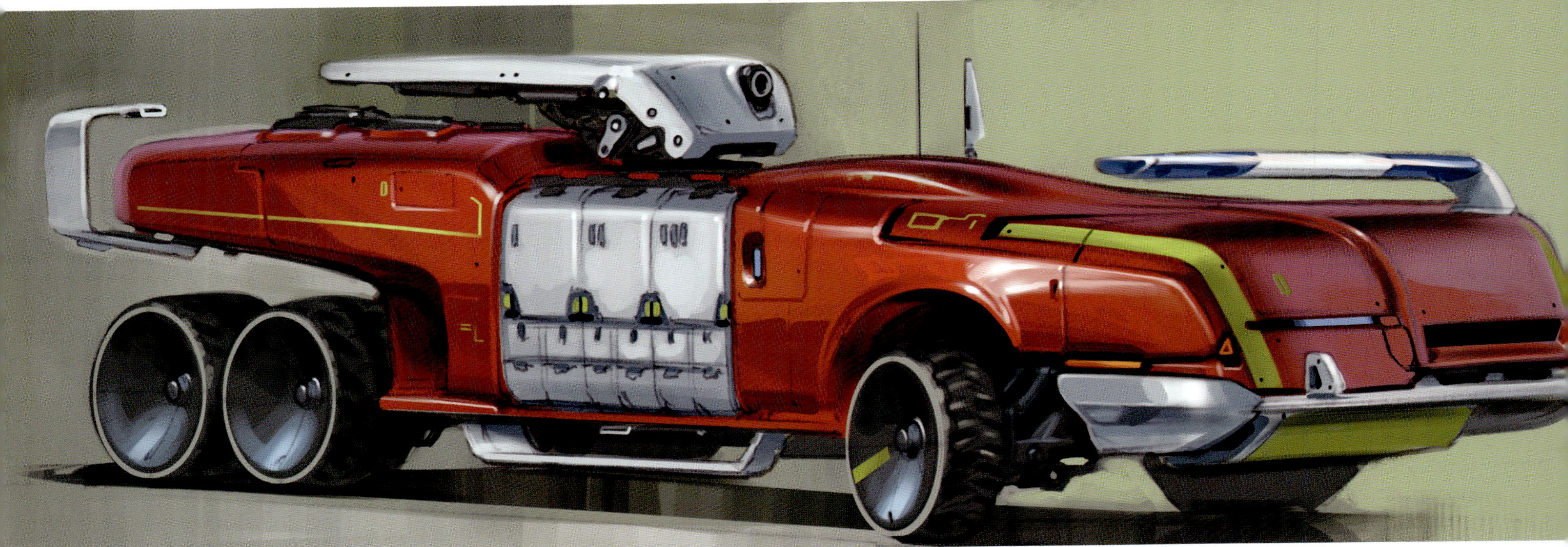

Besides clattering small, diecast cars together on the flowery green carpet at home in Oregon, one of my earliest childhood memories was experiencing the diesel roar of a fire engine passing by our house with full lights and sirens on. It was probably the most intense sensory experience I had at that age. I think fire trucks tend to make a similar impression on a lot of kids, and produce excitement and fascination with the rumbling, weighty speed, along with the noise, all that light, color, and chrome. Seeing a fire truck makes me want to draw them over and over again.

Here, I've playfully experimented with some future forms of fire engines, leaning toward the cab-over-engine layout, with the mass of the driver's compartment hanging over the front axle, as that proportion has an edgy imbalance that feels more futuristic but is also very function driven. The fire trucks used at airports are good reference, sporting taller wheels, higher ground clearance, and an aggressively sloped chin for driving over debris and uneven terrain.

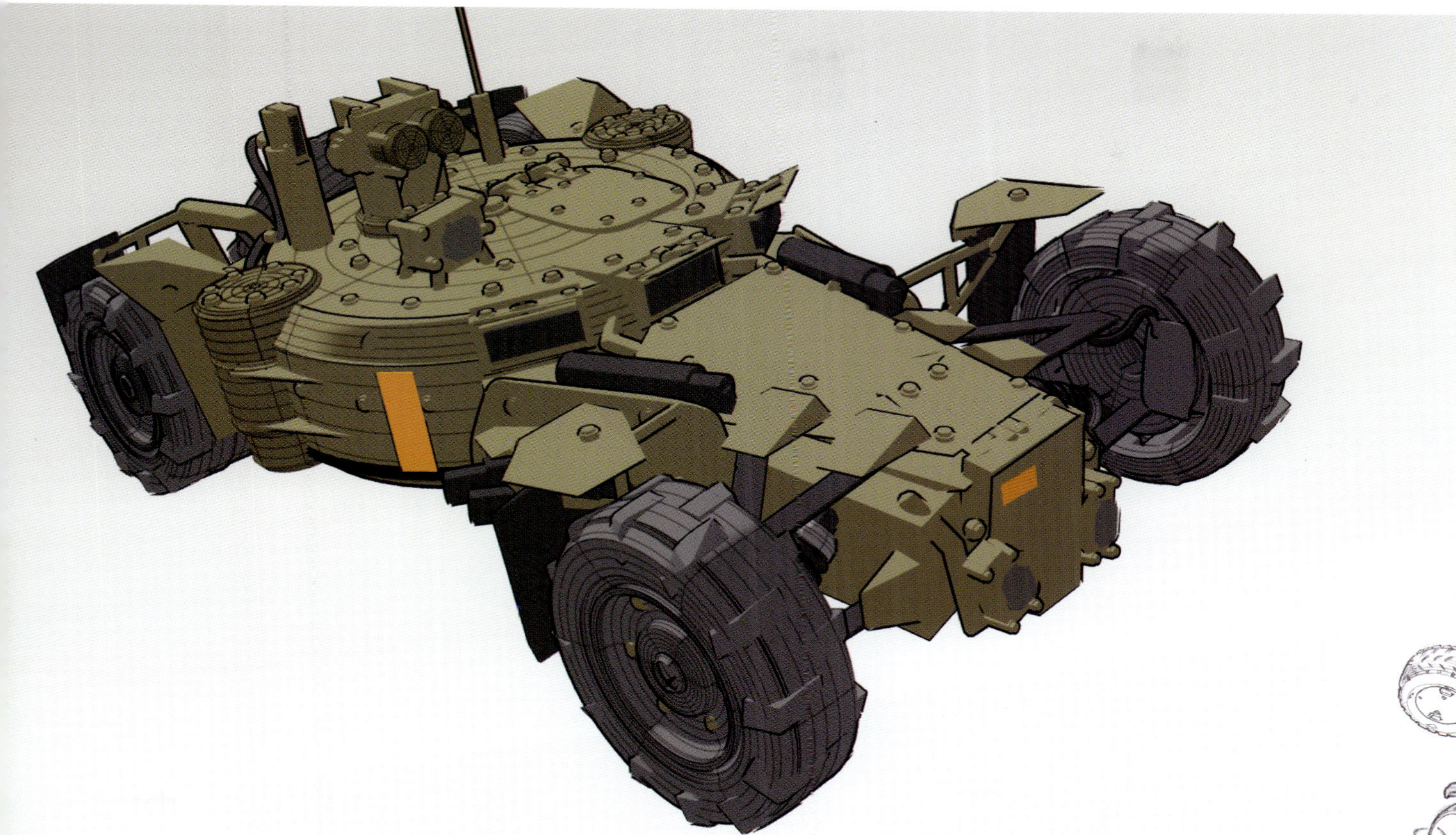

Some of the most effective designs are those with the simplest shapes—primitive forms with a practiced and intentional allocation of detailing. This design focused on knee-high roof height and a simple cabin volume as if the turret of the tank became its own wheeled vehicle. This was sketched quickly in iterations on paper, and then explored digitally in virtual-reality-modeled form with Gravity Sketch.

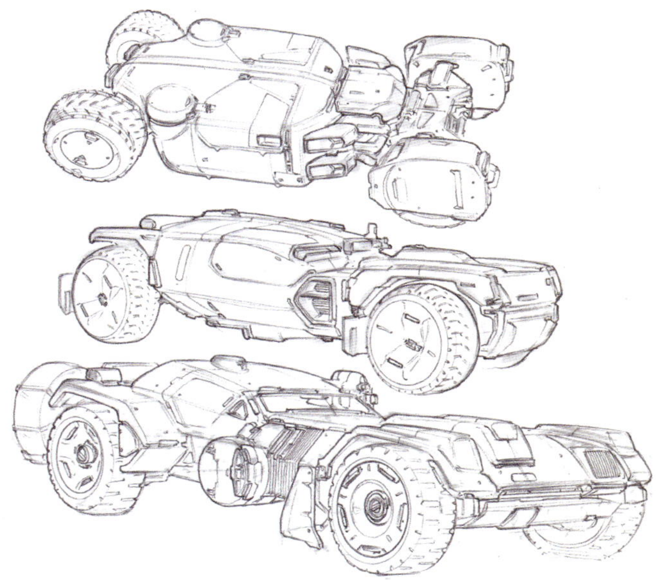

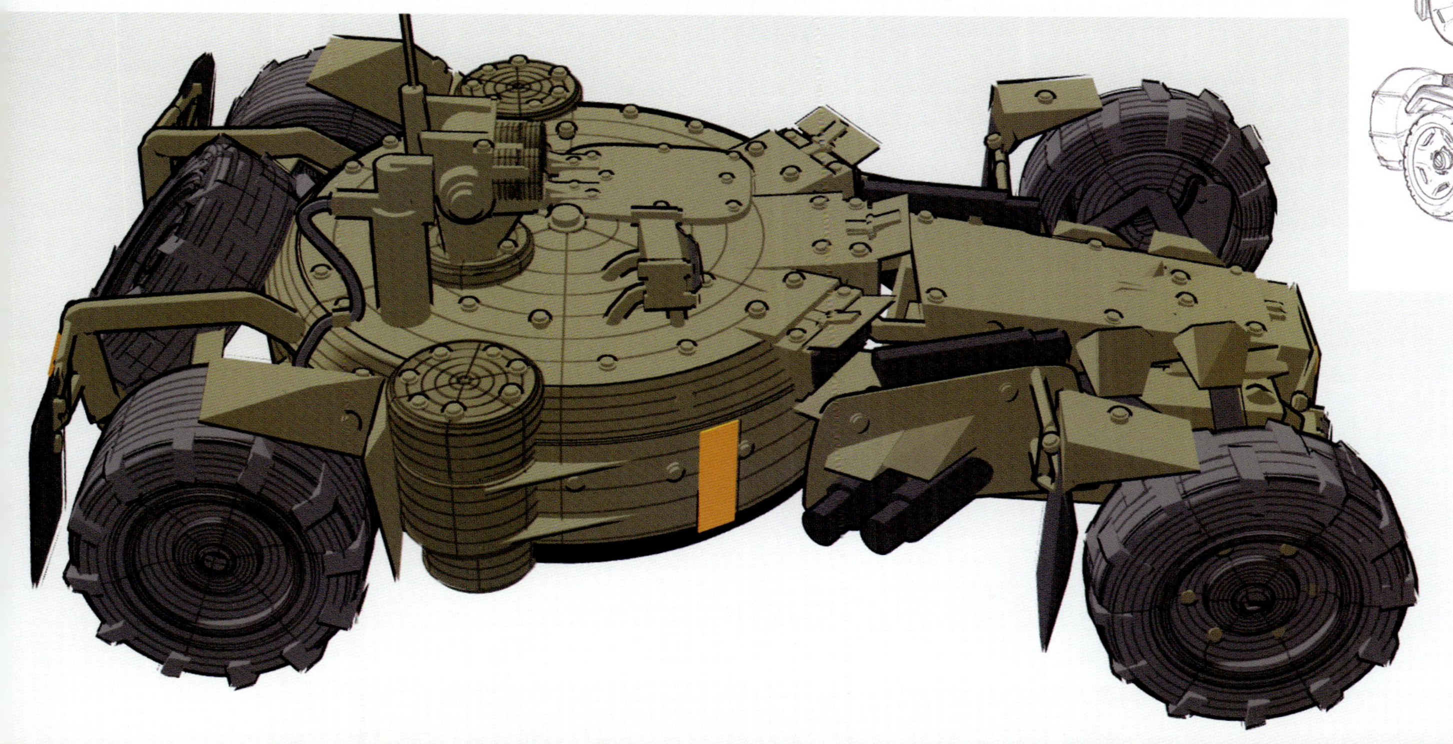

SLOTRIG

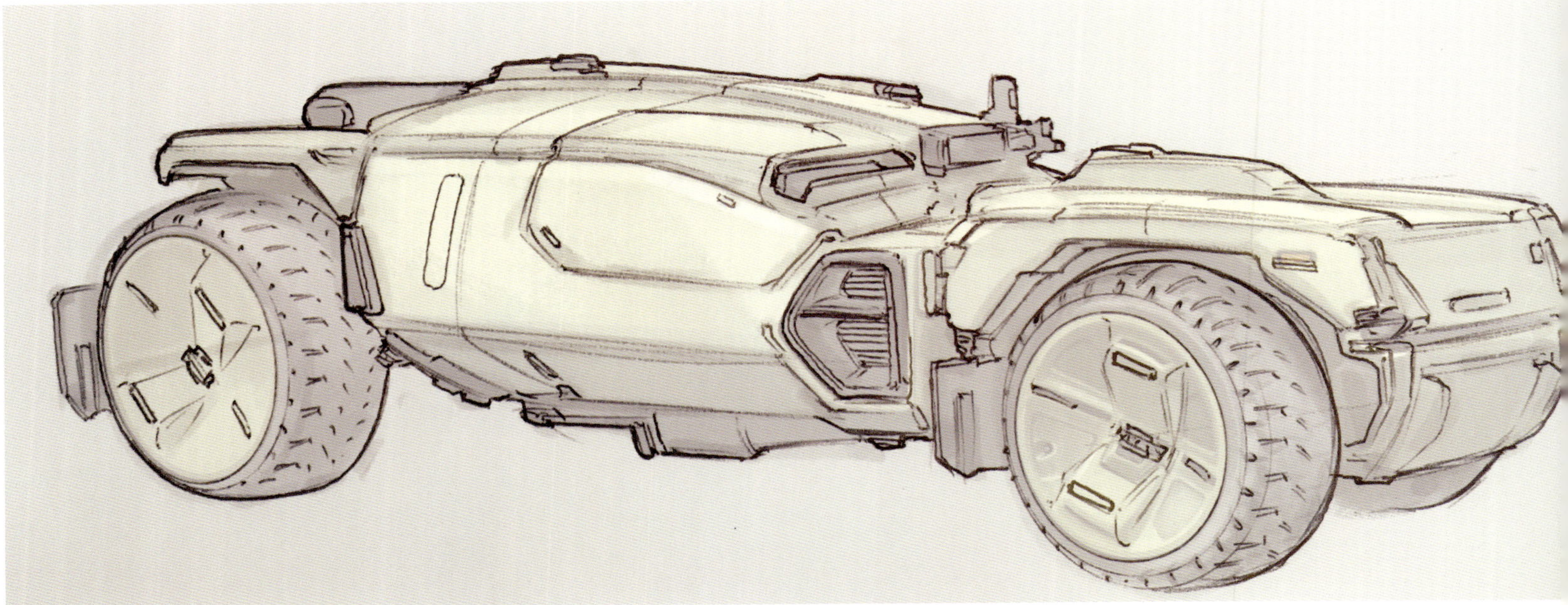

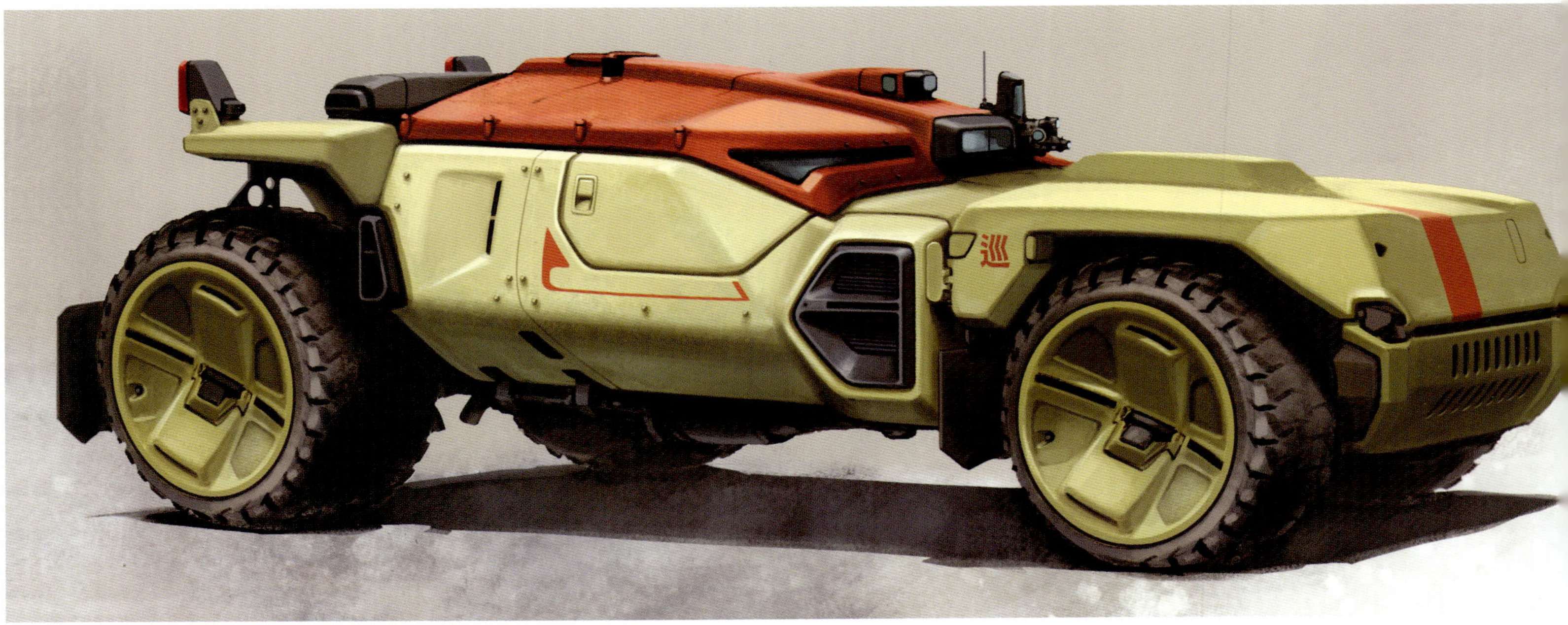

I move pretty quickly from one sketch to the next, often sketching out an idea on scratch paper that gets tucked away in a file and forgotten until I come across it again. Sometimes, after a couple years, a fresh review of an old idea sketch instigates some new ideas for executing the design in color and finished rendering. This is one of the flapjack sketches that I dismissed for at least four years before it got a thorough workover in color here, with minor modifications to the design to suit a more finished illustration.

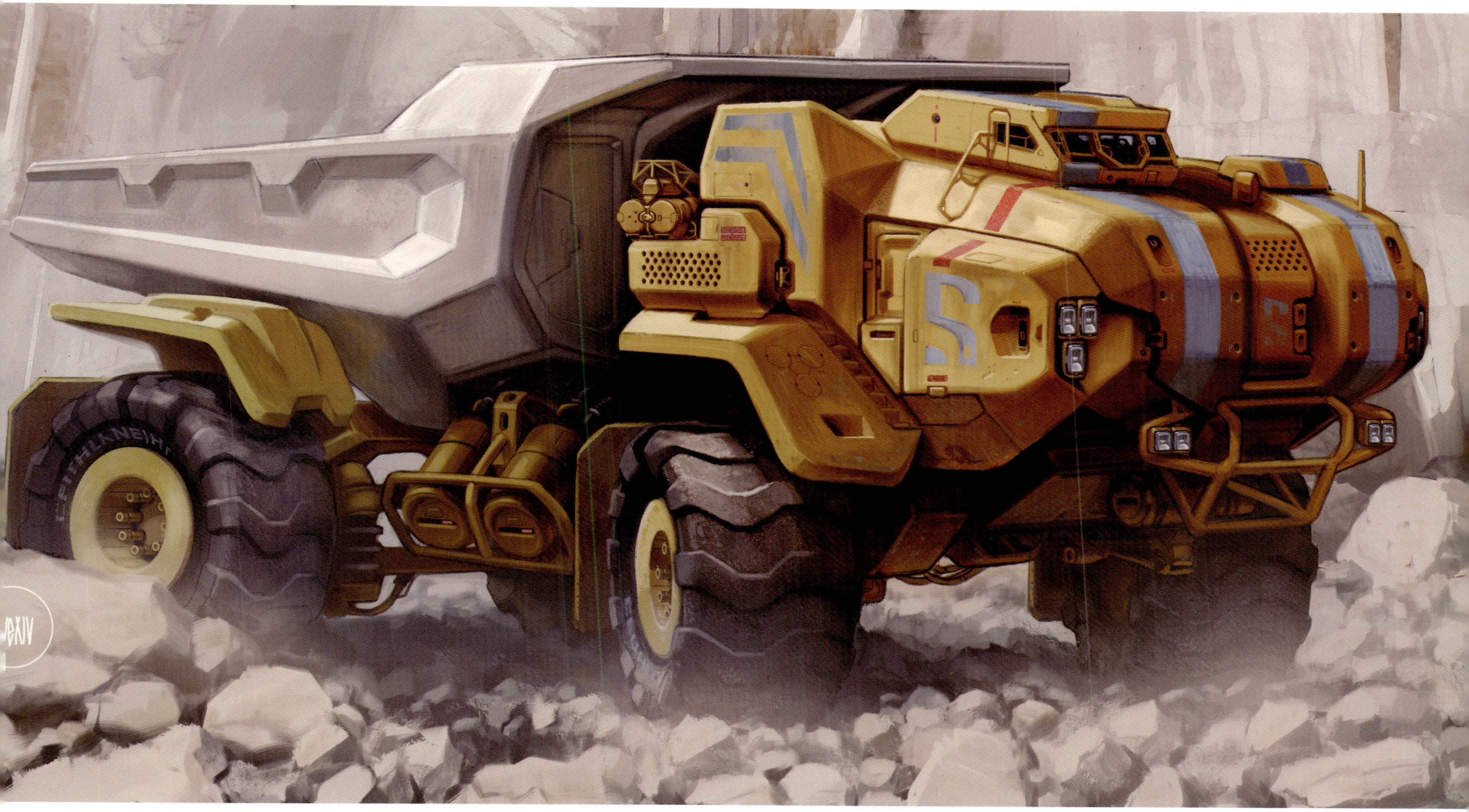

Movin' marble, 60 tons at a time. Powered by propane, driven by heavy metal. Mining vehicles are fantastic in their scale and proportion. Some vehicles for mining are designed to be as low as possible so that they can fit into low-clearance passageways carved into the earth, while other vehicles, such as digging equipment and dump trucks like this one, are massive in scale to haul tons of soil and rocks in fewer loads. As they drive exclusively within the mining area, their giant size is not restricted to the proportions of city streets and highways. This design is presented among the slabs of white stone in an Italian marble quarry. Showing that a vehicle is built sturdy and able to withstand heavy loads is accomplished by putting large contact patch tires at the far four corners of the vehicle and creating body surfaces that appear thick and meaty. Tubular frame structures show added protection and tell the story in the image that this vehicle gets used in rough environments. When I sketch heavy vehicles, I often listen to heavy, doom metal music to set the creative studio ambience and produce the weightiest designs.

MCLANDISH MB23: 1976 HUNTER TEST

Light gray marker is my advisable way to safely stick your toe in the water and do some exploration before you ink. While pencil can be erased, it puts down a precise line that ends up dictating the final ink line location too specific and deliberate at the earlier "sketchy" phase. I prefer to have a wider light gray marker line that gives me some range of options of where I should apply fine line ink.

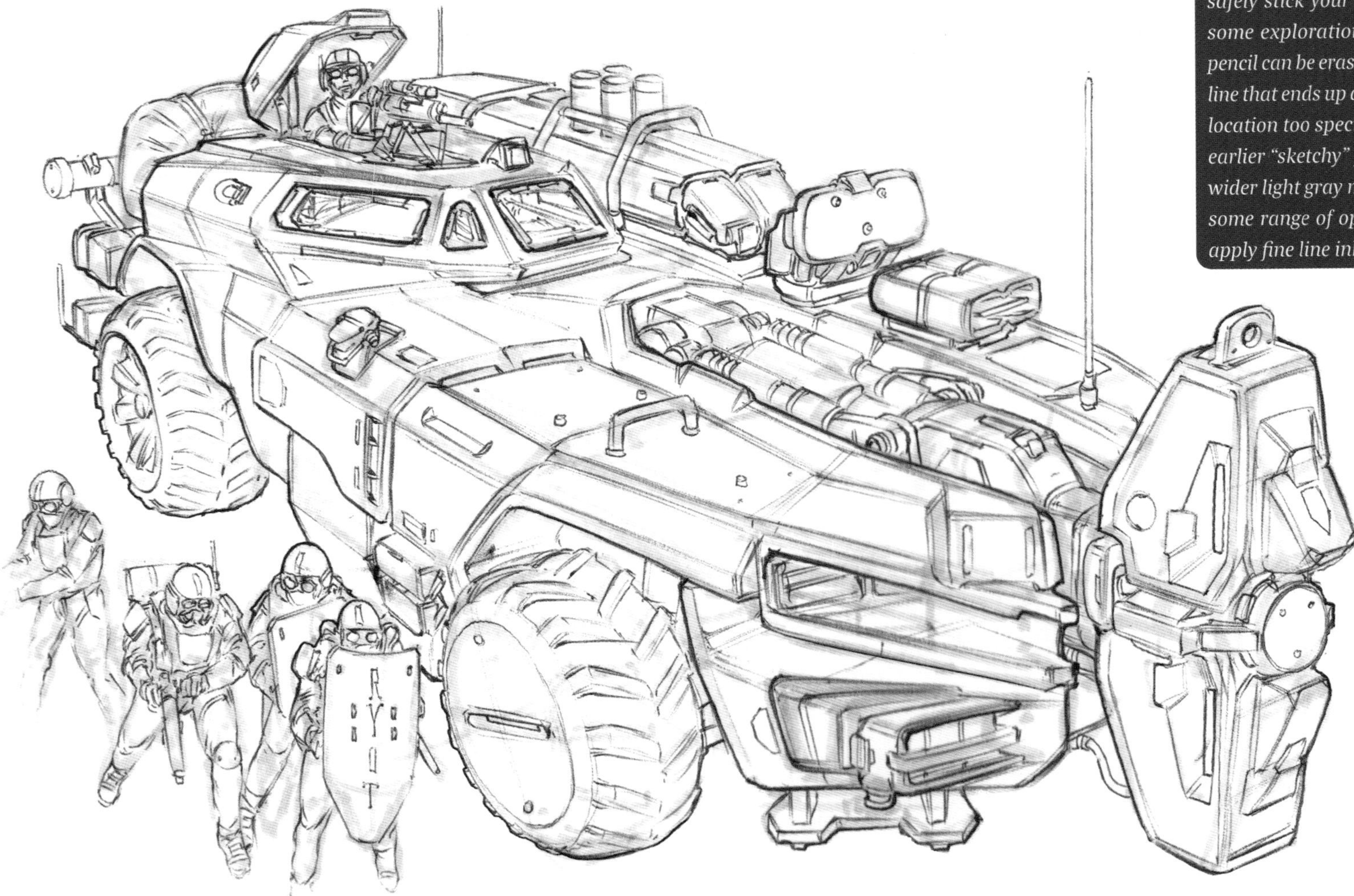

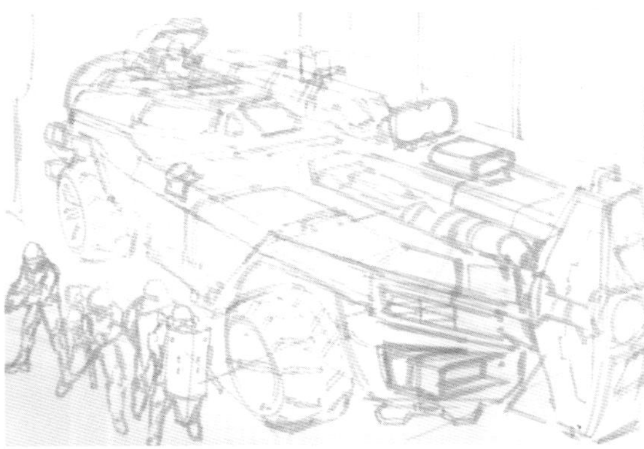

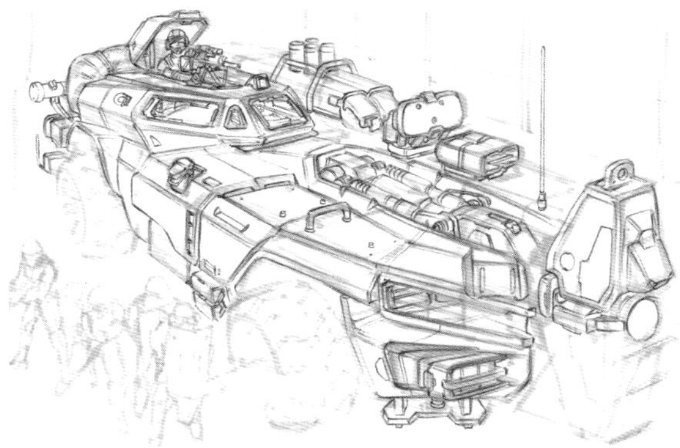

The three drawing "stunts" exercised here –drawing in little sketchbooks, drawing people, and high eye-level perspectives– made my brow sweat a bit, given my normal drawing comfort zone. I'm much more at ease at standing-height eye levels and sketching on individual pieces of paper: if I screw something up, it goes in the trash, and I can pretend it never happened instead of my gaffe being forever preserved in a leather-bound sketchbook!

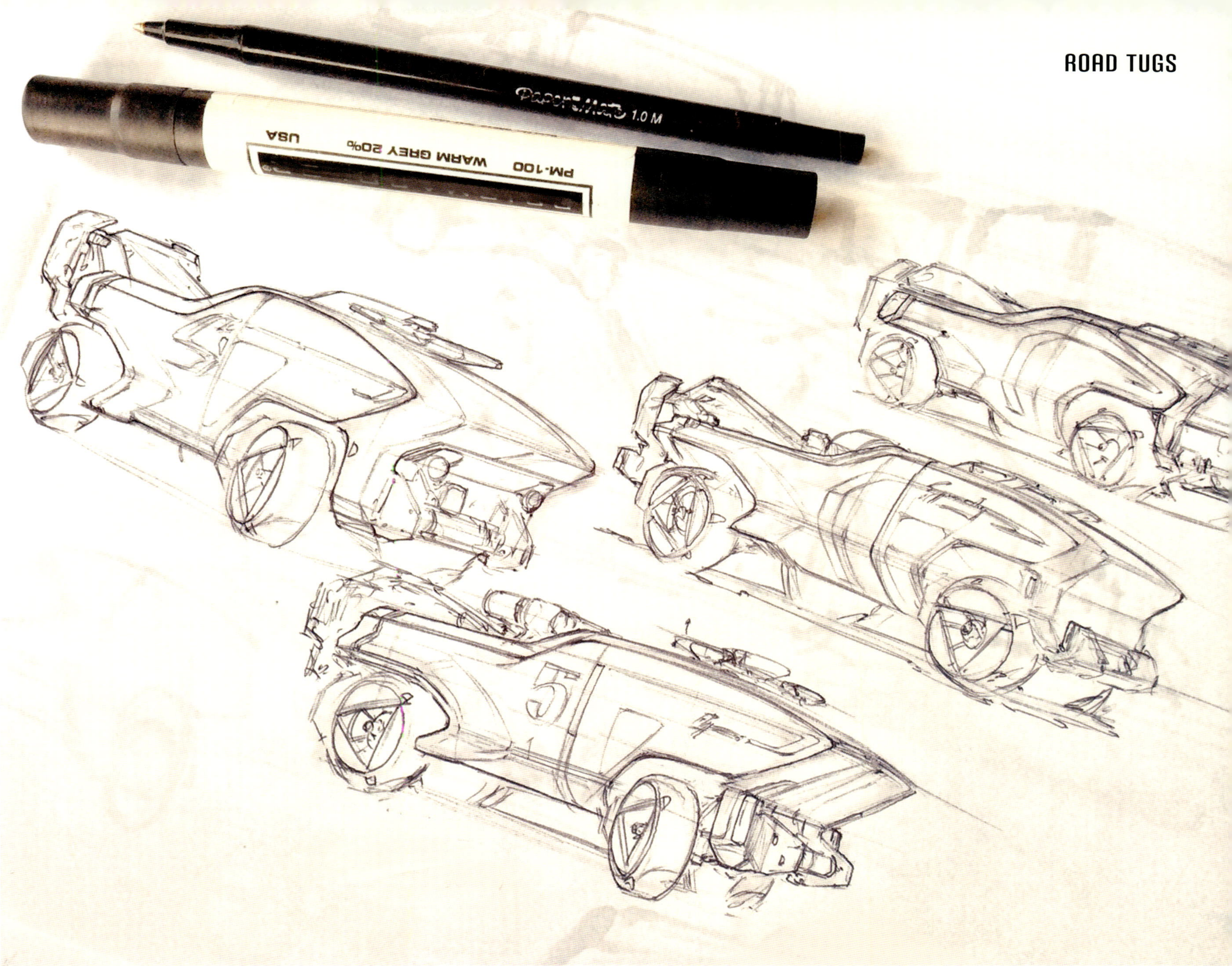

My ideation page of some tall and chunky tow trucks next to my drawing tools gives you an idea of scale. Notice the distinct cleaving-forward shape as a theme for the cab that is echoed in the rear fender. As I sketched these, I had the idea of playing off of the colors and shapes of one of my favorite chronograph watches, the Omega Speedmaster Mark III, with its thick conical stainless-steel case, deep metallic-blue dial, and touches of Day-Glo orange. Even when I sketch with line, or in black and white, I see the color of the finished image in my head. The color idea and some of the form language ideas were developed into van form as one of the Speedmasher concept sketches on page 169.

Metallic paint in a particular set of hues takes my mind back to the 1970s as a kid, when the custom van culture was prevalent. This took three hours to go from sketch to rendering. It gets its life from apple-green flake paint and contrasting chrome wheels and accents. Beyond that, it's all about a speedy-looking angular box with a strong forward wedge and paddled sand tires. Simple!

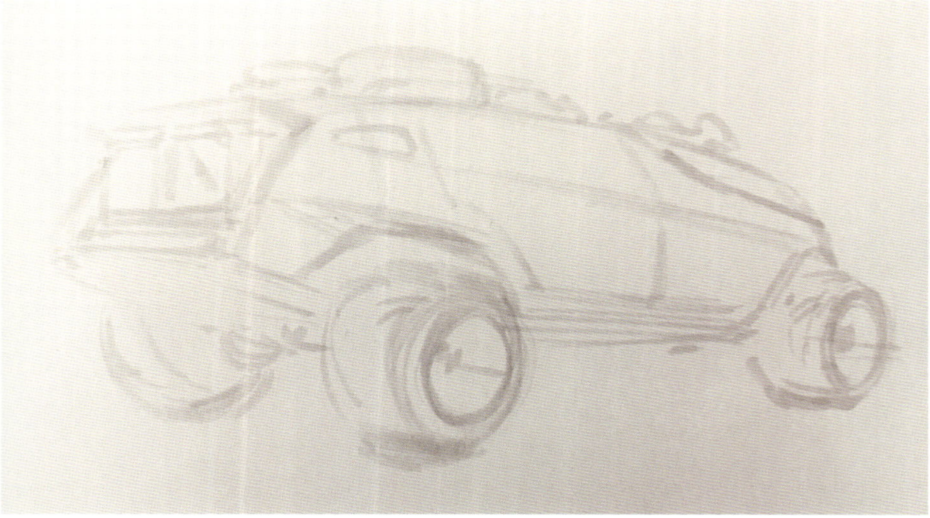

1) Sketch the thumbnail.

Starting out here by sketching a three-inch thumbnail with a broad-tip light (#2) Copic marker. Gesture, feeling of directionality, dynamic image, dynamic perspective drama, and wide, solid off-road **stance** are all crammed into the scribble. Many earlier exploration sketches at this level are often discarded before coming up with the "it" sketch that pulls everything together. I usually am able to see the potential very quickly at this stage before I commit to any ink.

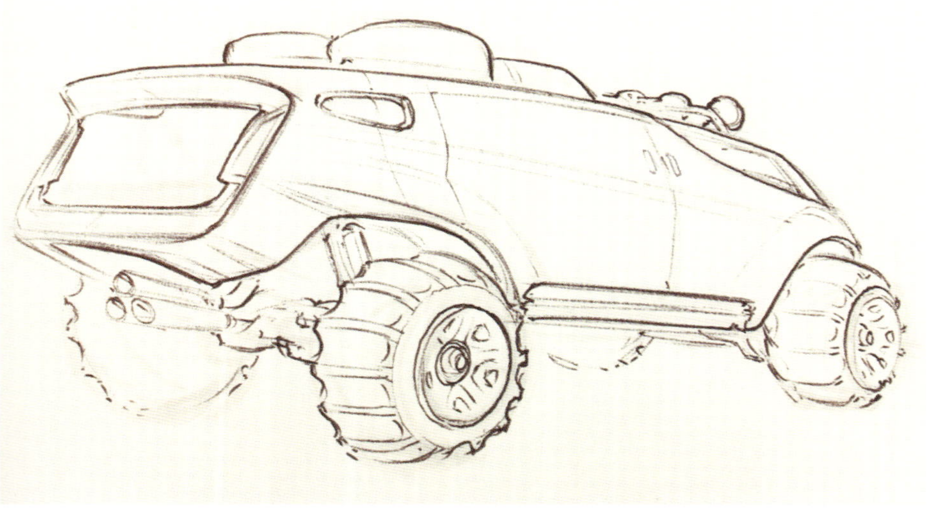

2) Apply ink.

Linework in a Paper Mate Medium Point ballpoint pen clarifies the marker sketch. I'm considering details like the definition of surface edges: Are they sharp or radiused (rounded)? The **glass to body breakup**, the chrome **moldings** that separate the glass and body, and exhaust-roof details are worked out. In the previous marker rough, I had considered jerry cans (steel liquid container) nestled onto the rear hatch area. Once in pen sketch, I instead simply located a large piece of glass and set of taillights there.

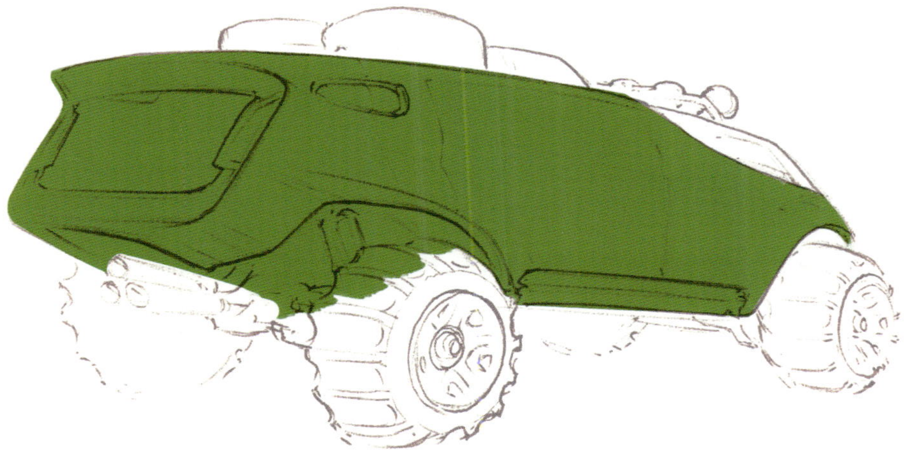

3) Add foundation color.

Most of the quick rough work is set up with the foundation color, or the base solid tone of the green paint. Once the area is filled in, the Photoshop feature layer pixel lock allows me to be rough and gestural with the next steps without going outside the boundaries of the vehicle body **block-in**.

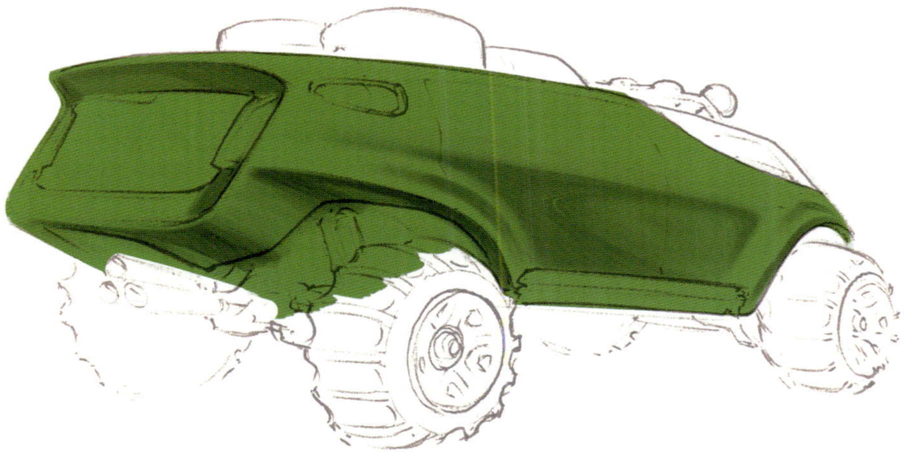

4) Apply darker value.

To produce the appearance of metallic paint, after the base color has been laid down, I add darker value in areas of shadow and surfaces that angle down below the eyeline to simulate shading and reflections of the darker ground.

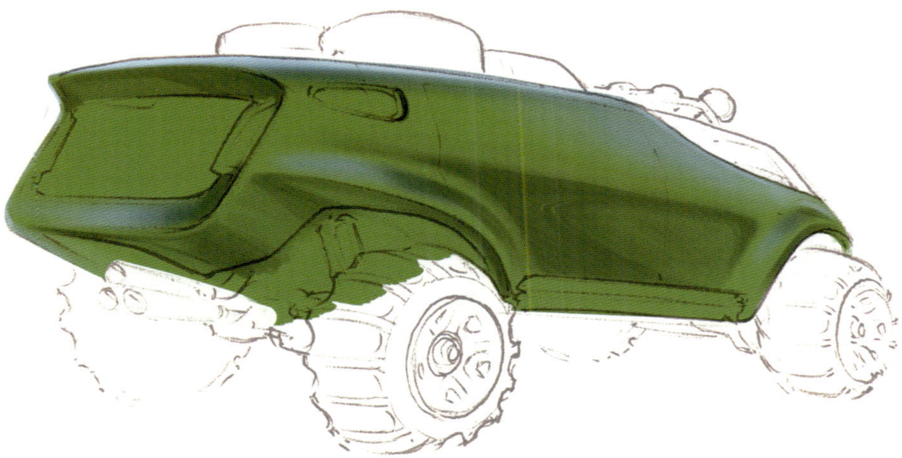

5) Add reflective tone.

As surfaces roll away from the viewing angle, they become more reflective due to the **Fresnel effect**, so surfaces that roll over toward the upper side of the vehicle get sky tone reflection. The metal flake also picks up sky tone, so usually metallic paint is very expressive of the color of the sky on the upper surfaces.

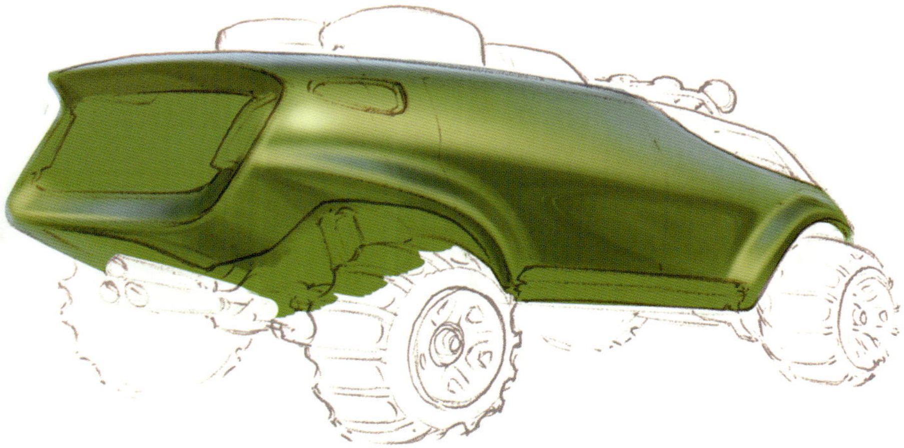

6) Layer on flake paint.

Metal flake paint may include its own coloration on top of the base color with colored metal particles, such as pearl flakes or, in this case, gold. When sunlight hits the flakes, the shimmering yellowish color lights up, giving an illuminated area where the light is reflected the strongest.

Usually it is good to do this–illuminating an area–in a focal point close to the viewer, as the near part of the car appears to come off of the 2D plane in the area of high contrast and focus.

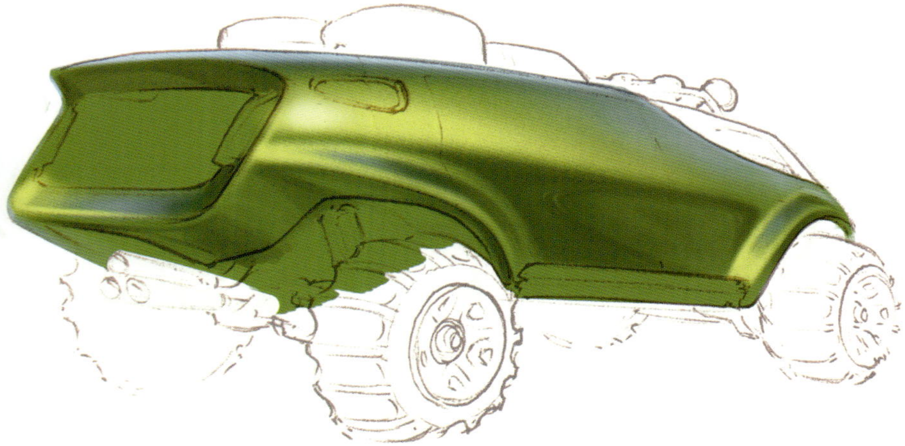

7) Duplicate and refine highlights.

Big flakes! I duplicated the previous golden highlight color layer in Photoshop and set the mode of the new layer to "dissolve," which gives the layer a particulate noise appearance similar to shimmering metal flakes in paint. Rasterizing the layer softens the effect enough so that it does not look too artificial or distracting.

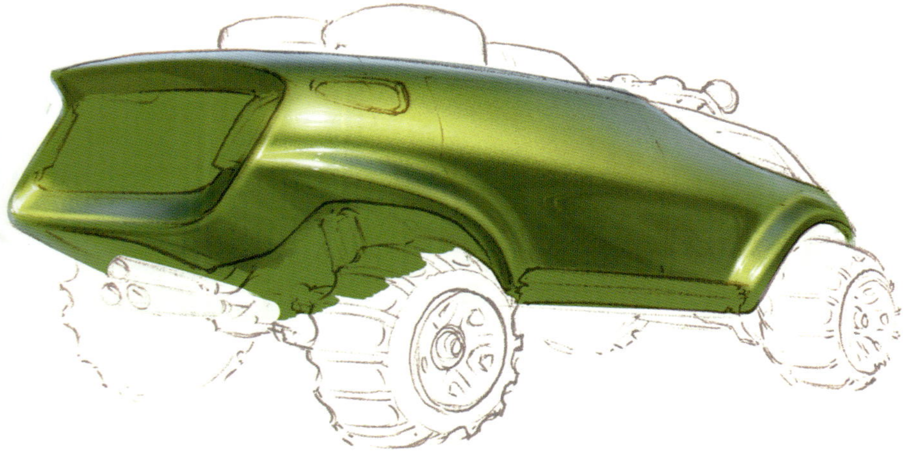

8) Dazzle with pure white!

Pure white is used as a dazzling hot spot sun reflection centered in the brightest area of the flake illumination. The shape of the "hot spot" simulates the sparkling and noisy effects of the appearance of bright light in the viewer's retina or in a camera lens.

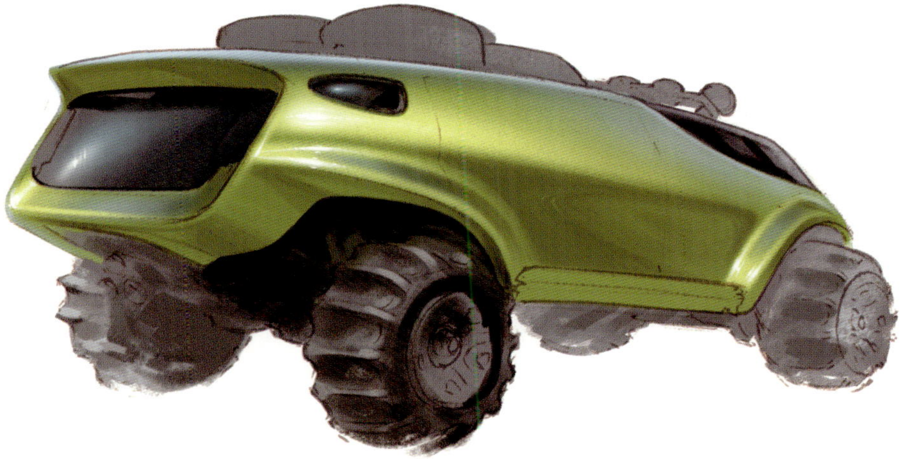

9) Block in tires and underbody.

Keeping a feeling of looseness from the original sketch, I roughly block in the tires and underbody, and I also contrast the clean, smooth appearance of paint. I don't use the full darkest value black, but add enough to contrast the body. Full black is used usually only near the focal point, sparingly. Glass areas have a touch of aqua-toned tinting film in the highlighted areas for additional color interest.

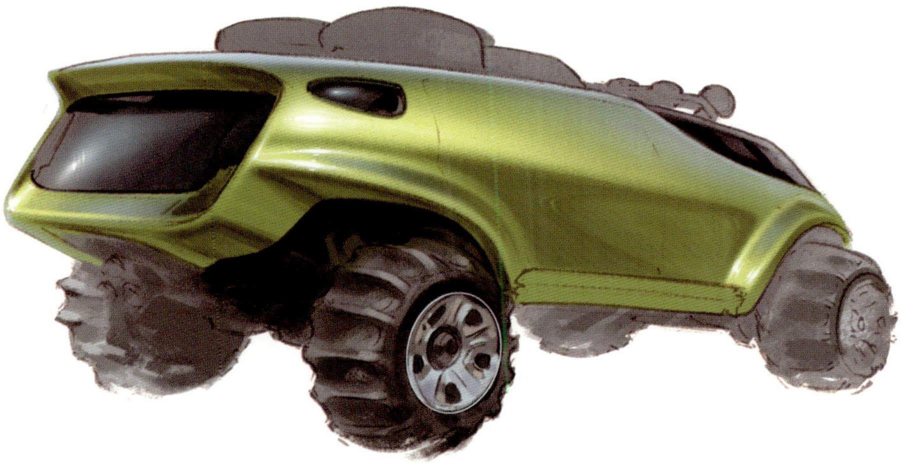

10) Define chrome hubcap and reflective tones.

I'm doing this very quickly and roughly, and letting the color and value provide the sense of form and materials. In the metal finish, I apply warm gray on surfaces that angle downward, reflecting the tones of earth: somewhat desaturated greenish blue to purplish darker blue on surfaces angled up toward the sky. Surfaces facing the zenith are best indicated with higher saturation of blue and more purple. Atmospheric haze pushes the blue toward a lighter neutral and green.

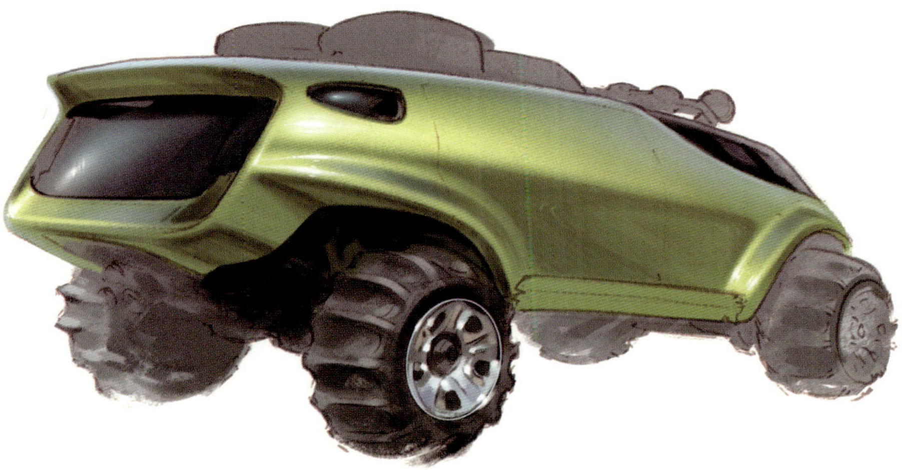

11) Create solar reflections.

Dabs of white indicate solar reflections on the wheels, dazzling the eyeball by breaking the boundary edges of the surface and bleeding into the tire area.

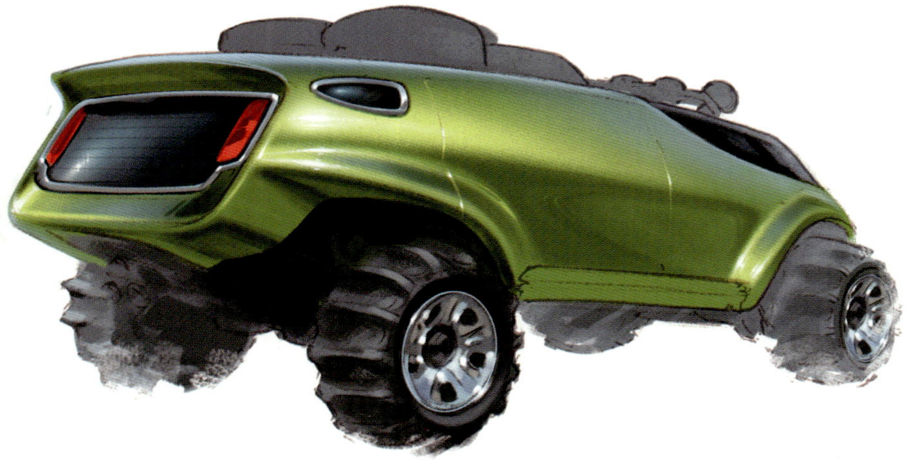

12) Add chrome trim.

Chrome trim around the glass forces me to slow down this rapid sketch a bit to ensure the clean separating metal bands look sharp and distinctly border the glass and paint. Color again is dictated by the surface angle previously outlined by the wheel material rendering.

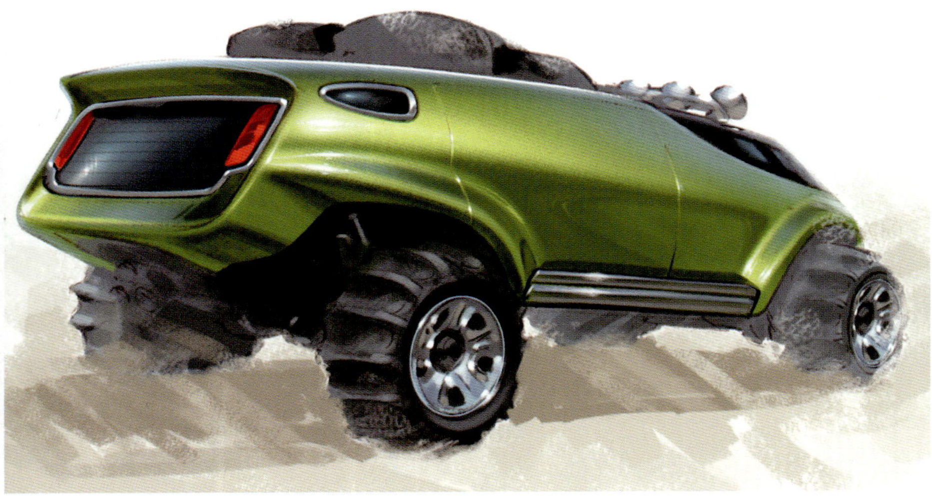

13) Rough a background.

Moving away from the focal point, the background is the most painterly and spontaneous area. Sand and sky are roughly indicated with low color chroma and value contrast, making sure neither is in competition with the vehicle itself. Where the rubber meets the sand, a dynamic blend merging the tire and the ground visually sets the vehicle into the earth.

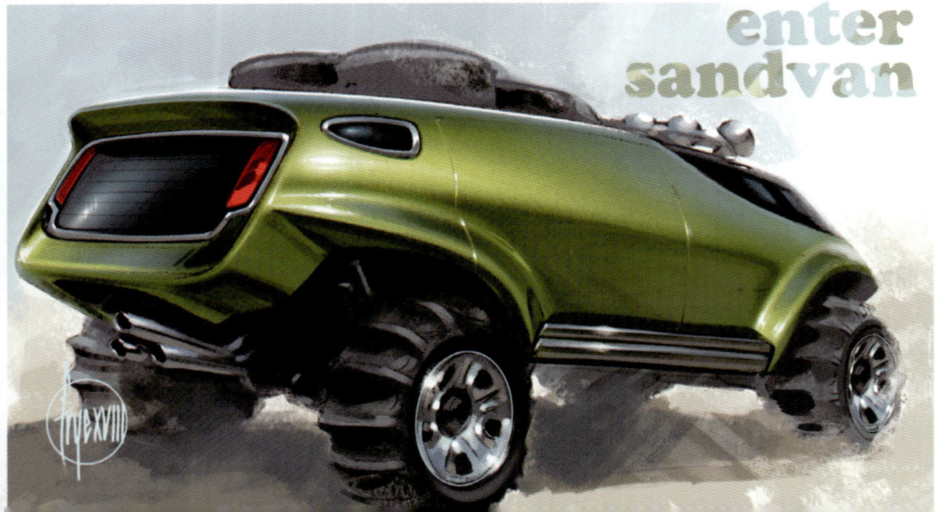

14) Refine and apply last details to finalize.

Final detailing, chrome trim on rocker, title graphic, and the overall paint color were considered in the context of the final piece. A choice was made to desaturate the green and push a tad toward the warm side of the spectrum.

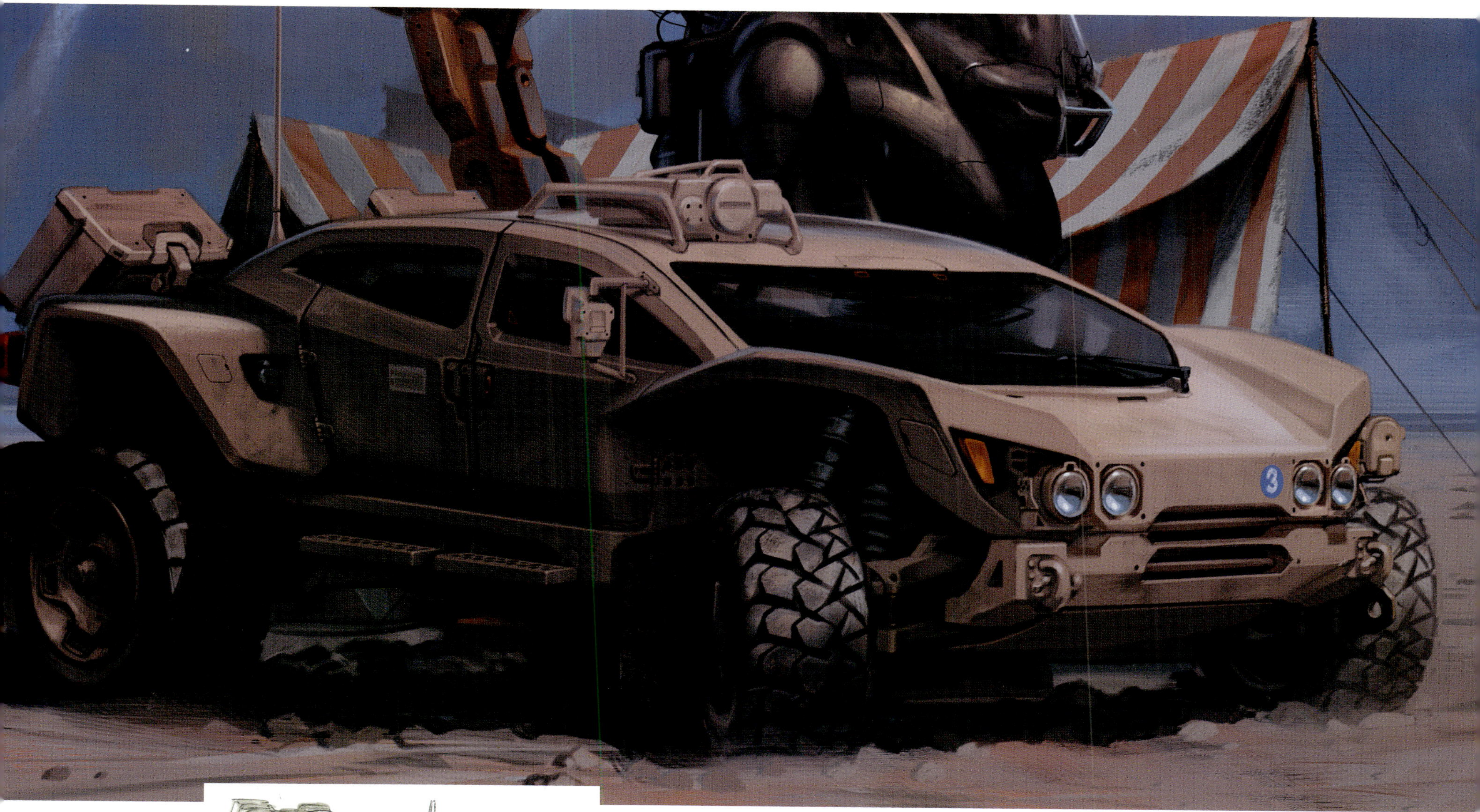

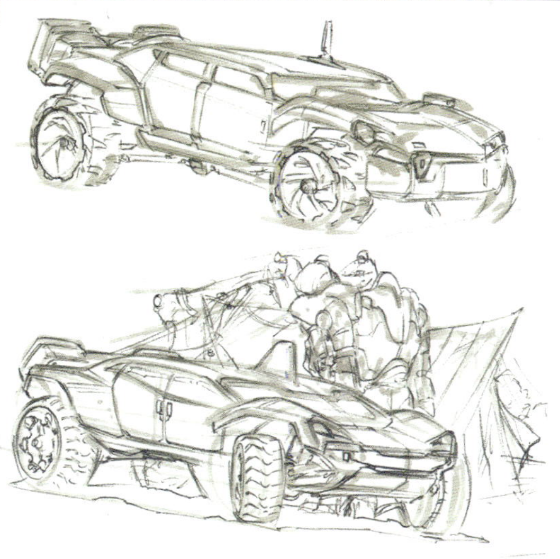

Rough little sketches for a hypothetical, government-contracted design for rough terrain led to this blue-hued moonlit color illustration. When I was a kid, I pored over the images in a series of Old West books that my parents had. The use of color and value to depict night lighting in the paintings of Frederic Remington and Charles Russell were in the back of my mind as I drew this. The wild and expressive fenders allow a huge amount of wheel jounce, suggesting a high level of performance at great speed on the roughest roads.

LB FEUERWEHR ENGINE NUMBER 14

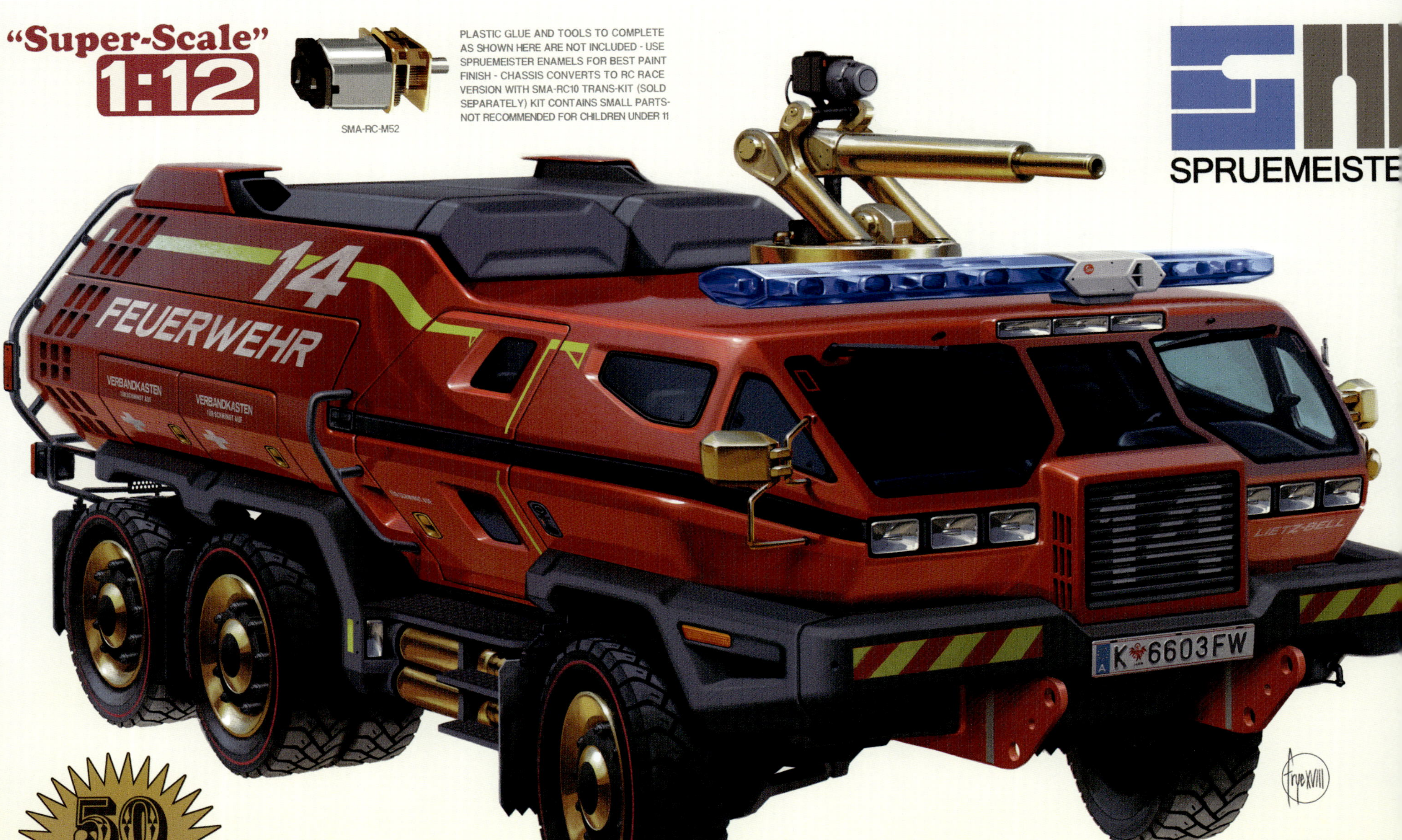

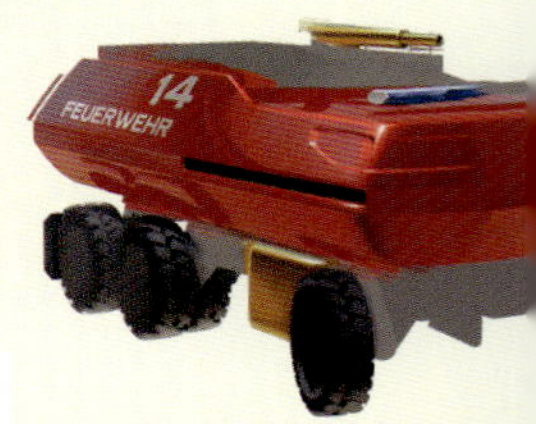

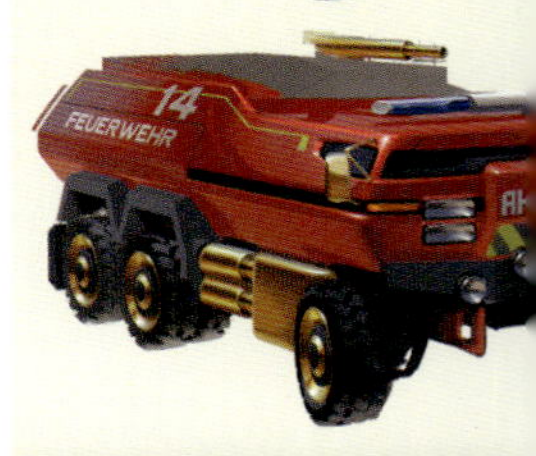

Fire trucks essentially end up being some sort of iteration on a big box, so while the details are important, the rendering of "The Box" needs to be engaging in itself. Starting with a quick color study of a **chamfered**, red-metallic extruded hexagon, I determined how to get a good feeling of depth by contrasting colors, with the near corner rendered with warm, sun-enlivened red flake and the sky blue-tinged Fresnel on the farther back portions of the vehicle. Getting a clear value change at the front edge, where the illuminated side folds around to a shaded front, enhances the feeling of volume. Quickly understanding the interplay of brass against the red paint was also important to visualize at the early stage before time was committed to the detailing. The flat front character was developed into something more dynamic, functional, and familiar.

TUŌ LĀ JĪ (拖拉机)

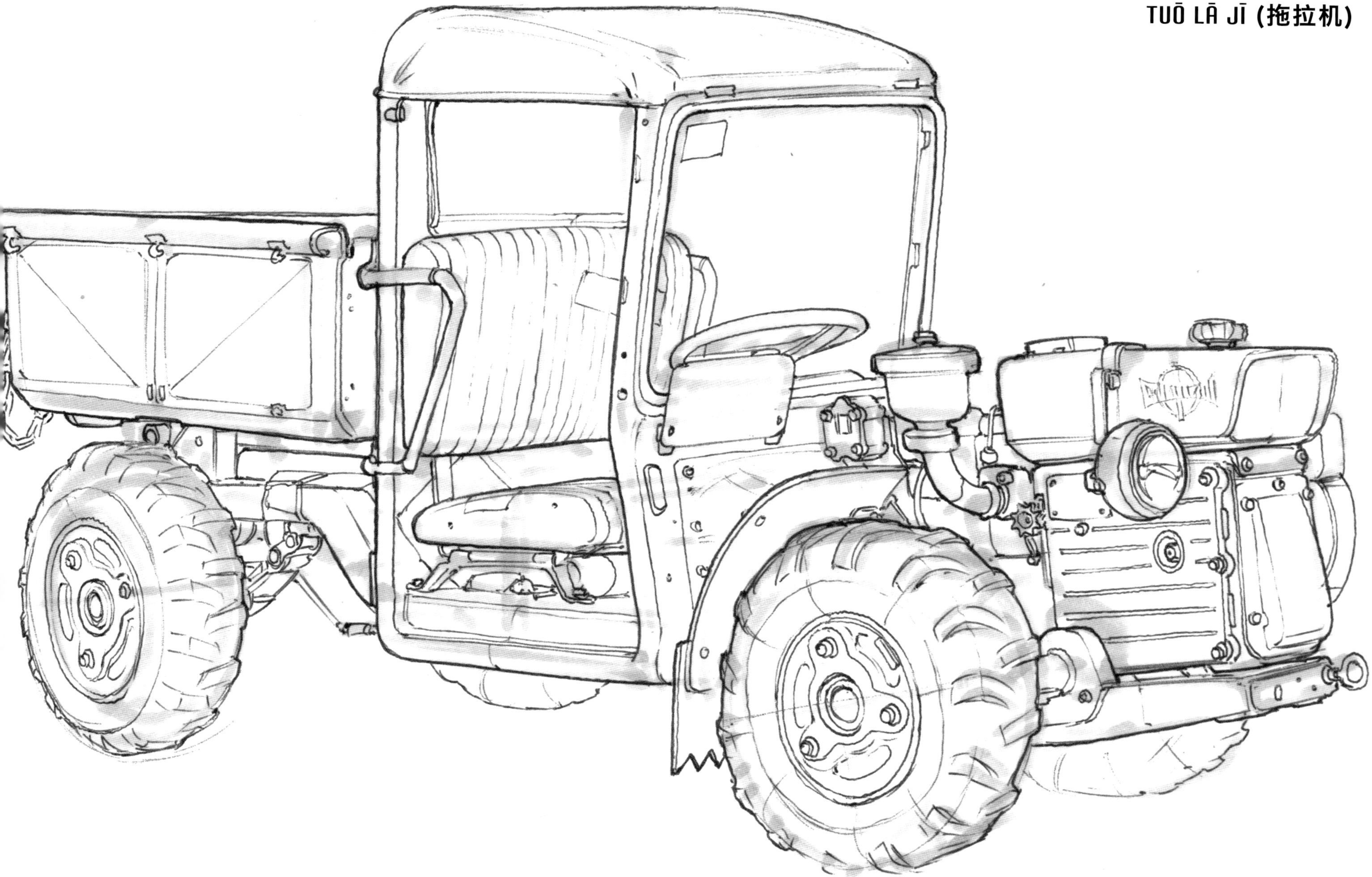

When I was in rural China, I started spotting these little agricultural utility critters everywhere. Tuō Lā Jī is essentially the generic Chinese term for a tractor, but the literal translation is "drag pull machine." There really isn't anything like them in the United States, so it was stunning to see something that was apparently so common in one part of the world that I had absolutely no familiarity with. While I initially caught fleeting glimpses of these tiller motor trucks out the window of the tour bus, I finally was able to track a few of them down on the street and study them closely. As the motor is completely exposed in the front, it takes on a rough hot rod or home-built appearance, but it's a factory-made machine. I took many photos of this type of vehicle over a period of weeks and eventually made this sketch based on the reference that I collected.

TRUCK SKETCHES

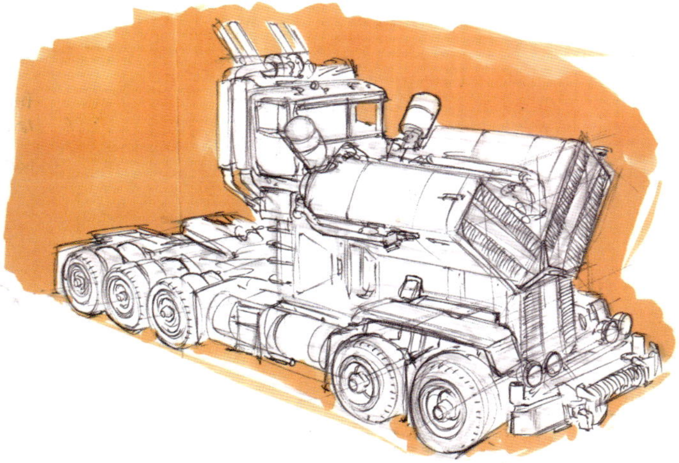

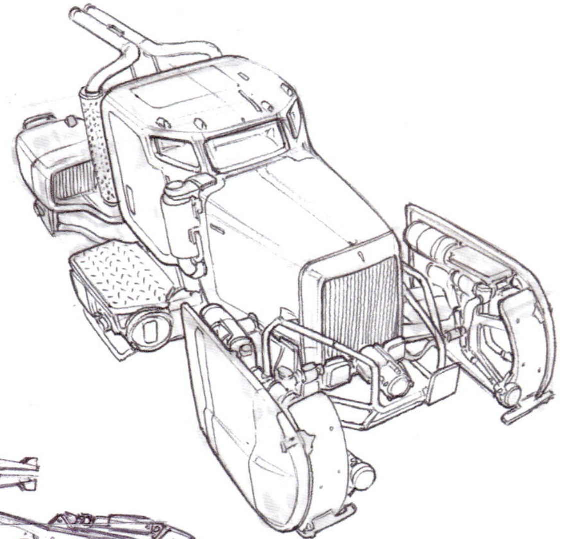

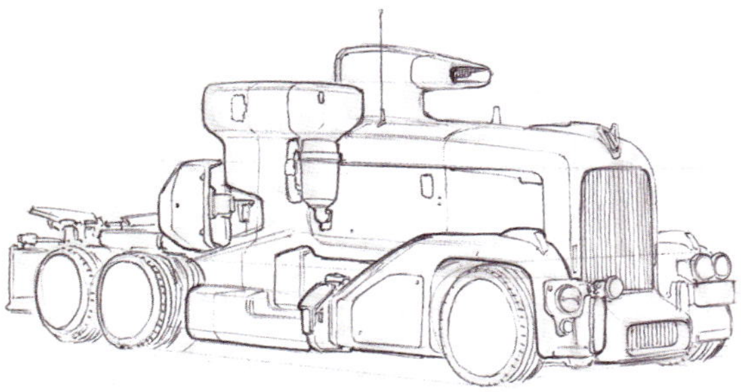

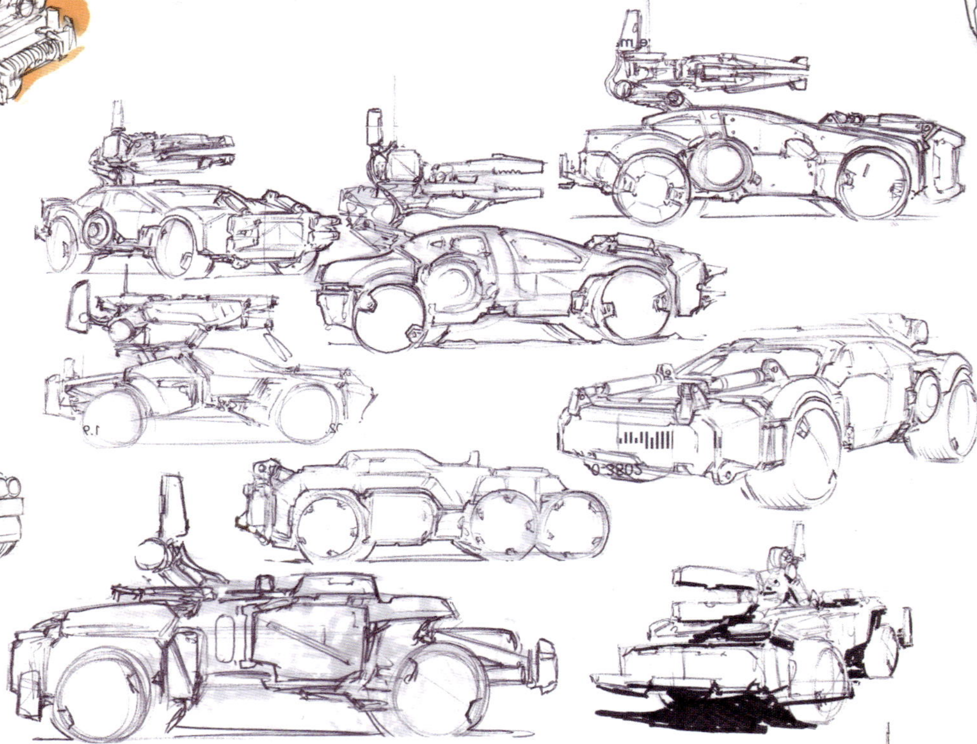

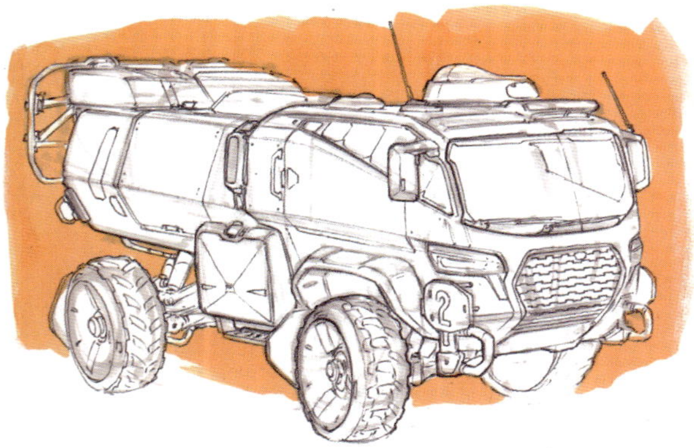

Little hard-edged stocky trucks are one of my casual for-fun doodle subjects. I enjoy decking them out with the utilitarian details. It's a zen sketching activity for me, particularly when picking away at the linework and patterns like on grilles and tires. When doing the small sketches, a little coffee can show its effects in the shakiness of lines. One of these sketches got the hover treatment, but even without wheels and knobby tires, it can retain its truck essence.

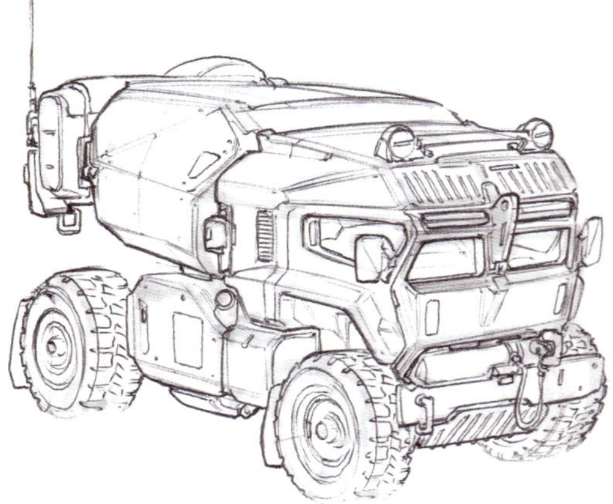

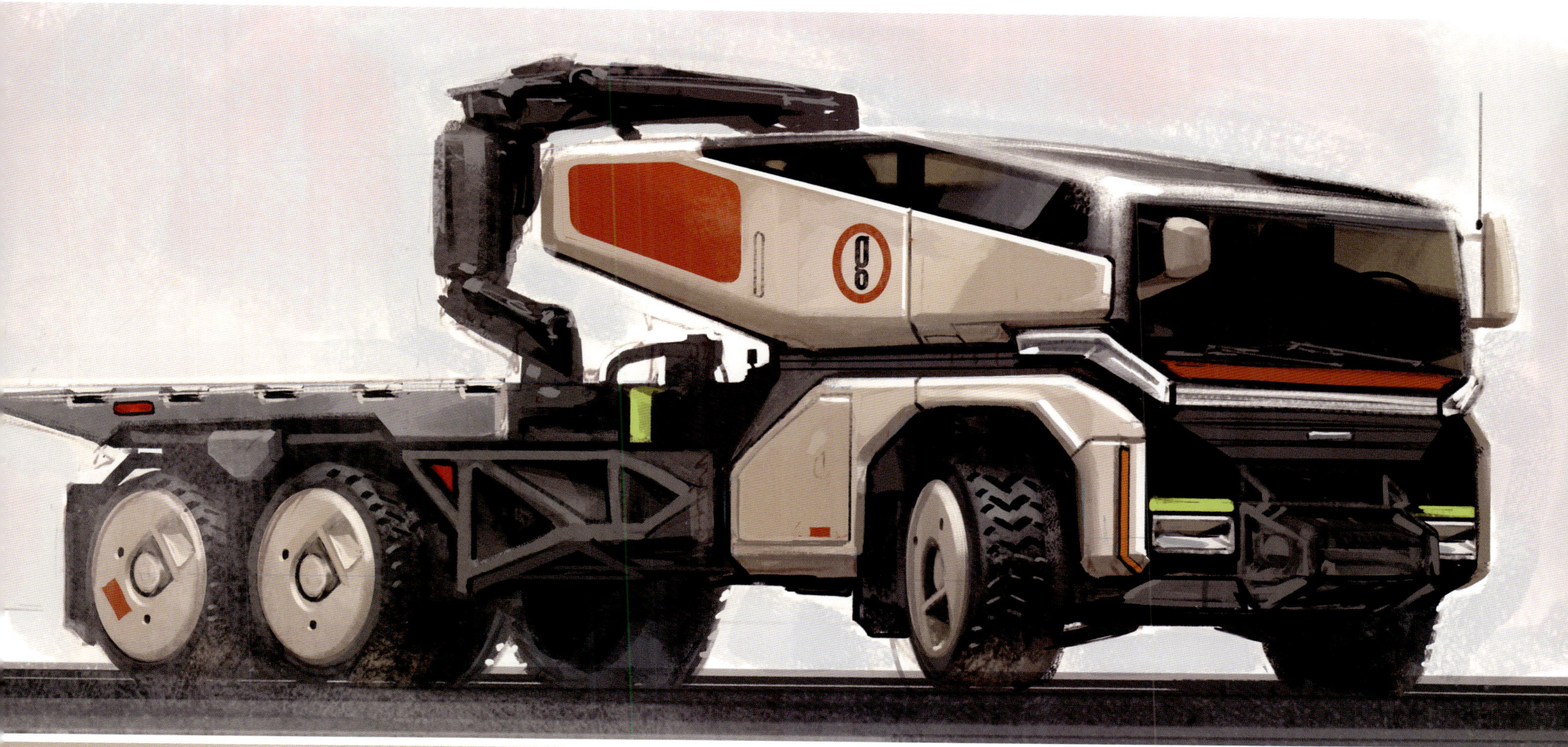

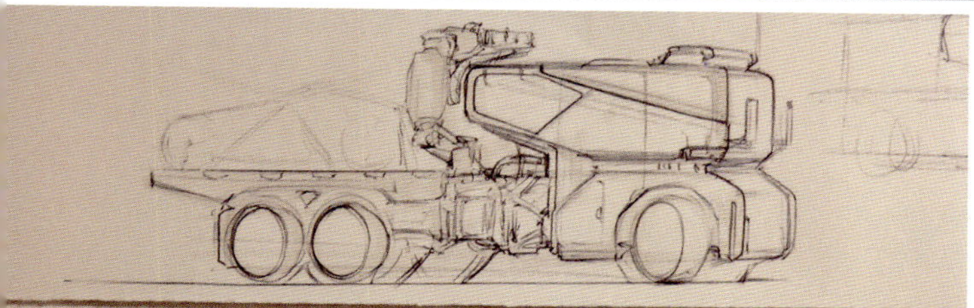

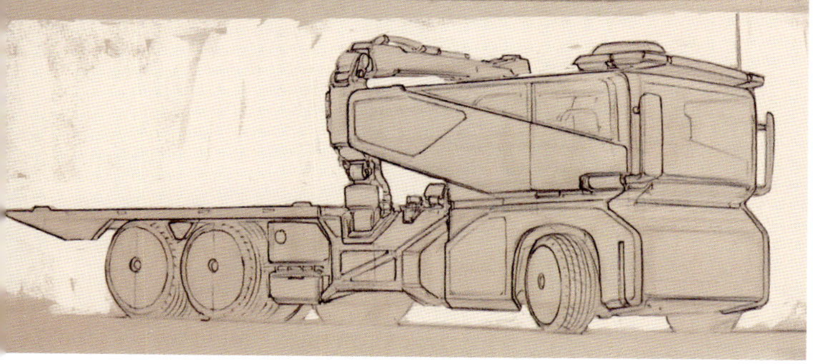

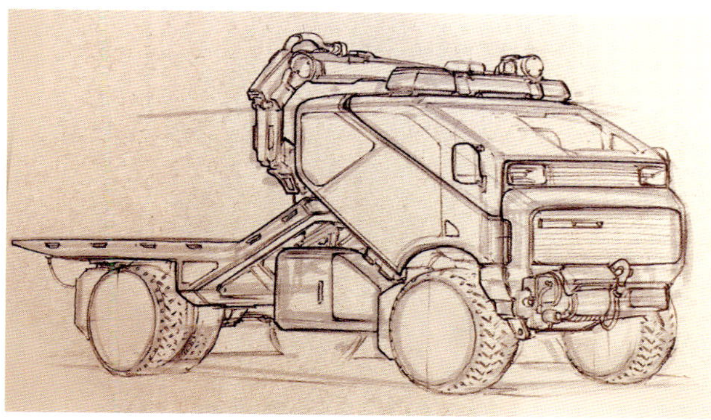

When drawing trucks, a ground-level eye point always helps present the large scale clearly.

For this exercise, I wanted to develop an idea for a track-side flatbed wrecker. I experimented with a strong diagonal graphic pattern to break up the cab design in a 1980s retro-future style. The final illustration has added character care of bold red graphics and heavily tinted slabs of glass that contrast the cream-white body panels.

TAPPAVA PUUKENKÄ

These rounded volume military vehicles are antithetical to modern common production methods that usually produce faceted, flat-surfaced body designs. The contrast to the typical folded-paper-form bodies was intended to distance these designs from reality, pushing into a sci-fi military aesthetic. My favorite style window (made as small as possible, much to the chagrin of any nervous driver) gets a lot of use in this series. The initial sketch process is captured here, starting with a quick progression from light grey marker exploration. Then building out with black ballpoint, tenuously at first, with thin, lightly sketched lines, and into more form, deliberate strokes, and finishing the line drawing with a hard-pressed, double-thick accent line to contrast thinner strokes.

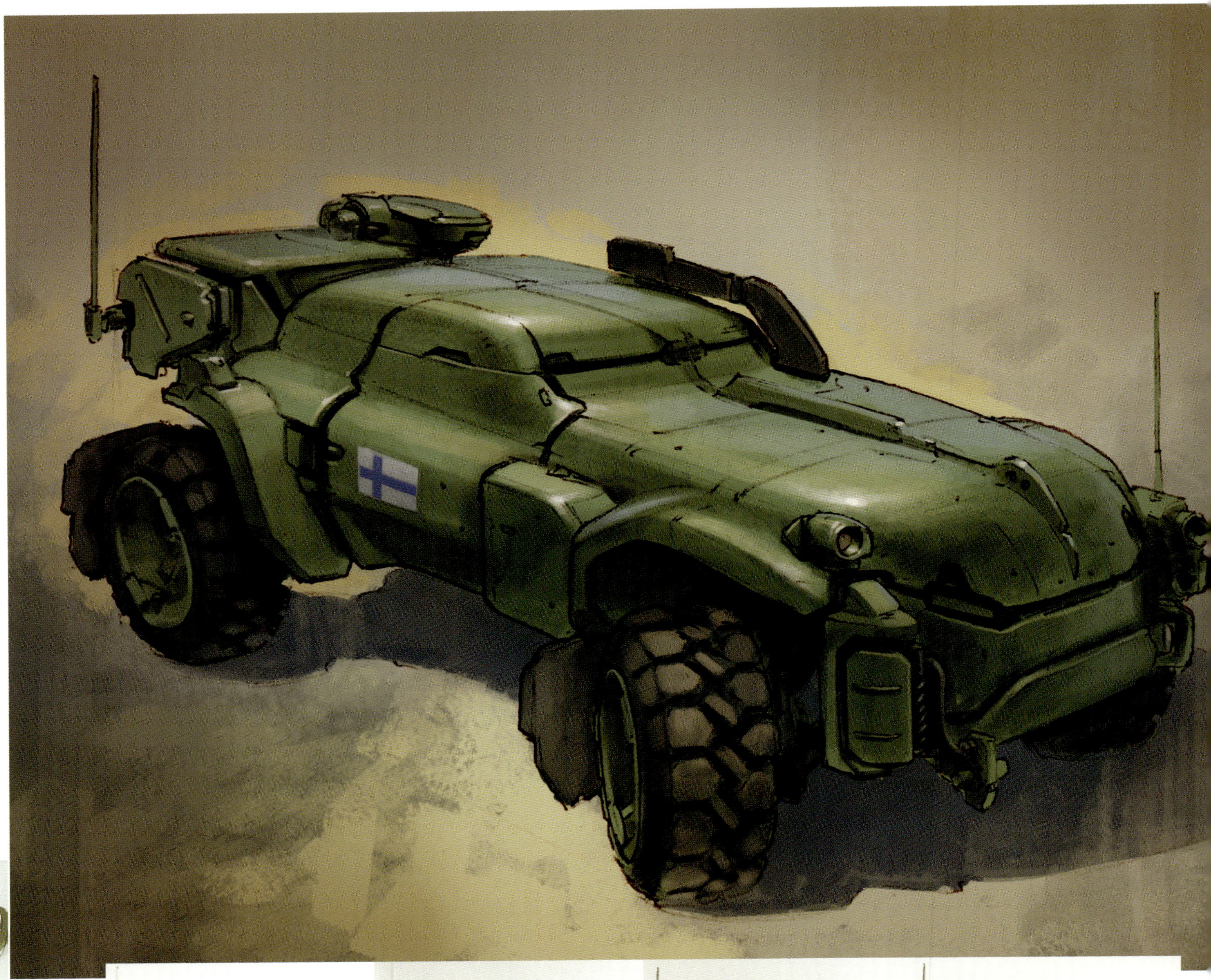

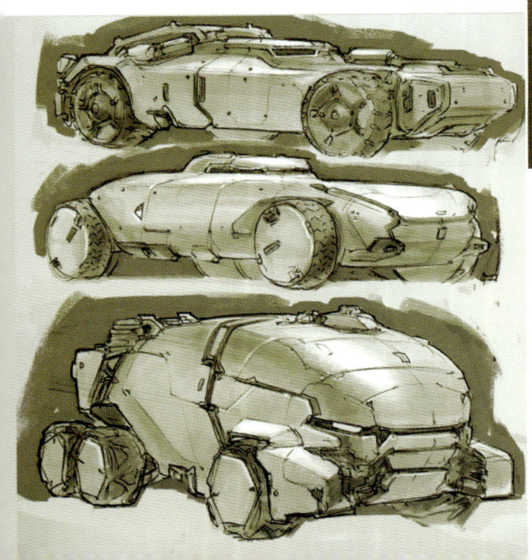

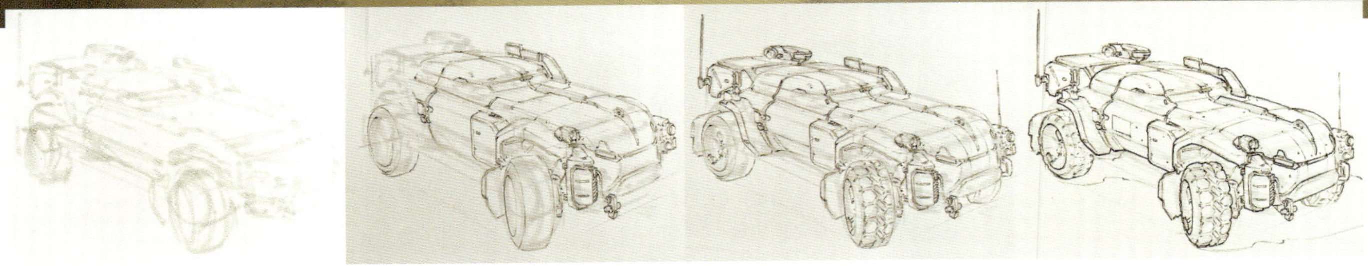

I'm always interested in the process of combining the strengths of 3D digital idea development with the enjoyable process of 2D drawing to produce a unique kind of image that does not immediately betray what method was used in its creation.

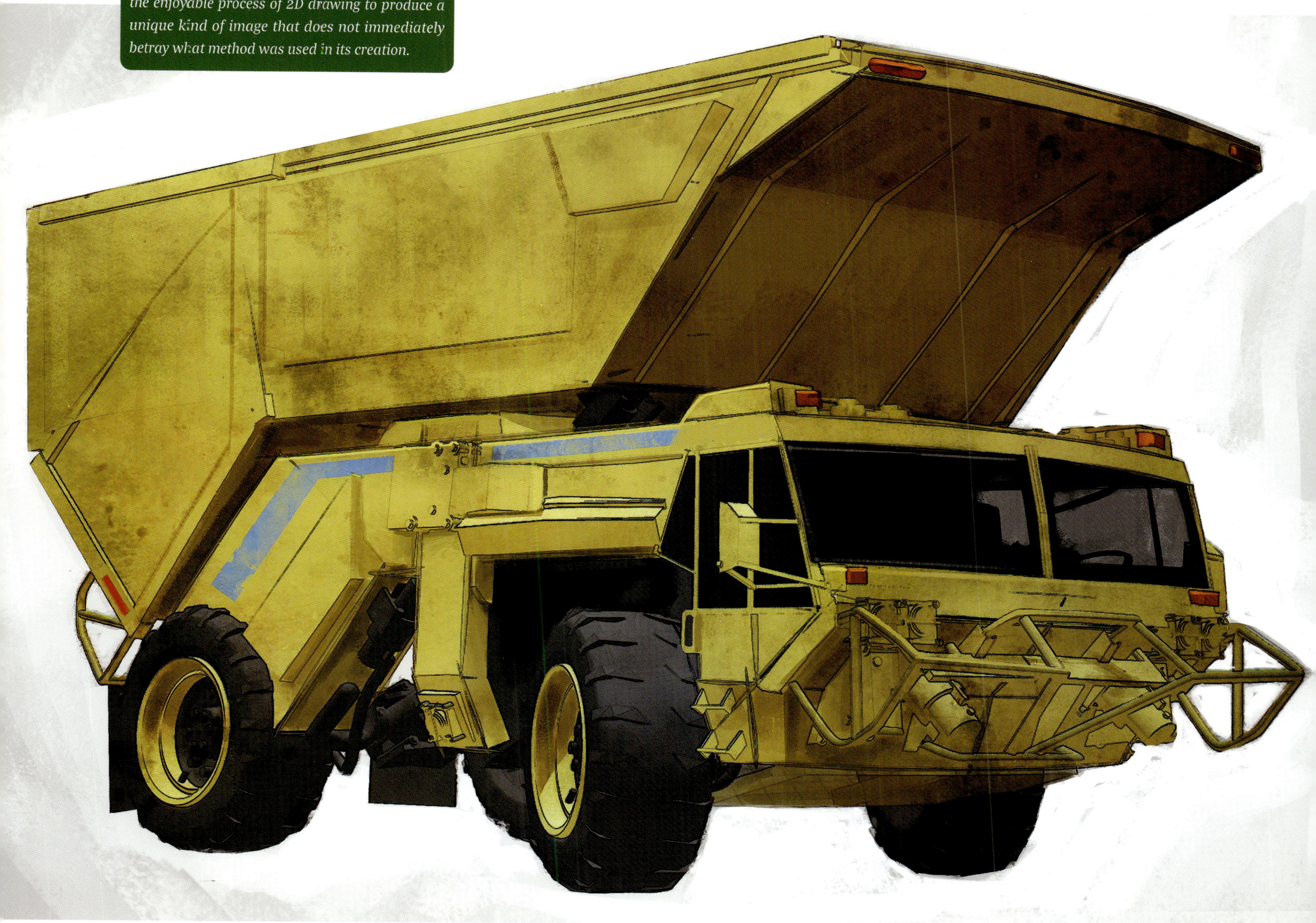

Some Gravity Sketch quick VR modeling, screenshots, and Photoshop 2D texture work and weathering.

ARMORED RIOT VEHICLES

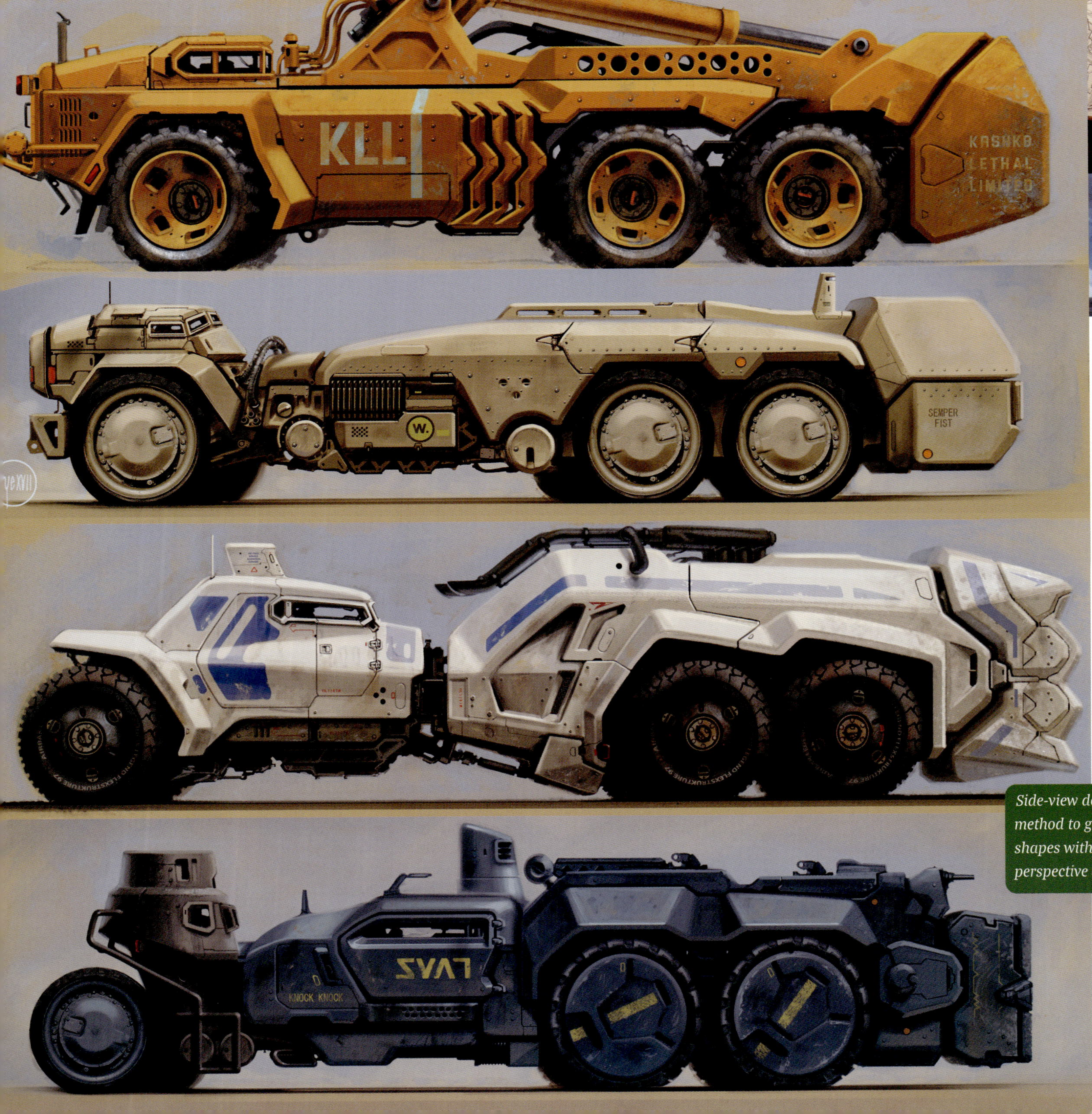

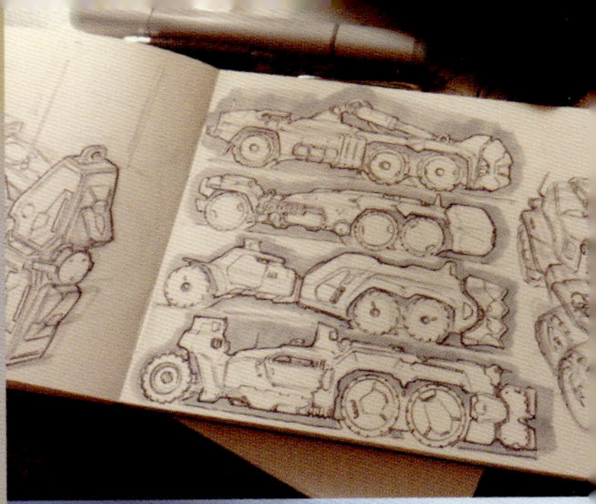

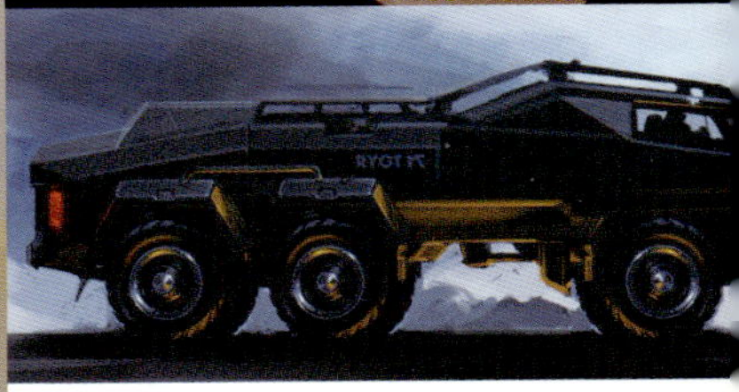

From sketchbook page to color rendering. Much of the character o vehicle can be seen in the direct si view, the longest proportion, so the success or shortcomings of a desig shape can be determined quickly from this flat angle. Taking the dire side view to finished illustration is a quick, though an angle view at this later stage is important to tell the complete story of the entire vehicle

Side-view design development is a quick method to get some distinctive and fresh shapes without slowing down to manage perspective drawing.

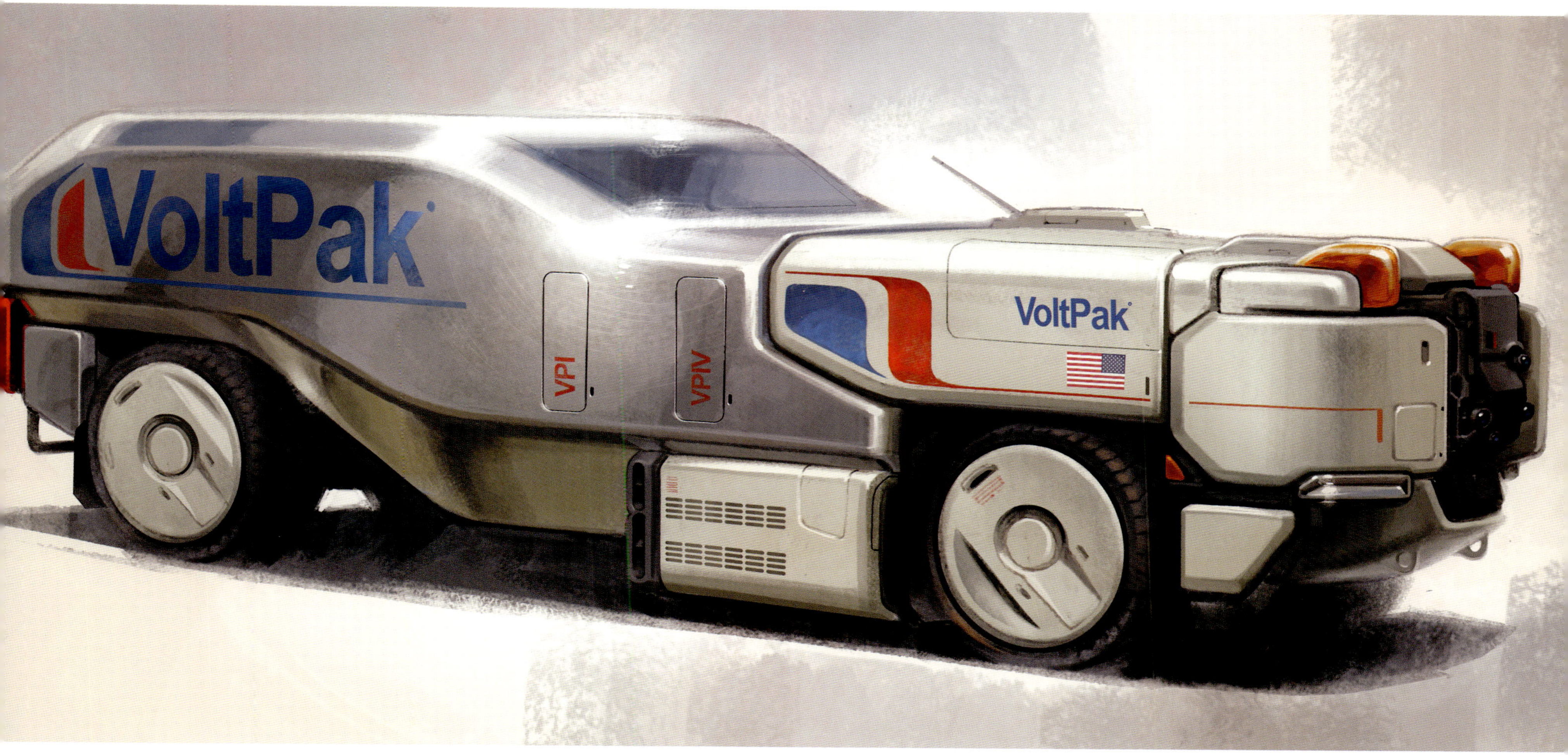

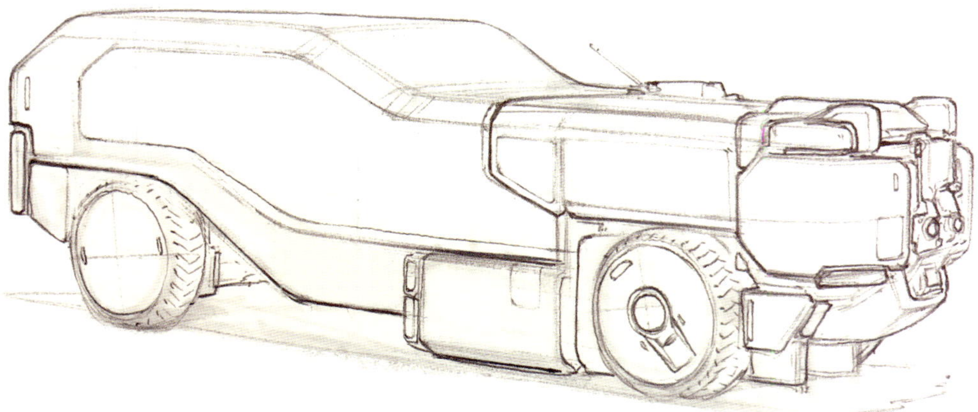

I briefly considered the design for a truck that could carry an electric charge to a location to aid depleted electric vehicles. The thinking was, If you don't have petroleum tanker trucks anymore, what would the electric equivalent be? In this case, without delving too deeply into the logic, I merged autonomous tropes with stainless-steel modern aesthetics in a rigid chassis battery delivery vehicle with graphics reminiscent of those used on travel buses in the 1980s.

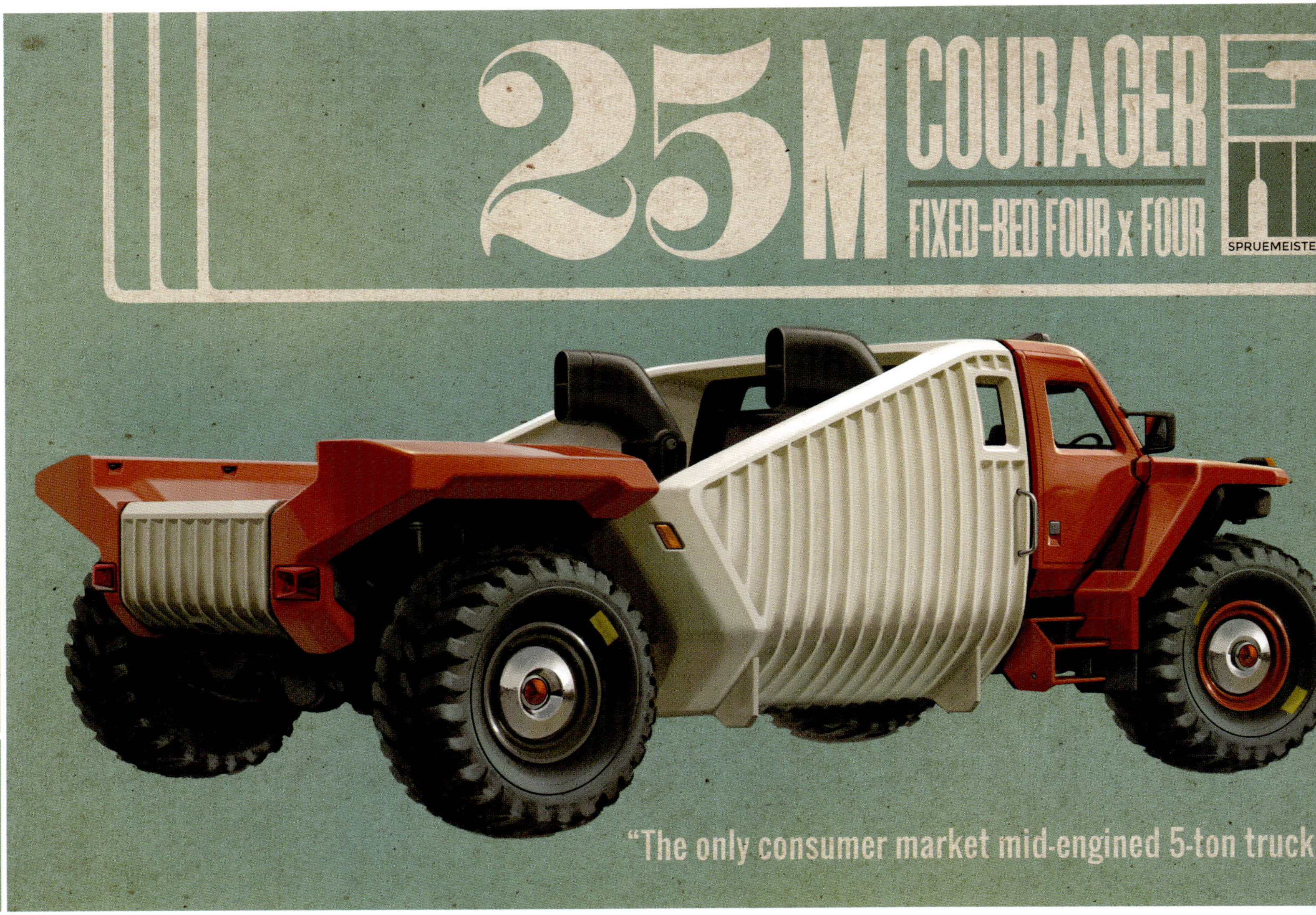

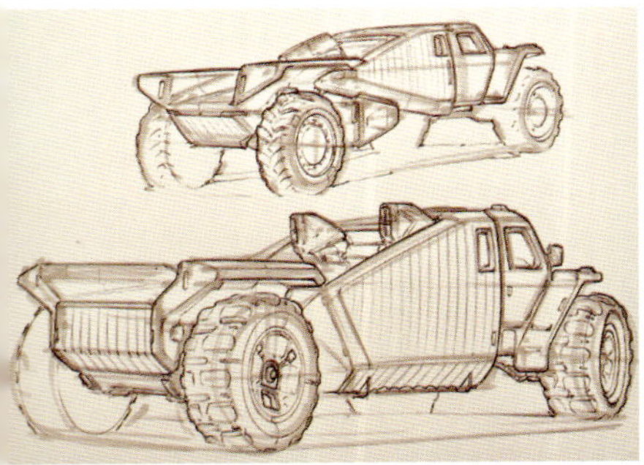

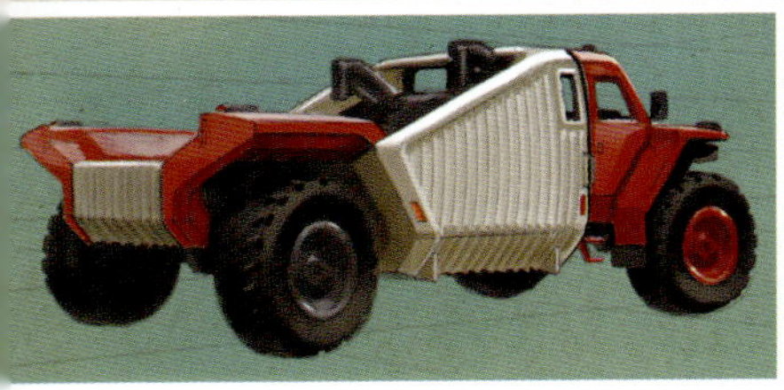

This concept direction came from observing the rough-looking shipping containers on the backs of trucks while I was on a road trip. I mixed the corrugated metal aesthetic with fuller (rounder) automotive surfaces and speculated what a pretty ridiculously large-sized consumer 5-ton truck could look like. I sketched some ideas a couple of years ago, including some marker roughs for a dual-axle version. Recently, I came across the old sketches and put them up for a vote along with a garbage truck on my Instagram account. People overwhelmingly liked the idea for this truck, so I went forward with a finished illustration. Using reference from a 1960s car brochure gave me a distinctively nostalgic color direction that I would not have normally come up with, red on a green background being a difficult color combination on the eyes, typically.

Ideation comes out of messy little sketches on any scrap of paper, such doodles that may have merit to pursue further. I sketch these throughout the day during any idle time—when waiting for a computer to boot up, sitting at the counter eating lunch. Creativity and idea generation are lengthy topics and, interestingly, difficult to pin down to the best methods. Everyone has their own process, but I have observed many approaches that have helped me.

I start with the subject. I have a very focused creativity for vehicles, so my mind already has a clear direction for considering automotive ideas. Second, the workplace is often not the best place to come up with the big concept direction. I can be watching TV, walking, driving, lying in bed drifting off to sleep and have some idea. For my own recreational drawing, it's very open because I am the sole art director. I may have watched a documentary on airports and started thinking about those cool pushback tugs that move the passenger jets in and out of the terminal area, and then consider transporting that general vehicle into a different guise to spice up the visual.

I'm always thinking about genres of vehicles that interest me but that I haven't explored as a designer. Working on the types of vehicles that I am unfamiliar with is exciting to me. I will do some cursory investigation to understand the basics of how that type of vehicle works, and the necessary functional elements that determine its appearance. I've given myself a generous safety net of "sci-fi" and "alternate reality" labels to allow for breaking away from the strict and limiting engineering aspects of the real product. This allows my imagination to run without too much worry or concern to create a new image.

I play with scale (height-to-length ratio)—big always is eye-catching. In this case, I write a short mental script. For instance, it's a passenger spaceport and ground equipment is moving giant spaceships much bigger than the jets we are familiar with. Then I have an idea for surfacing: big, **brutalist** blocky surfaces that read quickly and suggest some sort of giant, internal power source and a dearth of aero and streamlining as passenger vehicles normally would have on Earth today.

I sketch rapidly and loosely, but with logical restraint that guides and prevents senseless chaos. Functionality apparent, visual weighting interest, fresh and different forms, motion and direction to the shapes, camera angle to best show the design.

As I sketch, I am also leaping ahead mentally, thinking about the presentation of the finish. What is the color of the image? Is there an environment? Are there people interacting with the vehicle to help explain the scale and usage? Mentally, I color the sketch, a bluish dark background, industrial white paint with marking stripes and graphics zipping over the surfaces highlighting the strong diagonal chamfer. The cockpit glows from within with colored lamps and tinted glass.

This ideation process happens casually over a period of days—mentally thinking about the overall idea, playing with a design and illustration composition in my head, jotting those ideas on paper. The sketching may consist of dozens of scribbles, many scraps of paper, or it may come to fruition in an efficient single drawing. It's also very hard to explain on paper as the process of coming up with an idea is often unclear—sometimes I just see shapes and forms as I am trying to sleep. It is during those times that I know my creative energy is high and it's a good time to be sketching. While it's bad for creative work when a client has a tight schedule, it's good to recognize periods when the creative energy is exhausted and one needs to pause for a day, a week, or even a month to recuperate. I believe that we don't understand exactly how the brain works in terms of physical condition. You can't run marathons every day; you have to rest your muscles. This is also important for the creative part of your mental process.

AUTONOMOUS PUSHBACK TUG PROCESS

For the autonomous pushback tug, I was able to arrive at *the* sketch within a couple of drawings. This always gives me pause because I have a fear that I subconsciously cribbed an existing design.

Pictured here is the initial eye-level angled side view of the tug, with a very strong, simple, diagonally cut block. On the pale sticky note paper is a two-minute Q&A with myself:

"What if I tuck the vehicle under the wing of a spaceship so giant that it's completely off the page and show the difference in scale next to the tire and landing gear?"

"Oh, that's cool! The scale would really be impressive! But to get everything in the composition, the tug would need to get smaller or the page would have to get really wide."

More often than not, I will just focus on one vehicle. And my attention can remain on the main subject easier with a more abstract background. It's my area of expertise, for sure, and I think my short-term attention span is already fatigued when I consider a fully rendered background of architecture and other elements.

Tip: Working very roughly at first and tightening up incrementally in the digital drawing phase saves a lot of time and allows me to continue to develop elements of the design organically, all the way to the finish of the illustration.

It's impossible to go back through everything that I've ever seen in books and online to check, so I tend to push my designs far and into a less visually comfortable area so that I am more secure that I am covering fresh new turf.

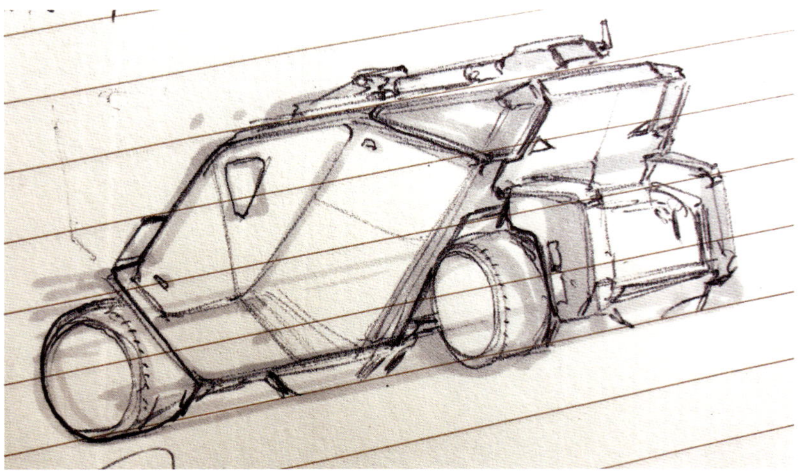

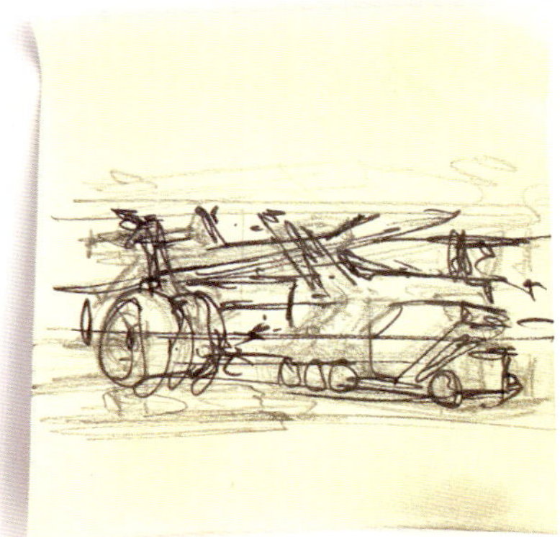

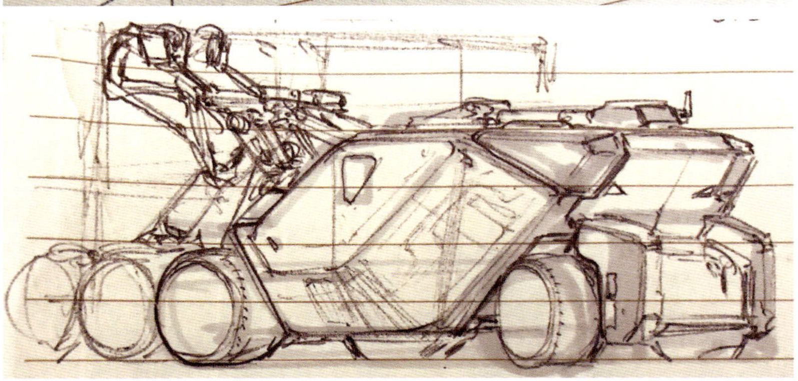

1) Further develop thumbnail sketch.

I took the initial sketch captured with a camera phone and chopped up and reconfigured it in Photoshop with more wheels and a tow arm in the rear portion, ready to use as an underlay for the working final illustration. Many years ago, I would do a very tight line drawing on a large piece of paper, which would take hours, and then capture that with a flatbed scanner and essentially color that in to finish the illustration, preserving the ink outline in the final image. Using a smartphone camera to quickly capture a small, rough sketch is much more time effective and keeps the process loose and relaxed at the beginning stages, which I find helps spur creative development of the design.

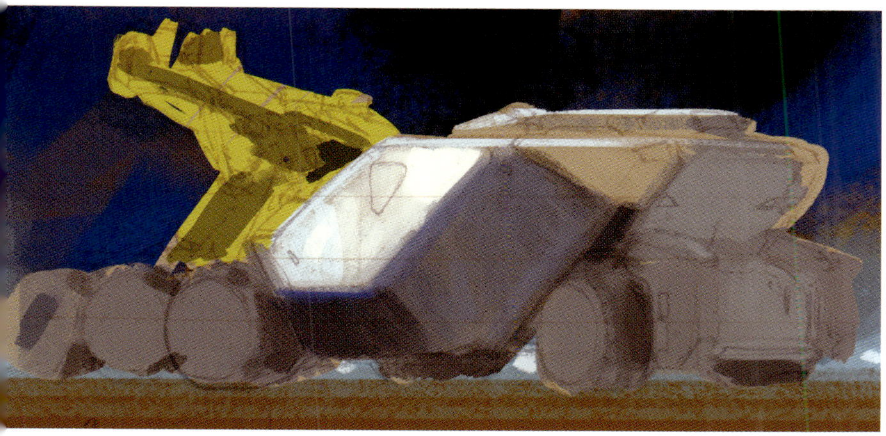

2) Establish initial color and value.

I use the rough sketch as a semi-transparent multiply layer that I can float on top of a color and value study. Light against dark is priority one. I am thinking about the direction of light, what kind of light is in the scene. I wanted to indicate multiple strong artificial light sources, casting different-colored shadows. Some bounce light from other directions, but I kept the strongest light on the side so that the front of the vehicle would be generally darker and I could get the headlights and interior cockpit light to glow intensely by contrast. At this step, that is still in process. I have quickly visualized the color contrast of safety yellow of the towing mechanism in back against a dark but pure blue. I also am suggesting a spaceport tarmac with some turquoise distant lighting that peeks between the silhouettes of the wheels. This establishes a scene roughly, but also helps highlight the number of wheels that is distinctive to the design.

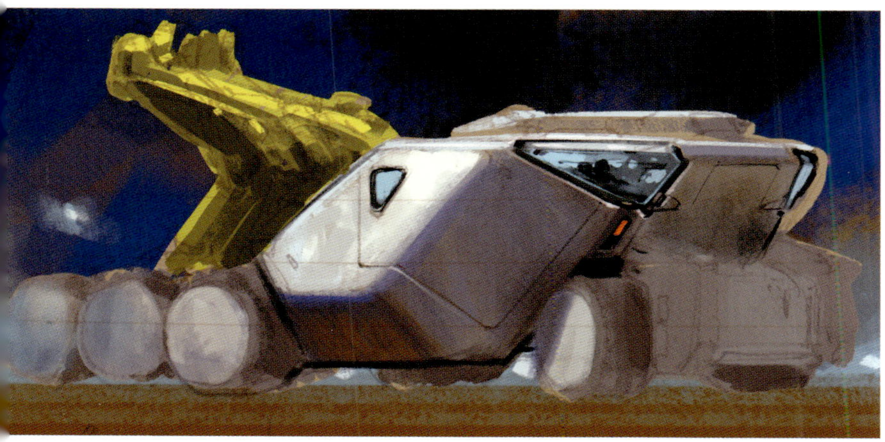

Working with strong and controlled value contrast ensures that you hold the image together without the little details.

3) Get the focal point and details to "read."

One of the great things about working digitally is being able to control the effort and level of detail during the illustration process by scaling the image. When working on physical paper, it was necessary to step away from the drawing table to see things from a distance while making the image. This distant viewing is an essential part of the process, as you can see the "far read" and make sure the image still has character and interest when the detail is removed. In these early stages, I am doing my work zoomed out in Photoshop and applying color and value quickly with broad brushes, being very aware of shape overlapping shape and getting the parts of the vehicle I want to be the primary focus by ensuring the value contrast is greatest. This vehicle has a giant slab of lit white that is unique to its character. I make that come forward by darkening the background right behind it. I begin to carve in some detail at a comp level, testing how things read, or appear to the eye. Does the material look like backlit glass with this brightness and color? Does it bring the eye to that area as a secondary focal point? Already, I can see that the little amber safety lights under the cockpit window are sufficiently noticeable. Putting the marker light in a black hole makes it pop even more.

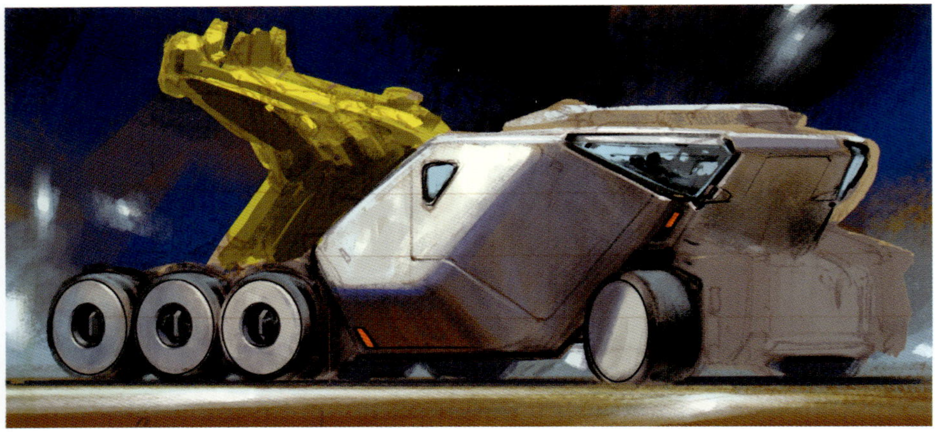

4) Work from the wheels up.

Getting the wheels and tires clarified is a big, important step. The contrast of the tire rubber to the face of the wheel and the body gives me a very clear idea of the overall impression of the vehicle to wheel balance. This is key to the expression of the design and visually determines the purpose and overall character. If the wheels are larger, they make the vehicle look physically smaller and can make the vehicle appear as if it is designed for all-terrain use. For this design, multiple axles and many wheels in back indicate that a large amount of weight that could be towed would be adequately supported. The lower profile tire could be a solid rubber, again, for heavyweight industrial use, but also showing that this vehicle is to be used primarily on a smooth, flat surface. Smooth covers help with safety–ground crew are less likely to get snagged by exposed lugs and bolts if the vehicle brushes against them while moving. Once the wheels are truly established in the illustration, I can clearly anticipate the look of the final image and understand what adjustments need to be made as I tighten up and add detail.

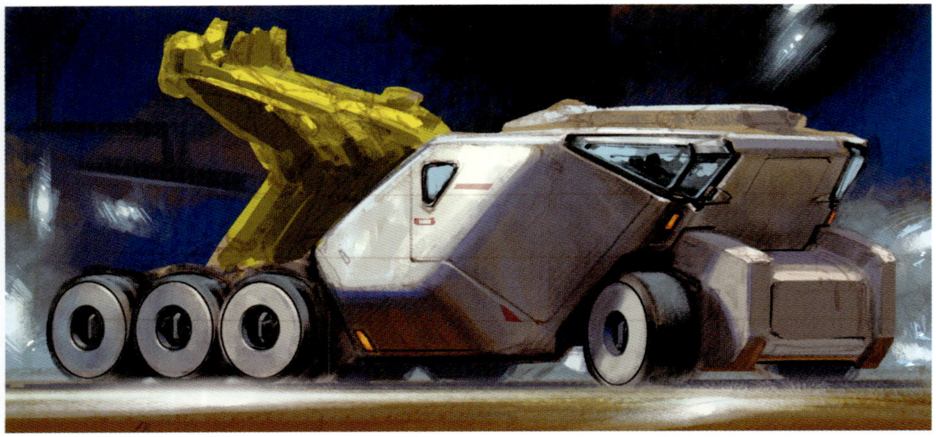

5) Develop the front of vehicle.

The front end of the tug gets the effort in this next step. The shapes are big and blocky, showing the strength and force that they are engineered around. The side lighting is catching bits of the front. Having a colored halo edge of the shadow was something that I wanted to experiment with in the image, so the front wheel both catches and casts light onto the front bumpers. While the bounced light into the shadow has orangish warmth, the edge where it transitions into the brightly lit surfaces is purple. This complementary color juxtaposition is much more interesting than just using gray to shade a white surface. Elsewhere, I am playing around with small graphic details in red on the body and carving into the cab to ensure sufficient clearance for the wheels to turn. The connection of the wheels to the ground is made less harsh with the addition of a low-lying haze that knocks down the strong value contrast between tire rubber and brightly lit tarmac.

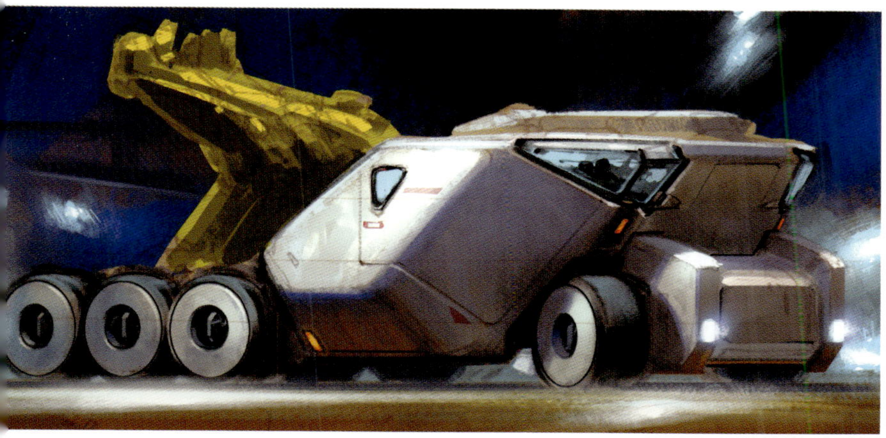

6) Punch up the image value contrast.

Some steps are subtle to the eye but very important. At this stage, the main elements of the vehicle, background, foreground, color, and value are all present. I flatten all the layers, and then work with punching up contrast in focal point areas (brighter, almost glowing lit areas of the front wheel and bumper, flicking on another set of lights on the lower bumper) and pushing back other parts (reducing value contrast of rear wheels relative to background, smoothing and cooling some of the warm shadows).

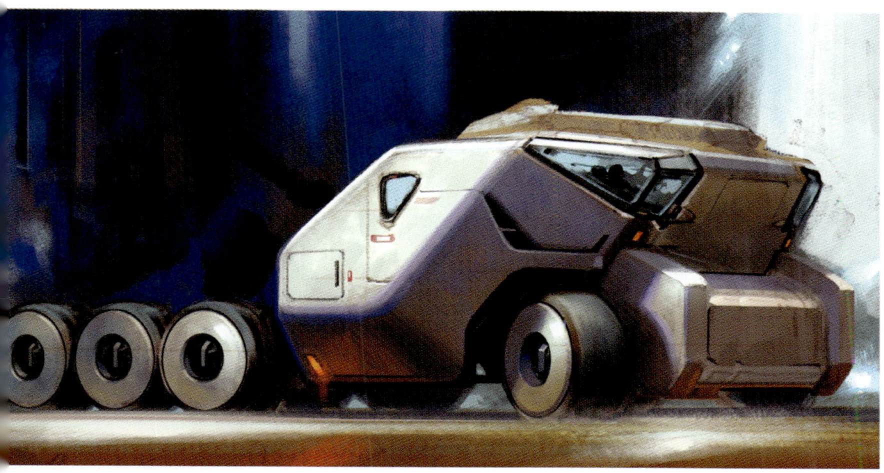

7) Add perspective.

Before I got into more detail, I wanted to add a bit more perspective to the image. Originally, the sketch on lined paper was very flat. While this still has the appearance of a telephoto lens shot, I've added more convergence to the side and front–the roofline angling down as it moves toward the horizon. More "suggested" detail is added in the background. Working with broader textured brushes in the background helps keep the focus where it is intended, in finely detailed focal point areas on the vehicle itself. The tow apparatus in back is wiped clean, as it had not been thoughtfully designed in the initial sketch, simply a general placeholder. I've also made some shape modifications to the bold side surface and adjustments to the mass of the cab that visually shortens it and gives more real estate for the rear tow area. I also wanted to show a front push/tow bar coupling activity in front, so I made space on the right side of the image for that and brought in a brightness in the background there to bring the eye to that area and clarify the shape of the far side of the cab.

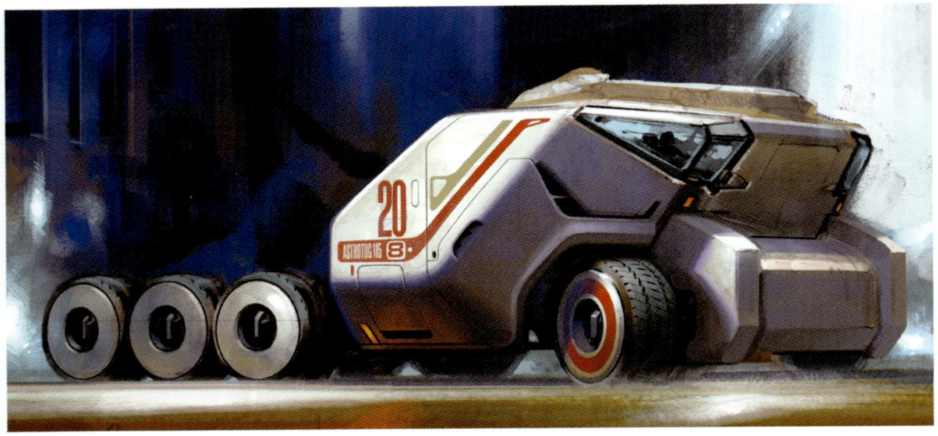

Detail should be applied in select areas; overdetailing can look unnatural and forced.

8) Ready for my close-up work!

At this stage, I'm working with the image zoomed in closer, using finer brushes and chipping away at detail. Small moves that take a lot of time. Throughout the process, I work from loose to tight, big to small, fast to slow. I like to retain some of that early, loose-process stuff in the final as texture that adds energy, if I can. If everything gets polished and tightened too tightly, the image loses some of its relaxed and painterly energy. Here, tires get stripes; a red stripe on the front wheel adds some fun and also is an area to be playful using the effect of the shadow color, going from a lit bright red to violet in the shade.

The side panel of the cab loses the window to give me more space to play around with graphics, but also leaves some broad areas clean. A curling lip highlights a visual connection of the cab to the front wheel and suggests some functionality, reducing the water splashing onto the cab. I tend to like to have logical clusters of detail around functional parts of the vehicle: the human provisions of the cab (windows, doors, hinges, ladders, and latches for egress and exit), engine areas (grilles, exhaust openings, warning labels, filler nozzles, and maintenance access panels), and moving parts (wheels and suspension, hydraulic or electrically actuated elements). The silhouette is always important. Finding ways to let light leak through or move along the edges of the vehicle adds distinct character. Behind the front wheel, a small triangle of light catches the eye, created by shapes in shadow—the **wheel-well** surfaces, a suspension or steering element, or horizontal frame member.

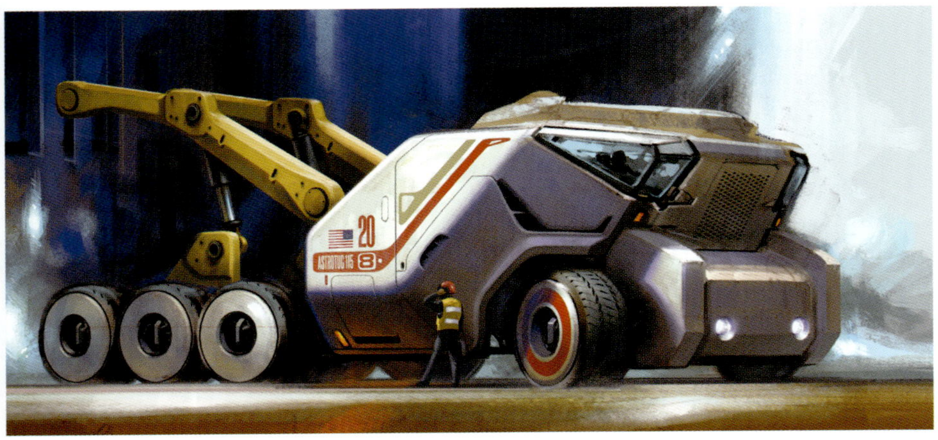

9) Tell a story with function and characters.

At this stage, it is critical to get the towing mechanism back into the image, as well as other storytelling items, such as a helmeted ground crew member with reflective vest. Adding people in the scene helps clarify the scale and also adds life, inviting more engagement with the image.

Further graphic work on the side of the vehicle includes the addition of the American flag in its somewhat awkward but technically correct "backwards" direction, as it is to be applied on vehicles as if it is flying in the wind from movement of the vehicle, such as on the right side of a space shuttle. As a setting-establishing device, the contemporary flag adds something familiar to an unfamiliar scene and vehicle design. It's also a quick way to add some colorful graphic detail without having to create unlicensed brand logos from scratch. The stripes direct the eye and reemphasize the essential, diagonally angled cab cube.

Generally, in the rare instance where I have people in the image, I will refrain from showing their faces; either I have them facing away from the camera or obscure their faces behind facial gear or helmets. The human face draws the eye too strongly, and if not executed perfectly, can bring down the entire image.

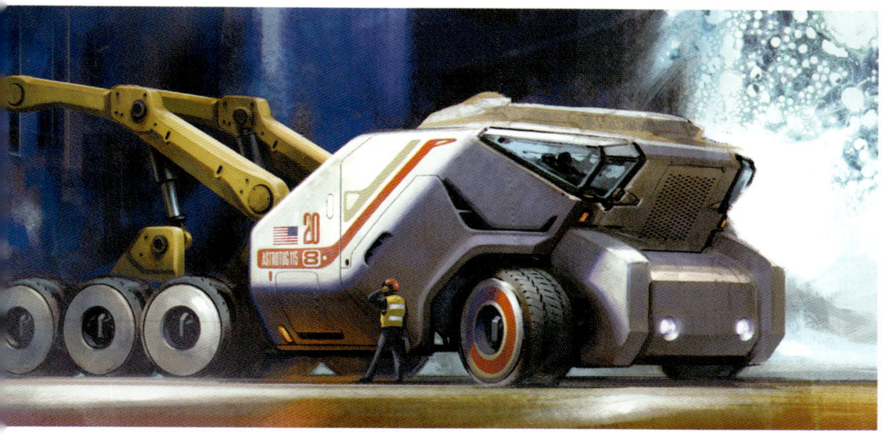

10) Decrease value contrast on one side and add texture.

Illuminated haziness toward the left side of the image reduces the dark to light contrast of the tires, background, and wheels. From right focal-point areas to the left side of the image, each wheel should appear less clear from an incremental reduction of value contrast, pushing the left side back in the image and pulling the front of the vehicle forward. I've brought in some liquid overlay textures as a contrast to the very mechanical and stiff vehicle. I create textures with paint or alcohol dyes on plastic film or paper, photograph them, and then manipulate in Photoshop to use as backgrounds. This process creates visually similar results to the toxic dye on vellum technique that was used in the auto design studios in the late 1960s to enhance and create excitement in car design illustrations.

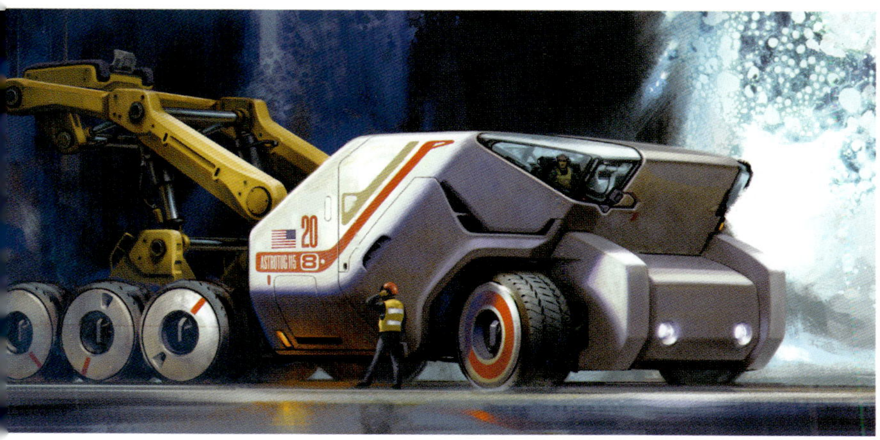

11) Detail the functional elements.

While the towing mechanism was added earlier, it wasn't fully realized. The tow mechanism suggested hydraulic rams, but the hoses have not been added. A secondary functional connector was also added. Heavy wear and lubricant leaks dirty up the yellow articulating arm, as well as rusty stains around bolt ends and bearing caps.

The contrast of saturation and value from right to left helps ensure the structure doesn't look flat in the image. The back wheels get some added detail: cutaway applied in the disc cover (valve stem access to add air) and a painted stripe to track tire to rim slippage. Clocking each wheel at a different angle instead of copying one to the next helps them feel more realistic. A nonrotating attachment system with a cam latch handle is unusual enough to imply that the technology does not exist in the near future. The cockpit cabin is executed in one go, carefully and precisely detailing the driver and his well-lit master control cabin. Single pixel dabs of precise red LED instrument panel indicator lights counterbalance the brutish and heavy-handed exterior. The ground surface got a bit of work as well, with a wet sheen now reflecting some of the light and color from the vehicle.

As I create an image, I don't necessarily complete one area and move onto the next. I'm usually moving around to different areas and refining, and then step back, zooming out to look at the overall image and determining where more detail or refinement is needed, and where color or value needs adjusting.

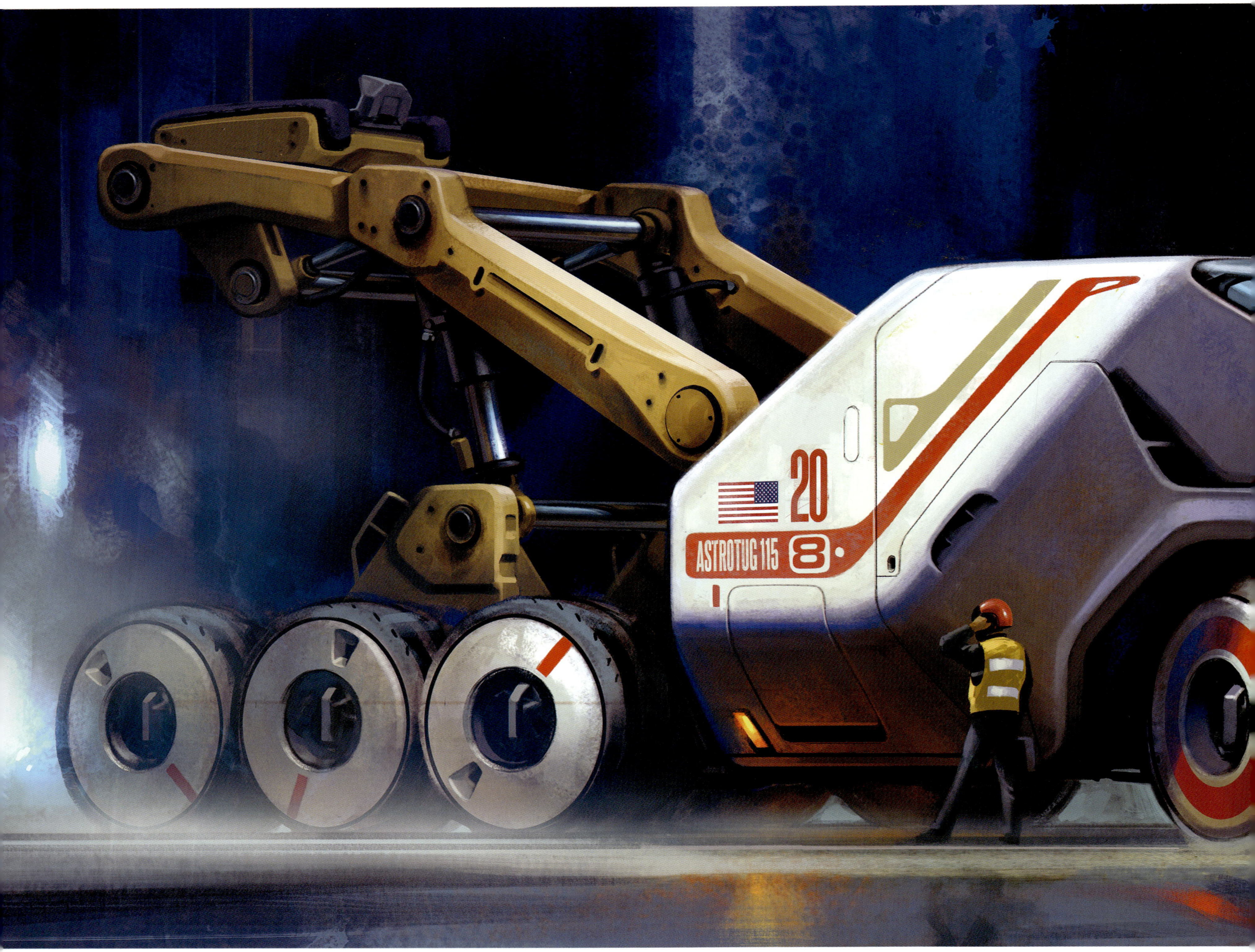
20
ASTROTUG 115
8

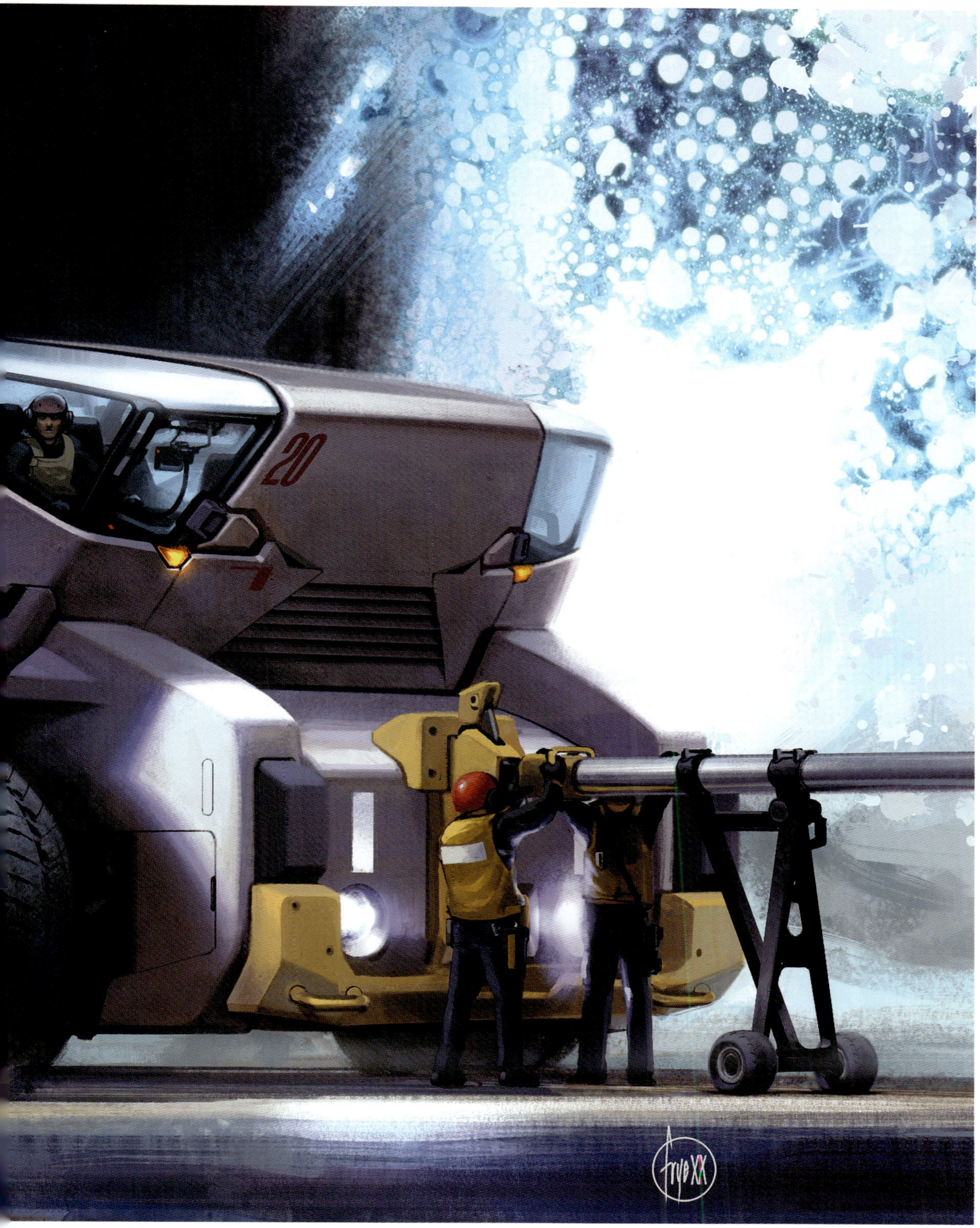

12) Finalize the storytelling.

In the final image, I added the activity of attaching the bar to the front coupling and some further detailing of the bumper and cab to give a finished feeling to some areas that had insufficient detail. Overall toning and contrast is adjusted. When the image is completely drawn, I usually spend quite a bit of time layering other copies of the whole image with darker values, less contrast. I then erase the focal point areas so that the original, brighter and more saturated image pops out in that area. Another layer of industrial haze lit by pale blue light out of frame on the left further pushes the focus back on that side.

5

CHAPTER 5 : OTHER EXTRAORDINARY VEHICLES

Some vehicles are tough to categorize, or they fall into unique areas of purpose that deserve some attention, as they are an essential part of what makes the Earth move. You'll see all sorts of specialized rigs in places that cars don't go: underwater, underground, in challenging terrain and environments. Vehicles that serve a very specific purpose other than taking passengers from one place to another often have a lot more character visually because their essential function determines the look. Something needs grabbing, needs to be dug or hauled; maybe a new planet deserves some scientific study, but the average vehicle isn't tough enough to withstand its hot and high pressure atmosphere. If you don't have paved roads, and the terrain is soft and slick like melted butter, what does the wheel and tire need to look like? If a rolling wheel won't have enough traction, what about giving the vehicle some mechanical legs, or tank treads? For many of these sketches, I have a brief snapshot of a story to go with the vehicle. Establishing the place and the purpose of the vehicle as I start to sketch helps guide me to a more problem-solving design workflow, as opposed to one that is purely stylistic.

It's a great exercise to take a more common vehicle like a city bus or a dump truck and drop it into an alien landscape and solve the problems that arise from having to function in its new environment.

MG7

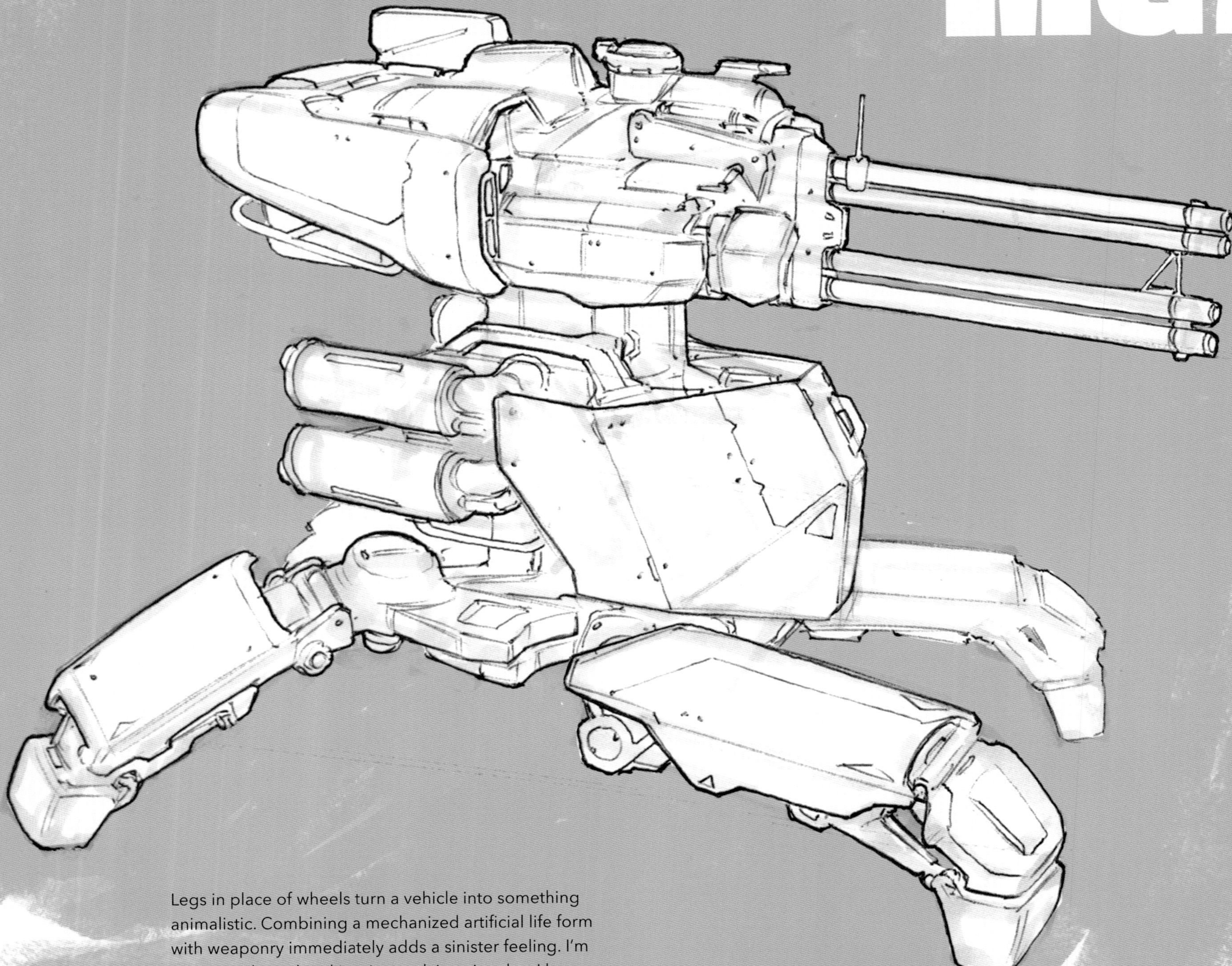

Legs in place of wheels turn a vehicle into something animalistic. Combining a mechanized artificial life form with weaponry immediately adds a sinister feeling. I'm not sure where this skittering tank is going, but I hope he's on my side of the battle!

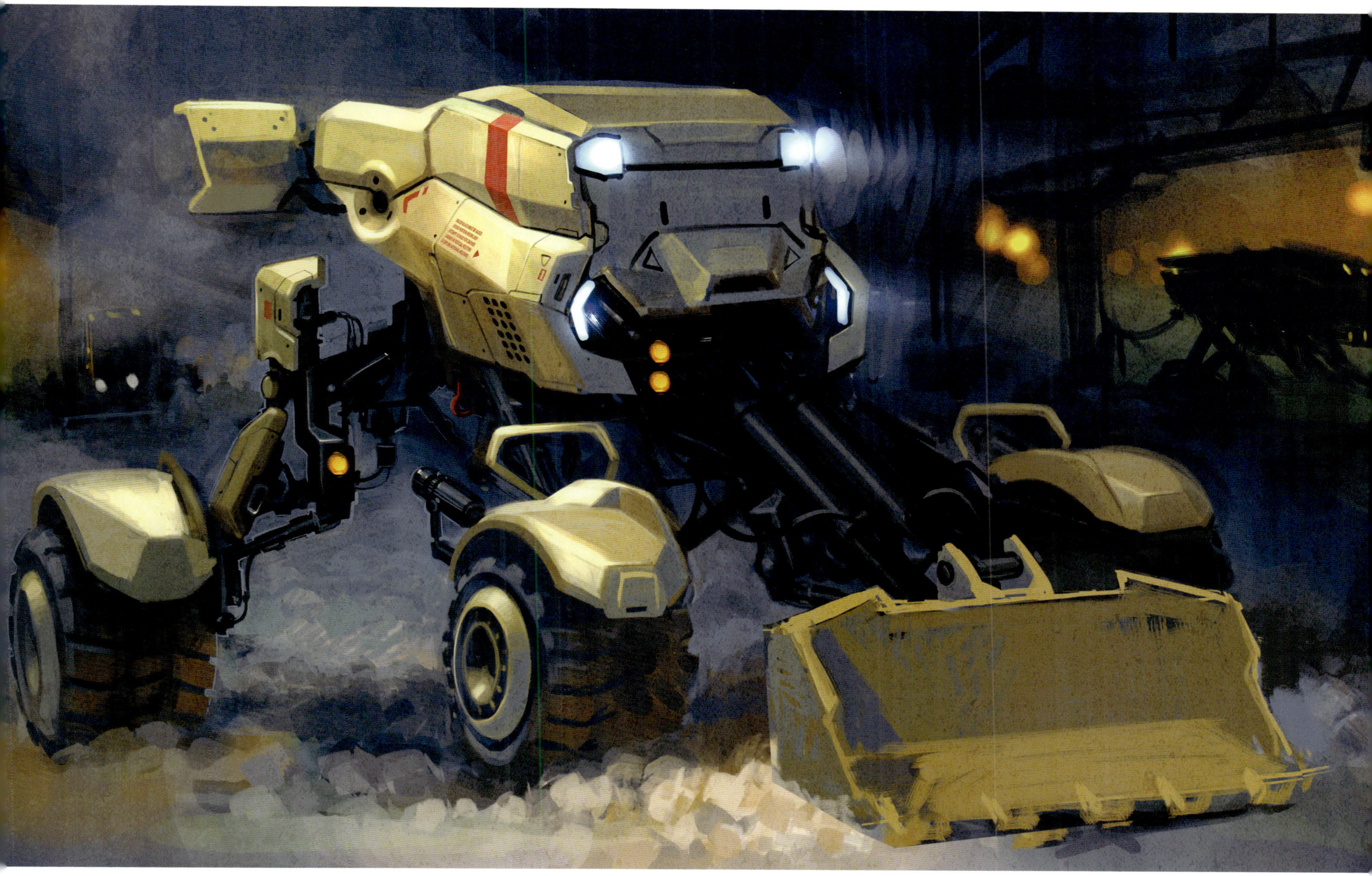

All through the day and night, restless and tireless robodozers hurriedly scuttle about the remote construction site, efficiently communicating as a team and quickly leveling the ground, pulverizing boulders and compacting soil. A week later, the human crew joins them at the site to begin laying the foundation for the rocket launch pad.

SUPERFUELER DETONATION AT MILE 16

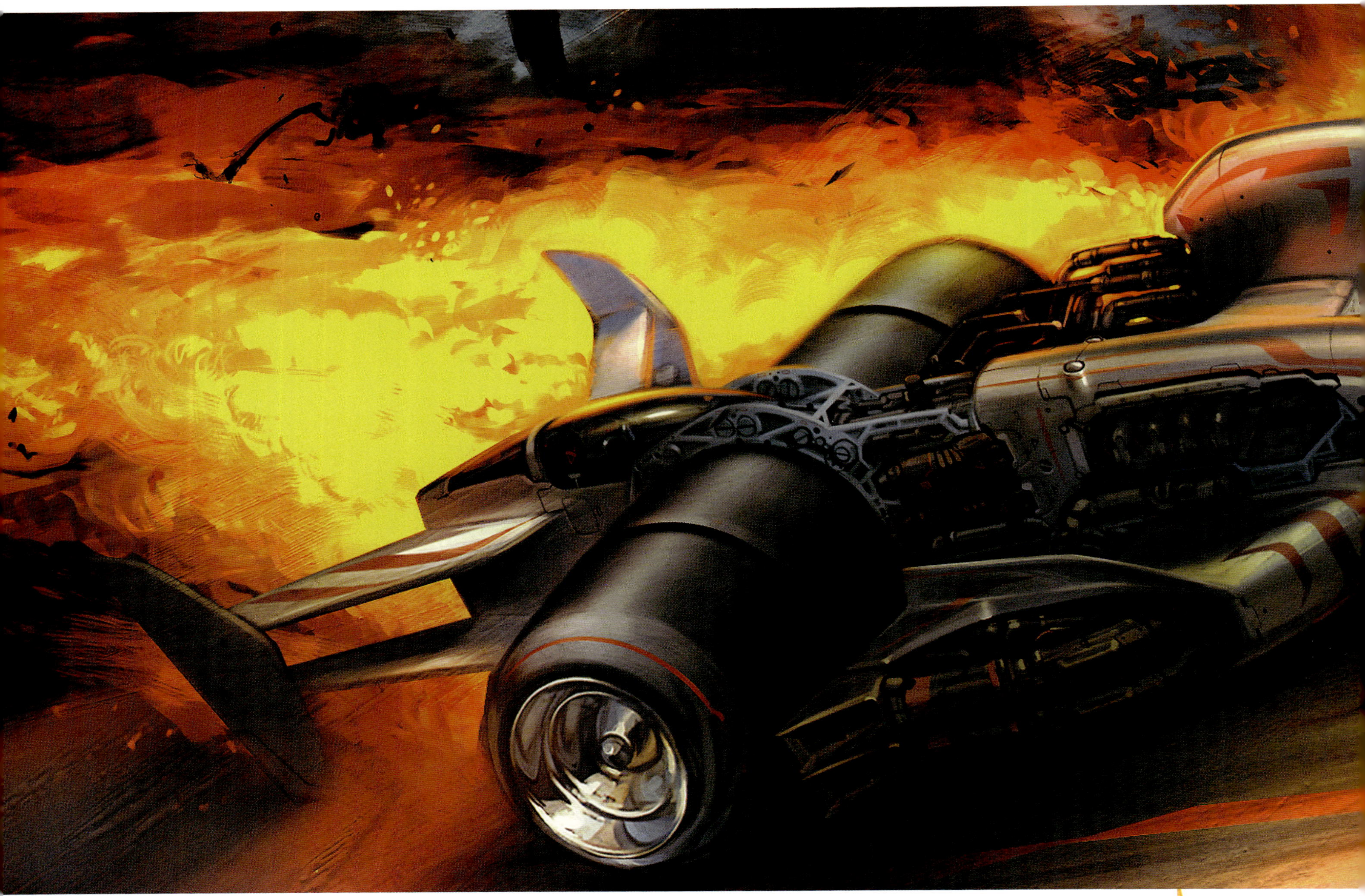

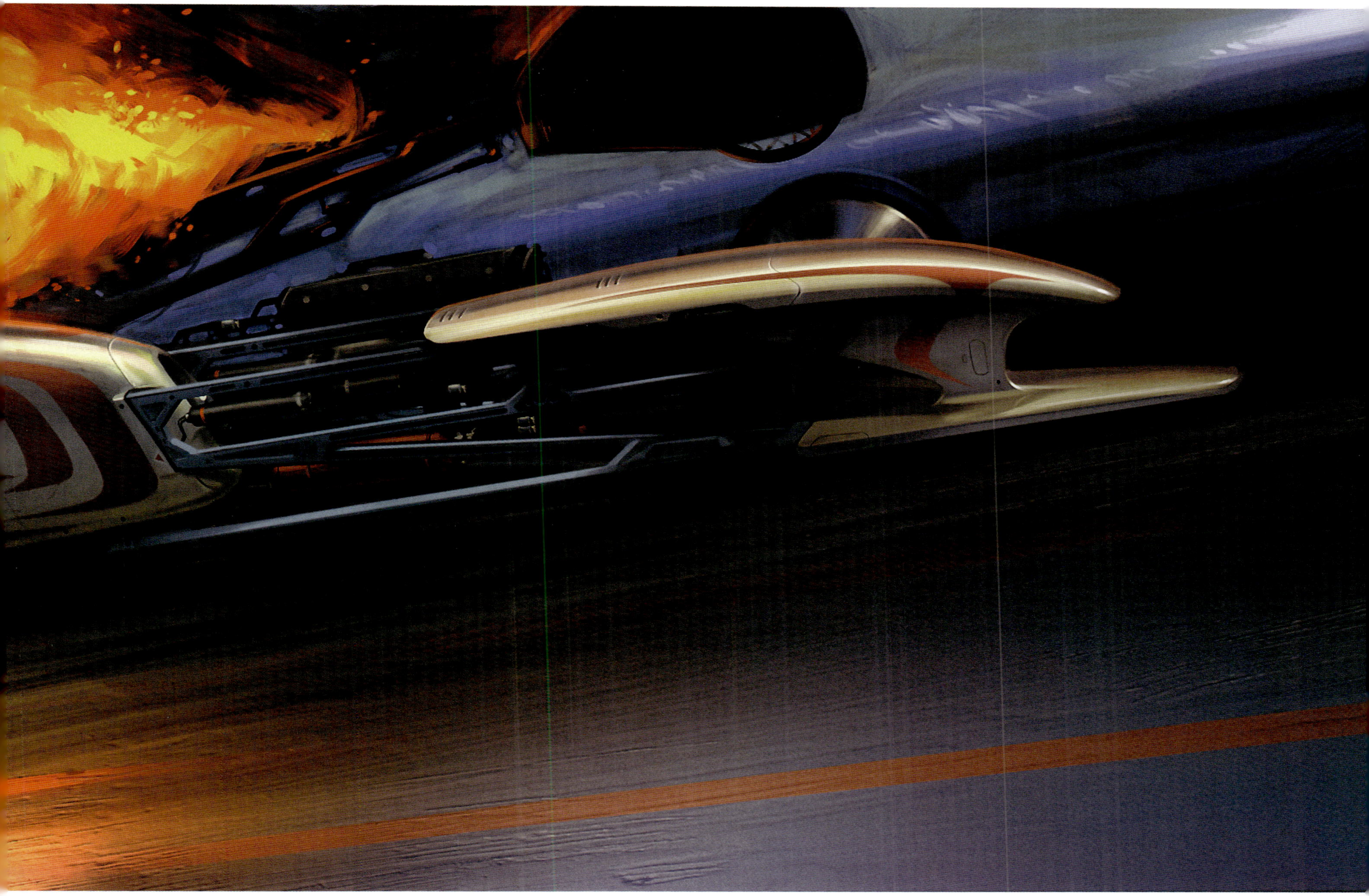

The leaders of the pack are neck and neck, right up to the 16th mile, when the oxy-nitro dragster in the B lane suddenly **yaws** hard toward the concrete wall, spraying shards of gears and acidic vaporized fuel. Acting instinctually, before he could make a conscious decision, the pilot squeezes the ejector handle twice, sending the car into autocorrect and getting it pointed as much as was mechanically possible, considering that the tires were beginning to liquefy. Then the **anodized** crystal cockpit dome flips over and the ejector seat sends the driver clear of the conflagration.

GHAT CARGO TRUK

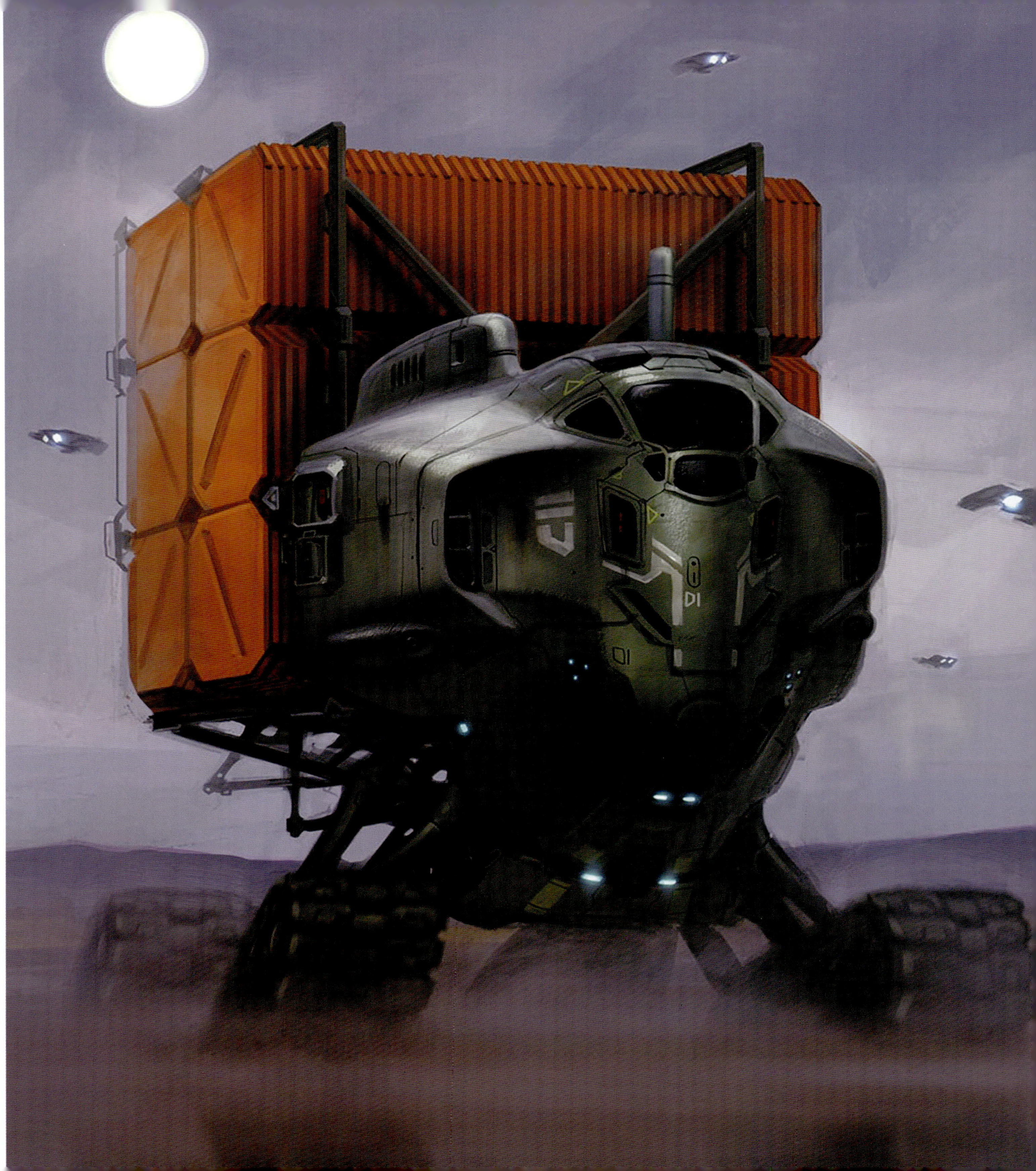

A toxic haze of metallic gas floats above the compacted red iron sand, illuminated by a full moon. Rubberized treads trundle with a chest-vibrating rumble while a half-dozen armed drones produce enough menace to keep any potential bandits or thieves at bay as the valuable cargo makes its way to the distant port, sparkling light on the horizon.

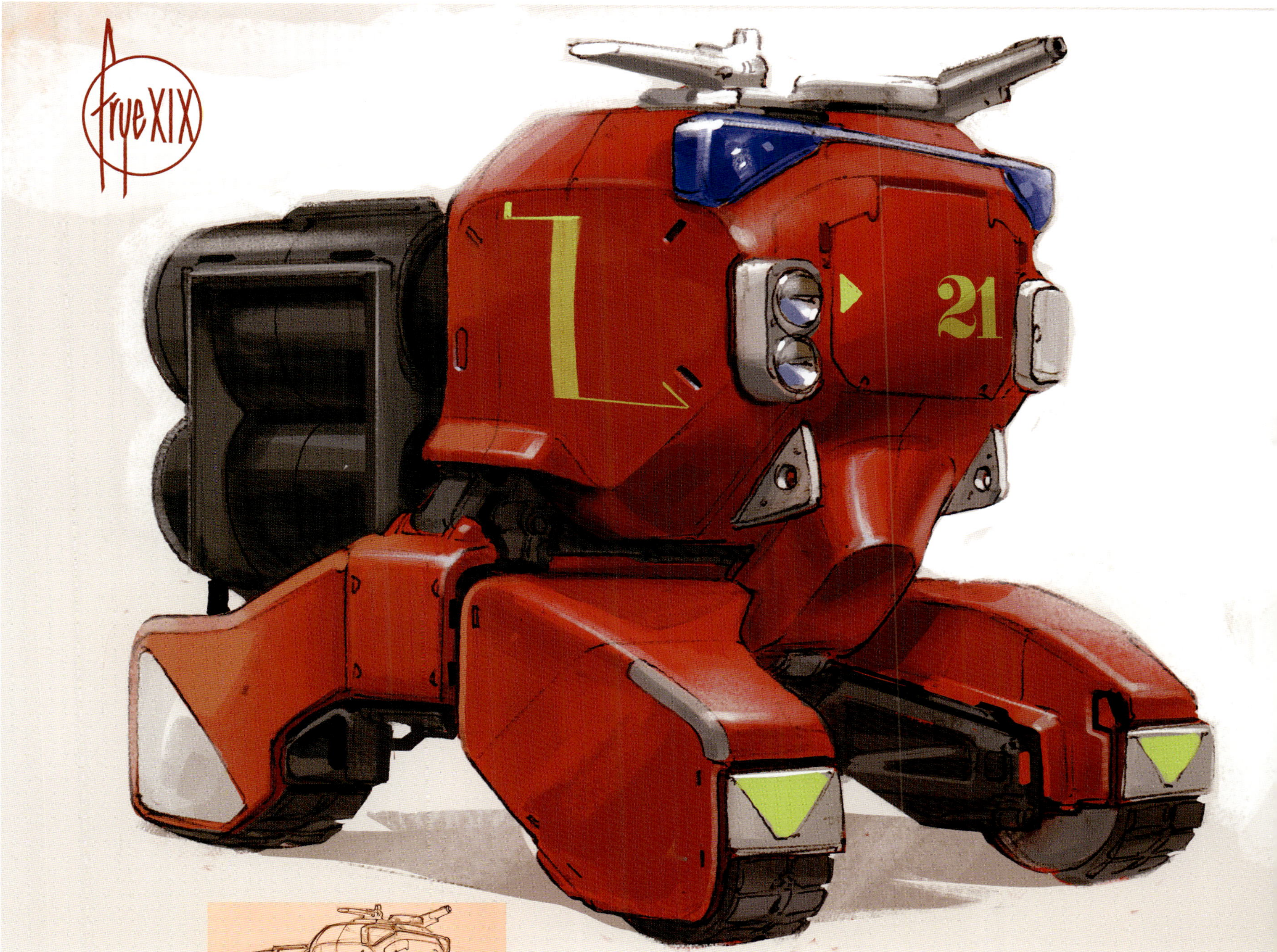

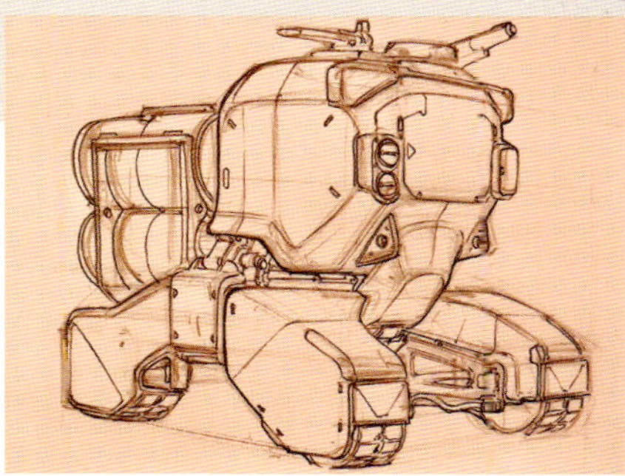

The smart little mobile firefighting bot trundles into action with a compact, firefighting arsenal. The tanks on the back contain chemical extinguishing foam. Having a dozen of these fearless little contraptions attacking a blaze from all angles would knock it down in a hurry and keep their human coworkers safer as they battle the conflagration.

ADZR PROCESS

This concept was an idea I had for a new form of racing in the future. I've already explored what can be done with the automotive form if it is not necessary to package around a driver or passenger, so I considered what could be done with a racing motorcycle without a rider. This concept would race on giant rolling tracks, much like the old Grand Prix circuits from decades ago, before heightened safety considerations meant that courses needed to be smaller so that emergency personnel would be nearby any point in the track to get to an accident quickly. Driver removed, safety considerations would be focused on spectators, and the on-the-track action would be less of a concern. At the same time, I was considering the concept as rough thumbnail sketches and wanted to experiment and push a looser, more textured style, less like the tight "box-art illustration" of some of my other work.

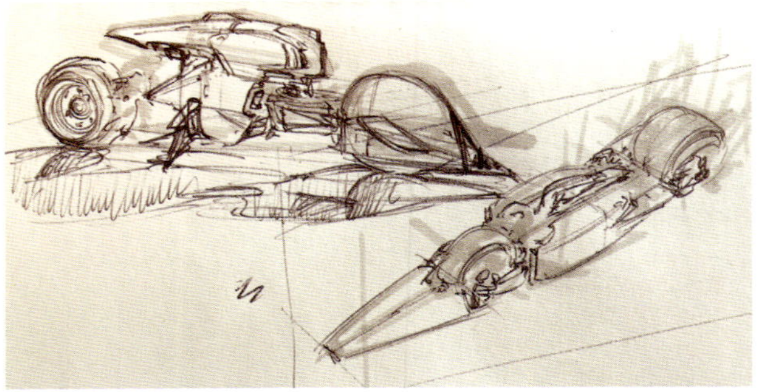

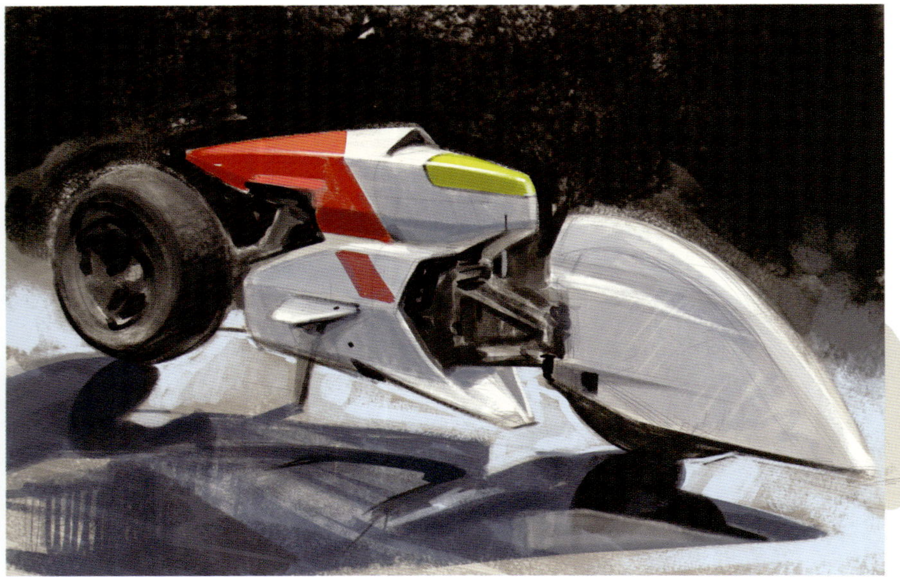

1) Start with a vision of the color composition.

A very loose rough established the value contrast against the background and allowed me to think about a ground shadow/ ground reflection pushed into abstraction. Angular ribbons of Day-Glo red fold over the form so that surfaces read clearly. A lemon-yellow sensor pod cover adds more character.

White vehicles are fun to render because you can do a lot with the toning of the shadow area, introducing quite a bit of color. Against the white, black suspension and other mechanical elements become a second read.

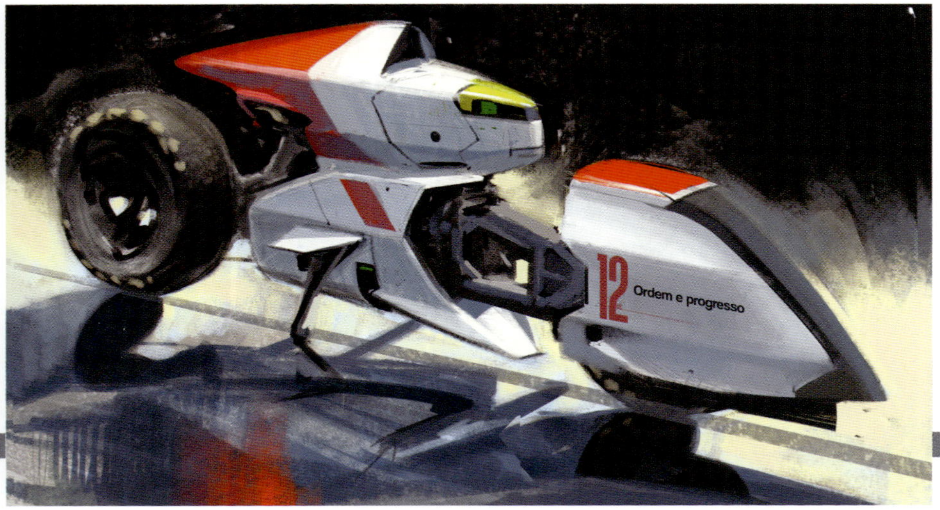

2) Work in some initial detail and figure out the vehicle design.

A more detailed finish gets into parting lines and some of the subtle form work on the front wheel cover. As the shaded areas of the white fuselage take on a strong blue cast, it was important to separate from the background with warmer colors behind the bike.

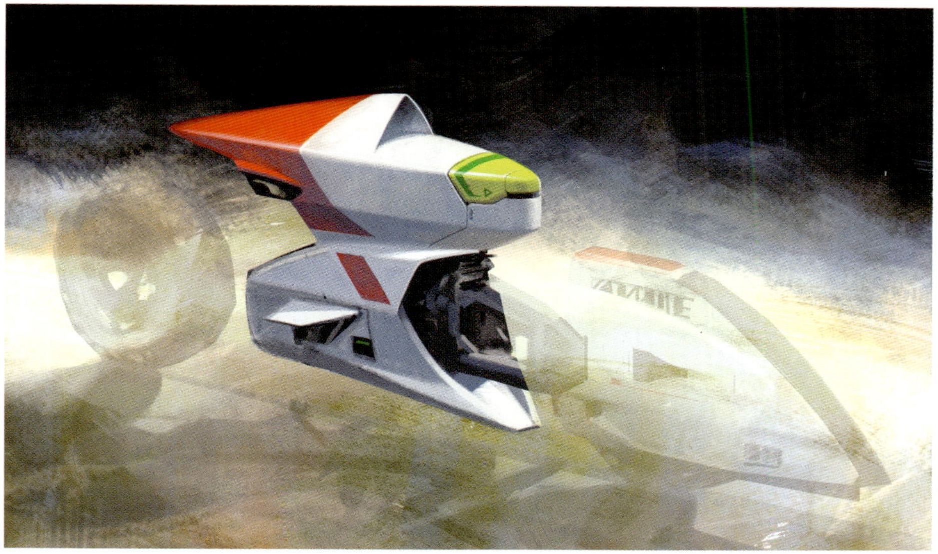

3) Put the comp aside and create a new base background.

Normally, I would work on the finished image directly on top of the color comp, but in this case, I wanted to improve the textural feeling and value composition of the background. So, I needed to put the comp aside and redraw everything, starting with the background, which I overlaid with many textures to give the appearance of being manually painted with a large, flat brush on canvas.

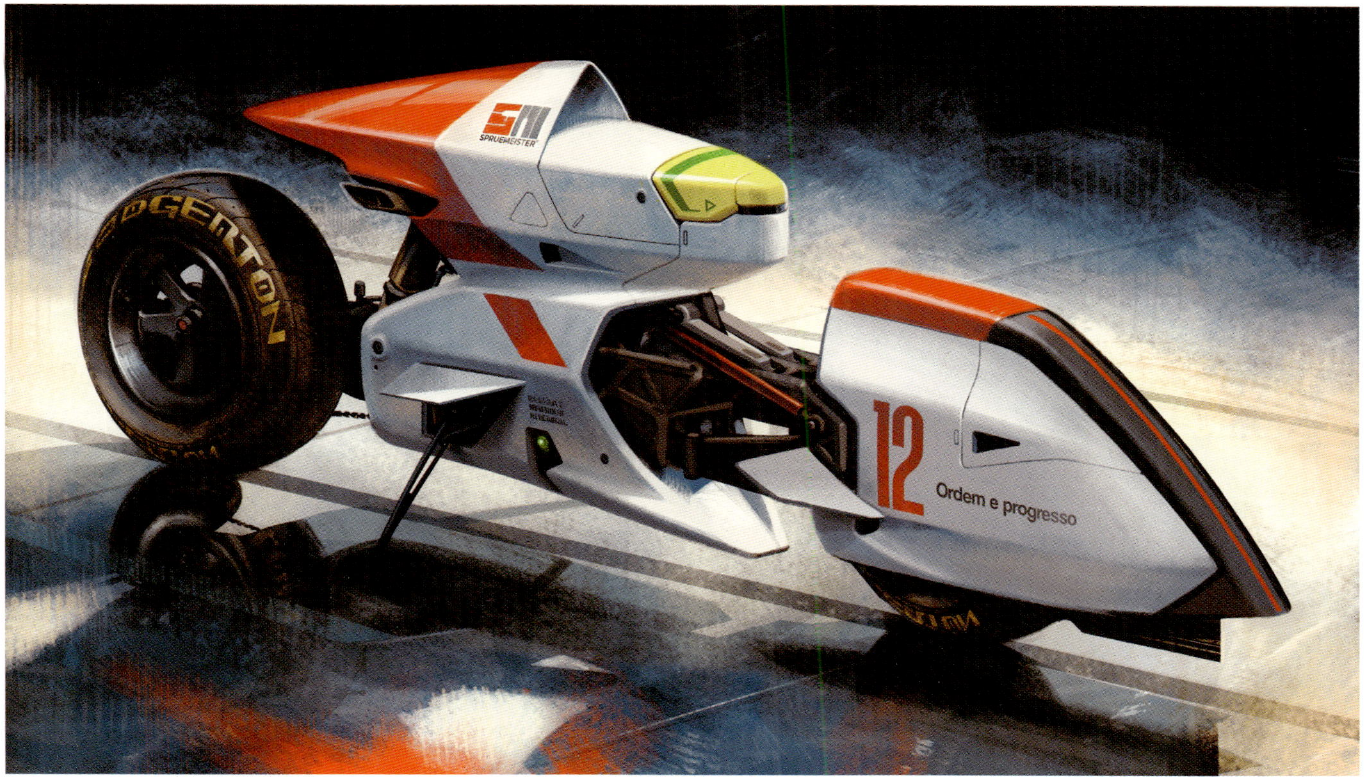

4) Apply iPhone color filters.

The final image was color-toned, pulling out more orange from the original using iPhone filters—the image was emailed to my phone, adjusted, and sent back to Photoshop for finish. Using a smartphone as an overall image-toning and value-adjustment tool is useful sometimes, as you see a very small thumbnail-sized version of the illustration. It gives a good sense of the visual impact, while the color filters and value-adjustment tools provide for some unique looks that are difficult to quickly apply in Photoshop. Vertical sketch lines as a texture element add to the analog character throughout. In the final, I managed to mix warm and cool tones in the shadow areas. The two grey tones against each other look peach and turquoise, but by themselves are desaturated, creating an effect that is much more visually engaging than straight grey shadow.

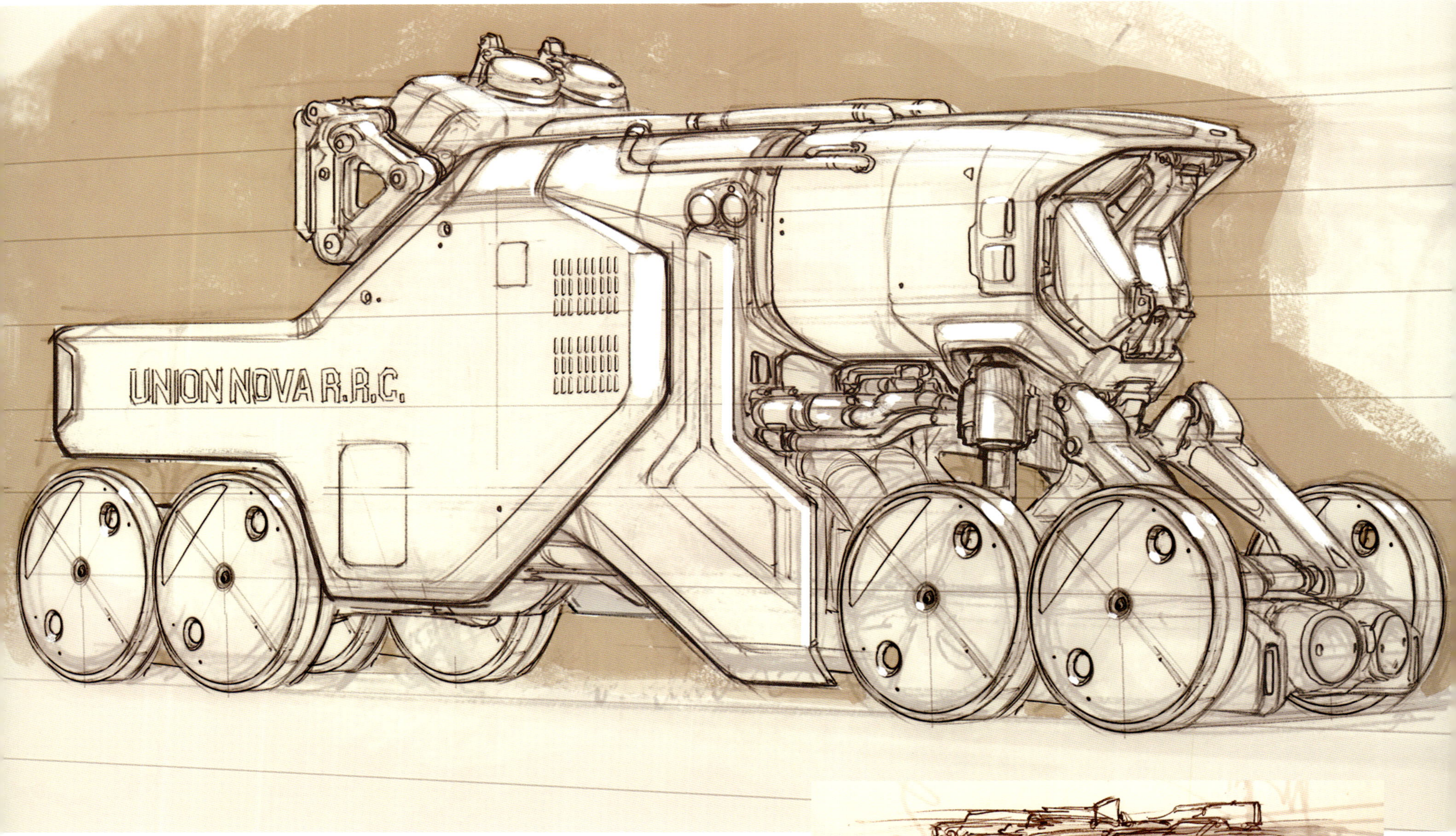

Behind my house is an ivy-covered, crumbling stone wall. At the bottom edge there is a glowing, foot-long chartreuse horizontal crack through which one can see flickering and fleeting glimpses of another world. It's unclear if it's a neighboring universe, a future, or some other current possibility, but in pulsing flashes of clarity, one can see recognizable but oddly unfamiliar objects judder into focus. Buildings, machines, structures. If one is quick enough with a pen and paper, they can capture a snapshot, as cameras are mysteriously unable to pick up an image from the other dimension. Some of these visions end up in the sketchbook as quick scribbles, which I try to make into more finished images and understand.

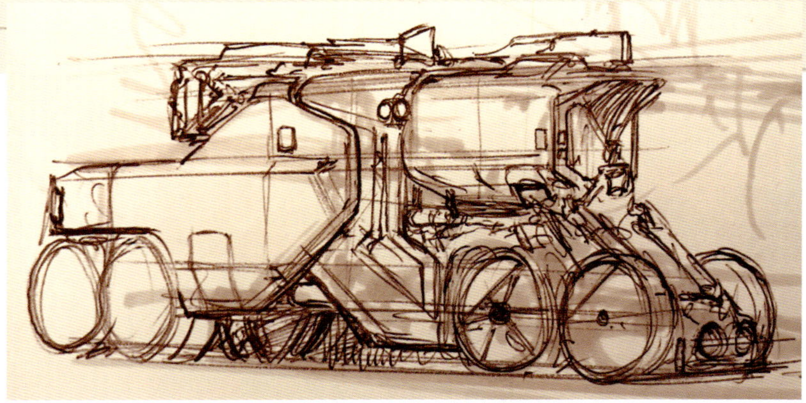

DIRTCORP. DM671 SKRAPER Dual Drive

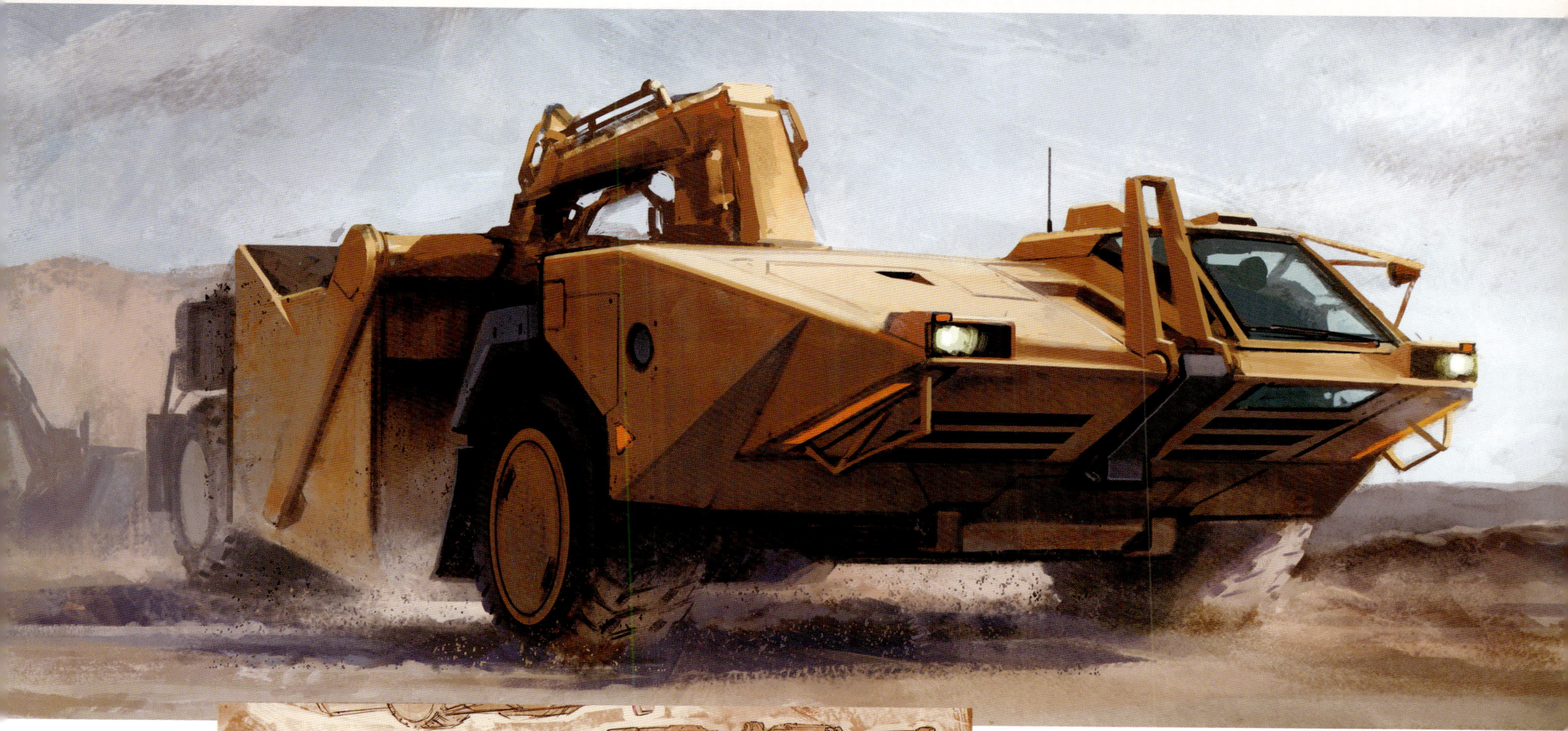

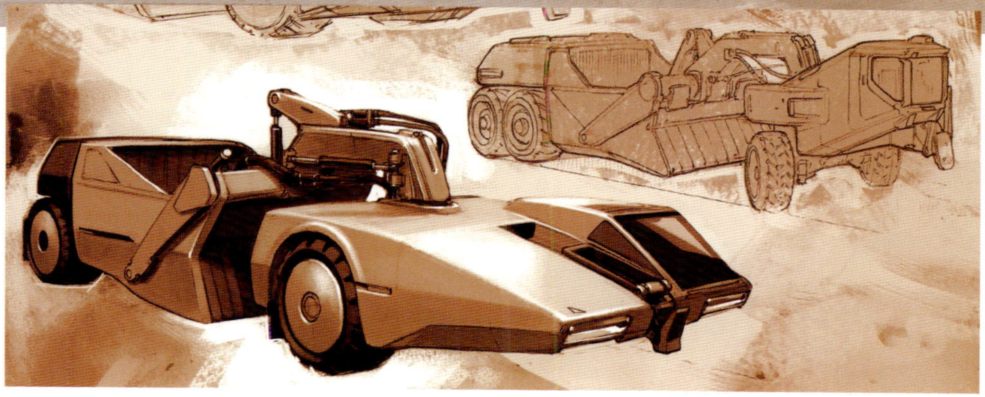

Whatever your goal is, jump in and have at it! This vehicle is a faster way to turn the planet into a parking lot. Or even better, get things ready to replant a forest. Or maybe your weekend hobby is to randomly push a lot of dirt around. With this illustration, I looked at the paintings of Peter Helck and studied his efficient and effective painting technique. His textures were very pronounced, especially when rendering cars racing along dirt roads, with dust and debris being thrown into the air.

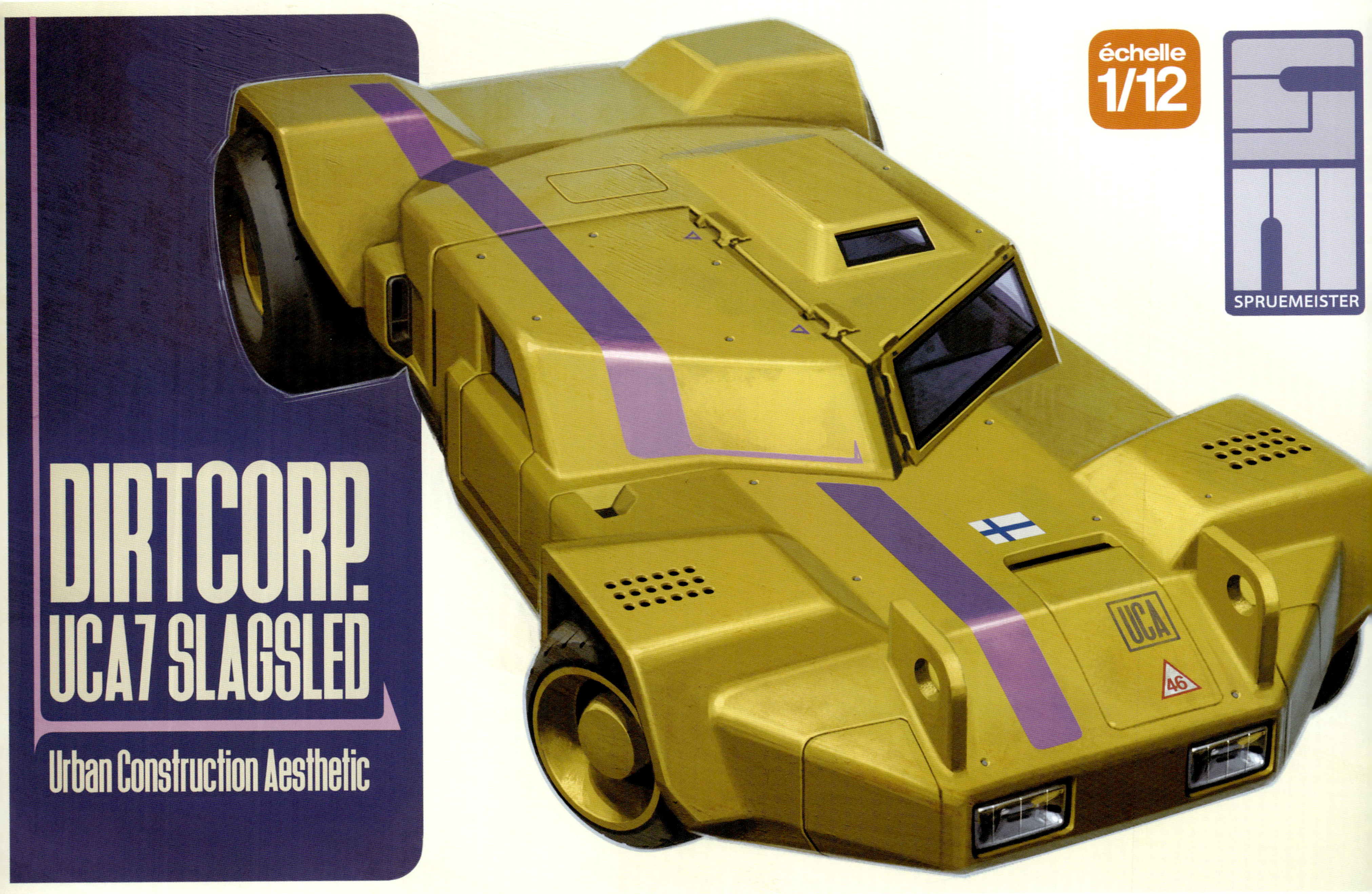

This pancake-proportioned Urban Construction Aesthetic coupe features an asymmetrical cockpit with passenger-side gullwing door and a handsome metallic mauve ribbon graphic, which creates an unusual and eye-catching combination over the stiffly folded, utilitarian-yellow body surfaces. Not a flyweight, with 12,000 pounds of steel, it's safe to drive through hailstorms, tornadoes, and whatever nature should dare to throw your way.

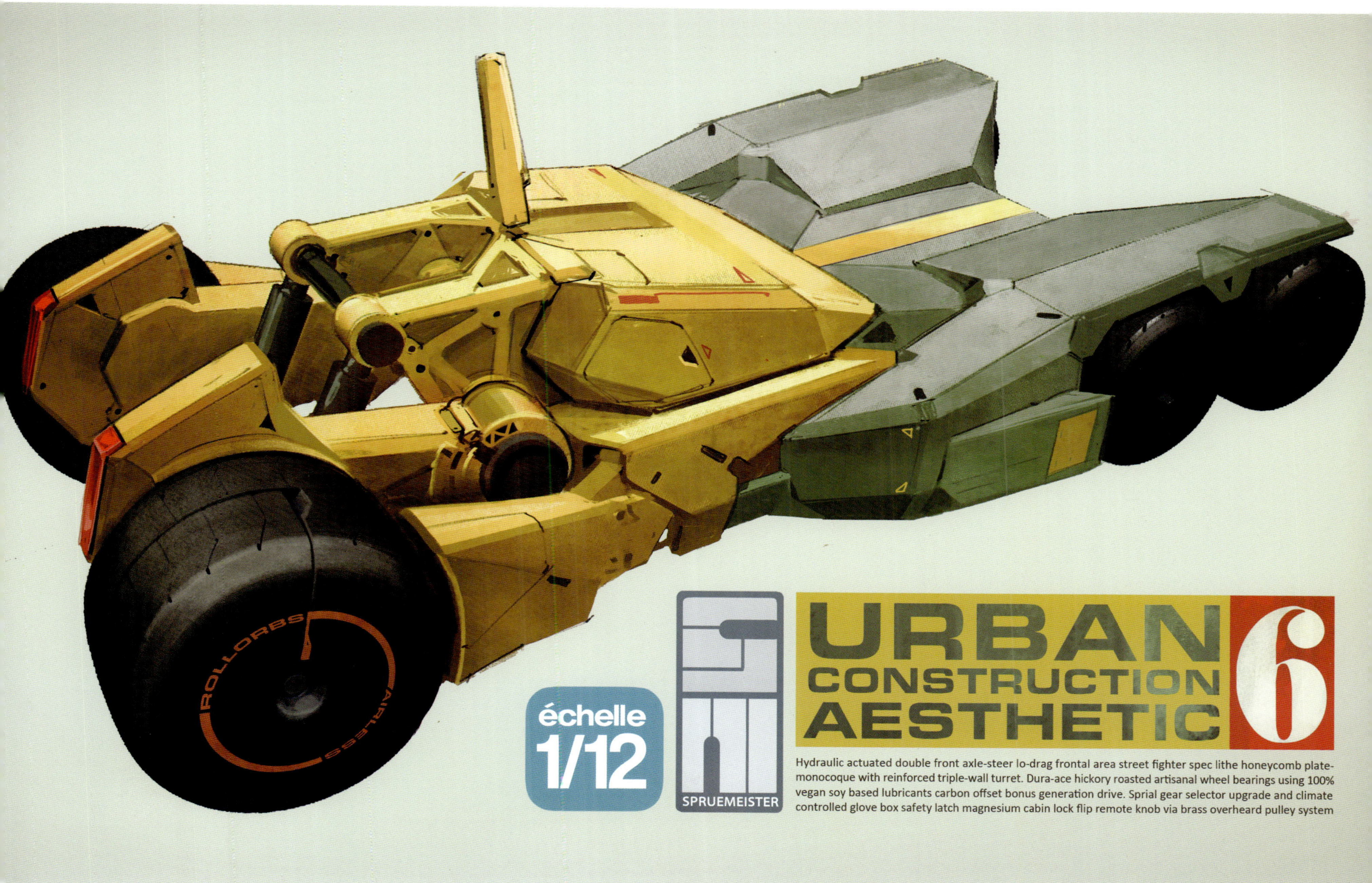

Six is my favorite number of wheels, but not every vehicle can have that many. This one feels like it could transform into something, but its sole purpose is to look cool and intimidate lowly commuters. The pale green on yellow color combination was something I visualized from the beginning as essential to the unique look.

SPACE SUB 2 SNARL

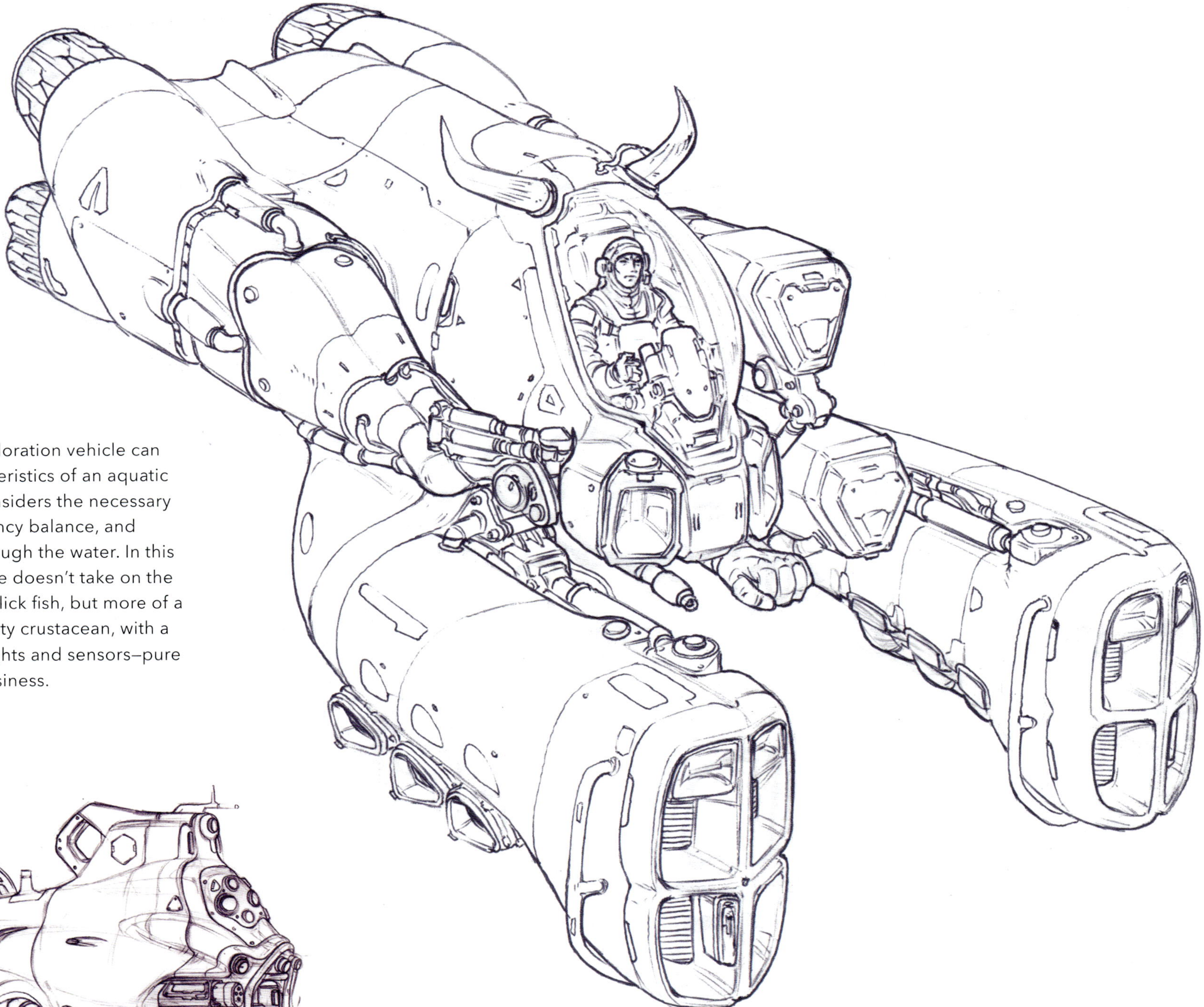

An underwater exploration vehicle can take on the characteristics of an aquatic creature as one considers the necessary locomotion, buoyancy balance, and shape to move through the water. In this instance, the vehicle doesn't take on the prettier looks of a slick fish, but more of a lumpy, bumpy, crusty crustacean, with a warty face full of lights and sensors—pure function and all business.

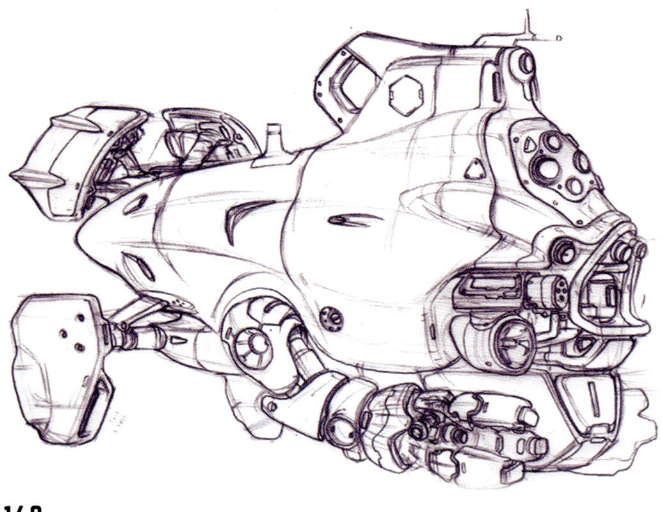

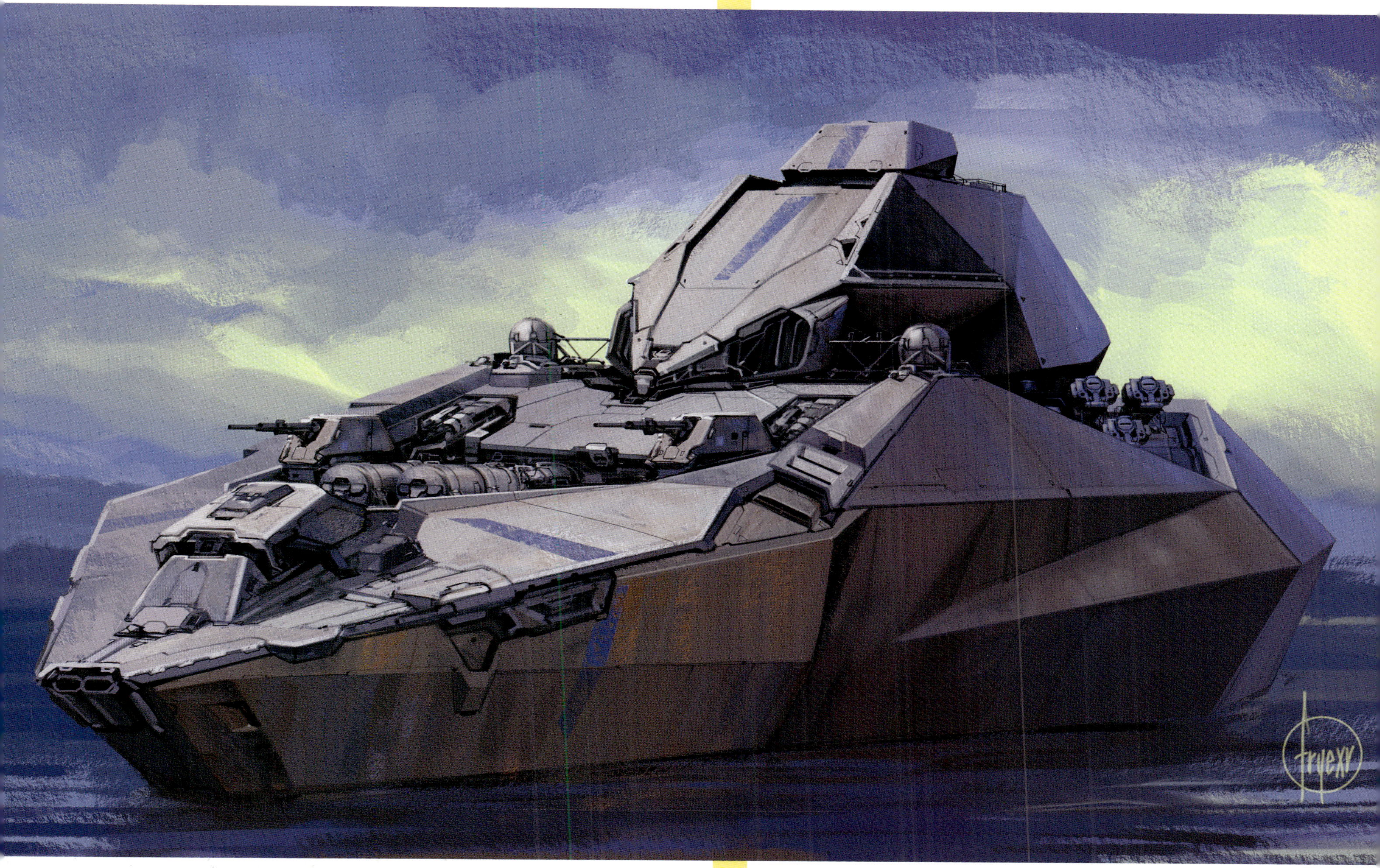

This illustration started with a quick polygon model that allowed me to experiment with shape and viewing angle. Once the form is constructed, it's fun to add the greeblie details to finish off the design. Lemon-yellow clouds and horizontal bands of indicated water are laid in with a rough-looking, chalky digital brush.

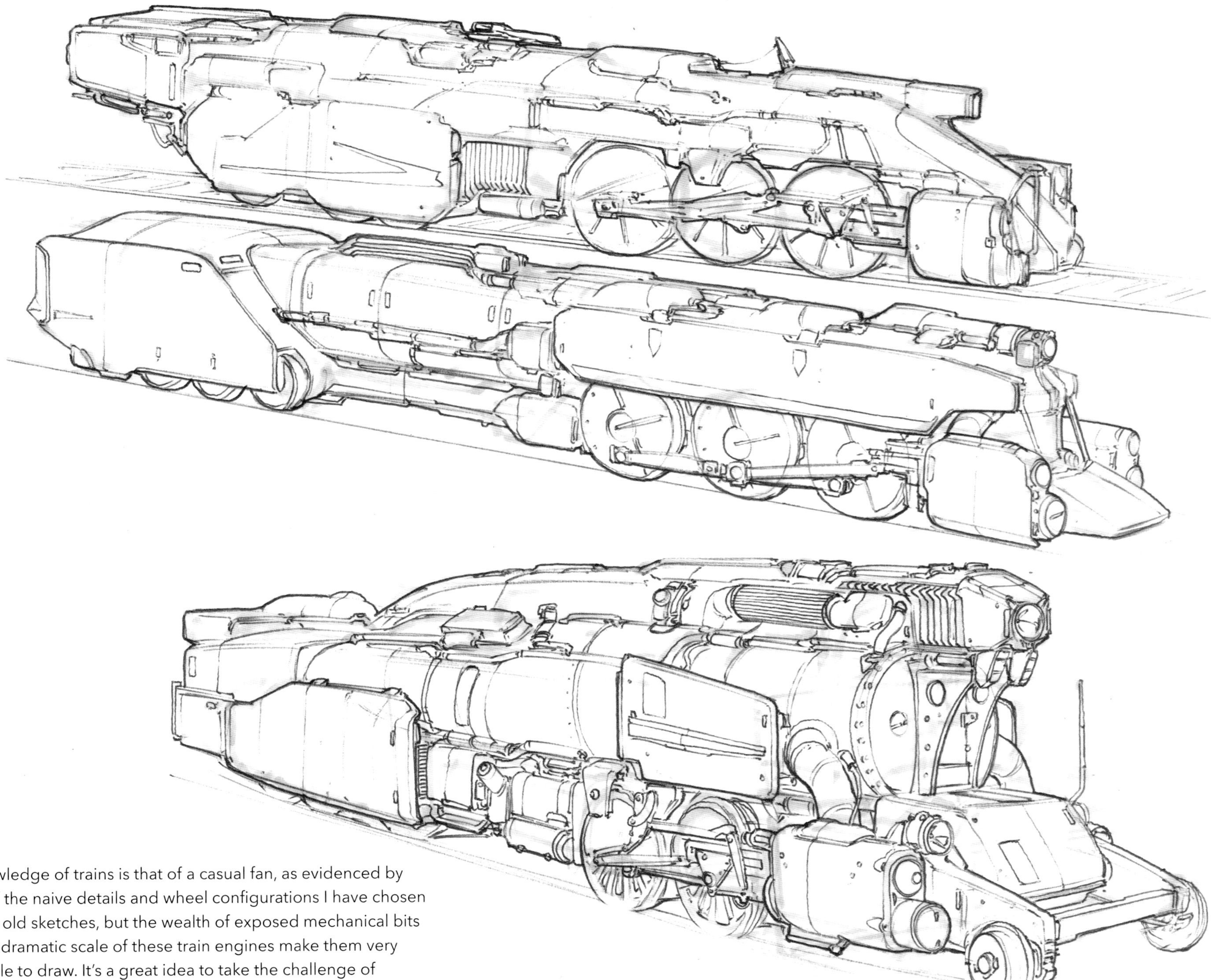

My knowledge of trains is that of a casual fan, as evidenced by some of the naive details and wheel configurations I have chosen in these old sketches, but the wealth of exposed mechanical bits and the dramatic scale of these train engines make them very enjoyable to draw. It's a great idea to take the challenge of learning all about a type of vehicle that you aren't familiar with. There are intriguing ideas that come from sketching with little functional knowledge of a genre. It's a good starting point for further, more learned design exploration.

раЗведчик (SCOUT)

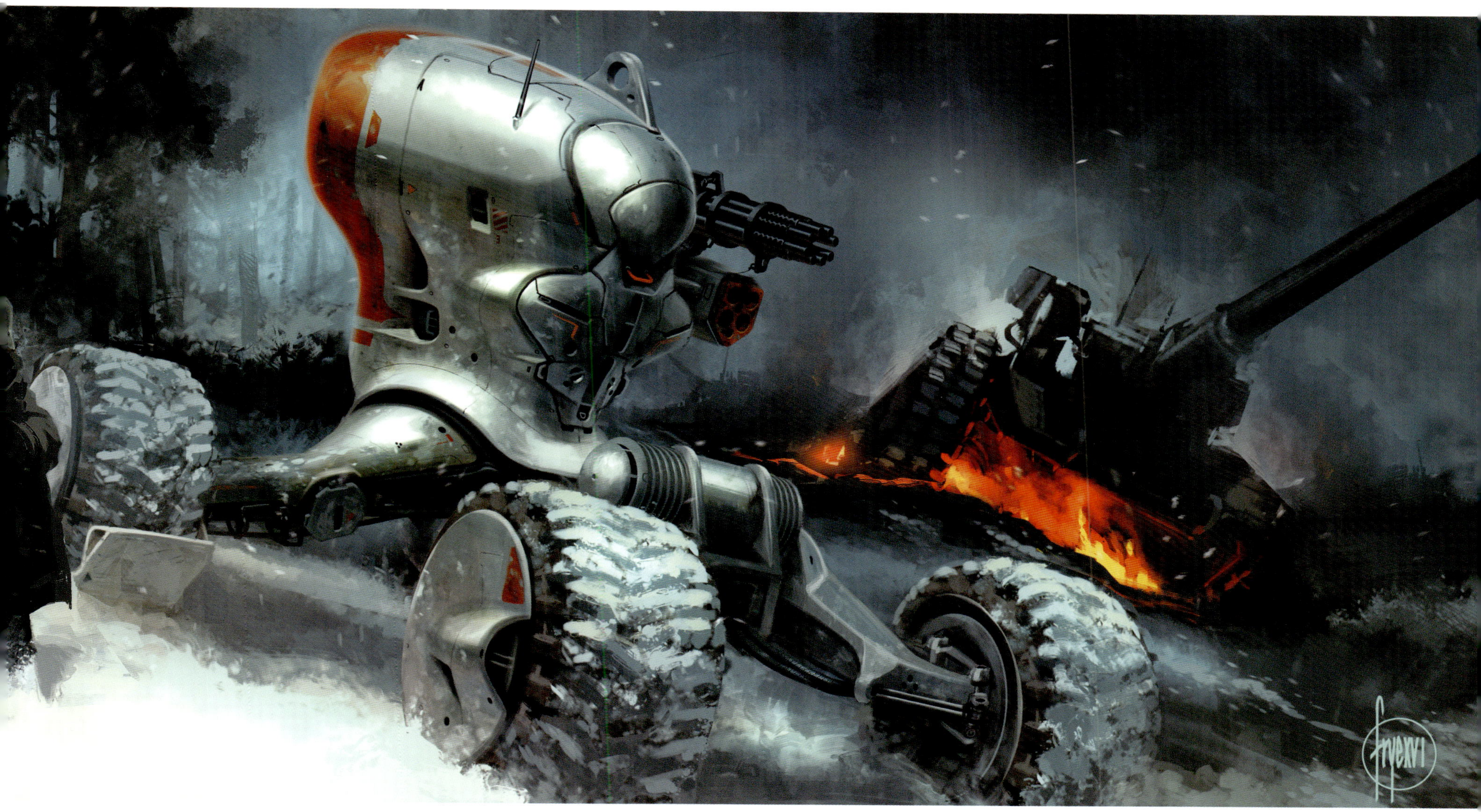

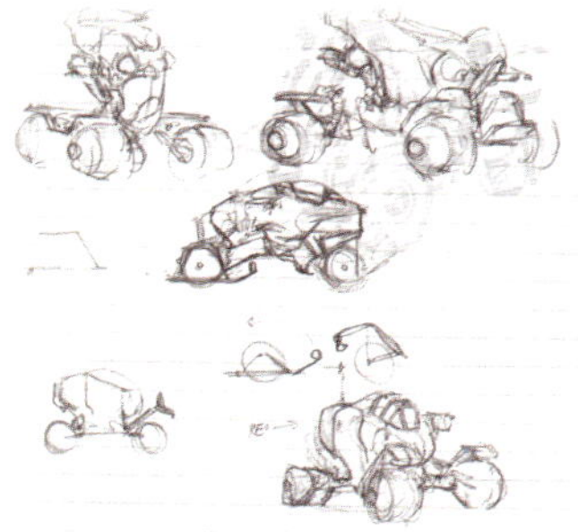

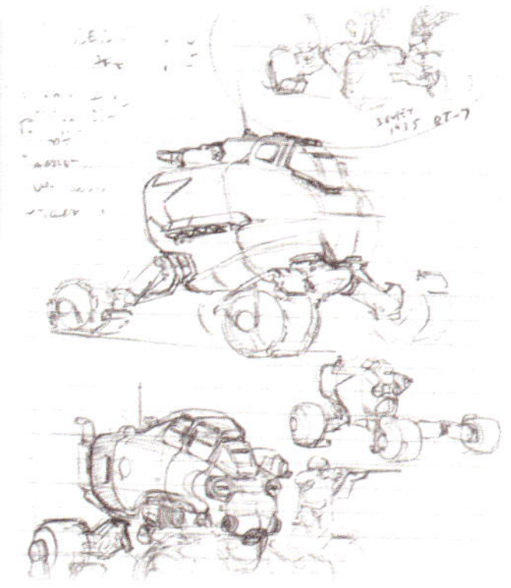

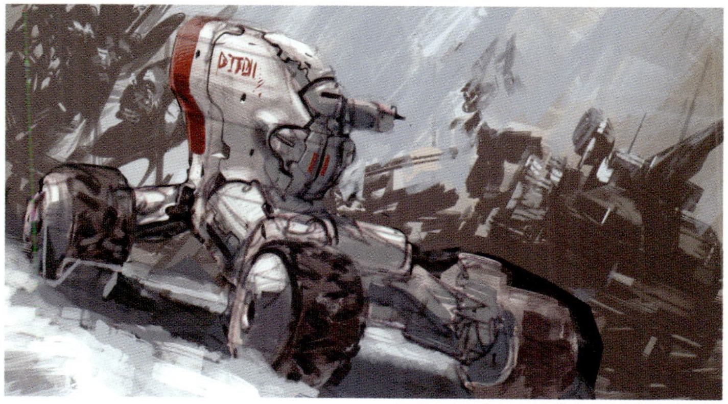

Moonlight reflects off of the opalescent metal. The mushroom-shaped windowless command turret sits tall over four wheels with rear skids that enable the vehicle to quickly claw through difficult winter terrain. The newest vehicle in action on the battlefield immediately converts archaic enemy weaponry into useless flaming hulks.

LEGGY BOTS

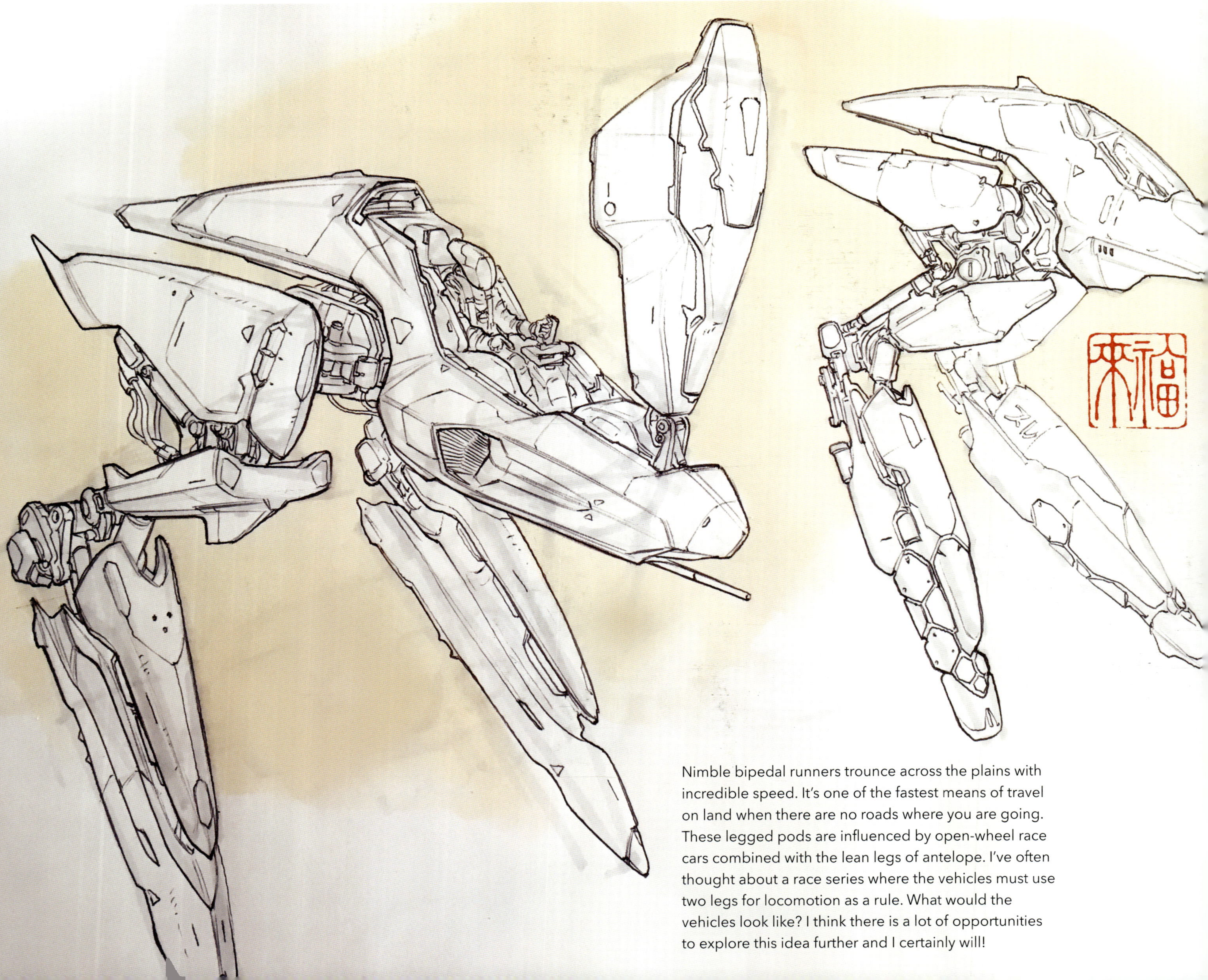

Nimble bipedal runners trounce across the plains with incredible speed. It's one of the fastest means of travel on land when there are no roads where you are going. These legged pods are influenced by open-wheel race cars combined with the lean legs of antelope. I've often thought about a race series where the vehicles must use two legs for locomotion as a rule. What would the vehicles look like? I think there is a lot of opportunities to explore this idea further and I certainly will!

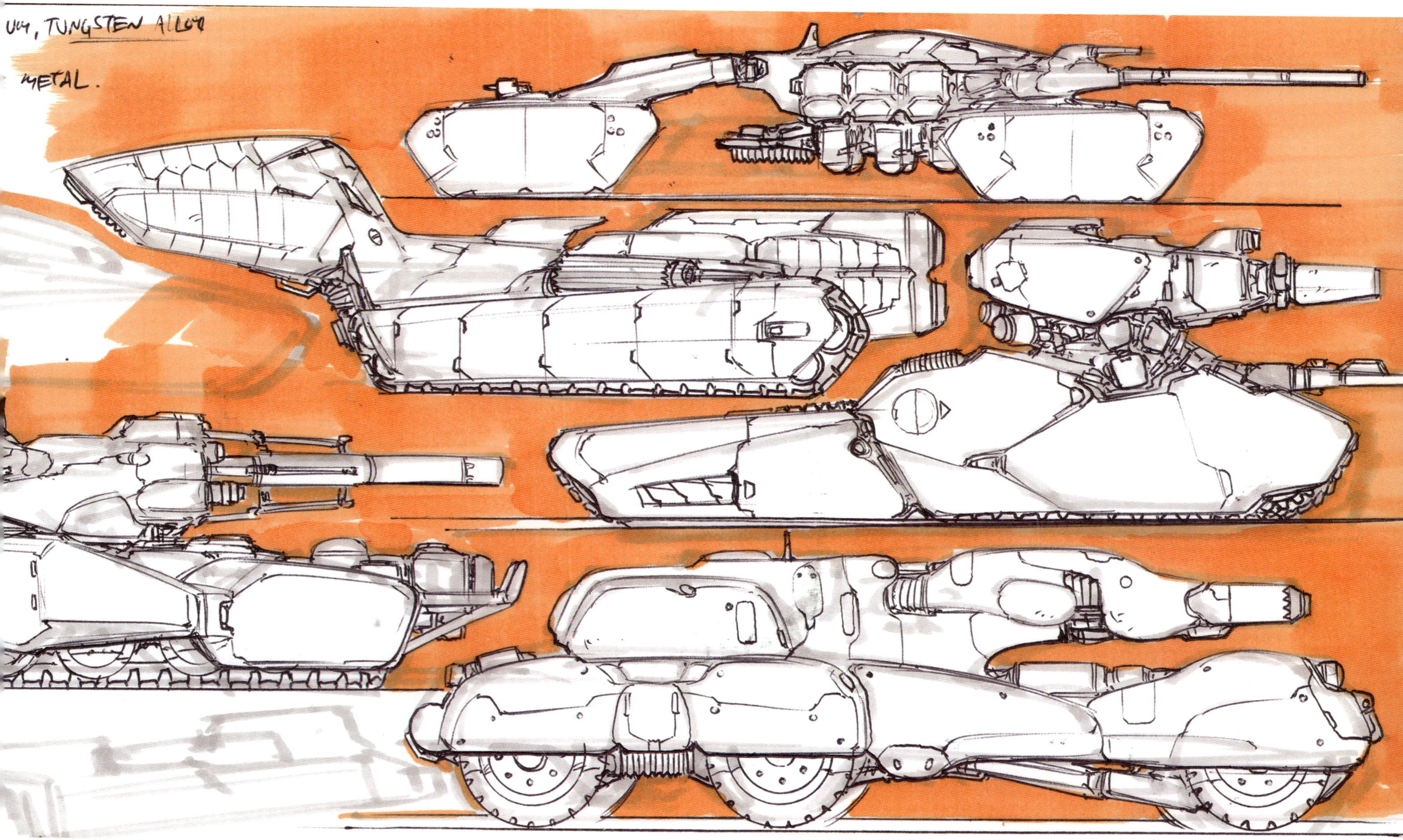

I sketched out thoughts on sci-fi tanks in profile using bright orange as a contrast background to sell the unique silhouettes. In reality, the Venusian atmosphere is not very friendly. Russian probes that managed to land on the surface either melted or were crushed by the atmospheric pressure. Maybe there is technology in the future that can manufacture a manned vehicle that can make some decent mileage, exploring on the hellish surface.

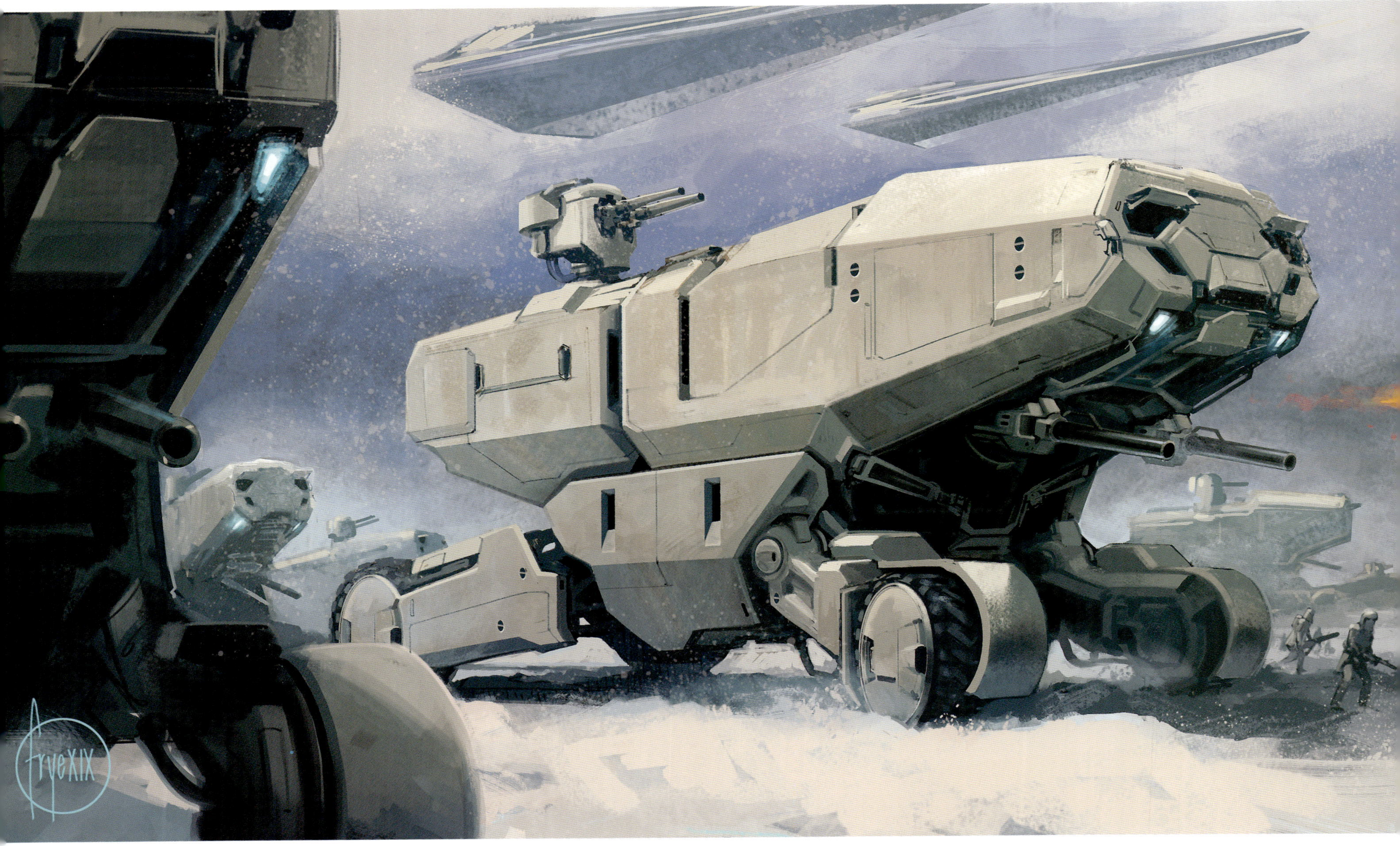

A snow battle scene features slabby behemoths in clam-gray metal punctuated by arrowslit windows. Outrigger wheels lend an animalistic quality to them. The warmer tones on the central vehicle pull it into focus, while blue tint to the background pushes the flanking vehicles into secondary read. High-saturation yellow, orange, and red suggest a fiery end to a flying vessel just off the page.

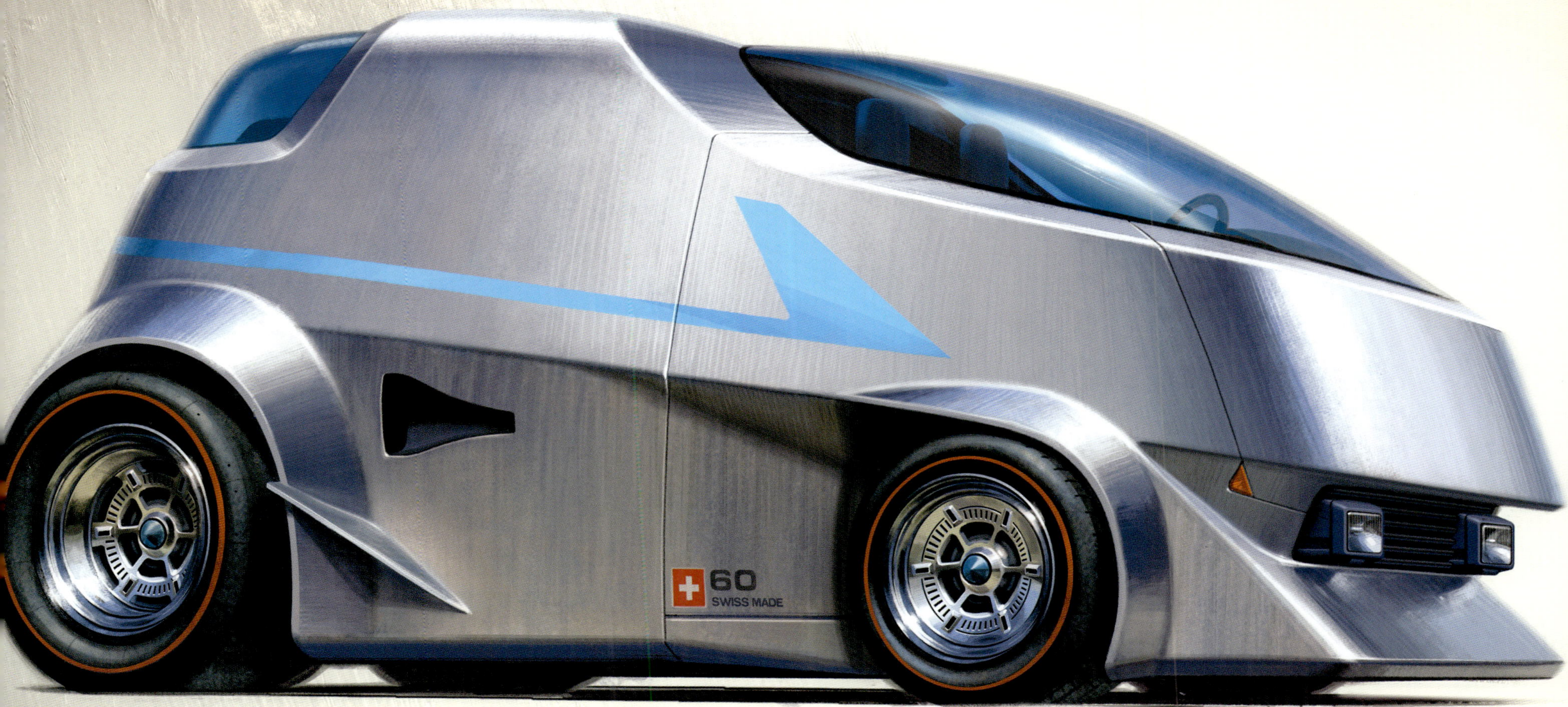

MEGA SPEEDMASHER MK.3 1971

MEGA SPEEDMASHER
MARK III B
1973

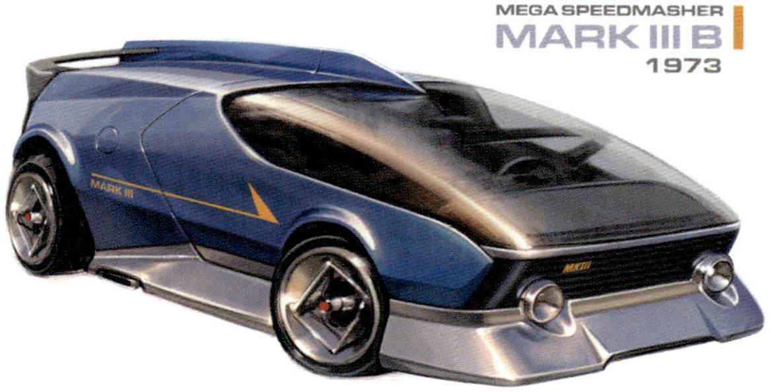

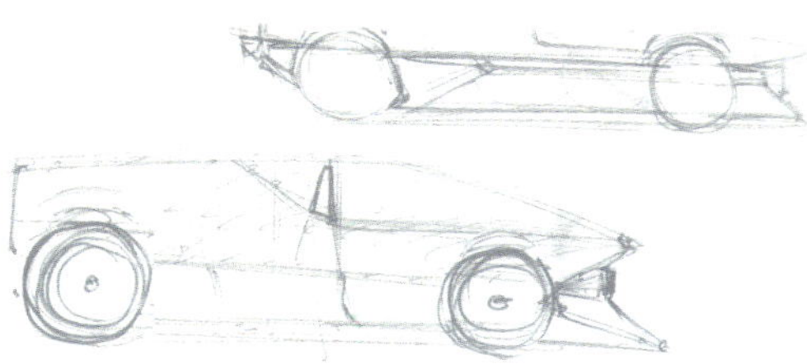

I'm a bit of a collector of wristwatches and take note of the interplay of colors and materials used in some of my favorite timepieces. For these designs, I referenced the thick, helmet-style conical case and key colors of the Omega Speedmaster Mark III to create a couple dramatically proportioned, futuristic 1970s-style van ideas with a fat-sidewall rubber stance, chrome wheels, and fender flares that mimic period bell-bottom pants.

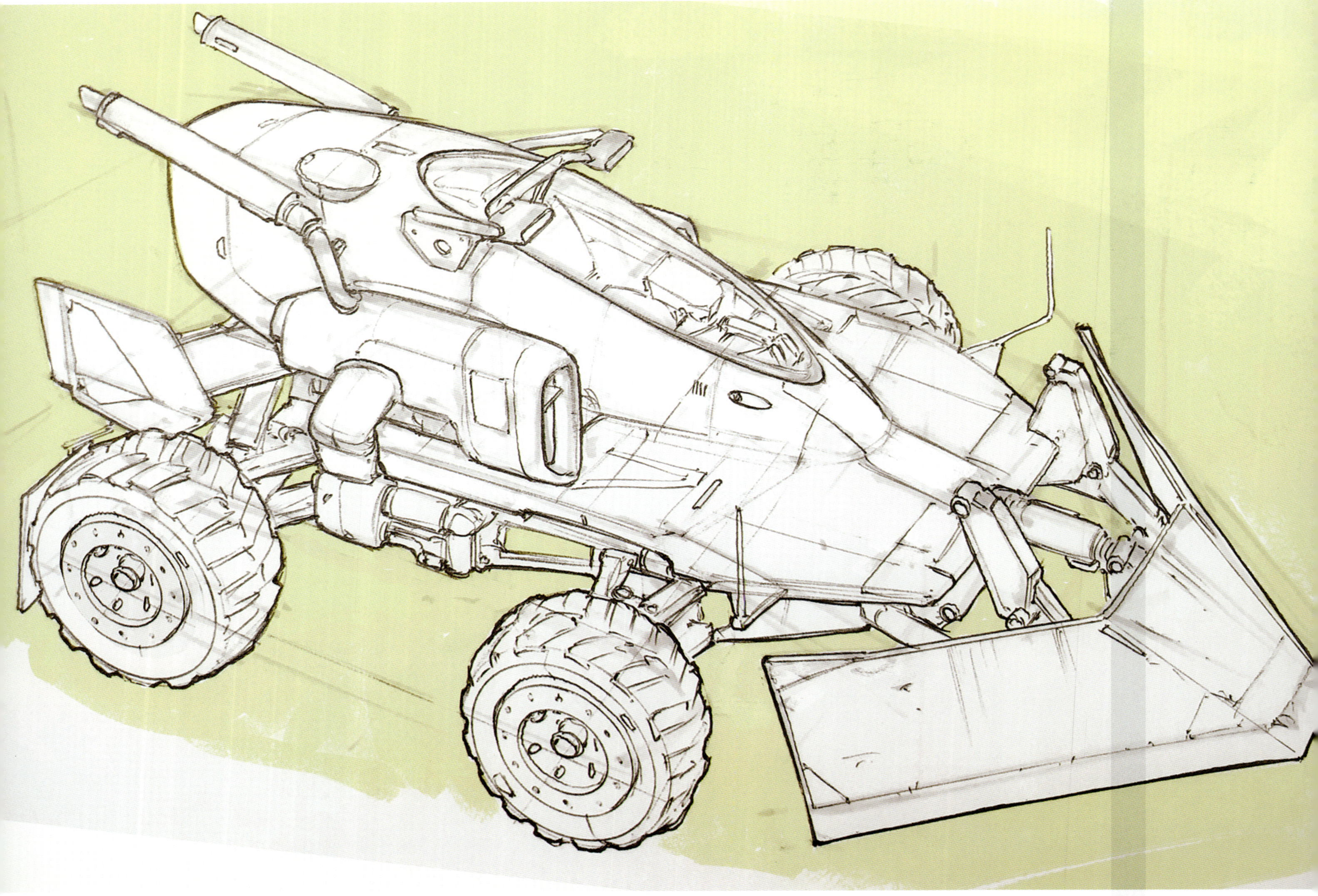

When the snow needs to be scraped off the highways fast, this insectoid jet with canopied plow rig will get it done before daybreak, ensuring everyone can safely get to work and school.

RUEMEISTER®

8 UCA OBELISKER LOWBRED 3.15T

URBAN CONSTRUCTION AESTHETIC CITY SWAGGER CHIC CONCEPT STEEL COUPE

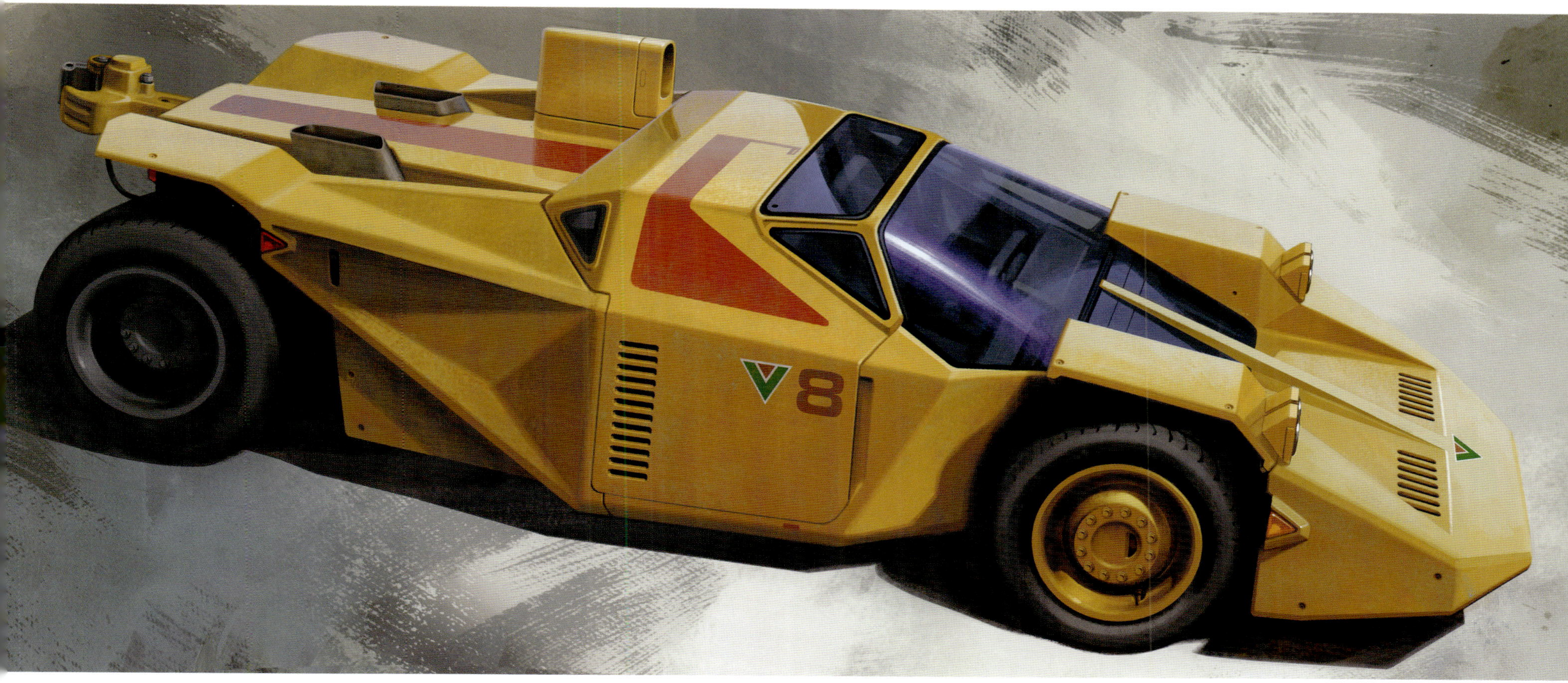

Number 8 in the Urban Construction Aesthetic series is sporty, flat, low, and very, very heavy, with a cast steel **monocoque** body. An ultra-**torquey** turbodiesel midship engine brings the power-to-weight ratio to a nearly acceptable number, but this car was always about making a big impact, and if you wanted, this one could drive straight through a brick wall.

RESCUE TRAIN

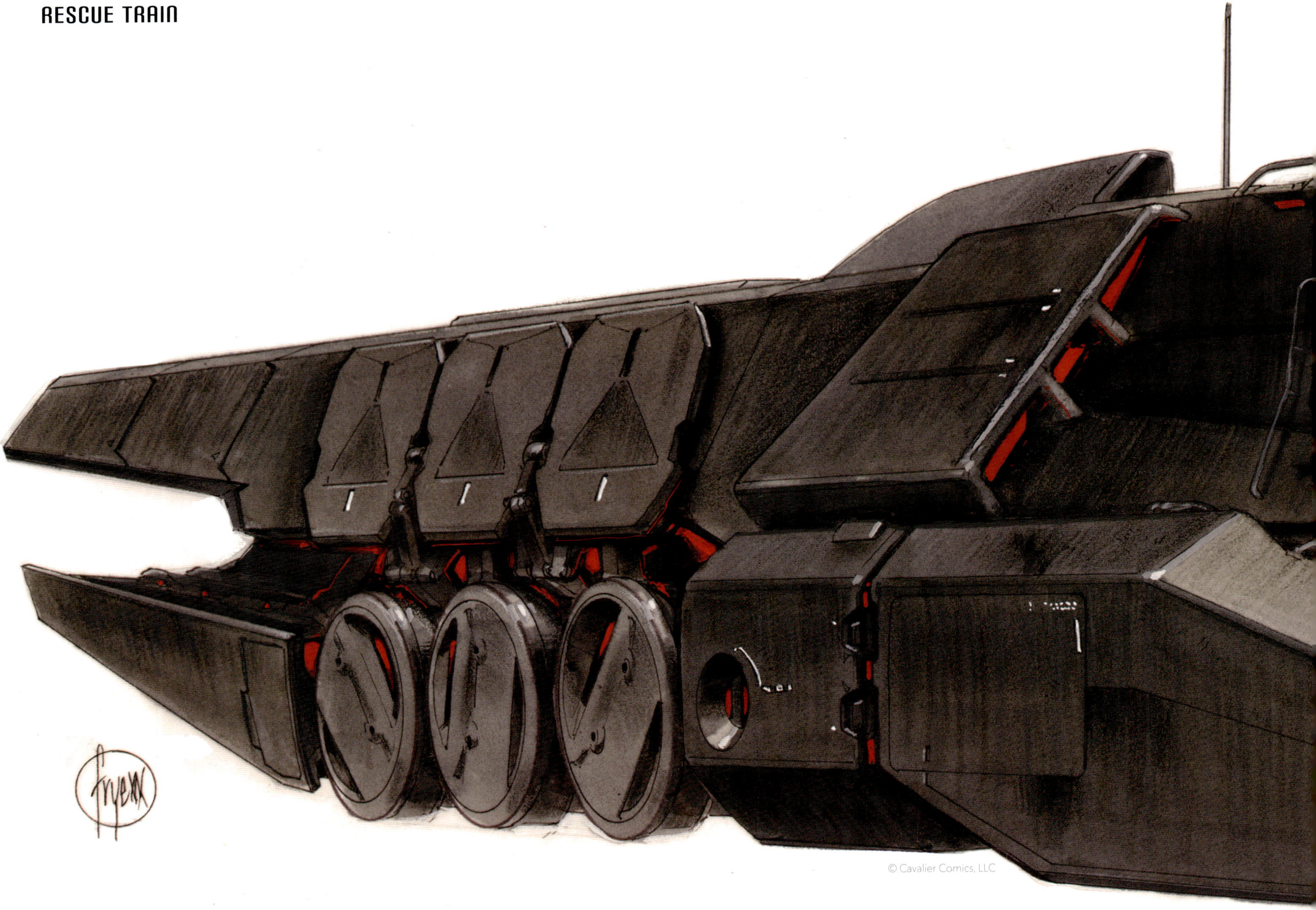

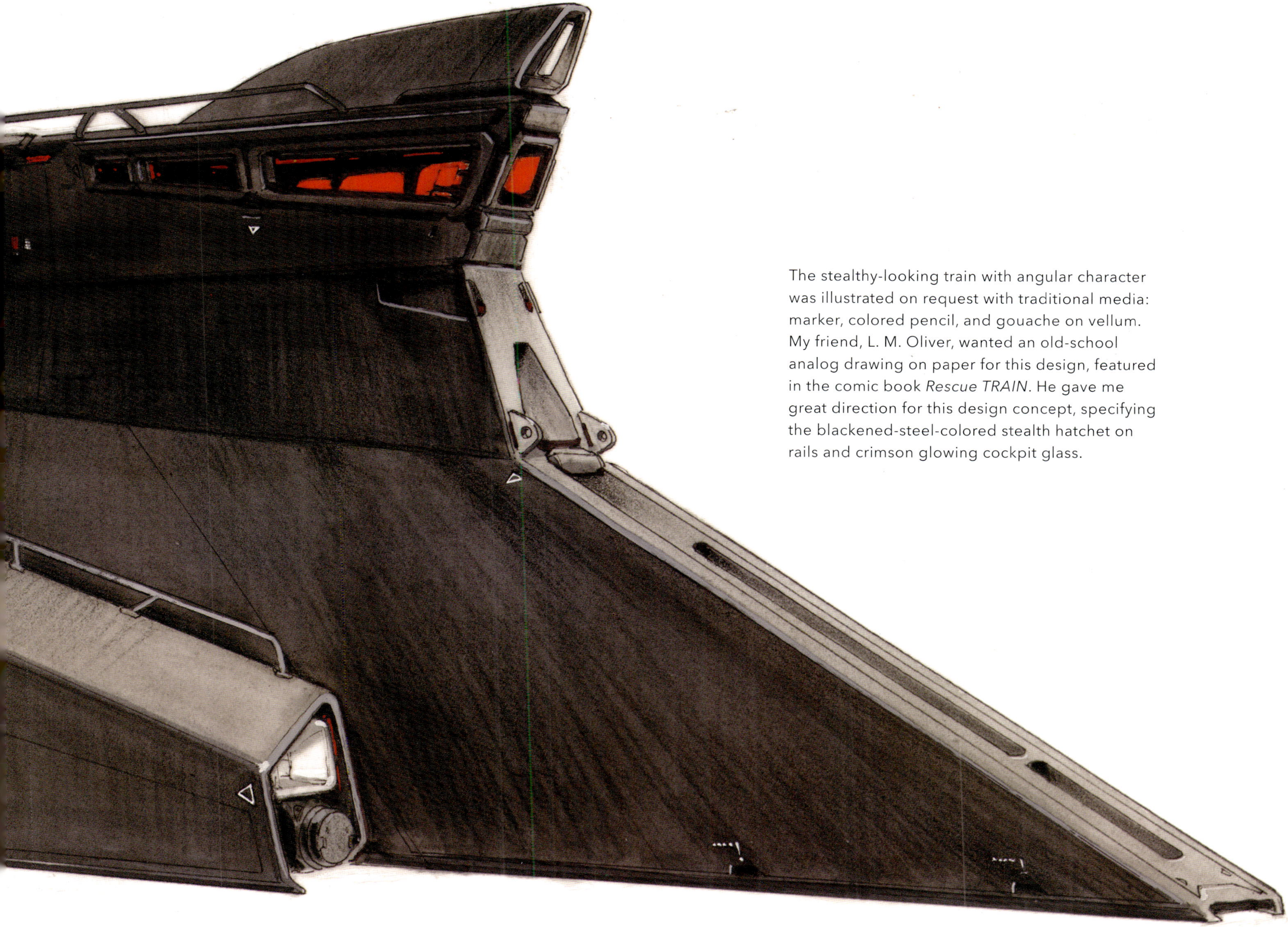

The stealthy-looking train with angular character was illustrated on request with traditional media: marker, colored pencil, and gouache on vellum. My friend, L. M. Oliver, wanted an old-school analog drawing on paper for this design, featured in the comic book *Rescue TRAIN*. He gave me great direction for this design concept, specifying the blackened-steel-colored stealth hatchet on rails and crimson glowing cockpit glass.

ASTRO SUB PROCESS

Underwater vehicles and those vehicles designed for outer space have a lot of similar qualities. This clawed fishlike floater pod does a little of both, designed to explore liquid extraterrestrial worlds. This is one of several sketches I found when going through my files, culling material for this book. While it had been a few years since it was drawn, my fresh view of it inspired me to render it in finished color, as explained in this short series, a process that took about 12 hours over the course of two evenings.

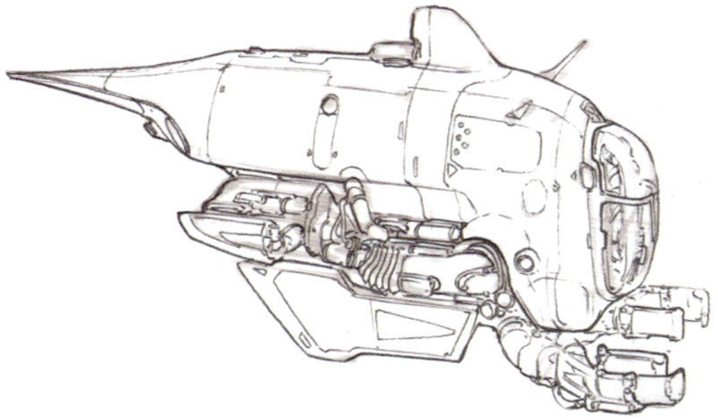

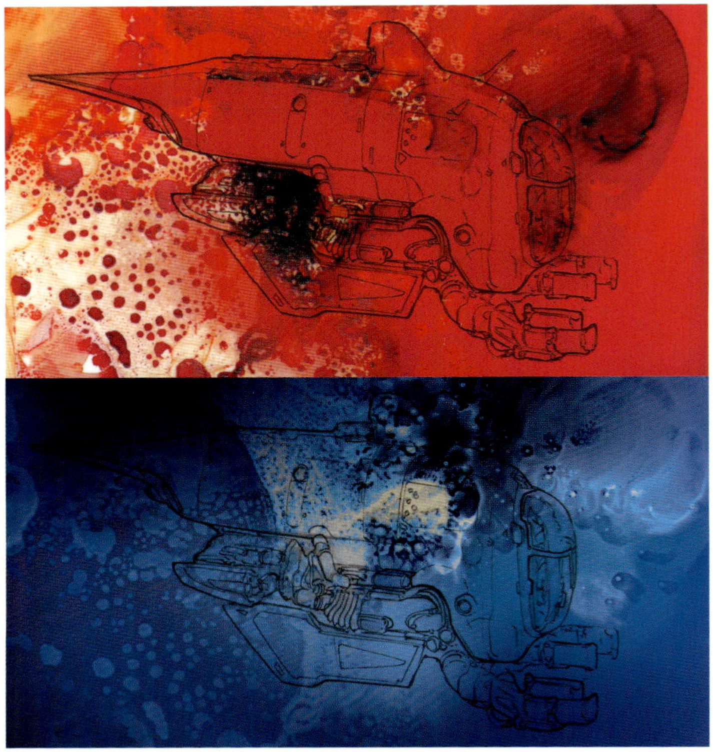

1) Establish the background texture, color, and value.

The first step was establishing a mysterious and moody environment–the value and composition to set off against the bright white of the vehicle. The main texture, unfiltered and unchanged, was yellow and red alcohol dyes on plastic sheet; this one I got some mileage on in other illustrations, but usually with downplayed contrast. In this instance, the droplets of color at the lower left and swirling flows of dye had the liquid effect I needed for the alien psychedelic liquid world. I simply inverted this texture layer, swapped reds and yellows for blue tones, and the darkest values became ethereal glowing swirls of energy. While this was not the finished background, it gave me enough foundation of color and value to begin to rough in the vehicle to see how the elements worked together.

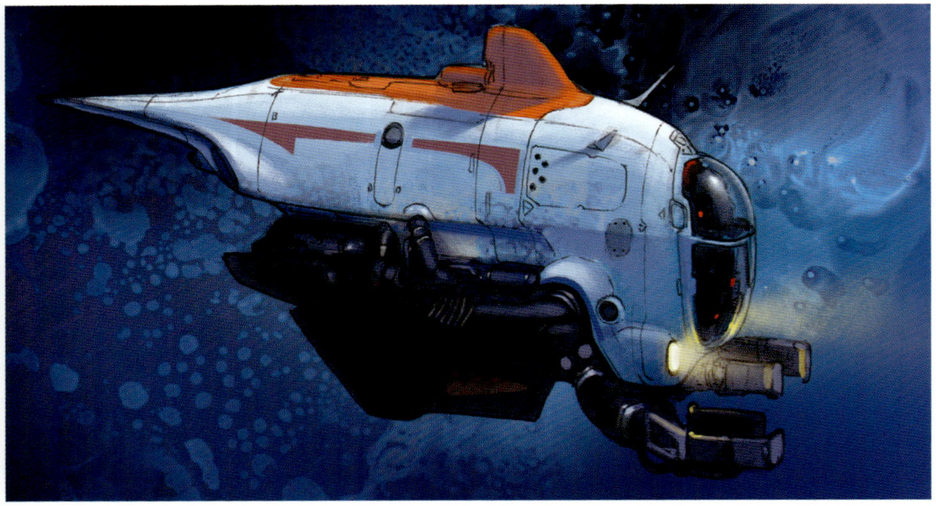

2) Develop color comp and underwater lighting.

Color rough-in, very quickly. In my mind, the main light source was directly above, so colors on the vehicle are darkened and toned to deep aqua blue on the downward-facing surfaces. Long shadows from the antennae and vertical dorsal fin stretch over the curved hull, emphasizing its volume. Glints of technical displays and warning lights are red dots under a human-proportioned front bubble canopy. While the vehicle functionally may need lights in a higher position, aesthetically, I didn't want the yellow glow and glare to obstruct the pilot area.

I briefly studied photographs of submersibles to get an idea of what they looked like underwater, and the optic effects that are quite different from when a vehicle is sitting on dry land. Generally, I observed that shiny surfaces appear much more matte, and fluorescent colors like yellow, red, and orange still have brightness but quickly get muddier and cooler in shadow.

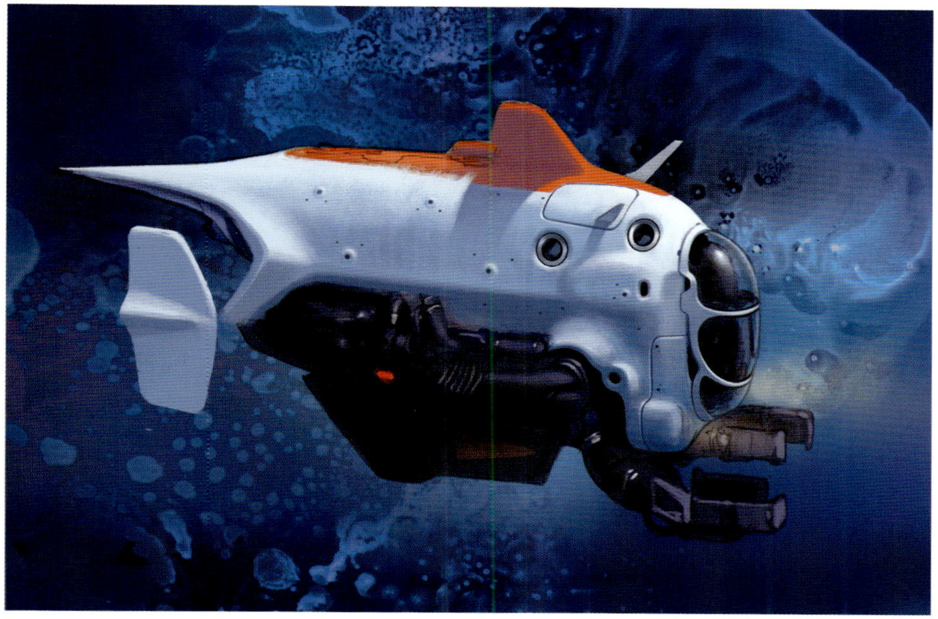

3) Build up the believable high-pressure fuselage shape.

Rendering over the color comp, I considered the overall formatting and gave myself more vertical breathing room to compose the vehicle. The shapes I modeled on the fuselage are soft and organic, somewhat rough and random with the intent of indicating a thick, high-pressure, cast-metal hull. Re-rendering the canopy glass, the framing became more bug-like.

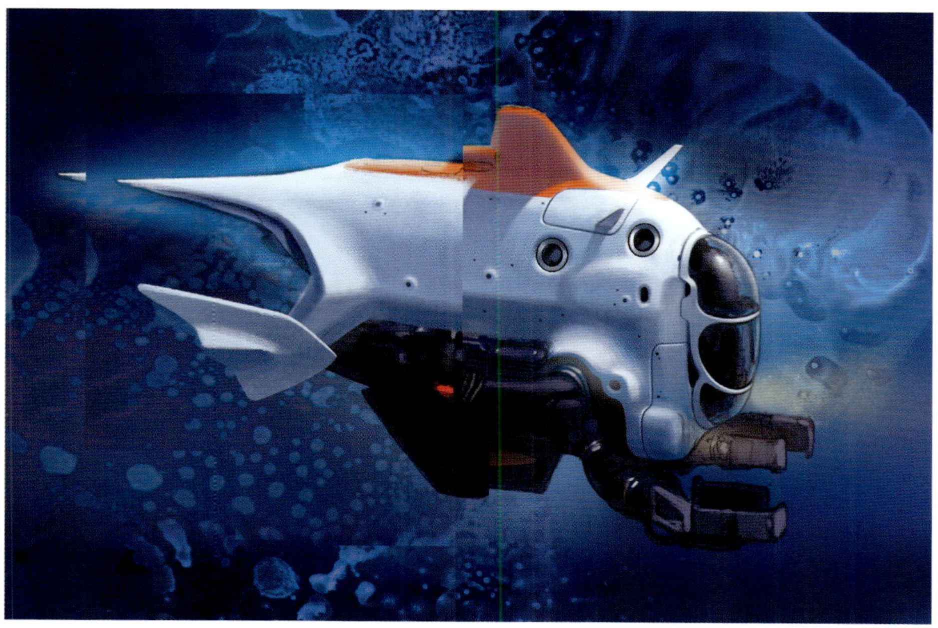

4) Adjust the overall dimension of the vehicle and add control surfaces.

Here, I've chopped and re-proportioned the overall shape as the shorter form connected closer to the look of tropical fish. Finlike stabilizers are functional and also allude to the fish reference. I roughed in a blue-white ghostlike glow on the top surfaces to test the look—an effect of bright light reflecting off and back into particles of the water.

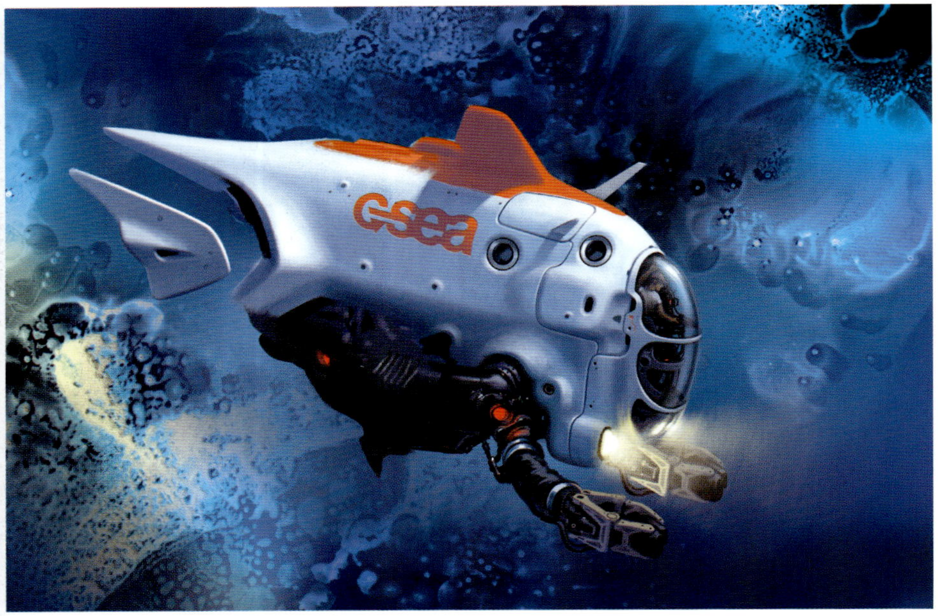

5) Get into the details, and tell some story with a logo.

With the increased compositional padding around the vehicle, I was able to rotate it slightly as if it was descending—a more interesting and dynamic presentation. Along with completed cockpit detailing and fleshing out the glinting, round metal coupling rings on soft material-shrouded arms with grappling claws, I did some storytelling through logo creation, "GSEA" being Global Space Exploration Administration. The background got some more layering to enhance a feeling of depth in the image, and the inner cockpit is shown. While the magnification effect of ultra-thick glass was something I observed in some of the contemporary submersible reference photos, I conveniently chose to invent stronger glass material, which could be used in high pressure without being very thick.

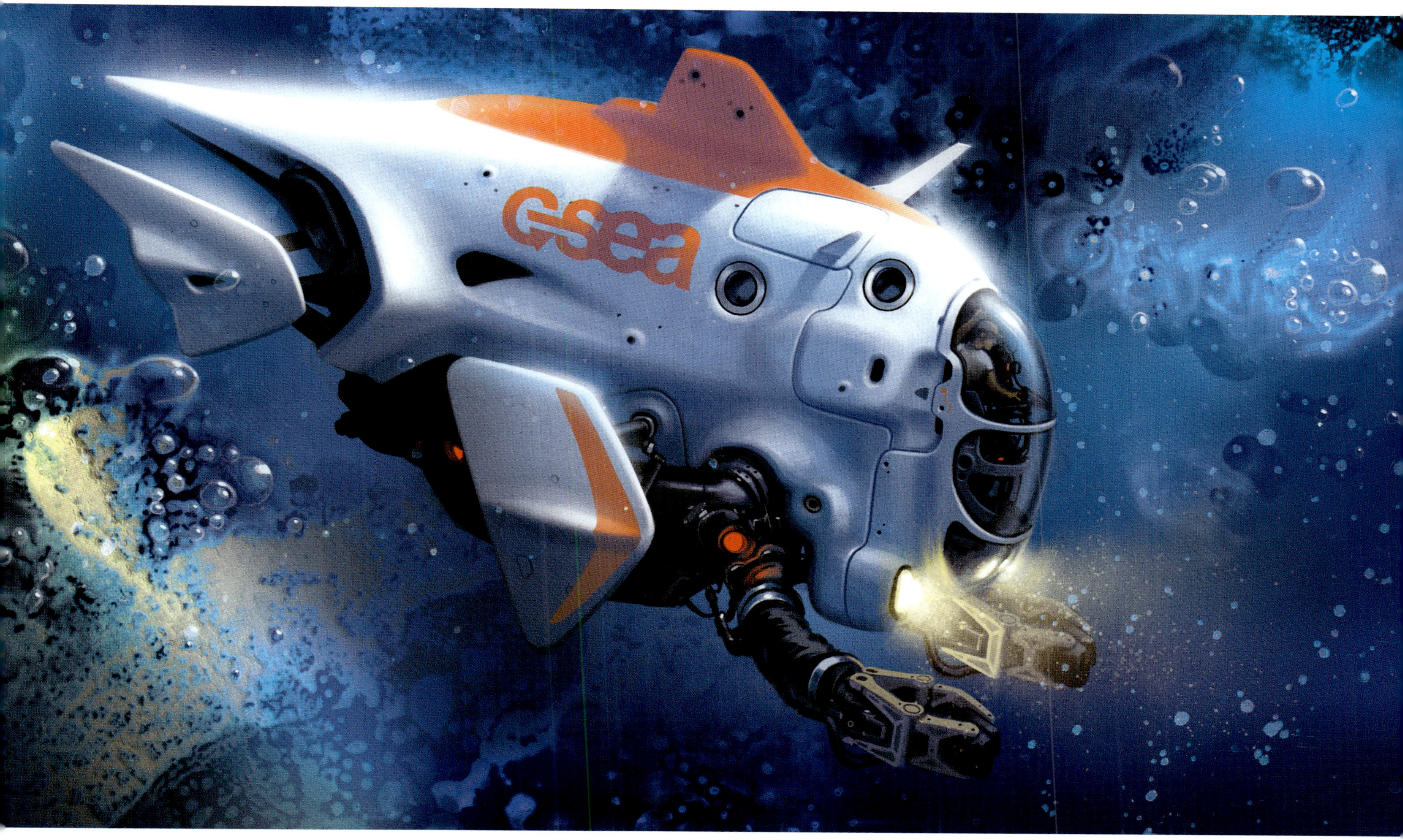

6) Make final adjustments to finish.

Final image finishes include detailing in the fin-stabilizer areas, adding a layer of illuminated floating bubbles and particles and pushing values darker in some areas so the brightly lit upward-facing surfaces of the sub have a stronger ethereal glow. Creating the appearance of bubbles was very quick—simply sketching in a white, light-refracting halo and single highlight on top of some of the paint splatters.

IN CONVERSATION: SCOTT ROBERTSON AND JOHN FRYE

Renowned designer, teacher, best-selling author, and founder of Design Studio Press, Scott Robertson (*How to Draw* and *How to Render*), talked with author John Frye about his creative processes and work. Combined, they have decades of experience working in the field of design and teaching the next generation of innovators.

Scott Robertson: There's only a handful of guys out there that inspire me to do work—and you're one of them. I'm very familiar with your work, but I'm sure readers would like to know how you developed it.

John Frye: This whole thing started with Hot Wheels designer Dwayne Vance when he wanted to do his hot-rod art book, *Masters of The Chicken Scratch: Volume 2*, about 12 years ago. He wanted a few illustrations from me, as he had remembered me from ArtCenter as a classmate and work that I had done. So, through enjoyment of that work I did for his book, I thought to myself, I should do more stuff for myself at home, because I've always seen the stagnation of designers once they get into the industry and stop all other art and design creation. They become focused on effectively producing ideas and work for a company, and then they kind of lose their own personal vision, their own personal drive that is so vibrant and alive when they're in school.

Robertson: Yeah, I've seen that a lot. And I think it's the designers, whether it be in the movies or games or automotive, that they only do the studio work once they get the job. And they try to derive all of their creative satisfaction in the day job, but the day job is not there to fulfill your creative satisfaction. That's not the function of that company as an entity. So what happens is that they're in conflict from that point forward for the rest of their career. They get grumpy and upset and then just become a disgruntled employee or designer artist by midpoint of their career. And so I totally agree that you have to retain a little bit of personal time, whether it's during the lunch hour or after hours, evenings, weekends, just a little bit. Like 10 to 20 percent of your time. Just do whatever you want to do without worry about creative overlords, basically.

Frye: Yeah, for sure. That's the difference between some sort of client work compared to doing your own creative work. With client work, there's something in the back of your mind where somebody's looking over your shoulder and you're thinking about them the entire time while you're creating a piece, whereas if you're doing something for yourself, it's you looking over your own shoulder, and you're tapping back into the childhood kind of sketching. When you're doing things alone, just focused on your own work and you're making yourself happy—not worried about anybody else's opinion—that really frees up your creativity.

I've always seen the stagnation of designers once they get into the industry and stop all other art and design creation. They become focused on effectively producing ideas and work for a company, and then they kind of lose their own personal vision, their own personal drive that is so vibrant and alive when they're in school.

Robertson: I agree. It's like we strive to return to what we were doing when we were 12 for the rest of our life. Basically, you're striving to get there with the potential carrot of retirement to fully achieve what you were doing when you were young. So, it makes you wonder, what's all the stuff in the middle for? Right? Because I was there when I was 12, I was doing it. We got to work to get all the way back to be able to do it again on the other end.

Frye: That's the real trick, to do what brings you the greatest joy and doing it with the most ease and confidence, and then just having somebody drop money in your lap at the same time. So managing real time work to replicate that in some way is a challenge.

Robertson: It's a big challenge.

Frye: You find the people to work with that are most aligned with your way of thinking, and if you're really confident, and you're really good at what you do, then you can pick and choose. And you can kind of find work that is most suited to your natural instincts and kind of joy, I guess, of creating.

Robertson: That's rare, and those of us that have been able to do that on occasion are very fortunate. That's why I think personal time and being protective of it is super important, because 80 percent of the time, even if the job starts out as that, you think it's going to be that sort of relationship two or three weeks in, you're like, oh, I see what this is.

Frye: Even the dream project can be spoiled by a nightmare schedule. I mean, you can be on the most fun project and that can ruin it all.

Robertson: Personal projects are super important. Anybody

That's the real trick, to do what brings you the greatest joy and doing it with the most ease and confidence, and then just having somebody drop money in your lap at the same time. So managing real time work to replicate that in some way is a challenge.

creative, whether you play music or paint or do design work or sculpt—any of those things, you got to keep a little bit in personal work. So, what gets you fired up to? Having a book is a really good project, like a receptor for everything that you create. I know when I'm working personally on stuff, I'm always thinking not about showing it in the end, but I'm sort of in the back of my mind. I help to justify the personal time and effort by thinking—oh, I can put this in a book someday. You're always still in the back of your mind kind of playing the client in a way, not so much judging the work but just the time investment, thinking, this is going towards something. That I have found to be very, very helpful.

THE JOURNEY VS. THE DESTINATION

Frye: Yeah, once I had a target of, "This will be published in some way," I started putting stuff on Behance. Behance is a pretty good community for industrial designers, specifically, as opposed to ArtStation, where it's a lot of entertainment design artists. But on Behance, I started to notice that people were interested in the process. Instead of just creating a piece and putting a piece out there, I would "snapshot," a capture of how I was arriving at a finished illustration, from the early thumbnail sketches to roughing in the color and all that. And I think people were learning a lot from it. I get a lot of personal messages of, "I'd like to see a video of how this is done." You start to understand that there's a lot of people interested in how things are done, the magic behind the scenes of a finished piece. It's not just about seeing a cool design; there's all that depth that goes behind it that people are interested in.

Robertson: And have you seen that Behance crowd skew toward the sort of thumbnail drawing and process versus, let's say, the ArtStation crowd, the finished piece?

Frye: Yes, you rarely see a tutorial kind of process on ArtStation. I think that's the way the artist page template was set up there; it wasn't really designed where you could interject bits of text between images. And Behance was set up pretty nicely to do that. They gave you the formatting behind that. My work kind of straddles two different worlds: the industrial design, straightforward automotive design, kind of aspect of it, and then more concept design, where you're thinking about environment and people and all that.

When I started my car design job, the first thing they asked me to do was a cartoon. They had seen that in a portfolio that this is a guy that doesn't just draw cars. And they're like, okay, finally, somebody that can do other than car sketching when we need it. So, I had to do an illustration showing the value of a concept car and how it draws customer interest to the brand as a five-panel illustration, which is actually my first ever illustration using a digital tablet. I was doing a couple of things right off the bat simultaneously.

Robertson: Yeah, it's a heavy lift right from the get-go, right out of school narrative piece, multi-panel with new tools.

Frye: I was quickly the guy that would draw the figures in a scene. If somebody needed to show the vehicle being used at a campsite and people at a picnic table unloading things in the background of mountain bikes and that sort of thing, I would do that aspect of it. And that's a storytelling process that I think a lot of industrial designers that come out of school, they can just draw the cool car, but the customer story is a little bit deeper than that. And I would like to have a lot more skill in the area of figurative drawing. Syd Mead, of course, is the master of seamless integration of product, environment, scene, character, and story.

THE VALUE OF NARRATIVE

Robertson: Have you found that being able to incorporate the narrative into your pieces still has a lot of value?

Frye: I think so. And then even at work I think, I start to see that as more recognized, as important, so I don't have to do that all the time. Design companies start to do more video- and animation-based customer image boards versus paste-up boards back when we were going to school. Before, you'd go to the newsstand and buy a bunch of magazines and cut out ad copy or images of buyers and paste on an illustration board. Now they'll do a video where they'll get clips of some fashion show and some materials, and they'll get a mood and they'll get some music behind it. And that storytelling process is so much more in-depth, I guess, than just showing a picture of a car sitting there.

> *Being in the car design world, you're thinking three to five years in the future and a contemporary kind of buyer. I stay out of the "one percenter" kind of product for the most part, and I focus on more of the mass-market stuff. But when I'm doing projects for myself, I'm thinking 50 years in the future, or 50 years in the past, or 500 million miles away from here.*

Robertson: That's interesting. So the new tools are new ways of getting people hooked into the narrative so they understand whom they're designing for. I still think it runs about 50/50, where half of the automotive designers just ignore all this stuff anyway and go and find a vehicle they want to do.

Frye: But all the sketching I do, I like to have some idea of the backstory behind it. Being in the car design world, you're thinking three to five years in the future and a contemporary kind of buyer. I stay out of the "one percenter" kind of product for the most part, and I focus on more of the mass-market stuff. But when I'm doing projects for myself, I'm thinking 50 years in the future, or 50 years in the past, or 500 million miles away from here. I'm thinking, Who's the buyer of this product in this very different world? What are their needs? What's the action that's happening? What's the universe and the story behind it?

Robertson: That's one of the things I've always loved about your posts on Instagram. A lot of times you include a little narrative about who these people are and what the things are used for. And I love all the made-up terminology. It's excellent. I always appreciate in your work that I can tell that there's thought that goes into it, and then it helps to justify a lot of what is going on with the design. It gives the viewer a place to appreciate it more, but also to understand it deeper. And then you realize why something is worn or something is weathered in a certain way, and you're like, "Oh, yeah, that's this thing that's been in use for 10 years, and it's changed hands three times, and this is the way this person is using it now. Of course, it should look like that." Whereas for a typical industrial designer, well, it has to be clean, it has to be new.

Frye: Well, the world is so complex, and having a background in real-world design is important. If I get some sci-fi project and they say, "You're making a spaceship," I want to know about the economy of the planet that's producing the ship. If they have a lot of money, how much are they going to put into the aesthetics of this thing? If they're pretty strapped for cash, of course, it's going to be super minimalistic and super functional and low-quality looking and simplified. It makes a huge difference.

Robertson: Huge difference. And that's what I think comes across in your work all the time—a consistency of intent. And that's what I love, you're able to change the intent based on shifting the different sliders of your narrative . . . to have a totally new POV for the new design and what it should and shouldn't look like and how it should and shouldn't function. I find that that's one of the things that sets your work apart from almost everything else I see online.

INFLUENCES AND INNOVATIONS

Frye: My biggest fear is recycling something, because these ideas come out on paper a lot easier than they used to for me. And I'm always afraid that I don't know where it came from, and that I'm grabbing it from somewhere and subconsciously plagiarizing it. I don't know if you ever have that issue, but sometimes you'll sketch something, and it's like, This was too easy and it looks too right, that it's got to be from somewhere else.

Robertson: Actually, recently I've had that feeling just in the back of my mind. That is one of the reasons it's important to stay current. It's a double-edged sword, right?

Frye: Right. You want to separate yourself from it so you're producing more of your own ideas, but you have to be aware of it.

Robertson: Exactly. I still have my old subscription to *Auto & Design* magazine. You have to stay relevant and aware. Then, to your point, you have to put it aside and ignore it. And when it starts to maybe come through in your subconscious, it's because you looked at it in the magazine. The last thing you want to do is have it come through in your work, because a lot of times there are alignments in technology or trends. It's very common for design studios, totally unbeknownst to each other, to hit on a common theme.

It's actually quite difficult to be aware, yet ignore it. It's like checks and balances in your own styling and in your own work and color palette and graphics. But at the end of the day, the community is pretty small and it is quite iterative. Historically, industrial designers went to movies to find advanced, interesting styling to influence their products. There was always that flow from entertainment into industrial design. I don't think it's a bad thing either. If you're doing an homage to somebody, that's what it ends up as.

Frye: If it's conscious, for sure, yeah.

Robertson: You just say, Oh, yeah, I totally see the familiarity. Then you say, That must have been in my subconscious, and I'll make that homage to Syd Mead. It's not uncommon, but people shouldn't feel too bad about it. But I do have that sneaking feeling in the back of my mind, questioning, How did this thing come to be?

Frye: I remember when I was at ArtCenter, and I was looking at something and remarked, "That looks like some animal or something," and Mac (Strother MacMinn, famed ArtCenter instructor) stopped me and asked, "Why does it always have to look like something?" It made me try to be aware of how I look at and criticize things. But I think the human mind always wants to connect something new to something familiar to understand it.

Robertson: Correct.

Frye: When people see something new, they'll want to categorize it as something. So, they'll often look at color first. More often than not, if somebody says that car looks like another car, it'll be the similar color, and they'll bring up a picture of it, and it'll be the same type of vehicle. Then you look at the details, and they're not really similar. But I've learned to take those comments and be a very good listener and make sure that I'll go check them out and make sure I didn't accidentally grab it somehow from the back of my mind. The feed of imagery that we get these days is absolutely insane. And I don't know where it all goes and how much your brain tosses out, how much of it retains, how it mixes it up, but that's my biggest phobia for sure, is accidentally, totally plagiarizing something.

I remember when I was at ArtCenter, and I was looking at something and remarked, "That looks like some animal or something," and Mac (Strother MacMinn, famed Art Center instructor) stopped me and asked, "Why does it always have to look like something?" It made me try to be aware of how I look at and criticize things. But I think the human mind always wants to connect something new to something familiar to understand it.

Robertson: You're [always] trying to push and push and push for originality. I think that's a really excellent character trait in your own work. But a lot of times you have to consider the audience. That 98 percent of the viewing audience are non-designers, and you have to become more familiar with the vernacular of that group. It sort of stops at the type of vehicle and color. There's no nuance beyond that. There's no subtlety to the silhouette or the surfacing at all. It doesn't matter if it's a radius or a chamfer or where's the weight of the proportion. None of that is even on the table as part of the discussion. It's really, "Oh, that's a red sports car. I've seen a red sports car before. You're designing a red sports car, right?" Yes, I am designing a red sports car. So I would just accept that part of it.

"COMFORT FOOD" DESIGN

Frye: Which brings up the whole idea of pandering for likes and doing the whole kind of fan art thing. There isn't a lot of fan art in industrial design like there is in entertainment and concept design. I guess if there is, it's going to be branding kind of stuff. Like designing a Lamborghini.

Robertson: Like illustrating old Porsches or something.

Frye: Yes. Like the entertainment design field, you have people that will do fan art of Iron Man or Spiderman or something, and you start to get into doing work based on branding. And as soon as you do a recognized property, you immediately gain a lot of attention. Partly because you'll do tags and people follow the tag that goes to that. And I've never wanted to get into that kind of aspect of it. But it's an interesting kind of area because it makes a lot of people happier to see that type of work.

Robertson: Yeah, I think that it's quite interesting. The whole topic of fan art, I've never been interested in doing it myself on the illustration side or design side, but I understand the value of it for not only artists but also the viewing audience. It's a way to deepen the connection to that property. The property only puts out X amount of content, and once you've absorbed all of that, you want to have a deeper connection to the work of that universe. Then you have this hunger and a desire to consume more things from that universe.

So, if somebody, an artist, comes along and has actually the same desire, like, "I'm such a fan of that universe, I'm going to create my own vision of more content from that universe," it actually satisfies a need and promotes happiness between both of those people. The person doing the fan art gets really more connected to their character, or their vehicle, or architecture, whatever it is in that world. Then the person either buying that original piece of art or just looking at it in their Instagram feed all of a sudden feels some level of gratification. So I don't think it's a bad thing. No, I don't think it advances the things that we're interested in.

Frye: I think it ends up being an easy outlet because it is a comfort area for people. It's like the Marvel universe. I know the characters. I can consume that and not be confused or challenged or whatever. And I do recognize that the entertainment for myself that I consume, that's kind of comfort areas, like car racing or watching *The Office* or *Seinfeld*. It's familiarity that brings you comfort. But at the same time, creatively, you need to challenge people in the right way by creating some new genre.

Robertson: That's not going to create likes when you challenge people. I think it's not a great game to chase likes, if you're wanting to be original. At the same time, they don't go together at all. So I think that fan art is kind of the equivalent of comfort food. And what we're into is eating vegetables. It's like we're eating it for nutrition and we're doing the design work and the styling in search of originality.

Frye: Right. So, it's a long-term approach, I guess.

Robertson: Yes, it is long-term, but I think it's a worthwhile endeavor because there needs to be some pioneers out there that are pushing and trying to advance and challenge people with their aesthetics. But not only that, the design, narrative, all those things blended together are important. That's one of the reasons I love your work so much, is because I think it does that even though there's some work that has nostalgia to it, which is a little bit of the comfort food coming in. But I love that because I'm a fan of history and a fan of older machines, etcetera. For me, that feels really comfortable. And then there's always that little 20 or 30 percent twist, right, that takes it in a slightly different direction, whether it's graphics or usage or an old-school, '60s-looking open-wheel race car. But it's autonomous.

Frye: Right. So that's the element of surprise that I want to introduce . . . a little bit of mystery. You don't quite understand how it works. You don't know the scale of something, or you don't know the technology behind it necessarily. So, there's got to be a little bit of engagement, because if you look at it, and you understand it right away, then it's not going to hold your interest. So, there's got to be that kind of intrigue into the work you do.

Robertson: That's right from the beginning? When you're doing your first thumbnail sketches, are you at the same time working on your twist or your surprise?

Frye: I think my process, it's so random sometimes, but the sketching is loose enough that even I don't understand the whole design the whole time, but I usually understand the functionality behind it. But I'm working in masses, and I had a great conversation with [designer] Tom Fritz at the Grand National Roadster Show. He really enjoys just dealing with volumes and the composition on the page. And I do the same thing with a vehicle, too, where I'm massing in, I've got the wheels or the wings of the layout, and then I start to just scribble in with the big gray marker. I'm seeking newness of form and shape in the abstract first.

I may sketch something on one side that's really heavy, and on the other side that's light, it's a contrast, and sometimes that will resolve into something. Sometimes, I understand what it is, but other times it's representing some mysterious technology that you don't need to understand. I can't explain it to you because this is 200 years in the future; it would take too long to explain it to you. But there is a mass to this vehicle, and it looks right to have this mysterious functional shape here. So it's a mystery box. It's a MacGuffin part of a sort in this vehicle. And then generally I know what the vehicle is for, the vehicle's purpose in its universe. So, if it is some ship that breaks up asteroids, an element of the design may be some solution for doing that. And we'll get a glimpse of it in grappler claws to grab the asteroid, but we don't actually see what it does with it later. But there's this volume in the back of the ship that has some eventual functionality that's going to solve all the problems in the future, where you just have a visual expectation that it's going to happen.

It's familiarity that brings you comfort. But at the same time, creatively, you need to challenge people in the right way by creating some new genre.

ON PROBLEM-SOLVING

Robertson: Yeah, and inevitably we all have run into challenges throughout evolving a design or illustration. Do you have a go-to on how to break through when things are going poorly?

Frye: The terrific thing about designing for yourself is you're not stuck with the timeline, but that means you can end up never arriving at a solution when you're stuck. So, I do a lot of these Agorapode Contest challenges because it is a very specific directive and it has a date. If I have a deadline, I actually work a lot more efficiently, because I can target that deadline, hit my sketch and my rendering timeline points, and achieve that with no problems. But if I'm sketching for myself, I'll just power through the problem of not being completely engaged with the design. I'll just have piles of 8 x 11 paper with iterative scribbles on them and just keep on producing stuff with no time limit until I find an idea that I want to take to the next step. It used to be that the problem was I wouldn't find a solution that I wanted to illustrate, and that the ideas just weren't any good. In the last, I don't know how many years, it's been the opposite thing, where I have a lot of good ideas, but the problem is I don't know which good idea to illustrate. It's fantastic to have that issue, so I file away lots of good ideas that I can revisit and fully illustrate later.

I don't know if you know Brian Eno's Oblique Strategies. There's a box of cards that he used for coming up with ideas when he was doing production with David Bowie, or YouTube, or whatever. It's these abstract ideas on cards. It'll be like, take the idea and do the opposite, or some really abstract way of rethinking a task. And I started using those cards for a while to give me some direction, and I started to get interested in the random kind of inputs for things. I had a piece of paper that I could roll a die and come up with new ideas for different types of vehicles. So, I had one row that was time frame . . . one row for the number of wheels, and one row for the type of propulsion, because I felt like I had so many ideas in my mind, but I needed the focus of the design directive. When you have a project where somebody is requesting a design, they already have a very specific direction. But when you're working for yourself, and you have, like, this high-volume creative fountain coming out of you, you need to specify and kind of target that energy. So, I found that I sometimes need that type of direction from an arbitrary source.

Robertson: I've used that in the past as well. I did that a lot with David Levy and Sparth when they were back in the old Steamboat [Studios] days. We had a randomizer that they used where you could put in all your terms and then just roulette wheel . . . mixes, and so, the same thing. You can do three different channels, then you hit go and, bing, bing, bing, and you have direction. A lot of times I make good headway on a project by starting with writing just bullet points, because it's so fast to write down a couple of words. And I find that having a framework, much like what you're talking about and how you're using the cards, is very beneficial to give yourself some parameters early in the project. In a lot of cases, it's not a problem of the creative process and how to come up with 100 versions of how to solve that one thing. It's really about, well, how do I narrow it down to one thing versus 1,000?

I really like the parameters, and that's why I did it. On my hot rod, the narrative parameters were about who was the builder of the hot rod, and it really helped; all my decision-making then fell into place. You just have to be decisive and move forward.

Frye: Yeah, being decisive is an important skill for creatives.

Robertson: I think it's a discipline, and you have to sort of make it a habit. What's that saying about a bad decision is better than no decision, or any decision is better than no decision?

Frye: Yes. And it's really difficult to teach that as well. I do a lot of instruction for students who have good technical skills and are getting to the level where they're just executing. I guide them into aesthetic decision-making, helping them make the correct aesthetic choices—it's very difficult because one solution is nearly as good as another. But, in the end, that decision has to be their own. And sometimes you're not able to easily justify one being better than the other for any specific functional design reason. It's a challenge to judge the merits of style because it's subjective.

Robertson: Have a framework to quantify your decisions on a daily basis, because if I hit an interesting narrative at the beginning, much like I see in your work, then it gives you that ability to make those decisions on the fly. You can always reach back. And you say, oh, yeah, this satisfies my initial mission or my narrative . . . that's the decision I should go with, because that's the one that matches my goal. So, it's critical to have those very clear, concise goals, however you arrive at them. But once you do arrive at them, and then try to fulfill them all the way to the end before making changes to that core idea.

REIMAGINING AND BUILDING ON HISTORY

Frye: I think that's why some of my thematic projects have worked pretty well. I did the autonomous race cars that were in the 1960s. I would start out with an idea of some specific actual car from the era that would give me a general feeling about the chassis, the surfacing on it, be it planar or streamlined cigar-shaped, or a kind of exposed minute suspension and minimized body. Or you get to the 1980s, everything's a little bit chunkier, a little bit more cab forward.

And then once you establish a couple vehicles in that world, then you start to design the technology that's typical of this conceptual world. So, I have these pods that are on the vehicles. That's a sensor pod of some sort for seeing the track and other vehicles. You start to say, well, the vehicles of this era have this kind of important, unique technology, and this is the aesthetic that develops around it. You can start to see, once these designs are stacked next to each other, do these vehicles seem like they belong in the same universe? And that starts to build a framework that I can design around.

Robertson: Are you a history buff?

Frye: Yeah, it depends on what kind of history. I really like local history, and I like to understand what was in some place 50 years ago, or where the street went. I was just driving home from the store the other day, and I was going down Huntington Boulevard, and I know that the "Red Car" railway system came through on Old Mill Road and hit Huntington. And you can see where the road is doubly wide for no specific reason. It's because there's a train that ran through there. So, that always interests me to be able to go back and see what existed generations before.

Robertson: You draw a lot on historical knowledge around building these sort of design briefs. I don't think a lot of people, a lot of younger students today spend much time considering how historical, whether it's economies, or politics, or even the weather, can influence the design of an object.

Frye: The GP Ten series that I have in the book, the whole premise is that there was no World War I. So, all the airplane technology went into racing in the early 1900s. So, 1917 wasn't the height of WWI–it was the height of racing. In my world, they were taking out airplane technology, merging it with automotive technology, which is what they did in, like, the late '60s. They started strapping wings on the cars. But what if they had done that in the 1900s, earlier on? And started to think about downforce and that sort of thing? That's kind of fun to play with. My dream is always a better world in the future, but also possibly a better world in the past as well.

Robertson: Alternate realities are just the best. And if you can put together a short description of your alternate reality, like, I have an ongoing book idea called *Hot Rods of Another World*. And *Hot Rods of Another World* is just all it needs to say. It's wide open, but it's a hot rod. So, you bring all of that history, and then you get to just twist it slightly–that puts it into another world.

Frye: Yeah, that removes the constraints of contemporary and Earth technologies. And you don't have to do wheels necessarily, or internal combustion, but you still have that combination of the hot-rod aesthetic.

Robertson: Simple themes, much like your chapters, are really important to have and provide structure. You can always go and create more content because you have the hero vehicles of that subject, but then you also have all the support vehicles of that subject. You can just broaden out the universe around that.

TEACHING THE NEXT GENERATION OF DESIGNERS

Robertson: I see you're teaching, on and off. Can you tell me a little bit about what you find gratifying and satisfying about that?

Frye: Yeah, I've been doing it for a while, and as you know, when you teach, you become more conscious of your own process. So drawing and being creative is a very right-brain kind of activity. But I found that I'm very internally vocal when I draw and sketch. I'm talking about more value, more color in this area, or I need to straighten that line. I have an internal dialogue and understand my process a little bit more. I think I've improved that by teaching and being able to explain how I do things. I realized that my process is actually more logical than I ever thought it was. So, it's really nice to be able to share that, and it's great that people are interested in that. Being able to make that internal critical discussion audible to students helps them understand the logic of the process.

For industrial design and for concept design, I kind of get the idea from students that people are a bit intimidated by sketching mechanical objects. When they don't have a mechanical kind of engineering background, they're a little intimidated by it. So, I like to teach that. For concept design, you have a pretty big range of realities and accuracy that you can play with. You can go from Flash Gordon and Star Wars to *2001: A Space Odyssey*, where you have NASA as a consultant, and you can play around creatively depending on how specific and accurate you need to be. It doesn't have to be as scary as people think it is. They don't have to be rocket scientists to draw rockets for sci-fi. I'm always happy to see students that don't know anything about vehicles start to get really interested in them.

In the class that I've taught at Concept Design Academy, and the one I taught at Beaux-Arts and Entertainment in Paris, I went through the history of airplanes and cars. I was able to show them what car design looked like from the early 1900s to modern-day times, and how aesthetics were added to what was a mostly function-driven automotive design. Then, for airplanes and jets, I showed students the functional elements that you need to have in an airplane if you're designing a realistic flying vehicle: what are the control surfaces, that sort of thing. And then, given the caveat of designing for a video game reality, you may be able to play around with the physics. For instance, the weight balance of where the center of gravity is on an airplane versus where your lift is, where the wings are located, thrust, and that sort of thing. So, it's kind of cool to share that there's a lot of creative freedom with a few simple functional design constraints.

For concept design, you have a pretty big range of realities and accuracy that you can play with. You can go from Flash Gordon and Star Wars to "2001: A Space Odyssey", where you have NASA as a consultant, and you can play around creatively depending on how specific and accurate you need to be. It doesn't have to be as scary as people think it is.

The teaching process helps you organize all those thoughts that you have in the back of your mind. I'm always learning about stuff, buying books and magazines all the time. I'm on a WWI airplane kick right now because I started to get really familiar with the fantastic colorful graphics and the paint jobs on these WWI planes. They started to do different kinds of camo on everything and super wild wing layouts and different overall proportions and so many designs that I was never aware of. And it just makes me want to sketch more and more. But I like to get students turned on to that—to get caught up in specific eras of design that spark ideas. I have some historical presentations that give an overview of planes and vehicles that are unusual in many eras that may get them to research and add to their knowledge bank.

If you really want to understand something deeply, try to teach it to somebody else. The student is going to ask you "why" every class and "how," and then you have to come back a week later with an honest answer of how and why. So, on a weekly basis, they force you to go do the research and quantify and organize your thoughts so that you can present them back in a concise way.

Robertson: I think you hit on one of the most gratifying and important reasons for people to teach is to selfishly improve their own skill sets. If you really want to understand something deeply, try to teach it to somebody else. The student is going to ask you "why" every class and "how," and then you have to come back a week later with an honest answer of how and why. So, on a weekly basis, they force you to go do the research and quantify and organize your thoughts so that you can present them back in a concise way. Teaching really helps you to organize your thoughts, and then your own process just gets better and better, just as a byproduct. You're never done learning.

Frye: And I think with that also comes a little bit of consciousness about the process itself and quantifying time. And that's been important for doing any kind of work for someone else. To be able to give somebody an estimate of how long it's going to take is being accurately aware of how long it takes to get through the sketch phase and ideation phase into the illustration phase. I know how much time it takes to illustrate an image that's 6,000 pixels wide versus a 2,000-pixel image. It's kind of like the difference between women who have been making lasagna for generations in Italy and not thinking about it, versus taking that recipe and making it into something they can put online by quantifying and measuring everything in the process. It becomes a shareable skill that people can understand. People ask, "How long does it take to do that? And how do you get from that scribble on a piece of paper to that finished image?" Many years ago, I couldn't tell you, but now I can explain the process a lot more clearly.

SKETCHING WITH INTENT

Robertson: Would you find that there's some value to automatic drawing, and just letting your mind go, and your hand go, and search? Or do you find that you really only get the best stuff when you sketch with intent?

Frye: The intent is focused into the genre vehicle as the most basic kind of limitation. So, I don't go with a piece of paper and a pen, not knowing if I'm going to sketch a wheel, versus, like, a spaceship. So, I have something like that. But beyond that, it's pretty scribbling. And the whole idea of pareidolia (visualizing a specific image in something abstract like seeing an elephant in a cloud) as an exercise to get an idea out is really, really powerful, because people tend to end up sketching the same type of things repeatedly. Car designers, especially, after many years, they'll just start to sketch the same perspective, same proportion, and they'll sketch the same key lines over and over again. I'm trying to get away from that kind of sketching on autopilot, as much as possible, and introduce a little bit of chaos into the process to come up with new ideas and shapes. The exercise of doing left-handed sketches that you show in your books, for example, is a terrific way to throw in some different gestures into your drawing, because the brain really wants to automate. It wants to make life easier for you.

Robertson: I use exercises, mental exercises for that, such as the left-handed example. It's a physical exercise because I just can't draw the same lines. I just physically can't do it. So, that opens up new windows. I will start like you and begin with a vehicle genre, wheels, or wings, or whatever. Then I try to pick a graphic-design style, but at a really simple level. This is going to be all rectilinear, right? Or it's going to be all circles, or it's going to be all flowing lines, and, a lot of times, I reference back to art history . . . an Art Nouveau theme or article. But that's at a very, very high level. That's as far as I go. And then you wander, and that's one of your style constraints to all the shapes and lines. Because, if you know your art history, then you know that that line quality or that type of line doesn't go with that historical reference.

Frye: And when you start to do that, the gesture you put down on paper becomes very specific as well.

Robertson: I even find that the sensitivity to line quality or the touch you can use, right? Even when you hold a pencil at the end, or you hold it in a writing style, can influence that early discovery phase in a sketch. And that's, again, back to a little bit of physical input. But it is a conscious decision if I'm doing really flowing Art Nouveau type of line work and shapes . . . I have a sketch with a much lighter touch, and it's really all about this rhythm of circles and forcing your arm to get into that. Then you sort of hold the tool in whatever gives you the best ability to make those kinds of shapes. It's fascinating. It's kind of an endless thing, isn't it? The endless pursuit of the how and the why.

Frye: Yes. And that's the challenge, keeping fresh and relevant as well. You don't want to get stuck in some era. A lot of designers, their stuff looks like it's rooted in some era. They hit a stagnation point or something.

Robertson: That's one of the worst feelings as a designer. If you look back at your own work, and you're like, I drew that when I was in school. I've already done that shape. I've already seen this thing, and I can't be doing this now, 30 years later.

Frye: Well, it's good if they can recognize that, at least, because I think some people aren't even aware that they're stuck.

Robertson: But it's important to educate people that it's a worthwhile pursuit. I don't want to sound like you have a moral obligation to advance the craft in any way. If you're going to contribute to this skill set in this industry, in this craft, help take it to the next level, help advance it, and then help teach it to the next generation to keep it going right to another place and another level.

EMERGING TECHNOLOGIES AND TOOLS

Frye: Which isn't designed necessarily by itself—it's also tools and processes.

Robertson: We should touch on new tools and processes, if you have any that you like. My favorite is Gravity Sketch. Virtual reality for me was like being 12 years old again and building models, right?

Frye: I have some VR projects in this book that I sketched out in there. And the great thing about the VR process is working in volumes. I talked about working in volumes before and how that's really important. You can start out with getting your wheels in there, your wings in there, and start to get the basic shapes and look at it from different angles as well. If you're sketching on paper, you see it from that one fixed perspective. But if you're able to turn it around in VR, you get a more cohesive feeling as an object from all angles.

Robertson: Correct.

Frye: And then the detailing that goes with that, it goes pretty quick. I initially started using VR modeling for simply getting the

3D form and getting the perspective established very quickly. I don't like a wonky perspective, but at the same time, I don't like to spend so much "non-design" time laying out perspective manually on paper. So, if I can just get the perspective laid out in VR, then I can screenshot it and add all the detail by sketching over the 2D image. But then I found out that with Gravity Sketch I can get more into the design beyond the basic perspective layout. I started to do more and more of the finished design creation in VR.

Robertson: Yeah, I think it's an incredible tool. And it's drawing. The thing about drawing is that you have to previsualize, especially when it comes to laying down ink lines. You're making the commitment; there's no "command z." Like, this is it. What it means is that [drawing] has honed and heightened your previsualization skills, especially with permanent media, like a Sharpie, for instance. Then, when you jump into something like Gravity Sketch, you have this superpower of previsualization already in your brain. And these new tools give you automatic mirroring to your drawing, but you already get it. You already know how to build a curve that's bending in two directions.

Frye: And it's more malleable as well. You can push and form and change what you have, as opposed to starting a new sketch. With Gravity Sketch or 3D applications, you can start to push and pull shapes and take the same design, and you can snapshot it. It's like, I like this, but I want to move on beyond it. So, I'm going to snapshot this, save a new file, and do an iteration on that and try doing tall versions this time, or start to tighten up the linework and make it more tense or more fluid.

Robertson: How much time and emphasis do you place on proportions versus surfacing and details?

Frye: Proportion is most important! I won't proceed with a design until the proportions are right. The proportion is pretty much nailed down as a thumbnail. I really get the sense of it and the feeling of whether it's successful or not in that mass that will appear as a scribble to somebody. But I'll see the shape in that scribble through pareidolia, and I like the gesture of that being further forward. Or maybe it's chunky and "off-roady" somehow. But the wheelbase means everything. The height to length of a spaceship means everything at that beginning stage. And the details are pretty secondary. But at that stage of sketching, I already see the color in my mind. So, I'm starting to put those two together and the graphics of light and dark of detail areas . . . that's kind of visualized already. And when I actually take that scribble, and I throw it in Photoshop, I start to do my color comp over it; I already know where I'm going with all my color. I just kind of validate it at that stage. But that's everything for sure. And then the whole level of detail, like functional detail, I think it's really similar to golden-ratio spiral, the little details you have in wheel wells or where folding wings connect, those little mechanical bits. It's just like when you see that golden-ratio spiral, and you have those little details in the corner, the tightest spiral versus the mass of big planes of surfaces. I think it's really similar. There's that feeling of it.

Robertson: I totally agree. I have a hard time getting students over the years, decades, to focus enough time early on getting the proportions right before they move on. No matter how many times you explain it, it's not until you've done it for a decade that you realize that that's where the real value is.

I have a hard time getting students over the years, decades, to focus enough time early on getting the proportions right before they move on. No matter how many times you explain it, it's not until you've done it for a decade that you realize that that's where the real value is.

Be your own best critic and cheerleader. During the creative process, you should cheer yourself along while also being introspective to improve.

This entire book was created from joy. All of these sketches and drawings were done for and fueled by my love of the creative process. Latch onto the joy of seeing a drawing take shape by hand. Don't rush it, and don't stop due to self-criticism. One can get metaphysical about art, but biologically, we are tapping into pleasure centers in the brain and releasing endorphins when we are effectively working and creatively performing at our best. This happy work that we used to do so well as children can be done as adults, with tremendous benefit to our health and well-being. Even busy professional artists who are happy with the work they do for clients should make time to unwind and be their own customer.

When you judge your own work, do so constructively with perspective on your experience level and goals that you seek to achieve as an artist. Beyond drawing, there are some specific habits that I strongly recommend to fortify your foundation as a creator:

- *Collect books.* You should incrementally build a library of images printed on paper. Loan and borrow them from your friends to engage in the images of the world around us and the worlds of fiction.
- *Collect art.* Surround yourself with inspiration and absorb the creative energy of other artists. Start with reproductions, neatly framed and deliberately hung in your workspace to inspire you and encourage you. Trade art with friends as well. Make a sketch for someone else in exchange and revel in the individualism of each artist's hand.
- *Work for yourself when the energy is high; recharge and refuel when your creativity tide rolls out.* Don't force yourself to create art all the time. If you aren't feeling engagement in front of the blank page, that is the day to visit a museum, walk around the city, dive into a book or art, and soak up the world.
- *Don't spend time just studying the contemporary.* Studying current design too much will leave you working with the limited visual palette of the banal "now."
- *Embrace the curiosity you had as a child*. As the director David Lynch said in an interview, "When you're a child, something as simple as a tree doesn't make sense. You see it in the distance and it looks small, but as you go closer, it seems to grow—you haven't got a handle on the rules when you're a child. We think we understand the rules when we become adults, but what we really experienced is a narrowing of the imagination."

Look toward the future of your own creation and gain inspiration from the past.

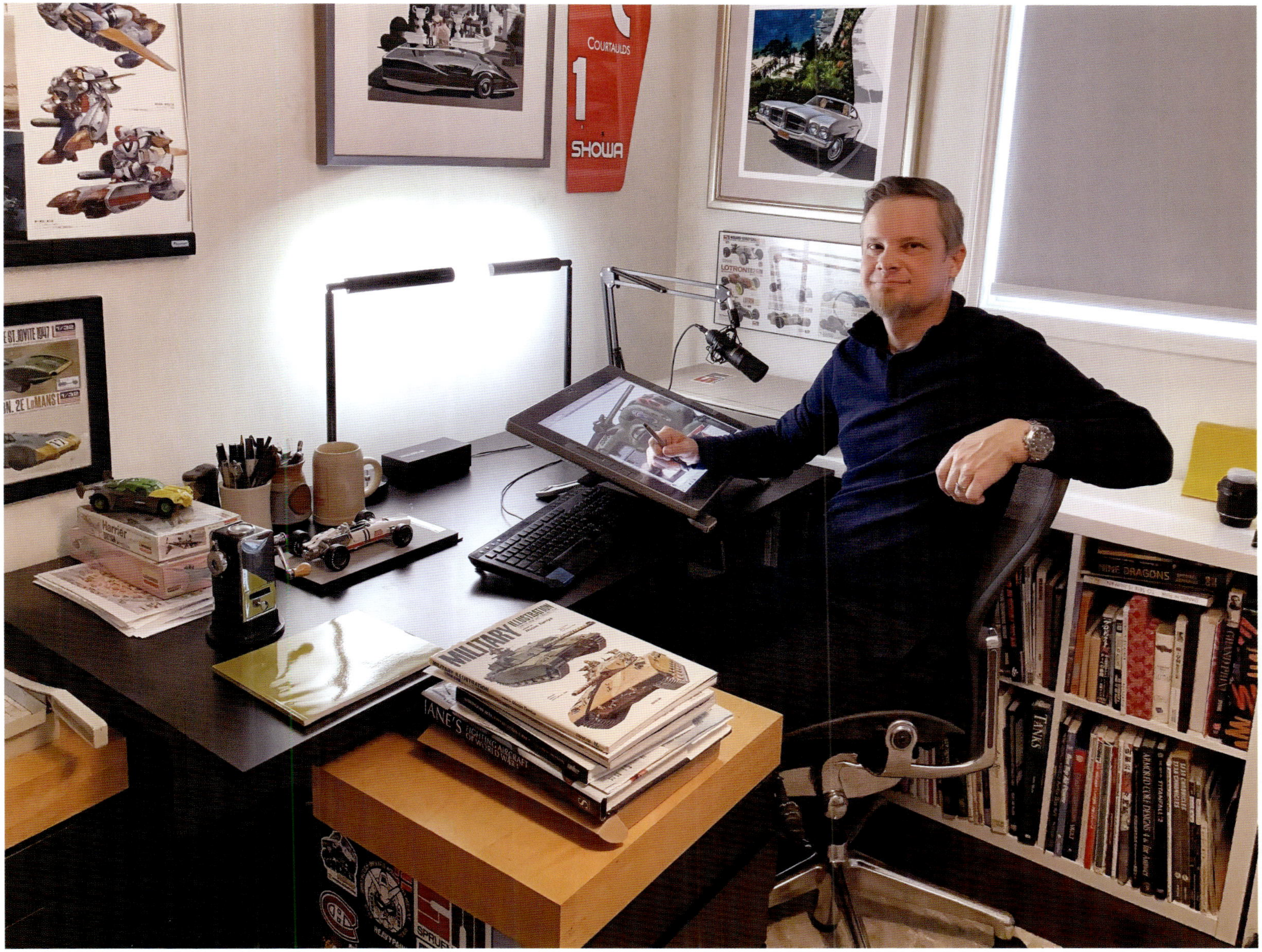

John A. Frye has been creating art and design for more than 25 years. His clients have included Hasbro, Teague, Activision, Boeing, and John Deere. He is currently team leader for the Digital Modelling and Visualization Group at Honda. John is currently and always a design student, and he has also taught and lectured at Concept Design Academy in Pasadena, California; College for Creative Studies in Detroit, Michigan; and Beaux-Arts & Entertainment in Paris, France. He resides in the hills above Southern California's San Gabriel Valley with his wife, Su, and dog, Bunny. His work can be found on Instagram @fryewerk and at fryewerk.com.

After drawing for decades, I've used a lot of different tools to create my images. Visiting an art supply store can be both exciting and daunting with the sundry of creative weapons to wield upon the page. With the advent of the digital workflow, namely Photoshop, I've been very happy to minimize the number of drawing implements that I need for the initial paper-ideation phase as my creative workflow tool kit is cheap, portable, and contains tools that aren't so obscure that you have to go to great lengths to replace them.

DIGITAL TOOLS

Photoshop CS5:
For the digital phase of an illustration, I use Photoshop CS5, which has pretty much everything I need for digital color rendering.

Autodesk Sketchbook Pro:
On occasion, I may use Autodesk Sketchbook Pro or the app Heavypaint to apply a different feeling texture and finish to my work.

Wacom Cintiq:
I churn out my digital work using a very old but very stable Wacom Cintiq 21-inch display.

Autodesk Alias AudioStudio:
3D form development is a good way to understand the volumes and mass balances of a design, and play around with finding the best camera angle to illustrate. If I want to rough something using 3D digital tools, I am typically using Alias AutoStudio, or strapping on a VR headset and using Gravity Sketch.

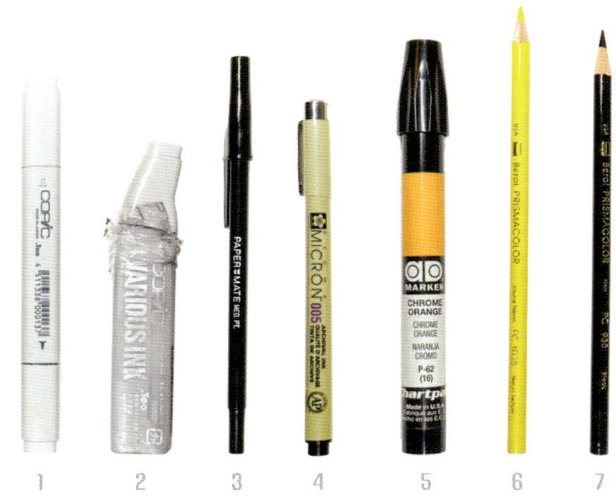

ANALOG TOOLS

1) Copic Sketch marker N2, neutral gray:
I use the chisel tip end for roughing in the general mass and volume of a design on paper, the foundation step of the majority of my design-sketching processes.

2) Copic Various Ink refill bottle:
You'll discover that the marker nibs will last a lot longer than the ink, so it's fiscally smart to buy the ink as a refill. Simply remove the nib on the marker and squeeze ink into the open end.

3) Paper Mate Medium Point Stick ballpoint pen:
This is my standard ballpoint for sketching, as this specific pen has a great variety of line thickness and value based on pressure and angle on the page. I recommend this pen because it is pretty common, cheap, and has terrific performance. I avoid gel-ink pens and higher-quality ballpoint pens because they are designed to create a very uniform line regardless of angle and pressure. For sketching, it's preferable to be able to vary the appearance of the line.

4) Sakura Pigma Micron Fineliner ink pen:
Occasionally, I may want a more uniform and sharper-looking drawing. Fine felt-tip pens, such as the Micron, will deliver a very clear and very black fine line that can emulate the work of illustrators such as Moebius and Kow Yokoyama.

5) AD marker or Prismacolor pencil, bright colors:
To add a splash of color to a sketch page or highlighting or complementing a line drawing, I will use an AD marker or Prismacolor. AD markers work well with ballpoint pens, as the marker doesn't make the ballpoint pen ink bleed. I recommenc AD markers only be used in well-ventilated rooms!

6) Black Prismacolor pencil:
If I want to have some sort of textural gradation or change up the feeling of a sketch and preserve an analog look, I may add some black-colored pencil for interest. Colored pencil works great on vellum paper with a bit of tooth to the surface for shading.

ACKNOWLEDGMENTS

Thanks to my love, my wife, Su, who supports me in every aspect of my life and brings me the happiness necessary for being a productive creative artist.

To my parents, who fed my artistic hunger from day one and were there to encourage my confidence, gave me all the paper, pencils, pens, books, and creative tools that I needed, and made the big sacrifices so that I could attend ArtCenter College of Design.

To all the great teachers in college and high school, who added something essential to my artistic personality and designer skillset at Mountain View High School, Central Oregon Community College, and ArtCenter: Mike Conley, Jerry Yahna, Douglas Campbell Smith, Cristina Acosta, Strother MacMinn, Harry Bradley, OK Ervin, Dave Solon, Dave Marek, Bruce Berkey, Harald Belker, Ricky Hsu, and Ed Natividad.

To Dwayne Vance, for his support and friendship, and getting me started as an illustrator by including me in his book, *Hot Rod Art Book: Masters of Chicken Part 2*.

To all the artists who shaped my brain and affected me over the years: Syd Mead, Ralph McQuarrie, Joe Johnston, Joe Mathieu, Robert Crumb, Katsuhiro Otomo, Bruce McCall, Wallace Wood, Bill Elder, Makoto Kobayashi, Moebius, Herge, Geof Darrow, Fitz and Van, Jack Leynnwood, Yoshiyuki Takani, Roy Huxley, Miles Davis, Michael Turner, James Clyne, Ed Newton, Ed Roth, John Berkey, Ron Cobb, Nick Pugh, Kow Yokoyama, and Marcello Gandini.

And to the artists and designers who are friends and helped me in my early career: Doug Halbert; Tony Ikeda; Jon Ikeda; John Dixon and Jose Wyszogrod at Honda; Kevin Chen, Vaughan Ling, and Darren Quach at Concept Design Academy; Tim Flattery at College for Creative Studies; the folks at Hasbro, Teague, from my fledgling intern years; and other important patrons of my work, Darko Markovic, Frank Soldo, Jerry Seinfeld, Lauren Oliver, Frank Schwartz, and Brook Banham.

To create my work, I use an ancient Dell Computer, a 15-year-old Wacom Cintiq, Paper Mate Stick ballpoint pens, El Casco pencil sharpener, Too Marker products, and Adobe Photoshop.

Everything hums along with the creative atmosphere provided by my Pro-Ject turntable, Tandberg amplifier, and depending on the location of the sun during the day, locally crafted beer or coffee.

Thank you, Tinti Dey and Teena Apeles at Design Studio Press, for the patience and guidance and the hard work to make sense of all this work that was dropped on their plate.

And thank you, for reading as well as absorbing the images—good luck to you in your creative journey!

anodized: A corrosion-resistant durable finish created by an electrochemical process. Anodized material often has a colored appearance.

block-in: To quickly add the essential key elements of a drawing or design—without much detail or refinement—in order to get an initial impression of the image.

body to glass breakup: The separation of the different materials on a vehicle, with the glass areas being the windows the driver and passenger see out.

brutalist: The postwar architecture style that rejected decorative elements, while embracing bold but simple utilitarian appearance, such as large, geometric shapes and exposed rough materials, such as concrete and brick.

chamfered: A transitional edge running along two planes at an angle between the two.

demi-streamliner: A type of race vehicle that has open wheels exposed to the airflow, as well as another set of wheels covered with smoothly formed aerodynamic bodywork.

dihedral: In aeronautics, the usually upward opposing angle of the right and left wings as viewed from the front.

Ed Newton: A notable hot rod designer, illustrator, and builder, known for his iconic custom car creations and collaborations with fellow designers Ed Roth and Dan Woods.

flying-wing jet: A jet-propelled aircraft with much of the fuselage integrated into a large, delta-shaped wing.

Fresnel effect: The amount of reflectivity of a surface due to the angle of viewing. Generally, a shallower viewing angle produces a more reflective appearance, while looking at a surface from a right angle produces the least amount of reflection.

greeblie: A term originating in the special-effects industry, it refers to small but plausible-looking mechanical details applied to the surface of a model to create areas of interest and imply functional realism.

jounce: The vertical range of movement of the wheel independent of the fixed parts of the vehicle.

lighting up (of tires): Spinning them quickly to break traction. Computers would need to control power and traction to fight the car's tendency to understeer because of the narrow, front-tire-contact patches. With the rear tires spinning up, sliding, and smoking, the spectacle would be fun for the spectators to watch.

monocoque: A vehicular fuselage structure created with a single rigid shell.

powertrain: The technology and mechanisms that propel the vehicle, be it gas, electric, nuclear, solar, or the like.

quantum-locked: Describes a surface that is rigidly fixed in space relative to another. Quantum locking is achieved by trapping a superconductor in place within a magnetic field.

ray trace: To calculate the path of waves or particles in a graphics simulation to produce an image that replicates how light, shadow, and color are projected from light sources onto objects.

shutlines: Linear gaps between body panels on a vehicle, specifically those between body and panels that open and close such as doors, hoods, and rear hatch.

scrub crawling: The movement of a vehicle at a parallel lateral angle by turning multiple sets of wheels in sync.

stance: The general appearance of a vehicle based on the relation of the mass of the body relative to the wheels and ground.

surface volume: The amount of roundness or flatness of a surface. For example, a flat plane has no volume while the surface of a sphere has substantial volume.

torquey: Having a lot of initial force and power to move something at rest.

wheel well: The space cut into the vehicle volume to permit placement of a wheel.

yaws: Movement of a vehicle when it rotates on a vertical axis.